THE EMERGENCE OF MAN

THE EMERGENCE OF MAN

A JOINT SYMPOSIUM OF
THE ROYAL SOCIETY
AND
THE BRITISH ACADEMY

ORGANIZED BY
J. Z. YOUNG, F.R.S.
E. M. JOPE, F.B.A.,
AND K. P. OAKLEY, F.B.A.

HELD ON 12 AND 13 MARCH 1980

LONDON
THE ROYAL SOCIETY
AND
THE BRITISH ACADEMY
1981

Printed in Great Britain for the Royal Society and the British Academy
at the
University Press, Cambridge

ISBN 0 85403 158 8

First published in *Philosophical Transactions of the Royal Society of London*,
series B, volume 292 (no. 1057), pages 1–216

Published jointly by
the Royal Society
6 Carlton House Terrace, London SW1Y 5AG
and
the British Academy
Burlington House, Piccadilly, London W1V 0NS

PREFACE

This book embodies the research and study into the origins of man that was reported at the third joint discussion meeting held by the Royal Society and the British Academy. Questions about human origins are obviously of concern to members of both societies, but they have not always shown adequate understanding of the evidence produced by their colleagues. Methods for investigating these questions have become much more precise and elaborate in recent years; as a result controversy has become more rigorous both in anthropology and archaeology. The study of the origin of man suffers especially from scarcity of evidence as well as from controversy. Because of this, strict requirements for careful, logical and statistical treatment of data are essential. Discussion of human origins is now usually at a scientific level but occasionally attitudes and language still intervene.

In organizing the symposium we tried to choose representatives from the various schools of enquiry that are today engaged in the search for the origins of man. The work of such experts is not always easy to follow as the techniques employed are often complicated, and they include for example atomic physics, electron microscopy, genetics and immunology. Nevertheless we hope that the information from such varied sources may provide a useful summary of some aspects of the state of our present knowledge. Research today into human origins is active and so it is especially desirable to provide a source in which each specialist is able to follow what is going on in other fields. It should also prove useful to the many people interested in this subject.

The meeting considered the emergence of human characteristics between 15 million years ago and the rise of modern man, from about 100000 years ago. It was therefore concerned with physical and abstract attributes that specifically pertain to man. We endeavoured to select for discussion topics that seemed most diagnostic for man in fields of research that ranged from the molecular level, through cells, to tissues and function, such as gait and eating, and so to socialization, the use of implements, the emergence of speech, syntactic thought and artistic expression.

The results of the research in these articles should convey some impression of the extent to which it is now possible to map and understand the stages of human evolution, especially over the last four million years. The contributions show the trends of advance in thinking about hominization that are now current. They also drawn attention to some serious gaps that remain in our understanding of how we became what we are. We hope this record will have some influence in shaping future enquiries into the Emergence of Man.

Several colleagues helped us with the early stages of planning the meeting, notably Professor C. B. M. MacBurney, F.B.A. (who but for his untimely death would have added his name to this preface as a co-organizer). Professor J. Desmond Clark, Professor Bernard Campbell and Professor P. V. Tobias.

January 1981

J. Z. Young
E. M. Jope
K. P. Oakley

CONTENTS

[Six plates]

PAGE

J. Z. Young, F.R.S.
Introductory remarks   3

MAN'S IMMEDIATE FORERUNNERS

G. H. Curtis
Establishing a relevant time scale in anthropological and archaeological research   7

    Discussion: R. Burleigh, T. Molleson   19

E. L. Simons
Man's immediate forerunners   21

P. V. Tobias
The emergence of man in Africa and beyond   43

    Discussion: B. Campbell   56

DIET AND TEETH

A. Walker
Dietary hypotheses and human evolution   57

B. A. Wood
Tooth size and shape and their relevance to studies of hominid evolution   65

    Discussion: Lord Zuckerman, F.R.S.   75

LOCOMOTION

E. H. Ashton
Primate locomotion: some problems in analysis and interpretation   77

R. H. Tuttle
Evolution of hominid bipedalism and prehensile capabilities   89

Mary D. Leakey, F.B.A.
Tracks and tools   95

L. P. La Lumiere
Evolution of human bipedalism: a hypothesis about where it happened   103

2 CONTENTS

GENETIC CONSIDERATIONS

H. Balner
The major histocompatibility complex of primates: evolutionary aspects and
comparative histogenetics 109

E. M. Jope, F.B.A.
The emergence of man: information from protein systems 121

A. J. Jeffreys and P. A. Barrie
Sequence variation and evolution of nuclear DNA in man and the primates 133

J. M. Lowenstein
Immunological reactions from fossil material 143

THE HUMAN BRAIN

C. G. Phillips, F.R.S.
Chairman's introduction 151

R. L. Holloway
Exploring the dorsal surface of hominoid brain endocasts by stereoplotter and
discriminant analysis 155

R. E. Passingham
Broca's area and the origin of human vocal skill 167

EMERGENCE OF HUMAN BEHAVIOUR PATTERNS

G. L. Isaac
Archaeological tests of alternative models of early hominid behaviour:
excavation and experiments 177

P. R. Jones
Experimental implement manufacture and use: a case study from
Olduvai Gorge, Tanzania 189

R. W. Brown
Symbolic and syntactic capabilities 197
Discussion: Lord Zuckerman, F.R.S. 204

K. P. Oakley, F.B.A.
Emergence of higher thought 3.0–0.2 Ma b.p. 205

J. Z. Young, F.R.S.
Some tentative conclusions 213

Phil. Trans. R. Soc. Lond. B **292**, 3–5 (1981)

Printed in Great Britain

[3]

Introductory remarks

By J. Z. Young, F.R.S.

The Wellcome Institute for the History of Medicine,
183 *Euston Road, London NW*1 2*BP, U.K.*

We hope that in this joint meeting the special knowledge of each contributor will help towards solution of the questions: what is man? where, when and why did he begin? The organization of the meeting jointly by the British Academy and the Royal Society draws attention both to the nature of man and to the difficulties that he meets in describing himself. The characteristics by which human life is maintained are governed in man perhaps more than in any other creature by a double dependence – on capacities acquired by inheritance and on those learned later in life. Moreover, investigations of these two aspects requires different backgrounds and techniques, which we could perhaps characterize as scientific for the study of inherited features and humanistic for the study of learning and culture. To put it differently, study of somatic inheritance requires a knowledge of science while extrasomatic inheritance is concerned with human languages, history and civilizations.

The evolution of man has been very rapid over the last 2 Ma and, at least in the later part of this time, extrasomatic transmission of information has been a major feature of the changes. Since the invention of language, individuals have been able rapidly to acquire detailed information from many others instead of only from two parents. Man evolves fast because of this multi-parental inheritance of information about how to survive. Yet the two methods of transmission are not wholly separate. The capacity to pass information by speech or writing must depend upon very specific characteristics that are inherited through DNA. Certain features of the brain and mouth are needed for speech, and still more complex properties to allow understanding of even the simplest logical propositions. Again, the social system that is necessary for learning and transmission of culture depends upon properties of the brain and endocrine system that reduce aggression, impose restraint and allow cooperation. Five hundred apes would not sit quietly and listen to another ape like the audience at this meeting.

Unfortunately we know very little about the details of the nature or inheritance of the brain features that provide these capacities, though there is already much evidence that humans are genetically programmed for the production and understanding of speech, well summarized by the late Eric Lenneberg (1967). Even if we knew more about the physiological basis of such capacities it is hard to see how we could expect to discover when they first appeared. One clue is that there has undoubtedly been a very great increase in brain size during the last two million years. If the KNM-ER 1470 skull is accepted as belonging to *Homo*, having a capacity of *ca.* 750 ml and dated at *ca.* 1.8 Ma B.P., there has been nearly a doubling since then, with no marked change in body size. This must have been based on genetic changes. No other mammal has shown anything like so rapid an increase. This suggests that the large human brain has a very high survival value and that the capacity for extrasomatic inheritance is somehow connected with brain size, no doubt among many other features of internal cerebral organization that have promoted the exchange of information. Some basic features of operation of the brain in learning may be common to all humans. For example, as social creatures our brains may be programmed to pay special attention to human features, as a baby certainly does from birth. It is likely that the brain is especially liable to describe otherwise inexplicable phenomena as due to the operation of unseen man-like entities. Anthropomorphism is not a 'primitive' character. I know of no evidence that apes believe in spirits. This is a human characteristic. How far is it determined by heredity? When did it begin? What is its value as part of the human powers of communication and formation of a brain model of the world?

The transmission of culture also depends upon genetic factors that regulate the whole pattern of life of the species, in particular the very long period before the growth spurt and adolescence. A long childhood is found in apes, but that in man is much longer. This must be the result of the action of inherited timing systems, presumably in the neuroendocrine hypothalamus. The arrested development of the gonads ensures the long period of dependence and learning that is the basis of the acquisition of the culture of each group. My own very speculative hypothesis is that this whole human life pattern may be a product of an inherited condition of the pineal gland. The melatonin that it produces certainly inhibits development of the gonads in other animals. Tumours of the pineal may produce precocious puberty, especially in boys (Kappers & Pévet 1979). This inhibitory function may also explain why the pineal becomes calcified in the adult. By then it has finished its main job, if this is to delay puberty. It does not altogether stop producing melatonin, but that does not necessarily invalidate the hypothesis. So, if the pineal makes culture possible, in a sense it *is* the seat of the soul after all, though not for the reason supposed by Descartes! The delayed puberty is a fundamental basis for all human societies, 'developed' as much as 'primitive'. It is certainly controlled by genetic factors that produce endocrine balances specific to man (Young 1973).

I have selected these features of human actions, brains and hormones to illustrate briefly how knowledge about what may be called scientific and cultural aspects of man interact. The great amount of information of the two sorts now available cannot possibly all be acquired by one person, perhaps not even properly understood by any one of us. Yet they *do* interact and the two methods of study merge, especially when we come to examine how man evolved from creatures that had no culture as we know it.

An important question for our discussion will be to try to decide how rapidly man's ancestors passed through the critical stages. According to recent advocates of punctuational evolution great changes might have occurred in small populations even in a very short time (Gould & Eldredge 1977; Stanley 1979). Probably most workers still feel that such transitions were gradual, or at least did not involve very large steps. But we shall only be able to answer such questions when we can identify the nature of the changes that were involved. Some people still seem to think that the qualities to be used for the definition of man are so distinct as not to be open to any sort of scientific investigation. The position of many philosophers is that human beings are characterized as conscious souls who have the unique capacity to make intentional judgements about aims and standards of value. From the way certain people write about such matters you might think that the 'intentionality' and judgement of value do not involve the brain at all. It seems to me that all living things are guided by aims and show intention to achieve them. Is it helpful to use 'intentionality' as a criterion of humanity? The scientific position is that the more we find out about the brain the better we shall understand these and other human features. But of course that is not the only, or perhaps even the best way to study them. All such matters require the *joint* consideration by those who are expert in the humanities and in scientific study.

There may indeed be some human powers that can truly be described as unique, but most biologists probably believe that all features that we find in man can be traced back to *some* antecedents in animals. I suppose one of the questions for our meeting is: how far is it profitable to pursue this belief? For example, Dr Brown will be telling us whether attempts to teach American Sign Language to apes have helped to understand the origin of language.

If we agree that man emerged gradually, or even by small steps, in a sense it is silly to ask *when* he appeared. Has he fully emerged yet? Perhaps a few hundred thousand years hence our learned successors will laugh as they relate how the creatures of 1980 seem to have supposed that they were already *Homo sapiens sapiens*. However, the title of our meeting suggests that there are some characteristics that define this subspecies. I hope that each of the speakers will try to tell us what these characteristics are from his point of view. I suppose that in trying to find *when* they emerged those who belong to the British Academy will mostly look back from what man *is*, while those from the Royal Society will look forward from what man *was*. Is it possible for the two approaches to produce any agreed consensus about the dates? Perhaps it will be possible to answer that question when I try to sum up at the end of the symposium.

REFERENCES (Young)

Gould, S. J. & Eldredge, N. 1977 Punctuated equilibria: the tempo and mode of evolution reconsidered. *Paleobiology* **3**, 115–151.

Lenneberg, E. H. 1967 *Biological foundations of language*. New York: Wiley.

Kappers, J. A. & Prevet, P. 1979 The pineal gland of vertebrates including man. *Progress in brain research*, vol. 52. Amsterdam: Elsevier-North Holland.

Stanley, S. M. 1979 *Macroevolution. Pattern and progress*. San Francisco: W. H. Freeman.

Young, J. Z. 1973 The pineal gland. *Philosophy* **48**, 70–74.

Phil. Trans. R. Soc. Lond. B **292**, 7–20 (1981)   [7]
Printed in Great Britain

MAN'S IMMEDIATE FORERUNNERS

Establishing a relevant time scale in anthropological and archaeological research

By G. H. Curtis

*Department of Geology and Geophysics, University of California,
Berkeley, California 94720, U.S.A.*

From time to time, it is desirable to review a given field of research, its methods and accomplishments, and see what further advances in that field may be anticipated. Toward this end, physical and chemical dating methods applicable to anthropological and archaeological problems are reviewed and discussed here, particularly recent innovations, followed by a discussion of the present status of established calibration points in early hominid evolution.

Since the advent of the radiocarbon dating method in 1949, there has been an ever increasing application of physical and chemical methods of dating to anthropological and archaeological problems as new methods of dating have been discovered and as both old and new methods of dating have been improved. There are now available several overlapping methods that may be applied under suitable conditions to yield reasonably precise and accurate dates in the entire time range of hominid evolution, or, from 0 to about 15 Ma. Some of these dating methods can only be applied to the most recent part of this time scale, the last 10 000 a or so, but this is most fortunate, because it has permitted the dating with fair accuracy of a number of very important prehistoric events that occurred as human beings emerged from the stone age, developed agriculture, domesticated animals, made pottery, improved grains and other foods, began to mine and smelt metals, and evolved the complex social organization that attended these innovations.

Some dating methods are more precise and accurate than others, because they are based on fewer assumptions concerning the measurable parameters of the methods. It must be kept in mind, however, that primary assumptions are made about every dating method as well as secondary assumptions concerning the history of the sample to be dated during and after its formation. Accuracy, the approach to a true date, is limited by the degree to which the assumptions themselves are met in the application of a given method of dating. The necessary measurements of a method can be made with high precision but still yield low accuracy if the assumptions are not correct.

Figure 1 shows the more important methods of measuring geological time in the range 0–15 Ma and their limits under most conditions. Dashed extensions indicate the ranges of these methods under unusually favourable conditions. The logarithmic scale emphasizes the younger end of this time range, where most rapid change has taken place in human technological and sociological development. These methods are not all of equal potential accuracy, and at the lower or upper limits of any method the accuracy attainable falls to zero. The details of the dating

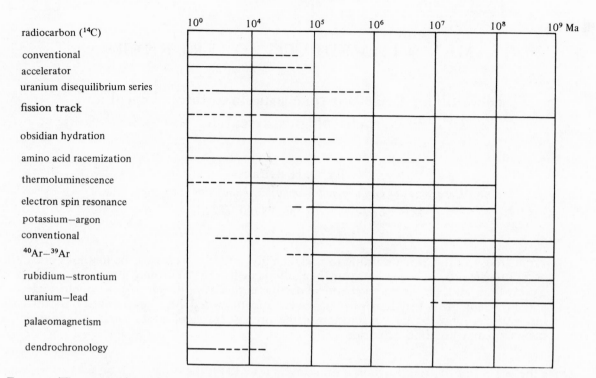

FIGURE 1. The ranges of the most common dating methods used in the calibration of the evolution of the hominids. Dashed lines indicate the ranges of methods under the most favourable circumstance.

methods have been described in a number of books and review articles. Faure (1977) is especially good for descriptions of the carbon-14, uranium disequilibrium series, uranium–lead, rubidium–strontium, potassium–argon and fission track methods. *World Archaeology*, vol. 7, no. 2 (1977) has review articles on amino acid racemization, obsidian hydration and dendrochronology methods as well as on fission track, carbon-14 and potassium–argon methods, together with a description of a new possible method of dating based on the rate of diffusion of fluorine into chipped lithic materials, a method that when developed would both support obsidian hydration dates and be applicable to a much wider variety of lithic materials. McDougall (1968) covers most aspects of thermoluminescence dating methods, while Cox (1973) reviews the history of the development of the geomagnetic time scale. Electron spin resonance research has been going on for more than two decades, but its application to dating geological materials was first described by Zeller *et al.* (1967). Owing to its potential for dating bone directly, the method will be discussed further here.

At the very recent end of the time scale, 0–10000a, radiocarbon (^{14}C), uranium disequilibrium, amino acid racemization, fission track, obsidian hydration and thermoluminescence, and, to a limit of about 7500a, dendrochronology, have been applied successfully to appropriate material to yield dates of fair accuracy. In the time scale 10000–75000a, the K–Ar method can be added to the above methods under favourable conditions. The extreme limit for both obsidian hydration and conventional radiocarbon dating by counting β-emissions of decaying radiocarbon is presently 75000a. Indeed, except in a few exceptional cases, 50000a is the virtual limit of the ^{14}C method. Thermoluminescence and electron spin resonance methods have been limited almost entirely to dating pottery or the stones forming ancient hearths in this time range, owing to the fact that these methods can only be used on crystalline material. Nevertheless, these methods have given some very important dates. Obsidian hydration, in theory, should be applicable to fresh glass over a period of several hundreds of thousands of years; however, hydration of volcanic glass results in expansion of the hydrated portion, and thin rinds often exfoliate from the specimen after a period of 60 000 to 75 000 a, permitting the process to start over again on the freshly exposed surfaces, thus leading to difficulties in obtaining accurate results. Although uranium disequilibrium series and amino acid racemization methods have been extensively used to date events in this time scale and beyond, both methods have inherent difficulties. With uranium disequilibrium series, there are large uncertainties in the assumption that the systems have remained closed to gain or loss of parent and daughter isotopes during the period of time after original isolation from the radio-active source uranium isotopes; and the amino acid racemization method is very temperature-dependent. So, unless there is some way to determine the temperature accurately during the entire period of time that the collagens to be dated have been in existence, the method cannot yield accurate dates. Radiocarbon dates have been used to calibrate racemization dates with great success, but extrapolations beyond the oldest ^{14}C date used for calibration in a given stratigraphic section can only yield approximate amino acid racemization dates, as mean temperatures for older periods of time can only be approximated.

The palaeomagnetic or geomagnetic time scale of the Earth's magnetic reversals has been an important adjunct to geochronological studies. It has been undergoing constant revision as new data are obtained concerning the calibration of the time scale itself and as new short-term reversal events are discovered (Mankinen & Dalrymple 1979). The successful application of the geomagnetic time scale in any given locality and stratigraphic section requires independent calibration by radiometric dating of at least one point, but preferably more, in the local strati-graphy. It requires also that the stratigraphic section to which it is applied be complete; that is, that sedimentation has been continuous in that basin, or, if it has not been continuous, that sufficient calibration points can be made, to correct for discontinuities in the sedimentary record.

Of the above methods applicable to 75 000 a, the most important has been and probably will continue to be ^{14}C, owing to the abundance of potentially datable organic carbon-bearing material available in this time range, the relative ease with which the method can be applied, and the high accuracy of the dates obtained. However, because of its importance for dating and its use in calibrating other methods of dating, the uncertainties in the radiocarbon method should be kept in mind. The amount of ^{14}C produced by cosmic ray bombardment of the atmo-sphere is not constant but varies as a function of changes in the intensity of the magnetic field of the sun. The residence time of ^{14}C in the atmosphere also varies, mostly as a function of climate; but there are other factors affecting the residence time as well. As a result of all of the factors involved, corrections have had to be made to radiocarbon dates of as much as 15% at 5000 a, the uncorrected dates being too young. These corrections have been based first on the careful dating of tree rings, mainly bristle cone pines, back to about 8500 a (the present limit of the pine record) and secondly on the dating of glacial varves beyond 8500 a. As there are uncertainties in the glacial varve record, corrections to ^{14}C dates beyond 8500 a are not as accurate as those younger than 7500 a.

Because of the large amounts of carbon required for old dates and the lack of other suitable material for dating at most sites 50 000 a of age and older, there is a rapid drop-off in the number of reasonably accurate dates that have been made beyond this time. A recent technological break-through in radiocarbon dating may soon change this, however. The increased precision and accuracy obtainable in measuring the amount of ^{14}C directly by means of mass spectrometers has been obvious to researchers for many years, even though there is only one atom of ^{14}C for every 10^{18} atoms of normal carbon in contemporaneous organic matter. The problem has lain, not in separating ^{14}C from other lighter carbon isotopes, however, but in separating it from ^{14}N, the nitrogen isotope from which it was formed and into which it decays. These two atoms differ in mass by only one part in 10^5, a mass difference too small for accurate separation by any mass spectrometer. This problem has now been overcome by making use of the different properties that these atoms have when ionized. ^{14}N ions slow down more rapidly than ^{14}C ions when they pass through matter at high energy; thus they may be filtered out. Xenon gas has been used successfully for such a filter. Also, it has been found that negatively ionized nitrogen, $^{14}N^-$, is fragile and quickly destroyed, while negatively ionized carbon is stable; and this property has been utilized in applying Van de Graff tandem generators to accelerate these atoms to high energies. In addition to the greater accuracy obtainable by the direct measurement of radiocarbon, there are other advantages afforded. Whereas large amounts of sample are usually required for β-counting, often 20 g or more, only a few milligrams of carbon are needed for accelerator dating, and the time necessary for a measurement can be very much less, only an hour in some cases. Many carbon-bearing objects heretofore undatable by conventional radiocarbon dating, such as carbon pigment in cave paintings, may now be dated by means of accelerator techniques. Presently the method has been used to date artefacts back to 75 000 a, but it may soon be extended to 100 000 a. See Bennett (1979) for an excellent review of the method.

Beyond 75 000 a, K–Ar dating has so far dominated the dating of archaeological and anthropological events, even though it is limited to use with volcanic rocks. Fission track dating, however, which also is limited to use with volcanic rocks in this time range, is being increasingly applied, and has given support to K–Ar dates, as will be discussed. Another method, formerly used only for rocks of great age, has also been improved recently to the point where it can be used to date igneous rocks in the range of a few hundred thousand years and older. This is the rubidium–strontium method (Rb–Sr) (Radicati di Brozolo et al. 1978).

The electron spin resonance (e.s.r.) method has been successfully applied to crystalline substances beyond 75 000 a and is also a method in which a major break-through has occurred. As the method is not well known, its general principle will be described. E.s.r. is somewhat similar in basic principles to the well known thermoluminescence dating method. Natural radioactivity in the mineral tears off electrons from nearby atoms by bombardment and produces structural defects. These radiation-induced defects, plus naturally occurring defects produced during growth of the mineral, serve as electron traps for the freed electrons, which attach themselves unstably onto such elements as oxygen and aluminium in the crystal structure, forming radicals. In a non-varying magnetic field, these unpaired electrons precess as they spin around the nuclei, grouping in two energy levels, the electron spin vectors of which are parallel to or anti-parallel to the magnetic field vector. If an alternating magnetic field is oriented perpendicularly to the steady field, it can cause 'spin flips' or transitions from one energy level to the other when the precession frequency of the electrons matches the applied microwave field frequency. Energy is absorbed or emitted when the electron spin vector is flipped from a direction parallel to the steady field or anti-parallel to it, as the case may be, the amount of energy being proportional to the number of unpaired electrons. An e.s.r. spectrometer is used to measure the energy absorbed. The absorption spectrum of the sample is compared with that of a calibration standard and with spectra obtained by treating the sample with known doses of radiation. The absorption spectrum of the natural sample is first measured, then the sample is irradiated with a known dose of gamma rays and the absorption spectrum is measured again. Several more irradiations are made, the natural amount being subtracted each time from the total to determine the amount of increase. Absorption bands that increase linearly with increase of dose are looked for. Linear increase indicates that the traps are not saturated, unsaturated traps being essential to the success of the method. To establish the annual amount of natural radiation in the sample, the content of natural radioactive contamination must be determined. By measuring how many radicals are produced in the sample by a known amount of radiation, the time required to produce the naturally occurring radicals by natural radioactivity may be determined.

Hydroxyapatite is an essential mineral in bone and teeth and is a repository for uranium absorbed shortly after death and burial of the animal from percolating groundwaters. Attempts to date bone by thermoluminescence have failed owing to secondary triboluminescence and chemoluminescence produced upon pulverizing the bone for the experiment. With e.s.r., however, the bone need not be crushed, only cleaned of soft organic material. Experiments performed so far by Ikeya & Miki (1980) have shown the feasibility of using e.s.r. on bone as old as 700 000 a. If further research bears out the great promise of these first results, it may lead to dating such important and heretofore undatable sites as those in South Africa and China.

With the development and perfecting of these dating methods, it is safe to say that in the future all critical points on the time scale will be acceptable only if they have been dated concordantly by more than one method. This is because, when two different dating methods give the same date for a sample, it indicates strongly that the primary and secondary assumptions have been met for each of the methods used for that sample. Without such concordancy or near concordancy by two different methods, any single date by any method must be suspect, even though it appears to have high precision. Replicate dates increase the precision but not necessarily the accuracy of a date. For instance, one of the assumptions of most radioactive decay systems used for dating is that there are no initial daughter isotopes in the materials to be dated, or, if there are, the amounts may be independently determined. If this information is unavailable for a particular sample that contains excess daughter isotopes, the sample will give too old an age; and it matters not how many times the experiment is repeated or how high the precision of the results, the ages obtained will all be too old. Similarly, if some of the daughter isotope is lost from a sample owing to diffusion after the time of formation and before dating of the sample, the sample will appear too young. In a succession of strata where more than one stratum may be dated, confidence in the dates is increased when the dates increase in age downward in the sequence of strata. Even so, the sequence of dates may have systematic errors that impair their accuracy. The precision of a single isotopic date is usually better than $\pm 5\%$ and if all assumptions are met this is its accuracy also; but this cannot be known with certainty unless the sample is dated by another method that gives a concordant date.

We may examine, now, the status of some of the dates obtained at various of the important earliest hominid sites that are being used to calibrate hominid evolution. The discussion is confined to hominid dates as there has been little added to the dating of the hominoids, the related apes, since publication of *Calibration of hominoid evolution* (Bishop & Miller 1972).

The ramapithecines are considered by some anthropologists (Pilbeam 1972; Simons 1972) to be the most primitive hominids, although the relationship of the ramapithecines to the more advanced hominids, *Australopithecus* and *Homo*, is not clear. *Ramapithecus* was first discovered in the Siwalik Hills in what is now Pakistan. It has since been found in deposits as far north as Hungary and southwestward in east Africa. Unfortunately, there are very few physically determined dates to calibrate this important early phase of hominid evolution. The oldest dated deposits are those at Fort Ternan, Kenya, where Evernden and Curtis obtained a K–Ar date of 14.0 Ma for a large euhedral biotite book in a tuffaceous bed just below the fossiliferous zone (Bishop *et al.* 1969). Later, Fitch and Miller obtained two K–Ar dates from this same tuff of 14.0 and 14.7 Ma (Bishop *et al.* 1969), confirming the date of Evernden and Curtis. Subsequent studies there, however, have shown that the tuff may be derived from older deposits, so that the vertebrate fauna containing *Ramapithecus* may be much younger (M. H. L. Pickford, personal communication). Fitch & Miller have recently completed a more extensive K–Ar and ^{40}Ar–^{39}Ar dating programme of the Fort Ternon beds, in which they conclude that the *Ramapithecus* beds are indeed approximately 14 Ma old. Their data are questioned by M. H. L. Pickford (personal communication), who is making an independent study of the area.

In the Siwalik Hills of Pakistan, *Ramapithecus* remains have been found with mammalian faunas ranging from Miocene to Pliocene in age. These have been under study for several years by a team headed by Pilbeam. The exact time span of *Ramapithecus* in the strata of the Siwalik Hills is not known, but a fission track date of approximately 9 Ma for a bentonite tuff in these beds, together with geomagnetic data indicating that *Ramapithecus* may be as young as 6 Ma there, shows a total time range of *Ramapithecus* of at least 8 Ma when the Siwalik data are taken in conjunction with the Fort Ternan dates (D. Pilbeam, personal communication).

Except for a few isolated hominid teeth, a significant gap of several million years presently exists in the hominid record between the youngest known *Ramapithecus* remains in the Siwalik Hills section and the oldest known *Australopithecus* bones in Africa. Whatever the relationship is between *Ramapithecus* and *Australopithecus* lies hidden in this gap, and until hominid-bearing volcanic strata of this age are found no calibration points can be determined.

Although the relationship of *Australopithecus* to *Homo* is being hotly debated, a large amount of fossil material of these two genera has been discovered in tuff-bearing strata at several localities along the East African Rift system, which has permitted accurate dating by isotopic methods. Most of the dating has been by the K–Ar and ^{40}Ar–^{39}Ar techniques, but recently some of these K–Ar dates have been supported by fission track dates, and in this support by an entirely different method the overall calibration of hominid evolution has been greatly strengthened.

South African hominid sites have so far not been dated directly by any isotopic method although an attempt to date them by the fission track method was made by Macdougall & Price (1974). The relative ages of the South African sites have been established by the mammalian faunal assemblages (Vrba 1975; White & Harris 1977), some of which have been dated by correlation with isotopically dated deposits in east Africa (White & Harris 1977). In this correlation, and for inter- and intra-basin correlation, the fossil suids have proved particularly useful (White & Harris 1977; Cooke 1976; Cooke & Maglio 1972). Vrba (1975) used the Bovidae in her study, and Cooke & Maglio (1972) showed the potential of the proboscideans for similar purposes, the family of Proboscidea having evolved rapidly over the past 7 Ma.

The oldest trace of *Australopithecus* (?) has been found at Lukeino, West Baringo, Kenya (Pickford 1978). *Australopithecus* has also been found at Lothagam and Kanapoi (Patterson *et al.* 1970; Behrensmeyer 1976), but the K–Ar dates controlling these finds have low accuracy and are stratigraphically remote from the hominid remains themselves and so cannot be used for accurate calibration purposes. All of these finds are probably older than 4 Ma and Lukeino may be as old as 6 Ma.

The oldest abundant *Australopithecus* remains closely associated with K–Ar dated tuffs are in the Laetolil beds at Laetoli, northern Tanzania (M. D. Leakey *et al.* 1976, 1978) and in the Hadar Formation in the Afar Depression of Ethiopia (Aronson *et al.* 1977). The accurate dating of these two deposits is of particular importance in the calibration of hominid evolution for two reasons: first, hominid footprints preserved in tuffaceous strata at Laetoli prove beyond question that hominids were bipedal at this stage of their evolution; and, secondly, on the basis of the hominid material found in both the Laetolil beds and the Hadar Formation, Johanson *et al.* (1978) have established a new species of *Australopithecus*, *A. afarensis*, which they believe is a direct predecessor of both *Homo habilis* and *A. africanus* (Johanson & White 1979).

The K–Ar dates and one ^{40}Ar–^{39}Ar date of the tuffaceous strata in the Laetolil beds were obtained from phlogopite, a magnesian-rich biotite, except for two whole-rock dates from a vogesite lava flow unconformably overlying the beds. Although the phlogopite dates range from 3.4 to 3.8 Ma, R. L. Hay (personal communication) believes that the strata were deposited in a shorter period of time than 400 000 a, probably no more than 200 000 a, as there are no palaeosols or disconformities in the sequence to indicate breaks in time between strata. All of these K–Ar dates have moderate precision, being based on more than 20 % radiogenic argon for each date. An excellent concordant date of 3.55 Ma was obtained by the ^{40}Ar–^{39}Ar incremental heating method on a split of a single large crystal of phlogopite for which K–Ar dates of 3.59 Ma and 3.62 Ma had been determined. This concordance would appear to confirm the validity of these K–Ar dates, but this is not necessarily so. The phlogopite-bearing xenoliths in these Latolil tuffs are holocrystalline and very coarse grained, the average grain size being often more than 1 cm, indicating that they have grown under uniform conditions of temperature and pressure. Such conditions are believed usually to obtain at great depth in the magma chamber. If this is true, ambient ^{40}Ar in the magma could be incorporated in the growing phlogopite crystals. There is a common belief that excess initial ^{40}Ar can be proved by the ^{40}Ar–^{39}Ar method when the isochron is extrapolated to intercept the ^{40}Ar/^{36}Ar ordinate at zero ^{39}Ar. If no excess ^{40}Ar is present, the isochron will intercept the ordinate at 296, the atmospheric ratio of ^{40}Ar/^{36}Ar; but if the mineral has excess initial ^{40}Ar, the isochron is supposed to intercept the ordinate at a value greater than 296. This, however, is true only if the excess ^{40}Ar is not in the same position in the crystal structure as the radiogenic ^{40}Ar. If the excess ^{40}Ar is uniformly distributed through the crystal structure, as it may be if incorporated during the entire growth of the crystal, the isochron will intercept the ordinate at 296, but its slope will be steeper, indicating an erroneously older age. All that has been proven by dating the phlogopite crystal by both K–Ar and ^{40}Ar–^{39}Ar methods is that the K–Ar dates for that crystal are quite precise; the accuracy of the dates will only be demonstrated when the tuff is dated by some other method.

The Hadar hominid-bearing strata in Ethiopia appeared at first to have superbly concordant dates for the BKT$_2$ tuff in the upper part of the section of 2.64 ± 0.03 Ma by K–Ar, the average of seven runs, and 2.61 ± 0.2 Ma by fission track, the average of 20 zircon grains (Aronson *et al.* 1981). This K–Ar date, however, was computed with use of decay constants for potassium that are no longer accepted. When new constants are used, this figure becomes 2.71 Ma, which is still good concordance. The lower part of the Hadar section has a less satisfactory whole-rock basalt date of 3.0 ± 0.05 Ma, the average of six K–Ar determinations of the 'massive black phase' of the Kadado Moumou basalt, and 2.62 ± 0.10 Ma for the 'sugary grey phase', the average of three K–Ar determinations. The black phase appears to be the better material for dating; and the 3 Ma date agrees with the magnetostratigraphy. It appears likely, thus, that the *Australopithecus afarensis* remains in these deposits are less than 3 Ma old. In view of the similarity of the hominids in the Hafar formation and Laetolil beds, it is puzzling that there is such a large difference in the ages of these deposits. The conclusion that hominid evolution was static for over 600 000 a during this period cannot be justified until the Laetolil dates are confirmed.

Extensive dating programmes of hominid-bearing strata have been carried out in the Lake Turkana area of northern Kenya and southern Ethiopia, where in the Omo River section of Ethiopia the earliest hominid remains have been found in unit 12 of the Usno Formation and in the slightly younger tuff B member of the Shungura Formation, both dated at over 3 Ma (Howell & Coppens 1976; Howell & Isaac 1976; Brown & Nash 1976; Cerling *et al*. 1979) and about 2 Ma in the lower member of the Koobi Fora Formation of the East Turkana section, Kenya (Leakey 1976; Fitch *et al*. 1978). These areas have been of great importance because of the large amount of hominid fossil material that they contain, cranial and post-cranial, as well as some of the earliest known stone tools and artefacts.

Isotope dating has been difficult in the Koobi Fora beds owing to the fact that all of the tuffs in that sequence have been derived from tuffs first deposited elsewhere then mixed with contaminating older minerals during transport to their present positions. Other problems have also arisen and, as a result, the very important KBS tuff containing early stone artefacts and overlying the remarkably complete skull, KNM-ER-1470, possibly the earliest *Homo*, has been dated no less than 60 times by K–Ar and ^{40}Ar–^{39}Ar techniques, and several times by the fission track method. Dates obtained for this tuff range from 0.52 to 223 Ma (Fitch & Miller 1976; Fitch *et al*. 1978); however, concordant dates by K–Ar and fission track methods indicate the age to be between 1.8 and 1.9 Ma (1.83 Ma, K–Ar (Drake *et al*. 1980); 1.87 Ma, fission track (Gleadow 1980); 1.89 Ma, K–Ar (McDougall 1980)). Using major, minor and trace elements, Cerling (Cerling *et al*. 1980) has correlated the KBS tuff with the tuff H_2 member of the Shungura Formation of the Omo area, for which Drake (Drake *et al*. 1980) obtained an age of 1.87 Ma, the average of four K–Ar dates. This is in good agreement with the concordant dates obtained for the KBS tuff, and these two members, the KBS tuff and tuff H_2, define an isochronous surface which is also well supported by proboscidean and suid fossils (White & Harris 1977; Cooke 1976; Cooke & Maglio 1972) as well as by the magnetostratigraphies in the two areas (Brown & Shuey 1976; Brock & Isaac 1976). By similarity of K–Ar dates, similarity of suids and probscideans, similarity of magnetostratigraphies, and similarity of stone tool and artefact assemblages, this surface can be extended to Olduvai Gorge, bed I. Indeed, it can be named the Olduwan Industrial Complex Surface (Isaac 1976). With this, then, as an accurately dated surface, correlations can be made with considerable assurance (figure 2) and conclusions drawn concerning hominid evolution, one of which is that stone tool and artefact making began before this time, the oldest dated stone artefacts being those found in the tuff D member of the Shungura Formation in the Omo sequence, dated by Brown at approximately 2 Ma (Brown & Nash 1976; Merrick & Merrick 1976; Chevaillon 1976). (Tools have been found in a bed in the Hadar Formation, Ethiopia, that have been tentatively dated at 2.6 Ma (Aronson, personal communication).)

If most of the taxonomic designations by the various workers are correct concerning *Australopithecus afarensis*, *A. africanus*, *A. boisei*, *Homo habilis* and *H. erectus* in the African succession, the

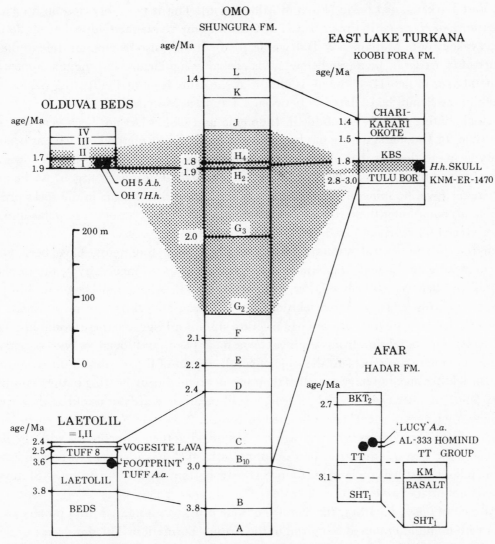

FIGURE 2. Correlations of dated stratigraphic sections at various localities in east Africa. The stippled area shows the biostratigraphic correlation (from Drake *et al.* 1980).

first appearance of *A. africanus* is calibrated by the date for tuff B of the Shungura Formation in the Omo sequence at close to 3 Ma (Brown & Nash 1976). The last appearance of that taxon is calibrated by the date for tuff G in the Shungura Formation at approximately 2 Ma (Brown & Nash 1976) The first appearance of *A. boisei* is calibrated by the date for tuff E in the Shungura Formation of slightly older than 2 Ma (Brown & Nash 1976) and its last appearance above the Middle Tuff at Ileret, East Turkana, cannot be calibrated more closely than that it is older than the Chari-Karari Tuff of 1.4 Ma (Drake *et al.* 1980) and probably close in age to the Koobi Fora Tuff, dated by Fitch & Miller at 1.6 Ma (1976). The first appearance of *Homo* (*habilis*?) is calibrated by the date of approximately 2 Ma for tuff G in the Shungura Formation, which is probably in close agreement with *Homo* below the KBS tuff in the Koobi Fora Formation east of Lake Turkana. *Homo habilis* appears below the KBS tuff in several places in the East Turkana section and possibly as high as tuff L in the Shungura Formation, dated at 1.45 Ma (Brown & Nash 1976). The first appearance of *H. erectus* is calibrated by the date for the Koobi Fora Tuff at Ileret, East Turkana, of 1.6 Ma (Fitch & Miller 1976). This is probably close in time to the first appearance of *H. erectus* in upper bed II at Olduvai, just above the Olduvai event dated at 1.67 Ma (Leakey 1961; Mankinen & Dalrymple 1979). It may also be close in time to the first appearance of *H. erectus* in Java (see below). It is probably significant that the first appearance of stone hand axes in bed II, Olduvai, is almost at the same level as the first *H. erectus*. They appear also in the Peninj beds, dated at between 1.4 and 1.6 Ma (Isaac & Curtis 1974).

The isotopic dating of early hominids in Indonesia and China has not been very successful up to this time. In Indonesia dating has been limited to the K–Ar method, which has been unsatisfactory owing to the fact that most of the volcanic rocks in Java are very low in potassium, and dates obtained from them have as a result relatively high atmospheric argon. At the major hominid sites in Java, no minerals with essential potassium in them occur in the rocks present. Of the minerals composing these rocks, hornblende has the highest amounts of potassium, but it does not exceed 0.3 % K.

At Sangiron, where several hominid fossils, mostly cranial fragments, have been found, possibly comprising two genera, *Pithecanthropus* and *Meganthropus* (Jacob 1973), the fossils are older than strata believed to bear tektites, although the tektites have not been found in place in the strata. Zähringer (1963) dated tektites from Sangiron and elsewhere in southeast Asia at 0.73 Ma by K–Ar, which would appear to put a minimum age on these hominids. However, the K–Ar ages of tektites from southeast Asia have been questioned on two counts: first, the ages obtained may not represent the time of emplacement of the tektites in the strata; and, secondly, the tektites may not have lost all of their initial argon during heating in the atmosphere when they fell (Schaeffer 1966), which, if true, would mean they are not as old as they appear to be. Fission track ages of the tektites obtained by Storzer & Wagner (1969), and corrected for annealing of the tracks by grass fires, average 0.7 Ma, making them concordant with the K–Ar dates. Possibly the first question can be discounted also. Tektites identical in composition to those found in southeast Asia on land are found in ocean-bottom cores at the Bruhnes–Matuyama geomagnetic boundary, well dated at 0.73 Ma (Cassidy *et al.* 1969).

A K–Ar date of 0.83 ± 0.04 Ma, the average of four runs, was obtained from pumice closely associated with hominid crania at Sangiron in the Kabuh Formation. The dates were obtained from hornblende in the pumice and ranged from 0.79 Ma to 0.90 Ma, and none of them had less than 98 % atmospheric argon (Jacob & Curtis 1971). Recently, a split of one of these samples was run at Berkeley under improved conditions and it yielded a date of 1.2 ± 0.2 Ma, with less than 90 % atmospheric argon (unpublished data). This date must be considered superior to the 0.83 Ma figure.

At Modukerto, where part of the cranium of a *Pithecanthropus* (*Homo*) *erectus* infant was found by Duyfjes in 1936 (Koenigswald 1936) a K–Ar date of 1.9 ± 0.4 Ma, the average of two runs, was obtained from hornblende separated from pumice fragments occurring some 50 m below the fossil site (Jacob & Curtis 1971). Again, the very high atmospheric argon content of these two runs, approximately 99 %, greatly reduces their precision and accuracy.

In China, at Choukoutien, the site of 'Peking Man' (*Sinanthropus pekinensis*, *Homo erectus*) and some of the earliest known evidence of the use of fire, as well as elsewhere in China, the geological context is unfavourable for isotopic dating, although a uranium–thorium date of 0.21 to 0.5 Ma has been obtained (Chang 1968). No details of this date are given, but it accords roughly with the Second and Third Glacials of Europe, as do the pollen profiles and associated fauna (Chang 1968). Evernden & Curtis obtained a K–Ar date of 380 000 a for Mindel II of the

Second Glaciation (Evernden & Curtis 1965) from a tuff on the Lower Main Terrace of the Rhine, which also tends to support an age of approximately 400000–500000 a for the age of *Homo erectus* at Choukoutien and, by mammalian correlation, at Lan-t'ien in east central Shensi.

In conclusion, it appears that very few isotopic dates being used to calibrate the early evolution of the hominids are as accurate as we would like them to be. On the other hand, several have higher 'accuracy' than the taxon designations that they are being used to calibrate. It appears probable that within a few years accurate isotopic dates will be available for calibration of all phases of hominid evolution. The late stages of hominid evolution and social and cultural development are dated better although not nearly as well as anthropologists and archaeologists wish. New improvements to dating techniques will soon help greatly to resolve problems at the younger end of the time scale.

REFERENCES (Curtis)

Aronson, J. L., Schmitt, T. J., Walter R. C., Taieb, M., Tiercelin, J. J., Johanson, D. C., Naeser, C. W. & Nairn, A. E. M. 1977 New geochronologic and palaeomagnetic data for the hominid-bearing Hadar Formation of Ethiopia. *Nature, Lond.* **267**, 323–327.

Aronson, J. L., Walter, R. C., Taieb, M. & Naeser, C. W. 1981 New geochronologic information for the Hadar Formation and the adjacent central Afar. *Nature, Lond.* (In the press.)

Behrensmeyer, A. K. 1976 Lothagam Hill, Kanapoi, and Ekora: a general summary of stratigraphy and faunas. In *Earliest man and environments in the Lake Rudolf Basin* (ed. Y. Coppens, F. C. Howell, G. Ll. Isaac & R. E. Leakey), pp. 163–170. Chicago: University of Chicago Press.

Bennett, C. L. 1979 Radiocarbon dating with accelerators. *Am. Scient.* **67**, 450–457.

Bishop, W. W. & Miller, J. A. (eds) 1972 Edinburgh: Scottish Academic Press.

Bishop, W. W., Miller, J. A. & Fitch, F. J. 1969 New potassium–argon age determinations relevant to the Miocene fossil mammal sequence in east Africa. *Am. J. Sci.* **267**, 669–699.

Brock, A. & Isaac, G. Ll. 1976 Reversal stratigraphy and its application at east Rudolf. In *Earliest man and environments in the Lake Rudolf Basin* (ed. Y. Coppens, F. C. Howell, G. Ll. Isaac & R. E. F. Leakey), pp. 148–162. Chicago: University of Chicago Press.

Brown, F. H. & Nash, W. P. 1976 Radiometric dating and tuff mineralogy of Omo group deposits. In *Earliest man and environments in the Lake Rudolf Basin* (ed. Y. Coppens, F. C. Howell, G. Ll. Isaac & R. E. F. Leakey), pp. 50–63. Chicago: University of Chicago Press.

Brown, F. H. & Shuey, R. T. 1976 Magnetostratigraph of the Shungura formation, lower Omo Valley, Ethiopia. In *Earliest man and environments in the Lake Rudolf Basin* (ed. Y. Coppens, F. C. Howell, G. Ll. Isaac & R. E. F. Leakey), pp. 476–483. Chicago: University of Chicago Press.

Cassidy, W. A., Glass, B. & Heezen, B. C. 1969 Physical and chemical properties of Australasian microtektites. *J. geophys. Res.* **74**, 1008.

Cerling, T. E., Brown, F. H., Cerling, B. W., Curtis, G. H. & Drake, R. E. 1979 Preliminary correlations between the Koobi Fora and Shungura Formations, east Africa. *Nature, Lond.* **279**, 118–121.

Chang, K. 1968 Archeology of ancient China. *Science, N.Y.* **162**, 519–526.

Chevaillon, J. 1976 Evidence for the techical practices of Early Pleistocene hominids. In *Earliest man and environments in the Lake Rudolf Basin* (ed. Y. Coppens, F. C. Howell, G. Ll. Isaac & R. E. F. Leakey), pp. 563–573. Chicago: University of Chicago Press.

Cooke, H. B. S. 1976 Suidae from Plio-Pleistocene strata of the Rudolf Basin In *Earliest man and environments in the Lake Rudolf Basin* (ed. Y. Coppens, F. C. Howell, G. Ll. Isaac & R. E. F. Leakey), pp. 251–263. Chicago: University of Chicago Press.

Cooke, H. B. S. & Maglio, V. J. 1972 Plio-Pleistocene stratigraphy in East Africa in relation to proboscidean and suid evolution. In *Calibration of hominoid evolution* (ed. W. W. Bishop & J. A. Miller), pp. 303–329. Edinburgh: Scottish Academic Press. Toronto: University of Toronto Press.

Cox (ed.) 1973 *Plate tectonics and geomagnetic reversals.* San Francisco: W. H. Freeman.

Curtis, G. H., Drake, R. E., Cerling, T. E., Cerling, B. W. & Hampel, J. H. 1978 Age of KBS tuff in Koobi Fora Formation, East Turkana, Kenya. In *Geological background to fossil man* (ed. W. W. Bishop), pp. 464–469. London: Geological Society.

Drake, R. E., Curtis, G. H., Cerling, T. E., Cerling, B. W. & Hampel, J. 1980 KBS tuff dating and geochronology of tuffaceous sediments in the Koobi Fora and Shungura formations, east Africa. *Nature, Lond.* **293**, 368–372.

Evernden, J. F. & Curtis, G. H. 1965 The potassium–argon dating of late Cenozoic rocks in East Africa and Italy. *Curr. Anthrop.* **6**, 343–364.

Faure, G. 1977 *Principles of isotope geology.* New York. John Wiley & Sons.

Fitch, F. J. & Miller, J. A. 1976 Conventional potassium/argon and argon 40/argon 39 dating of volcanic rocks from east Rudolf. In *Earliest man and environments in the Lake Rudolf Basin* (ed. Y. Coppens, F. C. Howell, G. Ll. Isaac & R. E. F. Leakey), pp. 123–147. Chicago: University of Chicago Press.

Fitch, F. J., Hooker, P. J. & Miller, J. A. 1978 Geochronological problems and radioisotope dating in the Gregory Rift Valley. In *Geological background to fossil man* (ed. W. W. Bishop), pp. 441–461. London: Geological Society.

Fleischer, R. E., Price, P. B., Walker, R. M. & Leakey, L. S. B. 1965 Fission-track dating of bed 1, Olduvai Gorge. *Science, N.Y.* **148**, 72–74.

Gleadow, A. J. W. 1980 Fission-track age of the KBS tuff and associated hominid remains in northern Kenya. *Nature, Lond.* **284**, 225–230.

Howell, F. C. & Coppens, Y. 1976 An overview of Hominidae from the Omo succession, Ethiopia. In *Earliest man and environments in the Lake Rudolf Basin* (ed. Y. Coppens, F. C. Howell, G. Ll. Isaac & R. E. F. Leakey), pp. 522–532. Chicago: University of Chicago Press.

Howell, F. C. & Isaac, G. Ll. 1976 Introduction. In *Earliest man and environments in the Lake Rudolph Basin* (ed. Y. Coppens, F. C. Howell, G. Ll. Isaac & R. E. F. Leakey), pp. 471–475. Chicago: University of Chicago Press.

Ikeya, M. & Miki, T. 1980 Electron spin resonance dating of animal and human bones. *Science, N.Y.* **207**, 977–979.

Isaac, G. Ll. 1976 Plio-Pleistocene assemblages from East Rudolf, Kenya. In *Earliest man and environments in the Lake Rudolf Basin* (ed. F. C. Howell, G. Ll. Isaac & R. E. F. Leakey), pp. 522–564. Chicago: University of Chicago Press.

Isaac, G. Ll. & Curtis, G. H. 1974 The age of early Acheulian industries in East Africa – new evidence from the Peninj Group, Tanzania. *Nature, Lond.* **249**, 624–627.

Jacob, T. 1973 Palaeoanthropological discoveries in Indonesia with special reference to the finds of the last two decades. *J. hum. Evol.* **2**, 473–485.

Jacob, T. & Curtis, G. H. 1971 Preliminary potassium–argon dates of early man in Java. *Contr. Univ. Calif. archaeol. Res. Facility* **12**, 50.

Johanson, D. C. & White, T. D. 1979 A systematic assessment of early African hominids. *Science, N.Y.* **202**, 321–330.

Johanson, D. C., White, T. D. & Coppens, Y. 1978 *Kirtlandia* **28**, 1–14.

Koenigswald, G. H. R. von 1936 Erste Mitteilung über einen fossilen Hominiden aus dem Altpleistocan Ostjavas. *Proc. K. ned. Alead. Wet.* **39**, 1000–1009.

Leakey, L. S. B. 1961 New finds at Olduvai Gorge. *Nature, Lond.* **189**, 649–650.

Leakey, M. D., Hay, R. L., Curtis, G. H., Drake, R. E., Jakes, M. K. & White, T. D. 1976 Fossil hominids from the Laetolil beds. *Nature, Lond.* **262**, 460–466.

Leakey, M. D., Hay, R. L., Curtis, G. H., Drake, R. E., Jakes, M. K. & White, T. D. 1978 Fossil hominids from the Laetolil beds. In *Geological background to fossil man* (ed. W. Bishop), pp. 157–170. London: Geological Society.

Leakey, R. E. F. 1976 An overview of the Hominidae from East Rudolf, Kenya. In *Earliest man and environments in the Lake Rudolf Basin* (ed. Y. Coppens, F. C. Howell, G. Ll. Isaac & R. E. F. Leakey), pp. 476–483. Chicago: University of Chicago Press.

Macdougall, D. & Price, P. B. 1974 Attempt to date early South African hominids by using fission tracks in calcite. *Science, N.Y.* **185**, 943–944.

McDougall, D. J. 1968 (ed.) *Thermoluminescence of geological materials.* New York: Academic Press.

McDougall, I., Maier, R., Sutherland-Hawkes, P. & Gleadow, A. J. W. 1980 K–Ar age estimate for the KBS tuff, East Turkana, Kenya. *Nature, Lond.* **284**, 230–234.

McDougall, I., Saemundsson, K., Johannesson, H., Watkins, N. D. & Kristjansson, L. 1977 Extension of the geomagnetic polarity time scale to 6.5 m.y.: K–Ar dating, geological and paleomagnetic study of a 3,500-m lava succession in western Iceland. *Bull. geol. Soc. Am.* **88**, 1–15.

Mankinen, E. A. & Dalrymple, G. B. 1979 Revised geomagnetic polarity time scale for the interval 0–5 m.y. B.P. *J. geophys. Res.* **84**, 615–626.

Merrick, H. V. & Merrick, J. P. S. 1976 Archeological occurrences of earliest Pleistocene age from the Shungura Formation. In *Earliest man and environments in the Lake Rudolf Basin* (ed. Y. Coppens, F. C. Howell, G. Ll. Isaac & R. E. F. Leakey), pp. 574–584. Chicago: University of Chicago Press.

Patterson, B., Behrensmeyer, A. K. & Still, W. D. 1970 Geology and fauna of a new Pliocene locality in north-western Kenya. *Nature, Lond.* **226**, 918–921.

Pickford, M. H. L. 1978 Stratigraphy and mammalian palaeontology of the late-Miocene Lukeino Formation, Kenya. In *Geological background to fossil man* (ed. W. W. Bishop), pp. 263–278. London: Geological Society.

Pilbeam, D. 1972 *The ascent of man.* New York: Macmillan.

Radicati de Brozolo, F., Huneke, J. C. & Wasserburg, G. J. 1978 $^{39}Ar-^{40}Ar$ and Rb–Sr age determinations on Quaternary volcanic rocks from the Roman volcanic province. In Short papers of the Fourth International Conference Geochronology, Cosmochronology, Isotope Geology 1978 (ed. R. E. Zartman) *Geol. Surv. open-file Rep.*, nos 78–701, pp. 344–346. U.S. Department of the Interior, Geological Survey.

Schaeffer, O. A., 1966 Tektites. In *Potassium–argon dating* (ed. O. A. Schaeffer & J. Zäringer), pp. 162–173. Berlin, Heidelberg and New York: Springer-Verlag.

Shuey, R. T., Brown, F. H., Eck, G. G. & Howell, F. C. 1978 A statistical approach to temporal biostratigraphy. In *Geological background to fossil man* (ed. W. W. Bishop), pp. 103–124. London: Geological Society.

Simons, E. L. 1972 *Primate evolution: an introduction to man's place in nature.* New York: McMillan.

Storzer, W. A. & Wagner, G. A. 1969 Correction of thermally lowered fission track ages of tektites. *Earth planet Sci. Lett.* **5**, 463–468.

Vrba, E. S. 1975 Some evidence of chronology and palaeoecology of Sterkfontein, Swartkrans and Kromdrai from the fossil Bovidae. *Nature, Lond.* **254**, 301–304.

White, T. D. & Harris, J. M. 1977 Suid evolution and correlation of African hominid localities. *Science, N.Y.* **198**, 13–21.

Wood, B. 1976 Remains attributable to *Homo* in the East Rudolf succession. In *Earliest man and environments in the Lake Rudolf Basin* (ed. Y. Coppens, F. C. Howell, G. Ll. Isaac & R. E. F. Leakey), pp. 490–506. Chicago: University of Chicago Press.

Zähringer, J. 1963 K–Ar measurements of tektites. In *Radioactive dating*, pp. 289–305. Vienna: International Atomic Energy Agency.

Zeller, E. J., Levy, P. W. & Mattern, P. L. 1967 Geologic dating by electron spin resonance. In Radioactive dating and methods of low level counting. *Procedures of the Symposium, International Atomic Energy Agency in co-operation with the Joint Commission on Applied Radioactivity (ICSU) Monaco*, pp. 531–540. Vienna: International Atomic Energy Agency.

Discussion

R. Burleigh (*Research Laboratory, The British Museum, London, U.K.*). The question of dating and time scales is the key to the ideas being discussed here over the next two days and we should be grateful to Professor Curtis for his clear survey, first of problems and methods (excluding, perhaps deliberately, palaeomagnetism), and secondly of the exact time scales that are now being established for the last 10 Ma. The dates and the time scales will, I am sure, be the basis of much discussion during this meeting and I would like to confine my remarks mainly to a brief commentary on the methods, and especially the potential application, of electron spin resonance (e.s.r.) to dating. If problems relating to the radiation history of the materials dated in this way can be resolved this is a most promising development since it offers the opportunity of making useful comparisons with other methods of dating based on different materials. It may also offer a chance to span the interval between the upper limit of, for example, ^{14}C dating and the lower end of the range of other methods such as K–Ar dating. Many of the methods that are now available to cover this critical period between about 50–100 ka B.P. when modern man, *Homo sapiens sapiens*, finally emerged, face severe technical difficulties, for example those to which thermoluminescence dating of burnt, humanly worked flint is subject, or the uncertainties of amino acid dating. Thus there is great scope for an alternative method that significantly overlaps the methods that are well established but have incomplete coverage within the period of greatest interest, such as the K–Ar and ^{14}C dating. The extension of the range of ^{14}C dating to perhaps as much as 100 ka B.P. by the use of Van de Graaff accelerator techniques (and the possibility of detecting by this means other natural radioisotopes with much longer half-lives, such as ^{10}Be) is also a development of the greatest importance in this context. But one of the advantages of using e.s.r. for dating of, say, bone would be the possibility of being able to date important fossil material directly (A.1 dating in K. P. Oakley's terminology) and I would like to ask Professor Curtis how destructive the use of this method, if it indeed proves workable, would be.

G. H. Curtis. The method is not destructive in the sense that one is still left with the sample at the end and measurements can be made on it any number of times, but one does have to grind up the bone first of all (a few grams only, though) to do the measurement.

T. MOLLESON (*British Museum (Natural History), London SW7 5BD, U.K.*). Dr Curtis remarked during his paper that fluorine and uranium elements accumulate in bone with time, and Dr Harmon has shown concern that uranium series breakdown should be used for dating fossil bones since we cannot tell when the uranium entered the bone.

It is not at all clear, however, that uranium and fluorine do in fact continue to accumulate in bone. During the process of fossilization of recently buried bone, mineralizing elements are taken up by bone as organic compounds are lost. The levels of fluorine, uranium etc. taken up by the bone reflect the ambient levels of these elements in the ground waters percolating over the bone. Equilibrium is probably reached comparatively rapidly. Once the sediment containing the bone has become indurated, little if any further chemical change can take place in the bone; although, of course, isotopic and amino acid breakdown continue. Bone from indurated impervious sediments can thus be considered a closed system for the purposes of quantitative measurements until rock erosion or excavation bring the buried bone to the surface again.

Phil. Trans. R. Soc. Lond. B **292**, 21–41 (1981)   [21]

Printed in Great Britain

Man's immediate forerunners

By E. L. Simons

Departments of Anthropology and Anatomy, Duke University and Duke Primate Center,
3705 Erwin Road, Durham, North Carolina 27705, U.S.A.

[Plate 1]

Discoveries of the last five to ten years have greatly expanded the number of remains of earliest *Australopithecus*, reaching back to nearly 4 Ma ago in Africa. In Eurasia a broad range of recent finds has greatly extended knowledge of the diversity, the distribution and the facial anatomy of a series of small *Ramapithecus* and of several similar-sized larger apes (with the usual proliferation of names, namely *Budvapithecus*, *Ouranopithecus*, *Sivapithecus*, and *Ankarapithecus*). All these new Eurasian fossil hominoids seem to come from around 8–15 Ma ago. Improvements in dating and fossil documentation emphasize the so-called 'Pliocene gap' in knowledge of higher hominoid evolution. The period from 4 to 8 Ma in Africa, and apparently elsewhere, is devoid of a single dentition, skull, or limb bone of any hominoid, other than the Lothagam mandible at 5 or 6 Ma (holding but a single preserved tooth.)

In §1 recent discoveries at three sites in East Africa, five in Europe and Asia Minor and two in Asia are reviewed. These discoveries document an unexpected and widespread occurrence of hominoids with *Australopithecus*-like cheek teeth having thick enamel and set in robust jaws. Although both dental and facial resemblance between *Ramapithecus* and *Australopithecus* has been demonstrated by recent finds, the proliferation of new finds has somewhat confused discrimination of subsets among later Miocene hominoids; also some workers have stressed similarities between *Ramapithecus* and *Sivapithecus* or between the latter and *Pongo*.

In §2 new temporal, ecological and morphological evidence relevant to determining the time of origin and the definition of the taxonomic family of man, Hominidae, are summarized.

1. Nature of the evidence

Fossils indicating the nature of the radiation of the higher hominoids between about 4 and 13 Ma ago are of wide distribution in the Old World, except in Africa, where only a handful of fossils from this time-span have been recovered. If these few African fossils were to be the only basis for inferring anything about hominid origins this contribution could be brief. There is strong evidence against the extreme recency of the diversification of higher Hominoidea advocated by a few exponents of molecular clocks. Moreover, the three African fossil teeth aged 5.5, 7 and 10 Ma respectively all have thick enamel and low crowns, which implies relation to the similarly constituted hominoids of the Eurasian radiation. There is reason to believe that from time to time faunal exchange between Africa and Eurasia took place, especially at about 2, 7, 14, and 17 Ma B.P. All these factors combine to suggest that in African and Eurasian sites from 10 to 17 Ma in age we have and may find information relevant to the problem of the immediate forerunners of African Plio–Pleistocene *Australopithecus*. It is to be hoped that the absence of evidence of any quality in Africa from between 4 and 14 Ma B.P. will soon be remedied by the discovery of new hominoid fossils that are relatively complete and can be made the basis of settling the exact line of ancestry of humankind. I am yet to be convinced that the molecular clock is accurate enough to require a split between *Homo* ancestry and that of *Pan/Gorilla* in

Africa around 7 or 8 Ma. Rather it should be stressed that, even if *Ramapithecus*, the taxonomic position of which has recently been made so controversial, is set aside, there is extensive evidence that split-point times among primates and particularly higher Hominoidea do fall before 14 Ma B.P. These considerations sustain the relevance of considering all the evidence about hominoid evolution from middle Miocene to middle Pliocene times site by site as follows.

(a) Sites in Kenya, East Africa

In contrast to the present extensive documentation of *Australopithecus* and *Homo* in Africa, running back to about 3.5 Ma B.P., evidence of immediate forerunners of man in Africa before that time is scant. Each of the three known finds (all from Kenya) is, or contains, but a single tooth. These specimens are:

(i) *Lothagam*, a partial right mandibular fragment containing roots of M_2 and M_3 as well as the whole of M_1 (Patterson *et al.* 1970);

(ii) *Lukeino*, a left lower molar (Pikford 1975);

(iii) *Ngorora*, a left upper second molar, described by Bishop & Chapman (1970).

Lothagam is located in northern Kenya, near the west shore of Lake Turkana, just southwest of the mouth of the Kerio River. The latter two sites are in the Baringo Basin, Northern Kenya Rift Valley.

(i) *Lothagam*

As far as it can be analysed, this right horizontal ramus with M_1 resembles early *Australopithecus* from Laetoli, Tanzania, and Makapansgat, South Africa. The age seems to be well substantiated at 5.5–6 Ma. In consequence the Lothagam mandible may be regarded as constituting the earliest evidence so far recovered of *Australopithecus*. Recent reports (Smart 1976; Coppens 1978) put the age back to perhaps 6 Ma. Neither M_1 nor proportions or structure in this mandible and molar roots resemble *Pan* or *Gorilla*.

(ii) *Lukeino*

This left lower molar (KNM LU 335) was found at a horizon in the middle portion of member A of the Lukeino Formation at Chepboit. A series of K–Ar dates indicate a probable age of about 7 Ma. The tooth is low-crowned, has thick enamel and is broad, with faint traces of a lateral cingulum. Resemblance is to both robust and gracile *Australopithecus*, but the size is distinctly smaller, which might be significant in view of the tooth being about twice as old as the gracile *Australopithecus*. Like that of later hominids and unlike that of many earlier hominoids, the trigonid is long compared to the talonid basin. The swollen, rounded cusps suggest that enamel thickness is very great. Molar morphology is reminiscent of M_{1-3} in A.L. 288–1 at Hadar, in some of the material from Laetoli and to certain late *Ramapithecus* such as the Hasnot, Pakistan, mandible. Although absolute size and length–width proportions are close to those from some *Pan*, crown morphology and enamel development is not at all like that of either of the African apes. In all probability this molar is definable as hominid even in a narrow sense and it is tentatively placed in Hominidae by Andrews in Pikford (1975).

(iii) *Ngorora*

Found in 1968, this upper left second molar is from a level in the Ngorora Formation, Baringo Basin, Kenya, that has been dated to about 10 Ma B.P. This tooth resembles that from Lukeino in being low-crowned and broadened or flaring lingually. As with the previous two specimens there is evidence of enamel thickness and a general resemblance to Laetoli *Australopithecus*, *Ramapithecus* and *Sivapithecus*. The tooth does not resemble those of *Pan* or *Gorilla*. (For further discussion see Bishop & Chapman (1970), Bishop *et al.* (1971), Bishop & Pickford (1975) and Pickford (1975).)

(iv) *Fort Ternan and Maboko*

Before the above three finds the next youngest African site that has yielded hominoid fossils is Fort Ternan, Kenya, at an age of about 14 Ma. There also a species with thickly enamelled teeth, *Ramapithecus wickeri*, exists. As far as these Kenyan finds at Lothagam, Lukeino, Ngorora and Fort Ternan provide evidence about hominid origins, they all indicate an African radiation of species with thickly enamelled teeth. Taken altogether, the fossil record from African sites ranging from middle Miocene to Recent provides not a single thinly enamelled tooth that would document the lineage of either *Pan* or *Gorilla* at any period in the past whatsoever. The only African fossil apes bearing any resemblance to modern *Pan* or *Gorilla* are the smaller and the larger described species of *Dryopithecus* (*Proconsul*) from the early Miocene of Kenya and Uganda, which do exhibit thin enamel. The face of *D. major* from Moroto, does bear specific morphological resemblance to *Gorilla* at an age of about 16 Ma.

Lest the unwary student should be inclined to the idea that *Ramapithecus* and *Sivapithecus* represent an Eurasian radiation, it is necessary to stress that these genera have both been recorded as occurring in Africa for many years. Recent evidence (Andrews & Molleson 1979) strongly suggests that the type of *Sivapithecus africanus* (Clark & Leakey 1950) came from Maboko Island, Lake Victoria, Kenya, where faunas are thought to be about 15 Ma old. The current view is that the type specimen of *S. africanus*, together with a few other fragments from Maboko, is correctly assigned to genus *Sivapithecus*. This point has been emphasized by Madden (1980).

There is an extensive literature about *Ramapithecus* (= *Kenyapithecus*) *wickeri* (Leakey 1962) from Fort Ternan, Kenya. Its lack of generic distinctiveness was recognized by Simons (1963) and the genus *Kenyapithecus* coined for it was dropped by later authors, for instance Andrews (1971). Although this find at Fort Ternan is not the type species of *Ramapithecus*, it should be emphasized that the material of it from the Kenyan site has played an important role in developing the concept of *Ramapithecus*. For instance, it documents in the African Miocene a form with small incisors and canines, thick enamel, transverse P_3 with distinct metaconid cusp and contact facet for canine anteriorly (no diastema). Interestingly there are large canines at Fort Ternan (KNM FT 28, 37, 41), one of which (FT 37) shows pronounced apical wear and curved, barrel-shaped body reminiscent of *Sivapithecus*. The approximate estimated volume of the crowns and of these canines is about three to four times that of the small upper canine (KNM FT 46) associated with the upper left maxilla of *R. wickeri* by Leakey (1962). Conversely, from Maboko there is a small upper canine (KNM MB 70) resembling that of Fort Ternan *Ramapithecus*.

(b) *Sites in Greece*

(i) *Macedonia*

During recent years de Bonis has located at the 'Rain Ravine' site near Salonika, on the left bank of the Axios River in Macedonian Greece, 12 partial or complete mandibular dentitions in jaws and one palate (with all save one tooth) of Miocene hominoids. These creatures occur in a fauna of about 200 other mammalian specimens that is judged by de Bonis & Melentis

(1977 a, 1978) to be of Vallesien provincial age, or about 10–11 Ma. Working on the assumption that the two size classes are of one species, they have named this species *Ouranopithecus macedoniensis*. As a whole these hominoids, of two distinct sizes, represent by far the most extensive series of hominoids from any single site in Eurasia, but not a single postcranial bone was found. At Rain Ravine fossils come from a sandstone channel deposit of limited extent. Apart from the hominoids the fauna consists mainly of jaws and limb bones of artiodactyls, including the genera *Mesembriacerus*, *Oioceros*, *Prostrepsiceros*, *Decennatherium*, *Paleotragus* of two species, and *Bohlinia*. The giraffids and bovids are considered by de Bonis to indicate a savannah mosaic environment where woodlands and grasslands were interspersed.

Perhaps the most important thing about these finds in Macedonia is the marked dimorphism indicated, if, in fact, the two morphotypes present at Rain Ravine do represent sexes and not a large and a small species. Arguing for the identity of the two morphotypes as one species is the similar morphology of postcanine teeth. However, differences in the canines and front premolars in the two morphotypes are at the extreme for highly dimorphic species now living. In the 'females' P_3 are more transverse and canines much smaller than in 'males'. Unlike *Ramapithecus*, P_3 metaconids are uniformly absent. If the Macedonian hominoids found so far may be taken as representative samples then the posterior teeth are more dimorphic than in any living species, including the gorilla and baboons. Also, apparently, absolute size increase posteriorly from P_3 through M_3 is greater in 'males' than in 'females'. Without personally revising this material it is difficult to have a certain opinion about the occurrence of one, or of two species at Rain Ravine. However, it is fair to say that, if Miocene hominoids had dimorphism that is both greater from and different to that seen in any living primate, then their taxonomic assessment is rendered most difficult.

As in African *Australopithecus* and in *Sivapithecus* from the Siwaliks of Pakistan and India, the upper central incisors in *Ouranopithecus* are large relative to upper lateral incisors. *Ouranopithecus* teeth all show very thick enamel with low, rounded cusps, and lower molars are, on average, broader relative to their length than is typical of most east Asian *Ramapithecus*, *Gigantopithecus* and *Sivapithecus*. Except for the third molars of the type specimen, a young 'female', most of the teeth in the other individuals are worn so that little crenulation can be seen. Symphyseal cross section and form of the horizontal mandibular ramus resemble more nearly *Gorilla* or *Gigantopithecus* than *Sivapithecus*. It would seem that the Macedonian hominoid represents at least one valid species. Were it not for the thick enamel one might consider that these have affinities with African apes. They come from a time and place where there is increasing evidence of African outmigrants (Azzaroli 1977). One such outmigrant, *Pliohyrax*, occurs nearby at Samos and apparently also at Pasalar, Turkey (Meyer 1978).

(ii) *Pyrgos*

At this site near Athens, which is also called 'Tour la Reine', was found a complete hominoid mandible with teeth that was later damaged by the World War II bombing of Berlin, where it had been sent for study. This specimen was described by von Koenigswald (1972) under the name *Graecopithecus freybergi*. Although according to von Freyberg (personal communication) this dentition was almost completely intact when discovered in 1945, now only right P_4–M_2 remain in the war-damaged find. On the basis of the limited associated fauna this site seems to be of Turolien provincial age, which would make this mandible the youngest of the European Miocene hominoids. Most students, having only seen uninformative casts, equivocate about this specimen. Nevertheless, it provides information. The posterior divergence of the tooth rows is about 20° and the front teeth are very small, while in contrast the molars are huge. Right M_2 appears to be broader buccolingually than is the jaw beneath it. My examination of the little-known type specimen of '*Graecopithecus*' *freybergi* at Erlangen, Germany, recently revealed the roots of the entire C–M_3 series on the left side, where all teeth have been broken away. The canine and similar-sized premolars are packed together and small. These and other features suggest assignment to *Ramapithecus*.

(c) Sites in Turkey

Finds of *Ramapithecus* and *Sivapithecus* at three different sites in Turkey have been made recently. These are (1) a mandible of *Ramapithecus* from Candir, about 60 km northeast of Ankara, (2) a palate with attached right lower face of *Sivapithecus* from the Sinap series, about 55 km northwest of Ankara, and (3) a considerable sample of isolated teeth of both *Sivapithecus* and *Ramapithecus*, recovered from deposits at Pasalar in eastern Turkey. The three sites appear to be of different ages, but since age estimates are made by faunal correlation some reservations must be retained. Pasalar seems to be the oldest (Vindobonian Provincial Age) at perhaps 15–16 Ma of age. The middle Sinap series fauna indicates an age of mid-Vallesian or perhaps 10–12 Ma. Candir has a fauna suggesting a Vindobonian age, or if *Hipparion* is actually present at the level of *Ramapithecus* a date as recent as 10–12 Ma B.P. is possible.

(i) Candir

Although Tekkaya (1974) originally assigned the well preserved type mandible from Candir to *Sivapithecus*, Andrews & Tekkaya (1976) as well as Simons (1976b) transferred this mandible to *Ramapithecus*. The main significance of this mandible is dual. It documents the presence of *Ramapithecus* in central Turkey and because of its completeness it provides or confirms interesting anatomical points about the genus seen less well in the east Asian materials recently reported on by Greenfield (1978, 1979) and Pilbeam et al. (1977). In size and morphology the Candir mandible is closely comparable to the best of the new finds from Pakistan, a mandible found near Gandekas and discussed below (see §1 (e)). The Gandekas mandible has been figured by Pilbeam et al. (1977) and by Simons (1979). Both mandibles show comparatively small and vertically emplaced incisor and canine sockets. There is a break across the right side of the symphysis so that the right ramus has been shifted slightly backwards and the right horizontal ramus bent towards the left ramus. This twisting has decreased somewhat the angle of posterior divergence indicated in the new find from Pakistan. In the Candir mandible the zygoma are situated further forward, arising at the front of M_2 rather than the front of M_3 in the Gandekas jaw. Left P_{3-4} in the Candir specimen are transversely broad and closed up against each other and the M_1. Although both the left and right canines have been lost there is a distinct contact facet for the canine on the anterolateral face of left P_3. Thus a closed C–M_3 tooth row is confirmed here as it is also for the Fort Ternan *Ramapithecus* mandible by a similar wear facet on P_3. There can hardly have been any gaps between lateral incisor and canine as the space that they occupied, judging from the position of canine and incisor roots, is small. The breadth across all four incisor roots between the canines is only 1.4 cm, while the estimated breadth across the outside of P_2 is 3.5 cm. Thus the Candir mandible provides strong evidence of a very reduced anterior lower dentition and a closed tooth row. Like Gandekas *Ramapithecus* this is a small creature with a small, flattened face and big molars. This mandible implies a face only about half the absolute size of that of *Sivapithecus* from Mount Sinap. P_{3-4} of the Candir mandible show considerable wear, so that there is no apex for a separate metaconid cusp; nevertheless, a distinct and extensive transverse wear facet is developed on the ridge running toward the inside of the tooth and the transverse long axis of left P_3 is almost parallel to P_4, as can easily be seen in fig. 3 of Andrews & Tekkaya. The general structure and orientation of P_3 is much as in *Ouranopithecus*, which on average shows no trace of a metaconid. Although P_3–M_1 are very well worn, M_3 wear is slight, and indication of the occurrence of differential wear. Mandibular morphology with double internal transverse tori strongly developed, an almost vertically orientated symphysis, closed-up tooth row with interstitial wear and large molars, thick enamel, differential wear, short face, and so forth, all show a clear model for origin of the *Australopithecus* dental mechanism. Even if jaws like those of Candir and Gandekas are regarded as only of female apes, it is difficult to see where resemblance to modern African apes, not seen also in *Australopithecus*, is to be found. Should males of *Ramapithecus* have had larger faces and bigger canines, later 'feminization' could have produced the condition seen in *Australopithecus*. It is less clear that dental/facial morphology of *Pan/Gorilla* could derive from such a species as occurs at Candir, Turkey.

(ii) *Pasalar*

This fossil-bearing site is located in western Turkey, about 125 km across the Hellespont, south-southwest of Istanbul. The probable age, as judged from the large associated mammalian fauna of over 45 species, would be 15–16 Ma. Primates are represented by 100 isolated teeth, which fall into two groups identified by Andrews & Tobien (1977). These are a smaller species, referred to *Ramapithecus wickeri*, and a set of larger species that they placed in the Vienna basin Vindobian species *Sivapithecus darwini*.

Morphologically each of these species appears to lie more or less between east African early Miocene *Proconsul* species and late Miocene *Ramapithecus* and *Sivapithecus* species from India and Pakistan. The larger species is about the same size as *Sivapithecus indicus* of the Siwaliks and the smaller stands close in size to *Ramapithecus* from Candir and Gandekas. Of the teeth, 14 are broken, which allows for measurement of enamel thickness. Both species have thick enamel and other advanced characters, such as partial reduction of upper lingual cingula. Consequently, Andrews & Tobien rightly referred them to the later Miocene genera and not to *Proconsul*. If the age correlation is correct, then this might be the oldest occurrence of *Ramapithecus* as well as of *Sivapithecus*.

(iii) *Mount Sinap*

This hominoid from the Sinap series northwest of Ankara was described under the name of *Ankarapithecus meteai* by Ozansoy (1957, 1965). It consisted of a symphysial fragment with crowns of left C–P_3 and right I_2–C; associated are broken-off left P_4–M_3. In 1967 a second specimen was found that was recently described by Andrews & Tekkaya (1980). This is an important find because of its completeness. MTA 2125 consists of a complete palate (with all teeth) and lower face that preserves most of the nasal region and parts of the right zygoma and orbit. The latter authors conclude from these two specimens that both belong to the species *Ankarapithecus meteai*, that this is the same species as *Ouranopithecus macedoniensis* from Greece, and that both genera belong in *Sivapithecus*. This face is clearly more advanced than any of the *Proconsul* group from the early Miocene of Kenya and Uganda. It combines a number of interesting features. The nasoalveolar clivus is long, so that the lower face is prognathic; the nasal opening is broad and the zygomatic process is very deep; central and lateral incisors are very different in size. Andrews & Tekkaya (1980) conclude from their study, not only that the Macedonian and Mount Sinap finds belong to the same species, but also that both of these species belong in genus

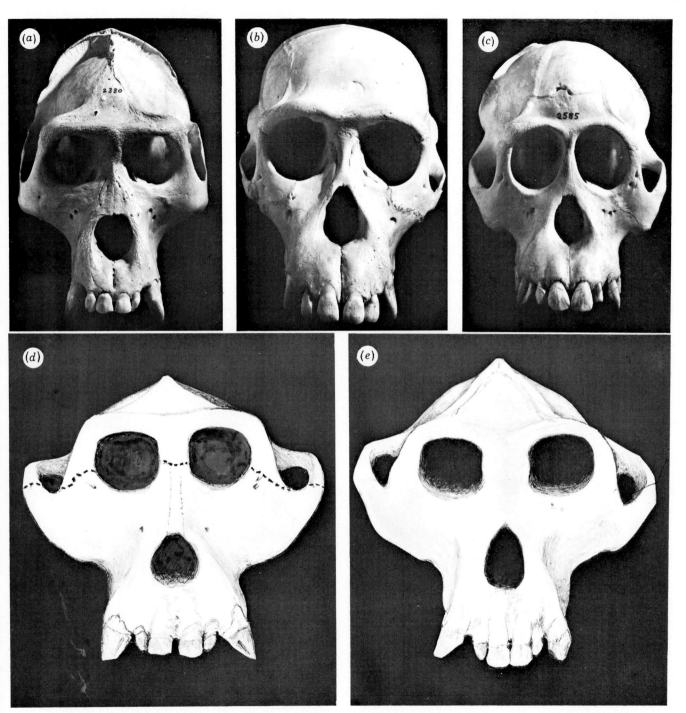

FIGURE 1. Comparison of the frontal aspect of the skull in the living great apes ((*a*) *Gorilla*, (*b*) *Pan*, (*c*) *Pongo*) with tentative restorations of two recently discovered skulls of *Sivapithecus* ((*c*) from Sinap, Turkey; (*d*) from Lufeng, China). All brought to the same approximate cranial height. ((*d*) Hypothetical above dashed line; (*e*) orbital and facial proportions partly hypothetical.) Cranial composition by F. A. Ankel-Simons, photographs by W. Sacco, drawings by E. L. Simons

Sivapithecus. They suggest further that the latter is very close to *Ramapithecus*. Nevertheless the face of *Ankarapithecus* shows considerable distinctiveness from that of *Ramapithecus*, for in the Turkish face the nasoalveolar clivus is long, not short, and prognathism is pronounced, rather than reduced. The zygoma of the Mount Sinap find arise much higher up and somewhat farther back than in *Ramapithecus* and the tooth rows in it diverge little posteriorly compared to those in the latter. In short, this face is as little like that indicated for *Ramapithecus* as are those of modern *Pan* and *Gorilla* like *Ramapithecus*. In the lower left corner of figure 1, plate 1, I have attempted a reconstruction by mirror-imaging the right side and correcting, as far as possible, for distortion.

The question of the relation of *Sivapithecus*, *Ankarapithecus* and *Ouranopithecus* is at present somewhat uncertain. My studies of the Macedonian ape and of Siwalik *Sivapithecus indicus* do not lead to the view that they are necessarily congeneric. *Ankarapithecus* shows little dental–gnathic difference from *Sivapithecus indicus*, but I believe that considerable facial differences may emerge with the description of the newly found face of *Sivapithecus indicus* from Pakistan. Tentatively, at present, the Mount Sinap species may be regarded as belonging to *Sivapithecus*.

One point should be developed about the face of *Sivapithecus meteai*. My study indicates that the upper face has been distorted by plastic flow and probably also by dislocation of the crack between the two halves of this face, which are glued together somewhat out of orientation. These distortions, which I detected on the original, can clearly be seen in Andrews & Tobien (1977, fig. 1 *a*, *c*). In both parts of this figure the tip of the maxilla running up between the ventromedial corner of the orbit and the nasal can be seen to go across a midline erected between central incisors onto the left side. Thus, any accurate calculation of width of nasals and interorbital septum in this specimen is impossible. As narrowness here would be an interesting similarity to *Pongo* the inadequacies of this specimen are regrettable. Walker & Andrews (1973) also contains a controversial interpretation of the orientation of parts of a crushed fossil, which I have analysed elsewhere (Simons & Pilbeam 1978). In an undescribed frontal fragment of Hungarian *Bodvapithecus* and both the newly discovered *Sivapithecus* face from Pakistan and the new *Sivapithecus* skull from Lufeng, China, the interorbital septum is broader, and none of these show the oval orbital outlines of *Pongo*.

In conclusion it is fair to say that some characteristics of *Sivapithecus*, *sensu lato*, may resemble those of *Pongo*, but the most probable meaning of this is that *Pongo* has retained certain resemblances to the middle Miocene radiation that evidently produced it. These features of similarity would be primitive retentions, not shared derived features. As long as the best specimens of most Miocene hominoid genera and species were known either from upper or lower dentition that were not directly associated with the respective opposing dentition (upper–lower), taxonomic judgments were hampered. This face from Mount Sinap, the undescribed jaws and face from Gandekas, Pakistan, and the new skull and jaws from Lufeng, China, all presently assigned to *Sivapithecus*, should make for better judgments as to whether all these finds represent one or more genera. Their full analysis will no doubt clarify the relationship of *Sivapithecus* and its relatives to the ancestry of man (see also Pilbeam 1979 *a*, *b*).

(d) Site in Hungary

Recent discoveries of Miocene hominoids at Rudabanya in northeastern Hungary have been summarized by Kretzoi (1975), who has proposed two new genera of hominoids: *Rudapithecus* and *Bodvapithecus*. Present also is a large species of *Pliopithecus*. The fauna and flora from this site are extensive and indicate a late Vallesian or early Turolian provincial age of approximately

9 or 10 Ma. *Bodvapithecus* is known from a not-quite-adult mandible Rud. 14, which preserves all lower teeth, save M_3, on one side or the other. The type, Rud. 7, is a maxillary fragment. These materials, although limited, are closely similar to *Sivapithecus indicus*. The other Hungarian form, *Rudapithecus*, is more *Ramapithecus*-like. Although much information is provided about *Rudapithecus* by the ten specimens reported so far, it is not quite clear whether placement of the species in *Ramapithecus* is warranted. Like *Ramapithecus* from India, Turkey and Kenya, *Rudapithecus* seems to show larger lateral incisors (above and below) than does *Sivapithecus*, as well as relatively small canines that are planed off by wear at an early dental age.

(e) Sites in Pakistan

From 1973 to 1980 joint research teams from Yale University and the Geological Survey of Pakistan have been carrying out a very broad programme intended to extend knowledge of the geology and paleontology of the Neogene deposits of the Potwar Plateau, Pakistan. In the course of this work the number of known fossil hominoids from the Indian subcontinent has been doubled. Extensive additions to scientific knowledge in the areas of dating, ecology and faunal assessment, summarized in Pilbeam *et al.* (1977), have been made through this project. These researches lead to many more new findings than can be dealt with in the few pages available here. I will therefore restrict consideration to the hominoid fossils. The major problem in interpreting the significance to human origins from the Siwaliks of north India and Pakistan before my expeditions in north India 1968 and 1969 and those of Pilbeam in Pakistan from 1973 onwards, was the problem of analysis of the very fragmentary hominoid fossils from scattered sites of different largely unknown ages. These finds had also been subjected to a proliferation of taxonomic names. Attempts to judge the meaning of various degrees of morphological intermediacy that were exhibited by the finds made before publication of the first revision of them by Simons & Pilbeam (1965) were largely futile. Since then Greenfield (1978, 1979), working largely with the same materials, has come up with further unsatisfactory conclusions that essentially derive from trying to rank fossils of unknown ages. Since they are synchronous samples of different species from the same sites the new finds from Pakistan can now be made the basis of more accurate deduction about the nature of *Sivapithecus* and *Ramapithecus*, both because they are more complete than earlier finds and because their ages, associations and relative stratigraphic positions are known. Nothing new has been added to knowledge of *Gigantopithecus* except for the possible reference to *G. bilaspurensis* of a large distal humeral fragment.

In understanding *Ramapithecus* from Pakistan the new finds there are informative. For *Ramapithecus* the best adult mandibles reported so far are GSP 4622/4857 (loc. 182) and GSP 9562/9902 (loc. 260). There is also an infant mandible from locality 260. Like the mandible from Candir, Turkey, the incisor root sockets are closely compressed between the canine root sockets. This condition indicates a small, closed, canine incisor row; premolar and molars are closely packed together against the canine without apparent diastema and mandibular corpora diverge posteriorly.

Andrews & Tekkaya (1980) discuss the front premolars of *Ramapithecus* as 'still primitively single-cusped', although this seems not to be so for the Siwalik type species, which Pilbeam *et al.* report as follows: 'P_3 has a small but distinct lingual cusp, and its long axis is orientated at some 45° to the mesiodistal line of the tooth row'. Shape and arrangement of P_3 in the jaw of the Siwalik species show an incipient bicusped structure that is not much more advanced in early

Australopithecus from Hadar or Laetoli, such as LH 4. Moreover, there is a distinct inner cusp on P_3 of Fort Ternan *Ramapithecus* (KNM-FT 45) and on Candir there is a transverse wear facet in this position. *Sivapithecus* species typically show anteroposteriorly orientated, not transverse, P_3 and, as is typically the case in *Gorilla* and *Pan*, the metaconid is rarely present. In *Ouranopithecus* P_3 is more transverse in the smaller morphotype, but in both 'sexes' there is no trace of a metaconid even though the tooth is extended inward. In many individuals of Siwalik *Ramapithecus*, when unworn, there is buccal flare in upper, and lingual flare in lower teeth. Tooth crowns become almost completely flattened out with advanced wear before dentine is exposed. This type of wear is associated with extreme enamel thickness, which is measured as between 2.5 and 3.0 mm on lower lateral cusps (Pilbeam *et al.* 1977). The mandible below the molars is typically robust (shallow, compared to thickness). The mandible diverges posteriorly at an angle of about 20°, while the symphysis is vertically attenuated, relatively vertically orientated, and has a shortened planum alveolare and well developed transverse tori. As I pointed out long ago (Simons 1964), these mandibular features of *Ramapithecus* (here newly confirmed) relate it morphologically to Plio-Pleistocene hominids. Finds from the new explorations in Pakistan have not confirmed that there is such a thing as a male *Ramapithecus*, with distinctly large canines, although, when taken together with other Indo-Pakistan finds, there is enough difference in size between individuals to allow for a moderate sexual size difference. It will be necessary, it seems, to find a male with large canines to attribute the progressive features of *Ramapithecus* to the expression of feminine and gracile qualities alone. My recent studies of *Pan paniscus* at Terveruren, Belgium, failed to indicate that there is a closer approximation between *Ramapithecus* specimens and female *P. paniscus* than there is between the former and female *P. troglodytes*.

Sivapithecus indicus finds made on the recent expedition (Pilbeam *et al.* 1977) are even more remarkable than those of *Ramapithecus*. These specimens include the only two individuals of this particular genus and species in which most of both the mandible and snout that come from the same individual are preserved. The first of these to be recovered, GSP 9977/01/05/9564, is figured by Pilbeam *et al.* (1977), but the second, yet to be described, includes much of the face, complete mandibles and all of the dentition. Although canines are large they are blunt compared to those of *Pan* or *Gorilla* and exhibit mesial, distal and apical wear. Central upper incisors are comparatively much larger than the laterals. There is moderate canine dimorphism; diastemata between C and P_3 is variably present; that between I 2/2 and C/C is typically present. Unlike in *Ramapithecus*, mandibular rami are deep, the planum alveolare and symphysis are long and at the top angled forward to hold procumbent teeth, and the inferior transverse torus is prominent relative to the superior buttress. Tooth rows are subparallel and concave buccally, incisor regions are broad and molar enamel is about as thick as in *Ramapithecus*, which, however, is a much smaller animal. Mandibular modelling is not reminiscent of the many mandibles of *Ouranopithecus macedoniensis*, in which jaw form is more like *Gorilla*. In *O. macedoniensis* the superior transverse torus is less developed, the jaws are less robust (narrower from side to side, although deep), and the tooth rows are straight with no buccal concavity, while molars are more rounded and have flatter crowns when little worn than in *S. indicus*. This suggests that the specific and generic distinction between *S. indicus* and *O. macedoniensis* should be sustained.

One of the most significant things that the new finds from the Postwar Plateau indicate is the confirmation of the important size and adaptive differences between *R. punjabicus* and *S. indicus* that occur at the same sites. I agree with Pilbeam *et al.* (1977), who state that a third species from the Siwaliks *Sivapithecus sivalensis* 'is the most enigmatic of the Siwalik hominoids and it is not absolutely clear that it exists as a separate species'.

One final set of discoveries from the Postwar is the series of 13 postcranial bones of hominoids recently reported (Pilbeam *et al.* 1977). Taken in sum these bones show some advanced morphological features similar to those of bones of living African hominids, at least they are advanced in comparison to what little is known from analysis of limb bones from the early Miocene of Africa. Particularly interesting is a large distal humerus, GSP 12271, which is said to have a size and morphology reminiscent of a female *Gorilla*. These bones have not been reported to resemble *Pongo* in any specific way. Unfortunately none of the bones was found in unequivocal association with cranial or dental material. In my judgement those materials recovered so far are inadequate to sustain the inference, by Pilbeam *et al.* (1977), that among these later Miocene apes postcranial bones are smaller relative to dental–facial size than in modern great apes. Moreover, these limb bone fragments are not adequate, it seems, to show whether or not *Sivapithecus* and/or *Ramapithecus* were knuckle walkers, incipient bipeds, or even arboreal climbers. This first discovery in Pakistan of many hominoid postcranials from known sites is to be applauded, but it seems that, in spite of these finds, almost everything is yet to be learned about the basic locomotor adaptation of middle and late Miocene hominoids. Without finding most of the fore- and hindlimb and pelvis one cannot say what was the locomotor adaptation of these Miocene hominoids, and I, for one, never have. Even if on recovery of better postcranial material no distinct, obvious bipedal adaptations could be discerned, we would still be in the clear for a full locomotor interpretation. Incipient specializations for arm swinging, knuckle walking or bipedalism might be difficult to detect. At present we have the whole period from about 16 to 6 Ma B.P. in which to look for the first traces of these modern adaptations.

(f) Site at Lufeng, China

Recent expeditions from 1975 through 1979 have been carried out from the Academia Sinica (I.V.P.P.) and the Yunnan Provincial Museum at a coal mine 9 km north of Lufeng, Yunnan Province, south-central China (Xu *et al.* 1978; Xu & Lu 1979). Fossils come from a stratum 6–7 m thick containing many alternating layers of brown coal and fine sand. The fauna is considerable, containing 30 species, which include varieties of *Hipparion*, *Stegodon*, rhinoceros, gibbon, *Sivapithecus*, *Ramapithecus*, sabre-toothed tiger, muntjac, takin and deer. The suggested faunal age correlation is 8 Ma.

Primate fossils have been described in 1978 and 1979 by Xu & Lu. These hominoid discoveries consist of two mandibles of different size, over a hundred isolated hominoid teeth, and an ape skull reported by Xu & Lu (1980). Because of their completeness these Miocene fossil hominoids are most important. The smaller mandible, number P.A. 580, has been assigned to a new species of *Ramapithecus*, *R. lufengensis*. This mandible preserves all teeth save the central incisor pair and it is at a young individual age. The lower jaw somewhat resembles the type of *Ouranopithecus macedoniensis*, but, unlike the latter, molars of the two morphotypes from Lufeng do not match each other. Therefore the two kinds of mandibles do not appear to be of different sexes.

Examination of a cast of the mandible of P.A. 580 indicates that relative to the molars, incisors, canines and premolars have nearly the same proportions as do these teeth in *Australopithecus afarensis*; that is, incisor size relative to cheek teeth is somewhat reduced compared to *Dryopithecus* or *Sivapithecus*. Paucity of evidence as to absolute and relative incisor size in *Rama-*

pithecus makes it unnecessary to speculate, as did McHenry & Coruccini (1980), that the supposed trend toward small incisor size would have to be reversed in any lineage relating *Ramapithecus* to *Australopithecus afarensis*. In fact, attached, intact incisor crowns are not known in any mandible of *Ramapithecus* described to date other than this one from Lufeng. We are hardly at a stage of knowledge to discuss reversal of trends in incisor proportions of *Ramapithecus* other than on the basis of this specimen, which is only a referred species. The Lufeng find of P.A. 580 is from a compressed coal seam and the canines and incisors have been splayed out and flattened away from P3. When restored by Xu & Wu the tooth series is closed and all anterior teeth contact without diastemata. The restored arcade that they figure is, in fact, arranged just as in *Australopithecus afarensis*. For instance, angles of posterior divergence of cheek tooth rows in the Lufeng jaw and that of the type of *A. afarensis* are very similar. Spacing between cheek tooth rows in the two is also nearly the same. P_4–M_3 length/inter-M_2 breadth is approximately the same in Lufeng number P.A. 580 as it is in the type of *A. afarensis*. In addition to showing interesting details of tooth crown anatomy (because of the early individual age at death) this specimen demonstrates that in this particular Miocene hominoid full canine eruption preceded that of M_3 (still not fully erupted in P.A. 580). This eruption sequence is that of *Australopithecus* and *Homo*, and not that of *Sivapithecus* or *Pongo*. In P.A. 580 lower canine roots are long, but canine crowns are small and do not project significantly above the level of the tooth row. Although somewhat pointed, these canines are about equal in crown volume to P_3 rather than have a distinctly larger bulk than P_3 as is typical in apes. As in some *Australopithecus* there is a small stylid cusp at the distal base of the canines (see, for instance, Sk 51 and Sts 50). An unusual feature is a posterior groove in the lower canine crown, running up and down the posterointernal face. The canine–premolar complex of this find appears to be structurally transitional between that of apes and *Australopithecus* as was explained for other specimens by Simons & Pilbeam (1978). There is some anterolateral extension of the P_3 in *Ramapithecus lufengensis*, implying a more pointed upper canine than usually occurs in *Homo*. Comparatively large upper canines are said to characterize *A. afarensis*. The long axis of P_3 in Lufeng P.A. 580 is situated more transversely and P_3 metaconid is larger (distinctly bicusped) than is typical of *Sivapithecus* or modern apes, while P_4 here is broader, compared to mesiodistal length, than in most Miocene apes. With a rather large heel, P_4 is somewhat molarized. The lower molars of P.A. 580 have rounder outlines, more rounded cusps and a much lower gradient of increase of anteroposterior size than in *Sivapithecus yunnanensis* from the same site. Molar metaconids do not appear to be significantly larger than in *Australopithecus africanus* or *A. afarensis*.

The mandible of *Sivapithecus* from Lufeng might be taken to represent a male of its contemporary at Lufeng, *Ramapithecus lufengensis*. Such a deduction would be based on the assumption that, as in *Ouranopithecus macedoniensis*, a very great sexual dimorphism obtained. Arguing against this are the clear-cut differences between *S. yunnanensis* and *R. lufengensis* in relative M_1–M_2 size and crown anatomy of molars, in contrast with *Ouranopithecus*, where both 'sexes' show almost identical molar crown anatomy and molar outlines. The very large sample of as yet undescribed isolated teeth from Lufeng should, when analysed, resolve the number of species present.

In spite of the resemblances cited above between a cast of P.A. 580 and the Laetoli materials of *Australopithecus*, *R. lufengensis* shows several differences from *Ramapithecus punjabicus*. In *R. punjabicus* lower molars are longer and have thicker enamel than in *R. lufengensis*. The pattern of crenulation on the molars of the Lufeng find appears also to be different from that typical of

R. punjabicus. Perhaps these two species should not be assigned to the same genus. Even so, both of these species show closer resemblances to early *Australopithecus* than can be found in females of such modern apes as *Pan paniscus.* Both 'Ramapithecus' species show the general type of morphology suitable for origin of the *Australopithecus* dental mechanism. This would be true even if there were larger and more ape-like males found for each of these species. Should this be proved in future to have been so, then the *Australopithecus* dental mechanism could be considered to have arisen through the 'feminization' of a previously dimorphic species.

In addition to the nearly complete mandible referred to *Ramapithecus* at Lufeng, the much larger species, *Sivapithecus yunnanensis,* already cited, is represented by many teeth, a mandible preserving all teeth save M_3, and a skull found in December 1978. This cranium is the most complete skull of an ape ever found in Eurasia.

Cranium and dentition are characterized by deep canine fossae and prominent canine jugae with outward flaring upper canines, lateral incisors are small compared to upper centrals, and there is a pear-shaped nasal opening beneath a very broad interorbital septum. The naso-alveolar clivus is long and front teeth above and below appear to be procumbent. Although crushed, orbits show angled corners, heavy outer margins and eye sockets that are roughly quadrate in outline but appear to be somewhat broader than they are high; the reversed V-shaped temporal crests on the frontal, the marked postorbital constriction of the skull, the vertically short upper face and the quadrate and widely spaced eye sockets are all reminiscent of *Australopithecus.* The large central incisors and blunt canine tips resemble both *Australopithecus* and *Pongo.* However, since *Pongo* shares to some extent the thickness of tooth enamel of the Eurasian later Miocene Hominoidea and of *Australopithecus,* the various resemblances between *Sivapithecus* and *Pongo* in the teeth and lower face may be primitive retentions or symplesio-morphies and not shared derived characters or synapomorphies as has recently been argued by Andrews (1980) for a specimen of the lower face from Turkey that he considers may belong to *Sivapithecus,* but which others have referred to genus *Ankarapithecus.* Certainly the overall appearance of the skull of the Lufeng ape, which has been referred to *Sivapithecus,* is quite different from that of *Pongo* in many regards, particularly in its robust interorbital septum and in its possession of quadrate, laterally buttressed eyesockets.

As an illustrative exercise I have prepared figure 1, plate 1, which contains a tentative facial reconstruction (*d*) of the find from Sinap, Turkey, and an even more tentative reconstitution (*e*) of the new skull from Lufeng. The two skulls appear to indicate that these finds had both distinct similarities and distinct differences.

(2) DEFINITION OF THE TAXONOMIC FAMILY HOMINIDAE

Three main considerations have figured in past attempts to diagnose the characteristics of our immediate forerunners exclusive of the apes, or, at least, each has had an influence on con-ceptualizations about hominid origins. These factors are (1) temporal, (2) ecological, and (3) morphological, both dental/facial and postcranial.

(a) Temporal considerations

It is not clear when or where the taxonomic subgroup of humans, the hominids arose. Recent discoveries by M. Leakey, at Laetoli, Tanzania, of trackways of presumed *Australopithecus* that are close to 4 Ma old, as well as the hindlimb structure of hominid fossils of similar age from the Hadar Formation of Ethiopia, show by then perfected bipedal walking in at least some hominids (Johanson & White 1979). I think that mammalian genera typically have a 6 to 8 Ma temporal survivorship. Therefore the generic characterization of *Australopithecus* at about 4 Ma B.P. need not then have been new, but could have been several million years old. Because of the general Pliocene gap in hominoid and other mammalian groups the first actual documentation of various genera of primates from around 4–5 Ma B.P. in all probability fails to record the time of initial emergence of any of them.

While finds in the Plio-Pleistocene of Africa have dated hominids back to about 4 Ma B.P. (Leakey *et al.* 1976), discoveries in Eurasia have extended the range of Miocene ramapithecines closer to the present. Many of the sites of occurrence of *Ramapithecus*, *Sivapithecus* and related form had been correlated with the appearance of *Hipparion* at 11 or 12 Ma B.P. While certain sites such as Pasalar, Turkey (13–15 Ma B.P.), and Fort Ternan, Kenya (probably 13.9 Ma B.P.), have yielded hominoid fossils with thick molar enamel that have been referred to *Ramapithecus*, other faunal correlations indicate ages of about 8 Ma at Pyrgos in Greece, Lufeng in China, and Gandekas in Pakistan. In the Haritalyanger region of India, ages are perhaps in the 9–12 Ma range. The youngest *Ramapithecus* fossils from the Potwar Plateau appear to be about 7 Ma old (perhaps even younger for one or two specimens).

There are at least two principal implications of the new evidence about time range for *Ramapithecus* and *Sivapithecus*. Earliest and latest occurrences are spread over such a long time period that certain species may prove to be outside the probable time spread for survivorship of a single genus. Consequently, a few species now assigned to either or both genera may prove to belong in other genera when more completely known. For instance, the type specimens of *Sivapithecus indicus* and *Ramapithecus punjabicus* seem to have come from the 9–11 Ma B.P. time range, while the type of *Sivapithecus sivalensis* from Jabi, Punjab, could well prove to be from 2 to 4 Ma younger than these. Depending on their specific ages, the former two could be 2–5 Ma younger than Pasalar and Fort Ternan. Likewise *R. wickeri*, at about 14 Ma of age, is much older than the referred find of *Ramapithecus*, *R. freyburgi* from Pyrgos, Greece, whose probable age is around 8 Ma.

The second important implication of the new radiometric dating is that the youngest 'ramapithecines' (at 7 or 8 Ma old) fall within the temporal limits imposed by advocates of the late split-point time for divergence of *Pan/Homo* ancestry. However, the attempt to create a controversy about the phyletic position of *Ramapithecus* in relation to *Pan/Homo* ancestry has, or should have been, a one-sided contention. This is because palaeontologists cannot deal in absolute phyletic judgements. The anatomy of the dentition and face of *Ramapithecus* bears sufficient similarity to that of *Australopithecus* to justify placement in the same family, but at all times the possibility has existed that the whole set of similarities could be due to convergence. Although I have considered the latter possibility from time to time it still seems to me unlikely. Nevertheless it will be the discovery of better anatomical evidence about *Ramapithecus* and its relatives that will shift them away from, or toward, particular associations with the African Plio-Pleistocene hominids.

One thing is clear. Strong advocates of the accuracy of 'molecular clocks' have shown a distressing lack of rigour in answering a sequence of problems posed by the series of seemingly late split-point times calculated generally throughout the family tree of primates. They need to come up with clearer answers to the numerous criticisms regarding confidence limits on dates, variance in rates of change and so forth. As I have stated recently (1977), the problem is not dependent upon whose ancestor is *Ramapithecus*, but is more general. There are at least half a dozen points in primate phylogeny where we have fossil evidence relating to branches of principal subgroups within the order. All of these are discordant with the dates determined by immunochemical distance by Wilson & Sarich (1969) or by Sarich & Cronin (1976). No adequate explanation of these discrepancies has yet been produced by proponents of 'molecular clocks'. Rather, extremists have begun to argue instead that split-point times determined by immunochemical distance have the same validity as radiometric determinations.

It is understandable that, as awareness of man's close biochemical similarity to the African apes has grown, later ancestral branch points between them should gain favour. The past twenty years has seen abandonment, by all authorities, of early divergence times of hominids from the apes. Living authorities have seriously advocated estimates that range all the way from a date before the end of the Cretaceous to the Oligocene. Now nearly all serious students of human origins agree that the ape–hominid divergence has to be much later. Estimates for this later split still spread between middle Miocene and middle Pliocene. It still seems to me that a split-point date in the Miocene around 12–15 Ma B.P. is more probable than a mid-Pliocene date of 4–5 Ma. Papers by Lovejoy *et al.* (1972), by myself (Simons 1976*a*), by Walker (1976), by Radinsky (1978) and by Romero-Herrera *et al.* (1979), as well as contributions not yet published (Baba *et al.* 1980; Korey 1980; Goodman 1980), all give reasons for inaccuracies or changes in rate of molecular evolution. These references and many others that could be cited forcibly call into question the validity of molecular clock dates. Interestingly, Goodman (1981) has demonstrated that, if one makes the assumption that molecular evolution proceeds in a clock-like manner, following the hypothesis originally proposed by Zuckerkandl & Pauling (1962), then a time of only 0.5 Ma was obtained for the *Homo–Pan* ancestral divergence. His method is based on counting the number of nucleotide replacements on four protein chains: α- and β-haemoglobin, myoglobin and cytochrome *c*. The new data summarized by Goodman indicate a clear-cut pattern of accelerations and decelerations in rates of molecular evolution throughout time.

It seems probable that higher primates, or most primates, show a slowed rate of molecular evolution. In Simons (1976*a*) I discussed the principal divergence times indicated from the fossil record. At least six of these present major difficulties for advocates of molecular clock dates for split points. These divergence dates are summarized in table 1.

Although various suggestions have been put forward as disallowing the relevance of the above indicated branching times, none of them have shown much rigour. The gelada baboon group traces back in Africa as far as does *Australopithecus*, yet it gives no immunochemical distance from common (*Papio*) baboons. The remarkable resemblance at 20 Ma B.P. of *Progalago* to modern genus *Galago* is so close as to hardly warrant their generic separation. Neither of these genera are lorisines, while *Mioeuoticus* is a lorisine related to *Perodicticus*. Small Miocene hominoids such as *Epipliopithecus* and *Micropithecus* show detailed specific resemblance to modern *Hylobates* and *Symphalangus*. The resemblance is particularly striking with *Epipliopithecus* from the European Vindobonian Miocene provincial age, where mandibles, face and skull can be compared (Zapfe 1960). The relationship between modern gibbons and *Epipliopithecus* has been explained away by the theories that all early apes would look like gibbons or that their primitive features, such as short forelimb and tail in *Epipliopithecus*, disqualify the relationship. Nevertheless, other early catarrhines whose face, jaws and skull are known, for example *Aegyptopithecus*, do not exhibit similarity to gibbons. New finds from the Fayum of parapithecid monkeys show them to have had many primitive features, but their advanced features resemble those of catarrine monkeys not those of the South American platyrrhines. These parapithecids are not very much like their ape contemporaries the Propliopithecidae from the Fayum, Egypt. For these two groups to have diverged as much as they have at 28 or 29 Ma B.P., the separation of Hominoidea must have been considerably earlier than the time of their existence and not, of

TABLE 1

divergence in ancestry of	fossil or geological evidence and date B.P./Ma		molecular clock date B.P./Ma
Papio–Theropithecus	age of oldest *Theropithecus* (= *Simopithecus*)	4	no immunochemical separation, therefore 0
galagines–lorisines	*Progalago* (galagine) and *Mioeuoticus* (lorisine) already separate at (see Walker 1978)	20	10
pongids–hylobatids	*Epipliopithecus* distinctly resembles gibbons facially and the same *Micropithecus*	16 20	10
hominoids–cercopithecoids	parapithecids and propliopithecids have evolved to level of distinct families at 29 Ma B.P. (allowing *ca.* 5 to 10 Ma for familial divergence)	34–39	22
catarrhines–platyrrhines	segregation of New and Old Worlds by North Atlantic rifting, and disallowing long distance South Atlantic rafting by ancestral platyrrhines	50 +	36
Ramapithecus–Sivapithecus from *Dryopithecus* regardless of whether each, or both are specially related to either *Homo* or *Pongo*	geological time of appearance *Ramapithecus* and *Sivapithecus*	*ca.* 15	4–8

course, at 22 Ma B.P. Although one or two palaeontologists have suggested that the New World monkeys could have left Africa by rafting to populate South America with platyrrhine monkeys at about the time the Fayum lower fossil wood zone was being deposited, that is, about 35–38 Ma ago, this is highly improbable (Simons 1976a). The South Atlantic was then at least two-thirds as wide as it is now. At typical east-to-west ocean current rates a raft of vegetation crossing the South Atlantic at that time would have had a voyage lasting a minimum of six weeks. This is far too long to satisfy water and other physiological needs of monkeys. Moreover, although the parapithecids share many primitive features with ceboids they have not one synapomorphy that would link them with each other, that is, they do not show any shared derived or advanced feature. Finally, even if the ramapithecine–sivapithecine assemblage is related to the ancestry of *Pongo* and not *Homo* it is discordant with a separation of 7 Ma B.P., determined by immuno-chemical distance since *Sivapithecus* appears 16 Ma ago. On the basis of present evidence it seems more probable to me that the few broad similarities so far reported between *Sivapithecus* and *Pongo* are symplesiomorphies not synapomorphies.

Looked at overall, advocates of molecular date determinations as well as students of the form of fossils are both morphologists. The former are trying to quantify the degree of difference in the form of molecules, and palaeontologists are those who assess macromorphological differences and similarities. Each approach can be closely quantified and this in turn tends to lead to dogmatic statements about the meaning of molecular and of phenotypic similarities. Each system also has an Achilles heel. For advocates of molecular clock regularity this is the demonstrated change in evolutionary rates. For palaeontologists the weakness is that evolutionary processes can bring about convergence, which masks the degree of relatedness between particular forms. Whether the split between the ancestors of man and the African apes was before or after the time when *Ramapithecus* lived and what actually happened in the early stages of the development of the Hominidae will only be confirmed with the recovery of new fossils. The search for this evidence is a true challenge and stands as one of the most exciting intellectual frontiers yet available for exploration by anthropologists.

One final point may be worth mentioning in regard to the time of emergence of hominids. For those who take it to have been at 6 or 7 Ma B.P. in Africa it is probably then synonymous with origin of genus *Australopithecus*. In spite of the morphological distinctiveness that living hominids like to attribute to themselves, a group of so recent an origin can hardly be given family status. Except for families that have no fossil record at all, and thus no documented origin, even the youngest mammalian families, such as Bovidae, Muridae or Elephantidae, had 12–15 Ma B.P. origin times. The peak time for appearance of mammalian families in the fossil record is early Oligocene and after early Miocene familial group origins decline abruptly (Lilligraven 1972).

(b) Ecological considerations

The ecological context for hominid origins seen in middle and late Miocene hominoids has been much discussed, but these discussions have led to few clear conclusions. In the early Miocene of East Africa and in the western European middle Miocene, forest-adapted apes with thin tooth enamel appear to predominate (Andrews & Van Couvering 1975). Such species include the various dryopithecine species of genus or subgenus *Proconsul*, *Micropithecus clarki*, *Limnopithecus legetet* and *Dendropithecus macinnesi* in East Africa, and in Europe the various species of *Pliopithecus*, as well as *Dryopithecus fontani* and *Dryopithecus laietanus*.

For the middle and late Miocene sites, much enlarged faunal lists have recently been published for sites where *Ramapithecus*, *Sivapithecus*, and *Gigantopithecus* occur. Particularly extensive faunal associations with hominoid species are known at Lufeng in China, the Potwar Plateau sites in Pakistan, Pasalar in Turkey, Rain Ravine in Macedonia, Greece, Rudabanya in Hungary, and Fort Ternan in Kenya. It would appear that forest fruit, nuts and vegetation were probably available at or near all such sites, none of which appears to have been in either gallery forest or dry grassland savannah. In some Miocene hominoid sites, such as Rudabanya, forest conditions seem to predominate, but even there we have evidence for open woodlands nearby. The best reconstruction appears to be that at least some of the many new populations of middle and later Miocene hominoids occupied a mosaic environment of woodlands interspersed with grasslands.

Many of these sites, such as several Indo-Pakistan localities, Candir, Rain Ravine and Fort Ternan, show, in considerable numbers, bovids adapted to woodland savannah, as well as other open country elements. Hominoids, however, have high water requirements and may seldom have strayed far from water. Although the presence of thick tooth enamel typically in almost all known later Miocene and Pliocene hominoids suggests a diet different from that of both early Miocene and present-day African apes, neither meat-, nor grass-eating is indicated for these hominoids by tooth microwear (R. F. Kay & A. Walker, personal communication). In fact, Kay (1981) has suggested that the predominant element evoking thick cheek-tooth enamel may be cracking into thick fruit rinds and the husks and shells of nuts. Whatever evoked this thick enamel in Tertiary hominoids, it is not needed by *Pan* or *Gorilla* today and is not found in any African apes. *Pongo*, on the other hand, does retain fairly thick enamel and, if its diet, when further analysed, shows distinctive features the reason for this retention will become clear. The molar crown enamel is approximately twice as thick in *Pongo* as in *Australopithecus*, *Sivapithecus* and *Ramapithecus*. Therefore, the modern east Asian ape cannot be taken as an exact dietary analogue for the earlier forms.

(c) Morphological considerations

(i) Dental/facial morphology

The structure of the dental mechanism as well as of the face and skull of man's immediate forerunners may be inferred by three principal approaches. The first is the traditional comparison contrasting modern and Pleistocene fossil man to the living great apes. Such definitions of the difference between hominids and pongids are characterized by LeGros Clark (1955). These definitions were done when almost nothing informative had been published about middle or late Miocene apes and when, as is still the case, nothing about the immediate (Pliocene, late Miocene) ancestors of living African apes was known. Inferring the nature of man's ancestor along these lines led to the expectation that man's forbears would somehow be intermediate between Pleistocene humans and the living African apes. Here the characters indicated for hominid emergence revolve around their acquisition of transverse, bicusped P_3, development of small canines, a small snout and a broadening of tooth rows posteriorly. Thus, when one takes this general approach the modern African apes, not fossil forms, are seen as the common starting point from which hominids diverged. A recent variant of this approach has been developed by Zihlmann *et al.* (1978).

Another manner of approaching the question of ancestral hominid facial and/or gnathic morphology is to bring in the evidence of past fossil forms that are older than earliest *Australopithecus* in an attempt to judge which show the greatest relation to the latter. To do this one has to skip back from earliest well understood *Australopithecus*, at about 3.5 Ma of age to the middle and late Miocene fossils, whose age ranges from some 8 Ma to about 16 Ma. On taking up this line of approach a number of features of resemblance to *Australopithecus* that can not be observed in modern African apes are found in Miocene forms. Such features are generally related to development of enlarged molars with thick enamel and to reduction of the size of the face, incisors and canines relative to cheek teeth. The findings that can come from this type of approach are summarized in Simons (1968, 1976*b*).

A third approach to the question of the nature of the dental/facial anatomy of earliest Hominidae and their immediate forerunners is to extrapolate backwards a set of primitive features that may be inferred from earliest *Australopithecus*. This third approach only became possible recently, with the dating of several sets of *Australopithecus* at earlier than 2 Ma B.P. Preliminary assessments of this sort have been made by both Johanson (1980) and White (1980). Out of this type of assessment also grows what is probably a most important issue, the new evidence about what not to expect in hominids earlier than those now documented from the 3–4 Ma B.P. period. Brain to body size ratios are difficult to estimate from fragmentary remains and it is also most difficult to demonstrate same site, that is contemporaneous body size dimorphism. However, there does seem to be growing evidence that the level of body size and canine size dimorphism may be higher in earliest *Australopithecus* than in later hominids (Johanson & White 1979). It is also uncertain whether the brain in an immediate forerunner of *Australopithecus* in relation to body size would have been particularly larger than its ape contemporaries. My view is that it probably would have been, based on the present evidence from *Australopithecus*.

(ii) *Postcranial morphology* (locomotor mechanism)

The major outstanding question about man's immediate forerunners that could be clearly answered from the fossil record would be the time of emergence of the bipedal walking adaptation in these ancestors. Since the appearance of different aspects of the whole animal in structural evolution are not correlated, membership in the hominid family could be adumbrated first in dental/cranial features and later in a locomotor adaptation. An analogous case can be seen in

TABLE 2

name	locality	probable age/Ma	description
Dryopithecus fontani	St Gaudens, France	15	distal two-thirds left humerus
Proconsul africanus	Gumba, Rusinga Island, Kenya	18	distal four-fifths juvenile humerus
Epipliopithecus vindobonensis	Vienna Basin, Czechoslovakia	16	complete right humerus
?Dryopithecus (= Austriacopithecus weinfurteri)	Vienna Basin, Austria	16	central shaft of humerus
Dendropithecus mackinnesi	Hiwegi, Rusinga Island, Kenya	18	nearly complete humerus (lacks proximal two-thirds of head)
Proconsul nyanzae	Maboko Island, Lake Victoria, Kenya	15	central shaft of humerus

the gibbon group, where a strong facial and/or cranial similarity developed early in the middle Miocene; that is, *Micropithecus* from East Africa and *Epipliopithecus* from Europe have strong cranial resemblance of *Hylobates* and *Symphalangus*. We know that Miocene *Epipliopithecus* and the modern gibbons are closely similar in face and cranium and in the hindlimb as well. It is only in the forelimb that adaptations differ strikingly. From this, there is a strong inference that the taxonomic group of the gibbons segregated first (family Hylobatidae) and the forelimb elongation of this branch of the ape family tree came later. Incidentally this means that forelimb elongation and tail loss developed independently for similar, but by no means necessarily the same, reasons in the *Pan–Gorilla* and the *Hylobates–Symphalangus* lineages. By analogy the Miocene ancestors of *Australopithecus* could have been living and eating much as they did later, even before they were bipedal.

Another important point about Hominoidea before the Plio-Pleistocene is that the fossil record does not support the idea that all earlier Miocene apes had a primitive monkey-like postcranium, and that the barrel-chested, broad-shouldered condition of the modern hominoids developed in one particular branch of apes at a late date. Although the chest and shoulder region is not well preserved in the fossil record it would be necessary to show that all known Miocene Hominoidea are closely similar and uniformly primitive in the upper arm. Fortunately for establishment of this point it is the humerus that can be compared among a series of Miocene apes that are all 14 Ma or older, running back to about 20 Ma. The taxonomic assignments, localities, probable ages, and descriptions of these fossils are given in table 2.

These humeri fall into at least four general classes, indicated by differences in morphology and all in existence before 1 Ma B.P. Clearly, chests, fore- and hindlimbs and spines of early and middle Miocene hominoids were likely to have been diversified if such is the case for their humeri. The *Dryopithecus* humerus from Saint Gaudens, France, and that of *Proconsul* from Gumba, Rusinga, both subadult, are generalized, lightly built and straight shafted without being elongated. The Vienna Basin ?*Dryopithecus* humerus, like that from Maboko Island, Kenya, are both retroflexed as in terrestrial monkeys. Different from these is the well preserved humerus of *Epipliopithecus*, which is short and broad distally, possesses an entepicondylar foramen and indicates a generalized arboreal quadruped like *Aegyptopithecus*. In contrast, the humerus of *Dendropithecus* from Hiwegi, Rusinga, is longer, relative to its calibre, than any of the above, is straight (not retroflexed) and narrow distally, has no entepicondylar foramen and has an over-all morphology suggesting incipient suspensory use of the forelimb (Simons 1972).

In conclusion, one has to say that we do not know how to choose from which of these upper-limb morphologies that of the hominids arose, but we do clearly know now that hominoids do not show early monkey-like postcranial uniformity. This is a point unrecognized, or glossed over by, many palaeoanthropologists who have focused their attention on the unknown last 10 Ma or so of ape evolution.

Recent confirmation of a perfected bipedal walking ability at Laetoli, Tanzania, and in the Hadar region of Ethiopia at about 3.5 Ma B.P. does not say anything about how much earlier the adaptation arose. Certainly we have not yet found any real evidence that would show whether or not any early Pliocene or late Miocene hominoids were possessed of bipedal adaptations. About this important issue, in spite of the numerous postcranial bones newly found in the Potwar region of Pakistan, we know essentially nothing.

In conclusion I should like to thank my wife, F. A. Ankel-Simons, and Dr R. F. Kay for valuable discussion and review of this paper. Thanks are also due to Dr I. Tekkaya, who allowed me to study the well preserved type mandible from Candir (see §1 (c) (i)).

REFERENCES (Simons)

Andrews, P. J. 1971 *Ramapithecus wickeri* mandible from Fort Ternan, Kenya. *Nature, Lond.* **231**, 192–194.

Andrews, P. J. 1978 A revision of the Miocene Hominoidea of East Africa. *Bull. Br. Mus. nat. Hist.* A**30** (2), 85–224.

Andrews, P. J. & Molleson, T. I. 1979 The provenance of *Sivapithecus africanus. Bull. Br. Mus. nat. Hist.* **32** (1), 19–23.

Andrews, P. J. & Tekkaya, I. 1976 *Ramapithecus* in Kenya and Turkey. *IX Congr. Un. Int. Sci. Préhist. Protohist.*, coll. 6, pp. 7–21.

Andrews, P. J. & Tekkaya, I. 1980 A revision of the Turkish Miocene hominoid *Sivapithecus meteai. Palaeontology* **23** (1), 85–95.

Andrews, P. J. & Tobien, H. 1977 New Miocene locality in Turkey with evidence on the origin of *Ramapithecus* and *Sivapithecus. Nature, Lond.* **268**, 699–701.

Andrews, P. J. & Van Couvering, J. A. H. 1975 Palaeoenvironments in the East African Miocene. In *Approaches to primate paleobiology* (ed. F. S. Szalay), pp. 62–103. Basel: Karger.

Azzaroli, A. 1977 Late Miocene interchange of terrestrial faunas across the Mediterranean. *Memorie Soc. geol. ital.* **4** (2), 261–265.

Baba, M. L., Darga, Ll., Goodman, M. & Weiss, M. L. 1980 Cytochrome-C and rates of evolution in primates. *Am. J. phys. Anthrop.* **52**, 201–202 (abstract).

Bishop, W. W. & Chapman, G. R. 1970 Early Pliocene sediments and fossils from the Northern Kenya Rift Valley. *Nature, Lond.* **226**, 914–918.

Bishop, W. W., Chapman, G. R., Hill, A. & Miller, J. A. 1971 Succession of Cainozoic vertebrate assemblages from the Northern Kenya Rift Valley. *Nature, Lond.* **233**, 389–394.

Bishop, W. W. and Pickford, M. H. L. 1975 Geology, fauna and palaeoenvironments of the Ngorora Formation, Kenya Rift Valley. *Nature, Lond.* **254**, 185–192.

Bonis, L. de and Melentis, J. 1977a Les Primates hominoïdes du Vallésien de Macédoine (Grèce). Étude de la mâchoire inférieure. *Geobios* **10** (6), 849–885.

Bonis, L. de & Melentis, J. 1977b Un nouveau gener de Primate hominoïde dans le Vallésien (Miocène supérieur) de Macédoine. *C. r. hebd. Séanc. Acad. Sci., Paris* D **284**, 1393–1396.

Bonis, L. de & Melentis, J. 1978 Les Primates hominoïdes du Miocène supérieur de Macédoine. Étude de la mâchoire supérieure. *Annls Paléont.* **64**, 185–202.

Clark, W. E. Le Gros 1955 *The fossil evidence for human evolution.* Chicago: Chicago University Press.

Clark, W. E. Le Gros & Leakey, L. S. B. 1950 Diagnoses of East African Miocene Hominoidea. *Q. Jl geol. Soc. Lond.* **105**, 260–262.

Coppens, Y. 1978 Le Lothagamien et el Shungurien, étages continentaux du Pliocène Est-Africain. *Bull. Soc. géol. Fr.* [7] **20** (1), 39–44.

Greenfield, L. O. 1978 On the dental arcade reconstructions of *Ramapithecus. J. hum. Evol.* **7**, 345–359.

Greenfield, L. O. 1979 On the adaptive pattern of *Ramapithecus. Am. J. phys. Anthrop.* **50**, 527–548.

Goodman, M. 1981 Amino acid sequences of Primates: their contribution to understanding human evolution. In *Les processus de l'hominisation, Colloque International Centre National de la recherche scientifique, Paris, June 1980.* (In the press.)

Johanson, D. C. 1980 Odontological considerations of the Mio-Pliocene hominoids *Am. J. phys. Anthrop.* **252**, 242. (Abstract.)

Johanson, D. C. & White, T. D. 1979 A systematic assessment of early African hominids. *Science, N.Y.* **203** (4378), 321–330.

Johanson, D. C., White, T. D. & Coppens, Y. 1978 A new species of the genus *Australopithecus* (Primates: Hominidae) from the Pliocene of Eastern Africa. *Kirtlandia* **28**, 1–14.

Kay, R. F. 1981 The nutcrackers – a new theory of the adaptations of the Ramapithecinae *Am. J. phys. Anthrop.* (In the press.)

Koenigswald, G. H. R. von 1972 Ein Unterkiefer Eines fossilen Hominoiden aus dem Unterpliozän Griechenlands. *Proc. K. ned. Akad. Wet.* C **75** (5), 385–394.

Korey, K. A. 1980 Species numbers and molecular dates for primate evolution. *Am. J. phys. Anthrop.* **52**, 45 (abstr.).

Kretzoi, M. 1975 New Ramapithecines and *Pliopithecus* from the lower Pliocene of Rudabanya in northeastern Hungary. *Nature, Lond.* **257**, 578–581.

Leakey, L. S. B. 1962 A new Lower Pliocene fossil primate from Kenya. *Ann. Mag. nat. Hist.* (13) **4**, 689–696.

Leakey, M. D., Hay, R. L., Curtis, G. H. ,Drake, R. E., Jackes, M. K. & White, T. D. 1976 Fossil hominids from the Laetolil Beds. *Nature, Lond.* **262**, 460–466.

Lillegraven, J. A. 1972 Ordinal and familial diversity of cenozoic mammals. *Taxon* **21** (2/3), 261–274.

Lovejoy, O., Burnstein, H. & Heiple, K. H. 1972 Primate phylogeny and immunological distance. *Science, N.Y.* **176**, 803–807.

Madden, C. T. 1980 East African *Sivapithecus* should not be identified as *Proconsul nyanzae. Primates.* (In the press.)

McHenry, H. M. & Corruccini, R. S. 1980 On the status of *Australopithecus afarensis. Science, N.Y.* **207**, 1103–1104.

Meyer, G. E. 1978 Hydracoidea. In *Evolution of African mammals* (ed. V. J. Maglio & H. B. S. Cooke), pp. 284–314. Cambridge, Massachusetts, Harvard University Press.

Ozansoy, F. 1957 Faunes des mammifères du Tertaire de Turquie et leurs révisions stratigraphique. *Bull. Miner Res. Explor. Inst.,* Ankara **49**, 29–48.

Ozansoy, F. 1965 Étude des gisements continentaux et des mammifères du Cénozoïque de Turquie. *Mém. Soc. géol. Fr.* **44**, 5–89.

Patterson, B., Behrensmeyer, A. K. & Sill, W. D. 1970 Geology and fauna of a new Pliocene locality in northwestern Kenya. *Nature, Lond.* **226**, 918–921.

Pickford, M. 1975 Late Miocene sediments and fossils from the northern Kenya Rift Valley. *Nature, Lond.* **265** 279–284.

Pilbeam, D. 1979*a* Recent finds and interpretations of Miocene hominoids. *A. Rev. Anthrop.* **8**, 333–352.)

Pilbeam, D. 1979*b* Major trends in human evolution. In *Current argument on early man* (ed. L. K. Königsson). New York: Pergamon. (In the press.)

Pilbeam, D., Meyer, G. E., Badgley, C., Rose, M. D., Pickford, M. H. L., Behrensmeyer, A. K. & Shah, S. M. I. 1977 New hominoid primates from the Siwaliks of Pakistan and their bearing on hominoid evolution. *Nature, Lond.* **270**, 689–695.

Radinsky, L. 1978 Do albumen clocks run on time? *Science, N.Y.* **200**, 1182–1183.

Romero-Herrera, A. E., Lieska, N., Goodman, M. & Simons, E. L. 1979 The use of amino acid sequence analysis in assessing evolution. *Biochimie* **61**, 767–779.

Sarich, V. M. and Cronin, J. E. 1976 Molecular systematics of the Primates. In *Molecular anthropology* (ed. M. Goodman, R. E. Tashian & J. H. Tashian), pp. 141–170. New York: Plenum Press.

Simons, E. L. 1963 Some fallacies in the study of hominid phylogeny. *Science, N.Y.* **141**, 879–889.

Simons, E. L. 1964 On the mandible of *Ramapithecus. Proc. natn. Acad. Sci. U.S.A.* **51**, 528–535.

Simons, E. L. 1968 A source for dental comparison of *Ramapithecus* with *Australopithecus* and *Homo. S. Afr. J. Sci.* **64**, 92–112.

Simons, E. L. 1972 *Primate evolution: an introduction to man's place in nature.* New York: Macmillan.

Simons, E. L. 1976*a* The fossil record of primate phylogeny. In *Molecular anthropology* (ed. M. Goodman, R. E. Tashian & J. H. Tashian), pp. 35–62. New York: Plenum Press.

Simons, E. L. 1976*b* The nature of the transition in the dental mechanism from pongids to hominids. *J. hum. Evol.* **5**, 511–528.

Simons, E. L. 1978 Diversity among the early hominids: a vertebrate paleontologist's viewpoint. In *Early hominid of africa* (ed. C. J. Jolly), pp. 543–566. New York: St Marten's Press.

Simons, E. L. 1979 L'origine des hominidés. *Recherche, Paris* **10**, 260–267.

Simons, E. L. & Pilbeam, D. R. 1965 Preliminary revision of Dryopithecinae (Pongidae, Anthropoidea). *Folia primat.* **3**, 81–153.

Simons, E. L. & Pilbeam, D. R. 1978 *Ramapithecus*. In *Evolution of African mammals* (ed. V. J. Maglio & H. B. S. Cooke), pp. 147–153. Cambridge, Massachusetts: Harvard University Press.

Smart, C. 1976 The Lothagam I fauna: its phylogenetic, ecological and biogeographic significance. In *Earliest man and environments in the Lake Rudolf Basin* (ed. Y. Coppens, F. C. Howell, G. Ll. Isaac & R. E. Leakey), pp. 361–369. Chicago: University of Chicago Press.

Tekkaya, I. 1974 A new species of Tortonian anthropoid (Primates, Mammalia). *Bull. Miner. Res. Explor. Inst. Ankara* **83**, 148–165.

Walker, A. 1976 Splitting times among hominoids deduced from the fossil record. In *Molecular anthropology* (ed. M. Goodman, R. E. Tashian & J. H. Tashian), pp. 63–77. New York: Plenum Press.

Walker, A. 1978 Prosimian primates. In *Evolution of African mammals* (ed. V. J. Maglio & H. B. S. Cooke), pp. 90–99. Cambridge, Massachusetts: Harvard University Press.

Walker, A. & Andrews, P. J. 1973 Reconstruction of the dental arcades of *Ramapithecus wickeri*. *Nature, Lond.* **244** 313–314.

White, T. D. 1970 Hominoid mandibles from the Miocene to the Pliocene *Am. J. phys. Anthrop.* **252**, 292. (Abstract).

Wilson, A. C. & Sarich, V. M. 1969 A molecular time scale for human evolution. *Proc. natn. Acad. Sci. U.S.A* **63** (4), 1088–1093.

Xu, Q., Lu, Q., Pan, J., Chi, K., Zhang, C. & Zheng, L. 1978 On the fossil mandible of *Ramapithecus lufengensis*. *Kexue Tongbao* **23** (9), 554–556.

Xu, Q. & Lu, Q. 1979 The mandibles of *Ramapithecus* and *Sivapithecus* from Lufeng, Yunnan. *Vertebr. palasiat.* **17** (1), 1–13.

Xu, Q. & Lu, Q. 1980 The Lufeng ape skull and its significance. *China Reconstructs* **29** (1), 56–57.

Zapfe, H. 1960 Die Primatenfunde aus der miozänen Spaltenfüllung von Neudorf an der March (Děvinská Nová Ves), Tschechoslowakei. Mit Anhang: Der Primatenfund aus dem Miozän von Klein Hadersdorf in Niederoesterreich. *Schweiz. palaeont. Abh.* **78**, 4–293.

Zihlman, A. L., Cronin, J. E., Cramer, D. L. & Sarich, V. M. 1978 Pygmy chimpanzee as a possible prototype for the common ancestor of humans, chimpanzees and gorillas. *Nature, Lond.* **275**, 744–746.

Zuckerkandl, E. & Pauling, L. 1962 Molecular disease, evolution, and genetic heterogeneity. In *Horizons in biochemistry* (ed. M. Kasha & N. Pullman), pp. 189–225. New York: Academic Press.

Phil. Trans. R. Soc. Lond. B **292**, 43–56 (1981)   [43]
Printed in Great Britain

The emergence of man in Africa and beyond

By P. V. Tobias

Palaeo-anthropology Research Group, Department of Anatomy,
University of the Witwatersrand, Johannesburg, South Africa

Transformations of the nervous, masticatory, locomotor and manipulatory systems, with accompanying functional changes, marked the emergence of the Hominidae and of the genus *Homo*. Various systems evolved in a mosaic fashion. The manipulatory and locomotor systems hominized early, probably with the emergence of the hominid family. Major changes of brain form and size occurred later, with the emergence of *Homo*. The functional counterpart of brain change is often thought of as cultural behaviour (material and non-material). However, the evolution of a propensity for culture would not alone have ensured the perpetuation of culture. Only an advanced mechanism for social transmission could have handed on the culture itself: evolving speech was such an advanced mechanism. Direct and indirect evidence suggests that emergent *Homo* (though not *Australopithecus*) possessed at least the rudiments of a speech faculty about 2 Ma ago. Thereafter, biological and cultural evolution were in a positive reciprocal feedback relationship. In this autocatalytic system, speech was a crucial component: by making possible spoken teaching and learning, it enabled culture to evolve beyond what could be conveyed by grunts, snorts or nudges.

1. Definition of man

Without qualification, the term 'man' is vague. In one usage it may refer to the members of the family of man, in another to the genus of man and in yet another to the species of (recent) man. More precise terms for these three groupings are the hominids (or members of the Hominidae), the genus *Homo* and the species *Homo sapiens* respectively. Moreover, more than one usage is possible at each of these three levels.

For this discussion the broadest usage of the term 'man' seems most appropriate; accordingly, my contribution deals with a morphologically defined group of higher Primates, the hominids or members of the zoological family, the Hominidae.

2. Hominids in time and space

The recognition of the earliest hominids poses grave problems, both because of the paucity of available fossil remains dating from the period 4–10 Ma ago and owing to the fragmentary nature and hence morphological indeterminacy of the specimens that we do possess. Therefore, this discussion will confine itself to the fossil remains dating from 4 Ma B.P. to the present. Within this time span the primate fossil record is complete enough and sufficiently representative for the presence of the Hominidae to be recognizable. Thus, it is possible to claim with considerable assurance that the hominids were already in existence 3.77 Ma ago. The evidence from Laetoli testifies that they were an upright-walking group of creatures with canine teeth much smaller than those of the pongids (or anthropoid apes); both of these features are in evidence 3.0 Ma ago, in the fossils of that period from Makapansgat in the Transvaal and Hadar in Ethiopia. An additional line of evidence on the structure of these late Pliocene hominids is provided by remains from Makapansgat and Sterkfontein, namely that the brain size of these upright-walking hominids with moderate canine teeth was not enlarged, was in fact no bigger on average than that of the great apes.

(a) Distribution

By criteria such as dental size, shape and function, the size and form of the endocranial casts, the detailed anatomy of the cranial and postcranial remains, it has been possible to classify a considerable proportion of the hominid fossil record and to place it in time. After over 30 years of study of all the fossils concerned, the author's investigations, along with those of numerous

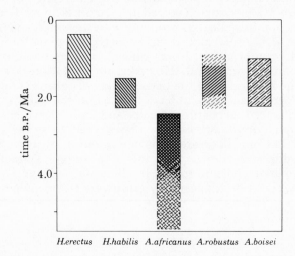

FIGURE 1. Schema of approximate distribution of five extinct hominid taxa in time (1979). The lighter shading on the *A. africanus* and *A. robustus* blocks indicates areas of uncertainty through incompleteness or indeterminacy of fossil record.

students of fossil man, with due allowance for regional or geographical variation, have led to the view that all of the hominid fossils between 4 Ma ago and the most recent past may be accommodated in two genera, *Australopithecus* and *Homo*.

The temporal distribution of three species of *Australopithecus* and of two extinct species of *Homo* is shown in figure 1.

On presently available evidence, the geographical dispersal of these hominid taxa (or taxonomic groups) is at earlier stages restricted to Africa. Thus, the fossil record of early hominids before 2 Ma ago is confined to the Transvaal, Tanzania, Kenya and Ethiopia. Many hundreds of fossil hominid specimens are available from this end-Pliocene phase (4–2 Ma ago) and all are derived from the six sites in southern and eastern Africa. These sites lie between 10–11° N and 26° S and thus embrace equatorial and subtropical localities.

Between 2 and 1 Ma ago, the African fossil hominid record remains rich. In addition, the earliest traces of hominids start appearing in Asia and in Europe. From the last 1 Ma, not only do we find fossil human remains all over Africa, Asia and Europe, but ultimately man has penetrated into the last great hominid-free parts of the earth, America, Australia and, very recently, the Pacific islands, including Melanesia, Polynesia and New Zealand.

If we dismiss the possibility that the dating and geographical spread of the finds are accidents of discovery and the freakish consequences of an incomplete geological record, it is reasonable to hold that the late Pliocene hominids were a peculiarly African manifestation. It further seems valid to state that recent searches, in India, Pakistan, Burma and elsewhere, have not upset the inference that the hominids (as discussed here) arose in Africa, evolved and diversified in Africa and spread thence to Asia and Europe in the early part of the Pleistocene.

(b) Variation

The fossil hominids available from Pliocene Africa are spread over considerable distances. The continent itself comprises 27% of the land surface of the globe. Between the northernmost and southernmost australopithecine sites in Africa (Hadar and Taung) there lies a distance of a little less than 4800 km, while between the two virtually contemporaneous sites, Hadar in Ethiopia and Makapansgat in Transvaal, there is a span of close to 4000 km as the crow flies. Laetoli in Tanzania is removed by almost 1600 km from Hadar.

Over such vast distances, it is to be expected that early hominids would have been subject to geographical variation, even as other mammals are. In discussions on the systematics of the early hominids, it would seem that this factor has not received sufficient emphasis. As with other mammals, including baboons, monkeys and other primates, it is highly likely that the species of *Australopithecus* would have undergone geographical subspeciation. As an example, the species *A. africanus* is best known from the Transvaal, where it is called *A. africanus transvaalensis*. If this species occurred as well in east Africa, as is true of many other Plio-Pleistocene mammals, it is very likely that the Tanzanian form of *A. africanus* would have differed somewhat from its Transvaal conspecifics 2400–2700 km to the south; these differences might have been sufficiently detectable to connote a different subspecies of the same species. A commonly observed procedure for the naming of subspecies is to add a geographical appellation to complete the trinomial name; an appropriate name for the Tanzanian subspecies of *A. africanus* might thus be *A. africanus tanzaniensis*, the nomen matching *A. africanus transvaalensis* to the south.

Similarly, another geographical variant of *A. africanus* could have lived in Ethiopia, say, north of Lake Turkana (formerly Lake Rudolf) and in the Hadar of the northeastern part of the country. A most suitable name for such a subspecies would be *A. africanus aethiopicus*.

This principle of recognizing and appropriately naming geographical subspecies has been followed for the Pleistocene hominid, *H. erectus*; thus, we recognize *H. erectus erectus* from Indonesia, *H. erectus pekinensis* from China, *H. erectus mauritanicus* from NW Africa, the suggested *H. erectus olduvaiensis* (= 'H. erectus leakeyi') from Olduvai, and *H. erectus heidelbergensis* from Germany.

When we take into account chronological differences within and among the fossil sites, the case for recognizing intraspecific variation becomes even stronger. Makapansgat member 3, for instance, has been dated palaeomagnetically to *ca*. 3 Ma. Sterkfontein member 4, found 320 km away, seems, on faunal grounds, to be somewhat younger, between 3.0 and 2.5 Ma old. These strata at both sites contain early hominid remains, and there are some morphological differences between the samples from the two sites. Once, when there was little appreciation of higher primate variability, these differences were thought to justify generic (Broom) or specific (Dart) distinction between the two hominid populations represented. In the fullness of time, the specimens from the two sites were deemed to have belonged not only to one species, but even to the same subspecies (*A. africanus transvaalensis*).

There are two lessons to be learnt from this case history. First, every site sample should be analysed separately, before decisions are taken on whether two site-samples may be pooled as representing a single population. Secondly, a moderate degree of variation is compatible with membership not only of the same species, but also of the same subspecies.

More specifically, on *a priori* grounds, one would have expected the east African representatives of *A. africanus* to have shown some differences from the Transvaal representatives and to have been classifiable possibly if not probably as distinct subspecies. Furthermore, between the northern and southern parts of east Africa (i.e. between Hadar and Laetoli), the same principle might have applied, with different subspecies in Ethiopia and Tanzania.

In sum, geographical and chronological variation within a species is a widespread phenomenon in the animal kingdom; it probably applied as well to early hominids; and insufficient note has been taken of this principle in some attempts to classify the early hominids.

3. Accommodating the Laetoli and Hadar fossils

Recently, an attempt, the latest of several, has been made to relegate *A. africanus* and, especially, its Transvaal subspecies, to a subordinate role in hominid phylogeny and, instead, to represent a succession of east African discoveries as the 'true' ancestral line of modern man. This attempt has been the claim of Johanson *et al.* (1978) and of Johanson & White (1979) that the 3.77–2.6 Ma old hominids of Laetoli in Tanzania and of Hadar in Ethiopia together represent a new species, '*A. afarensis*'. According to them, '*A. afarensis*' represents the common ancestral lineage of which *H. habilis* is the evolutionary continuation, while *A. africanus* affirms early stages in a specialized side branch leading to *A. robustus* (and *A. boisei*).

Unfortunately, some most unusual procedures have been employed by Johanson and his coworkers. First, the Hadar fossils have been 'pooled' with those of Laetoli before they (the Hadar specimens) have been described as a separate site sample, let alone as a succession of site samples, for the hominid-bearing deposits at Hadar span a time range 'from somewhat more than 3.1 Ma ago to somewhat less than 2.6 Ma ago' (Aronson *et al.* 1977). Thus, even within the Hadar deposits there may be a sequence of populations. Yet they have been treated as a single population and, for purposes of the creation of the species '*A. afarensis*', have been pooled with the Laetoli fossils, which are bracketed between 3.59 and 3.77 Ma B.P. (Leakey *et al.* 1976).

Secondly, in a most curious manner, a Laetoli mandible has been chosen as the type specimen of the supposed new species (apparently without the discoverer having given her consent), while the nomen '*A. afarensis*' is based on the Ethiopian site name, Afar. Thus, whatever subsequent revisions of classification these fossils undergo, we are left with the most unsatisfactory situation that an Ethiopian place name ('*afarensis*') is irrevocably attached to a Tanzanian jawbone and, by association and anatomical commonality, to all of Laetoli hominid fossils, unless, as the *International code of zoological nomenclature* allows, the nomen '*A. afarensis*' is suppressed.

Thirdly, in placing the Transvaal *A. africanus* fossils off the main hominid lineage and '*A. afarensis*' on it, Johanson & White (1979) have assigned too recent a date to the Transvaal *A. africanus*: they have shown the Transvaal sites as about 2.5–2.3 Ma, and, in one phylogenetic chart (Johanson 1978), as directly contemporaneous with *H. habilis*. The available evidence places the date of the *A. africanus*-bearing layers as 3.0 Ma B.P. at Makapansgat and 3.0–2.5 Ma B.P. at Sterkfontein. Moreover, they have erroneously assigned 'robust' elements to the Transvaal *A. africanus* populations, although such elements, used in a descriptive sense, have been reported in only a couple of Makapansgat specimens and not at all in the very large Sterkfontein site sample. Thus, the Transvaal *A. africanus* as a whole has been misdated and misrepresented as 'robust'.

A critical appraisal of the published diagnostic criteria of '*A. afarensis*' (Tobias 1979) has revealed that virtually every cited trait is to be found as well in the Transvaal samples of *A. africanus*. The supposed criteria, said to be diagnostic of '*A. afarensis*', do not distinguish the combined Hadar–Laetoli sample, at specific level, from *A. africanus* of the Transvaal.

Furthermore, it is by no means clear that the pooling, for statistical and comparative purposes, of the Hadar and Laetoli fossils is justified. Apart from the great distance separating the sites and the chronological distance of about 0.8 Ma between the midvalues of their time ranges, there appear, from the scanty anatomical data published on the Hadar fossils alone, to be indications of morphometric differences between them and the fossils of Laetoli, which have been well described by White (1977, 1980). For example there appear to be appreciable differences in tooth size, the teeth found at Hadar being smaller (like the smaller *A.* cf. *africanus* teeth from Omo reported by Howell & Coppens (1976)), whereas those of Laetoli are virtually indistinguishable in size from those of *A. africanus transvaalensis* (Tobias 1979).

Both procedurally, comparatively and morphometrically, it does not appear that a case has been established for the claims that the hominids of Laetoli and Hadar represent a single population and that that population has been sampled from a new species of early hominid.

It is recognized that, apart from Johanson's claimed criteria, some anatomical differences may exist between the *Australopithecus* of Sterkfontein–Makapansgat, of Laetoli and of Hadar, but it is indeed rather remarkable how slight those differences are, if we take into consideration the geographical and chronological distances involved. As an alternative hypothesis to explain those small variations among the three or four populations, it is proposed that the Laetoli and Hadar hominids belong to the same lineage as that represented by the hominids of Makapansgat members 3 and 4 and of Sterkfontein member 4. Moreover, it is hypothesized that the Laetoli and Hadar hominids cannot be separated morphologically, at the level of species, from *A. africanus* and that they represent two new subspecies of that species. Since the tying of the name '*A. afarensis*' to the Laetoli fossils is manifestly inappropriate and since it is considered that the case for '*A. afarensis*' has not been established, it is proposed formally that the name '*A. afarensis*' be suppressed. Instead, the author formally proposes the name *A. africanus tanzaniensis*, first proposed by him at the 41st Nobel Symposium (1978), on *Current argument on early man*, for the Laetoli hominids discovered by M. D. Leakey, and dated at 3.77–3.59 Ma B.P.

For the sequence of fossils from the Hadar deposits, the author proposes the name *A. africanus aethiopicus*; this subspecific nomen probably applies as well to the *A.* cf. *africanus* fossils from the older deposits at Omo, of which Howell & Coppens (1976) have spoken, as being somewhat smaller-toothed than *A. africanus transvaalensis*. Thus, from both Omo and Hadar, we have evidence for this somewhat smaller-toothed subspecies of *A. africanus*.

These newest east African discoveries afford confirmation of the hypothesis that *A. africanus* is the common ancestor of the two later hominid lineages, *A. robustus/boisei* and *Homo*.

4. SOME ANATOMICAL TRENDS

A voluminous and ever-growing literature on the morphology of the fossil hominids need not be reviewed here. However, three or four recent developments should be stressed.

(a) Mosaic evolution

It has become very plain that hominid evolution in the past four or more million years has been mosaic in character. If we consider the various complexes of characters that separate modern man and the apes, some of these complexes seem to have been early acquisitions and others late. There is now strong evidence, added to by the recent discoveries from Laetoli and Hadar, that the hominid locomotor system evolved before the majority of changes in the skull and teeth. Indeed, with Zihlman & Brunker (1979, p. 156), it seems fair to claim that, at least

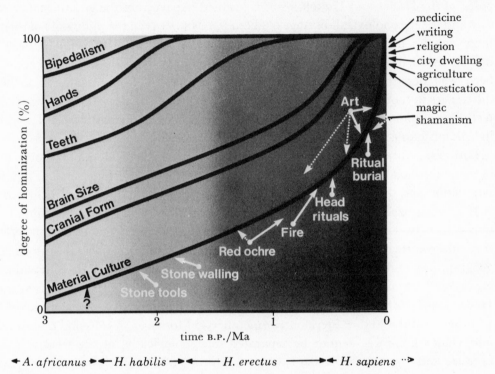

FIGURE 2. Schematic graphical representation of the degree and rate of hominization in respect of diverse structural and functional complexes and of cultural characters (100 % hominization for modern man). The various complexes underwent hominization at different times and rates, as shown by the fossils and the archaeological record. The figure illustrates the mosaic character of hominid evolution.

from an anatomical point of view, 'bipedalism initially defined the family Hominidae'. Figure 2 provides a schematic model of the suggested order of changes in the process of hominization: limbs changing early and teeth intermediately, while skulls and brains are the tardiest, in some respects, to attain modern form. The occurrence of development in this mosaic pattern adds to the difficulty in the identification of very early hominids, which might have begun to hominize structurally in a few respects but not in others. The case of *Ramapithecus* and the uncertainty about earlier claims for its hominid status may be illustrative of this point.

(b) Tooth material

The 'tooth material' of the premolars and molars as a whole may be portrayed as the sum of the 'crown areas' (mesiodistal diameter multiplied by buccolingual diameter) of the two premolars and three molars of the upper half jaw and of the lower half jaw. This is a modification (Tobias 1967) of Howes's (1954) measure of tooth material. When the means or sums of means are used for samples of systematically identified fossil teeth, the data arrange themselves interestingly. If we leave out the Hadar teeth because of some doubts about the published measurements, we find that the oldest hominid tooth samples have intermediate values within the total range of hominid means. For the mandibular teeth, these values are: Laetoli 869 and *A. africanus transvaalensis* 861, which are nearly twice as great as the value (485) in modern *H. sapiens*. From these early values it seems that changes occurred in two directions. On the line of the robust hominids we find an increase in summed crown areas.

A. robustus robustus (Kromdraai)	882
A. robustus crassidens (Swartkrans	960
A. boisei (E Africa)	1312

On the line of *Homo* the following values are found, testifying to a progressive decrease in summed tooth areas.

H. habilis (E Africa)	787
H. erectus erectus (Indonesia)	695
H. erectus mauritanicus (NW Africa)	665
H. erectus pekinensis (China)	608
H. erectus heidelbergensis (Germany)	544
H. sapiens sapiens (worldwide)	485

The reduction of cheek-teeth occurs in the lineage of *Homo* in a definite sequence, at least in African material. Early *Homo* (*H. habilis*) shows a striking elongation of the premolars and first molar; on the other hand, M2 and M3 are mesiodistally abbreviated. The process of dental diminution seems to start at the posterior end of the dental arch. This posterior tooth reduction is part of a general reduction of the posterior part of the maxillary arch, which has been shown to produce profound functional effects on the pattern of tooth wear.

(c) Tooth pattern and function in the Homo lineage

In the early 1960s, while studying the Olduvai hominids assigned to *H. habilis*, the author noted changing occlusal slopes along the tooth row and a slightly helicoidal occlusal plane, although these features had not been noted in other early hominids. Subsequently, Wallace

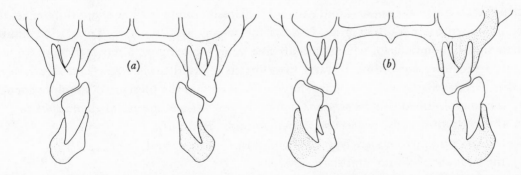

FIGURE 3. Relationship between upper and lower cheek teeth in (*a*) the more anterior and (*b*) the more posterior parts of the dental arcade. The changing relative widths of the maxillary and mandibular arcades, from front to back, leads to a change in the plane of the occlusal wear surface from mesial to distal; this changing plane is known as a helicoidal occlusal plane. It has been found in *Homo habilis*, in which there occurred reduction of the posterior part of the maxillary arch and of its contained teeth.

(1973) showed a total absence of the helicoid from the Transvaal australopithecines, and its presence in Swartkrans *Homo* (SK 45 and SK 80).

Recent studies on *H. habilis* confirm that all specimens studied, including Stw 53 from Sterkfontein member 5 (Hughes & Tobias 1977), show the helicoid. Hence this trait may help distinguish between *Australopithecus* and early *Homo*.

Of several hypotheses to explain the helicoidal occlusal plane, Campbell's (1925) proposal has gained widest acceptance, namely that the helicoid results from differences in upper and lower alveolar arch width. Measurements of maxillary arch widths of early hominids have shown that, whereas in *Australopithecus* arch widths increase to a maximum at M^3, in early *Homo* maxillary arch widths are greatest at M^2. The decline in posterior maxillary arch width is part of the general reduction of that region mentioned earlier.

It seems that the onset of posterior arch reduction, with the appearance of a helicoid, is a structural and functional concomitant of the transition from the presumed australopithecine ancestor to *H. habilis*.

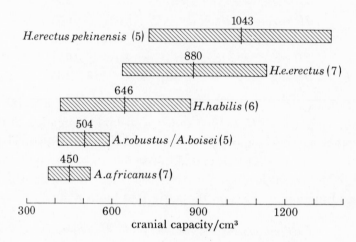

FIGURE 4. Means and 95% population limits for the cranial capacities of five samples of hominid crania.

(d) Brain size

The newest data on the endocranial capacities of fossil hominids show slight differences from earlier published estimations. Figure 4 shows the means and the 95% population limits in five taxa of early hominids for which data are available, while figure 5 shows the pattern of the changing trend in cranial capacity (and therefore in inferred brain size) from *A. africanus* to *H. sapiens*. Arbitrarily we may recognize four major stages in the increase of absolute capacity:

   (i) the small-brained or *micrencephalic* hominids, the various species of *Australopithecus*;

   (ii) the medium-brained or *mesoencephalic* hominids, *H. habilis*;

   (iii) the large-brained or *macrencephalic* hominids, *H. erectus*; and

   (iv) the *gigantencephalic* hominids, *H. sapiens*.

In round figures, the mean brain sizes of these four grades are respectively 1.0, 1.5, 2.0 and 3.0 times the sizes in the modern great apes.

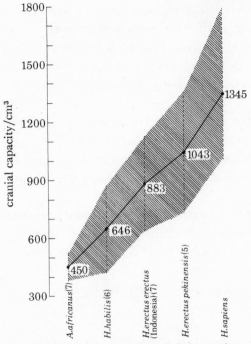

FIGURE 5. The pattern of the threefold cranial capacity increase over the past 2.5–3.0 Ma. For each of the five samples, the mean and 95% population limits are indicated.

(e) The pattern of brain enlargement

Whatever the causal factors or selective advantages favouring brain enlargement, it is clear that even an autocatalytic or positive feedback system operating between brain size and culture could not have been successful if there were not available mutations favouring belated postnatal brain expansion. It is true that, as Mayr (1963), Bielicki (1964, 1969) and the author (Tobias 1971) have stressed, a positive feedback system of this nature could have led to a substantial increase in brain size. However, if the pattern of antenatal and postnatal brain growth had remained much the same as in apes, this might have had biologically disastrous consequences.

In apes at birth the cranial capacity is about 300 cm³ or some 60–65% of the adult cranial capacity (Keith 1931). In *Australopithecus*, with about the same mean adult capacity, the neonatal capacity could likewise have been 60–65% of the adult capacity. However, if an *H. habilis* with an adult capacity of, say, 650 cm³ had retained a neonatal brain ratio of 60%, its cranial capacity at birth would have been about 390 cm³. On the same basis, *H. erectus* of Java would have had a neonatal cranial capacity of 530 cm³ and *H. erectus pekinensis* one of 625 cm³, while modern *H. sapiens* would have been faced with the daunting prospect of giving birth to a swollen-headed baby with a cranial capacity of 810 cm³. It is obvious that, had brain enlargement been achieved in this irresponsible manner, an increasing number of individuals would have had difficulty in giving birth to their large-headed babies. On the one hand, the feedback system could have proceeded wantonly to increase brain size, because of its great cultural advantages, while, on the other hand, such a pattern of increasing brain size would have been decidedly detrimental to survival. The deviation-amplifying system would have been powerless to overcome the high incidence of obstructed labours, and foetal and neonatal deaths. The system would have become not only counter-productive, but counter-reproductive.

Fortunately, we may infer that it did not happen like this. The bland agency of natural selection operated on the whole feedback system and allowed the brain size increase to be effected without such a menace to survival. Instead, it favoured the evolution of a new pattern of brain growth, whereby absolute brain size at birth seems not to have altered appreciably, the neonatal capacity of modern man being about 350 cm³, only slightly more than the value for modern apes.

If we accept 300 cm³, in round figures, as the neonatal capacity, a newborn *H. habilis* would have attained only 46% of its adult capacity (instead of 60% as in apes and as postulated for *Australopithecus*). In Java man, that percentage would have dropped to 35%, in Peking man to 29%, and in modern man to about 22%. At a neonatal capacity of 350 cm³ in modern man, the figure would be about 26%.

Natural selection clearly favoured variants showing belated brain expansion. Thus, there was a progressive drop in the percentage of adult brain size attained by birth, along successive stages in the human lineage. In this way, the biological equipment was brought into line with the demands of the positive feedback system. A corollary of this change is that the brain at birth became progressively more immature. Neonatal dependence on the mother accordingly became ever greater.

(f) Brain form

When the structure of the australopithecine endocast is compared with the structure of the endocast of the apes, it is seen that the hominid endocast shows some evidence of transformation, though its size is approximately the same. Of especial interest are the marked prominence of the inferior frontal convolution and a tendency towards expansion of the pairietal lobe. Though the position of the lunate sulcus remains, in this author's opinion, indeterminate, it does seem that the parietal enlargement affects both the superior and inferior portions more or less equally. There is no evidence of especial enlargement of that very basic secondary association cortex, the inferior parietal lobule. In fact, in several australopithecine endocasts, this region is rather flat, being overshadowed rather by the upper part of the parietal lobule.

However, in the endocasts of *H. habilis*, as the author first pointed out in 1973 (see Tobias 1975), there is a clearly developed rounded fullness of the inferior parietal lobule. This indicates a relatively strong development of part of the brain, comprising the angular and supramarginal gyri and containing one of the developmentally youngest parts of the brain. It includes part of Wernicke's area, known to be a part of the central mechanisms concerned with the control of speech. Unfortunately, the relatively poor endocranial marking of the lateral or Sylvian fissure has thus far prevented our detecting any signs of asymmetry of the length of that fissure or of the height of its posterior terminus, the Sylvian point.

Nevertheless, the striking development of the inferior parietal lobule in Olduvai hominid 24 and in KNM-ER-1470, together with the strong development of the posterior part of the inferior frontal convolution (Broca's area), strongly suggests that the structural and functional bases of articulate speech were present in *H. habilis*. In *Australopithecus* only a hint of an enlarged Broca's area, but not of Wernicke's area, could be detected.

Thus, just at the stage where the first allometric enlargement of the brain becomes apparent, in *H. habilis*, structural speech centres make their appearance. A further coincident phenomenon is that cultural manifestations appear in the record at the same time. What is the relationship among these phenomena?

5. ANATOMY, FUNCTION, SPEECH AND CULTURE: A NEW PROPOSAL FOR AN AUTOCATALYTIC FEEDBACK SYSTEM

Many adaptive advantages have been hypothesized as flowing from man's bigger and re-organized brain (see Gabow (1977) and Tobias (1980) for recent summaries). Some of these explanations could have applied if brain enlargement were a non-recurring event. However, encephalization was not a unique event; it was sustained for 2 Ma or more and it carried the lineage across a generic boundary into *Homo* and continued in the three consecutive chrono-species, *H. habilis*, *H. erectus* and *H. sapiens*. The brain changes transcended systematic categories, geographical dispersion, cultural diversification, ecological radiation and ethological variegation. Whatever selective and other causal agencies were operating, they must have continued influencing the hominid brain throughout the assumption of a bewildering array of new life styles and circumstances.

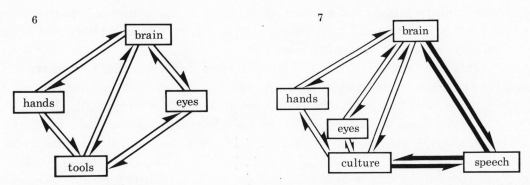

FIGURE 6. Positive feedback system featuring three biological components and a cultural component. This earlier version is now held to operate within a generation, but not necessarily across the generations, in respect of cultural progress.

FIGURE 7. Modified, trans-generational feedback system incorporating speech, the biologically determined faculty that enables cultural beliefs and practices of survival value to be transmitted to future generations. In this autocatalytic system, speech is believed to play a predominant role.

One pattern of causal factors that could stand up to this difficulty is the positive feedback system, for such an autocatalytic system, once established, could continue operating more or less under its own momentum, despite behavioural and ecological diversity, Mayr (1963) proposed that brain size and the duration of parental care were so related to each other. The author earlier stressed such a feedback relationship between culture and its genetic bases, between physical and cultural evolution (Tobias 1971). Bielicki (1964, 1969) suggested the interplay of two-way causal links or feedbacks between cultural and non-cultural components of hominization. However, as indicated above, this system does not operate in a vacuum and must be considered as still subject to the operation of natural selection.

It is proposed that the enlargement and reorganization of the brain in hominid phylogeny was in a positive feedback relationship with the rise and increase in complexity of culture. This is a deviation-amplifying system: a small shift or initial kick on one side of the feedback equation would have stimulated or favoured a shift on the other side, and so on. Certain material aspects of cultural evolution, very obvious in the archaeological record, required visual and motor skills as participants in this autocatalytic system: centrally, this involved specific parts of the brain; peripherally, it brought in the eye and the hand.

These were the components and the limits of the feedback system that the author earlier proposed. The whole autocatalytic system was under the influence of natural selection. At that stage the stress was on material culture, the implemental life, and on a generalized brain enlargement, together with efficient eyes and hands, as the three biological components. This feedback system was proposed to explain the persistence of brain enlargement and reconstruction, so that the advantages that applied about $2\frac{1}{2}$ Ma ago were still valid 1 and even $\frac{1}{2}$ Ma ago. The earlier formulation could be summarized thus: better brains made for better culture; better culture increased chances of survival; challenges to survival placed a premium on still better brains. The unstated assumption implicit in this formulation is that if the next generation had better brains, the culture would automatically persist. As this assumption is unacceptable a new hypothesis has been made.

The system now proposed has several new features.

(1) On the cultural side are included the whole panoply of non-material as well as material aspects of man's social heritage, for the concepts and social structure might have been as crucial to survival as material innovations and improvements.

(2) On the biological side, stress is laid on the special development of certain areas of the cortex, rather than on a generalized enlargement. The evolutionary benefits lay in having enlarged parietal lobes (and especially the inferior parietal lobule on the left), inferior frontal lobes and superior temporal convolutions. The ape's brain already has much localization of functions; therefore, it is suggested, in the hominid lineage the whole brain enlarged for the sake of highly desirable enlargement of certain areas. The very areas that have shown the most striking enlargement are those that provide the clue to the third new feature.

(3) The main new proposal is that speech be brought into the feedback system as a fifth and predominant component.

Enlargement of certain areas of the brain went hand-in-hand with the development of an increasingly complex culture, as a revolutionary new survival kit. So intricate a culture did man develop that only articulate speech could have transmitted it from generation to generation. It is suggested that the main natural selective advantage flowing from brain enlargement and especially of the lower frontal, lower parietal and upper temporal regions was the evolution of mechanisms for the transmission of culture, and that means primarily cognitive abilities and articulate speech. By making possible a new kind of inheritance, cultural or social inheritance, articulate speech facilitated the learning of the new techniques by children of the next generation and so helped ensure their survival.

This system of culture and cultural transmission was, in effect, a new kind of inheritance, cultural or social inheritance. It took the universal mammalian capacity for learned behaviour, refined it into a powerful mechanism for ensuring the survival, not merely of one current generation, but of future generations. The survival of future generations is precisely what evolution is all about.

The feedback system operated for approximately 120 000 generations of hominids. It continued until it produced a situation in which articulate speech was the ineluctable destiny of every normally developing individual, and even of most abnormal and defective subjects. It operated until, as Washburn & Benedict (1979) have put it, it is extremely difficult to stop people speaking. It operated until a kind of threshold quantity of relevant brain tissue to permit the acquisition of spoken speech was reached at younger and younger ages, as Krantz (1961) suggested. This meant that one's brain and one's speech mechanisms permitted active learning and participation in the cultural process from young childhood.

When these advanced stages were reached, the whole process slowed down. Beyond a certain point of cultural evolution, it was no longer an advantage to have bigger and better brains. Cultural sharing and the benevolence of social life had taken the place of nimble wits of the individual, as an insurance against extinction. Encephalization was no longer at a premium. One could manage and be as educable with 1250 g of brain as with 2250 g.

The transgenerational aspect of culture impels us to see in speech the cardinal factor in the evolution of the human brain and intellect. Differential enlargement of the brain enabled man to become not only culture-bound but speech-dependent: in a word, it made over a speechless animal into a speaking man.

REFERENCES (Tobias)

Aronson, J. L., Schmitt, T. J., Walter, R. C., Taieb, M., Tiercelin, J. J., Johanson, D. C., Naeser, C. W. & Nairn, A. E. M. 1977 New geochronologic and paleomagnetic data for the hominid-bearing Hadar Formation of Ethiopia. *Nature, Lond.* **267**, 323–327.

Bielicki, T. 1964 Evolution of the intensity of feedbacks between physical and cultural evolution from man's emergence to present times. *UNESCO Expert Meeting on Biological Aspects of Race, Moscow, August 1964*, pp. 1–3. Paris: UNESCO.

Bielicki, T. 1969 Deviation-amplifying cybernetic systems and hominid evolution. *Mater. Pr. antrop.* **77**, 57–60.

Campbell, T. D. 1925 In *Dentition and palate of the Australian aboriginal*, pp. 1–123. University of Adelaide: The Hassell Press.

Gabow, S. L. 1977 Population structure and the rate of hominid brain evolution. *J. hum. Evol.* **6**, 643–665.

Howell, F. C. & Coppens, Y. 1976 An overview of Hominidae from the Omo succession. In *Earliest man and environments in the Lake Rudolf basin* (ed. Y. Coppens, F. C. Howell, G. L. Isaac & R. E. F. Leakey), pp. 522–532. Chicago University Press.

Howes, A. E. 1954 A polygon portrayal of coronal and basal arch dimensions in the horizontal plane. *Am. J. Orthod.* **40**, 811–831.

Hughes, A. R. & Tobias, P. V. 1977 A fossil skull probably of the genus *Homo* from Sterkfontein, Transvaal. *Nature, Lond.* **265**, 310–312.

Johanson, D. C. 1978 A new species of man. *Australopithecus afarensis* from Eastern Africa stimulates major revisions in understanding human origins. *Further Evidence* **1**, 5–8.

Johanson, D. C. & White, T. D. 1979 A systematic assessment of early African hominids. *Science, N.Y.* **202**, 321–330.

Johanson, D. C., White, T. D. & Coppens, Y. 1978 A new species of the genus *Australopithecus* (Primates: Hominidae) from the Pliocene of eastern Africa. *Kirtlandia* **28**, 1–14.

Keith, A. 1931 In *New discoveries relating to the antiquity of Man*, pp. 1–512. London: Williams & Norgate.

Krantz, G. S. 1961 Pithecanthropine brain size and its cultural consequences. *Man* **11**, 85–87.

Leakey, M. D., Hay, R. L., Curtis, G. H., Drake, R. E., Jackes, M. K. & White, T. D. 1976 Fossil hominids from the Laetolil Beds. *Nature, Lond.* **262**, 460–466.

Mayr, E. 1963 *Animal species and evolution*. Cambridge: Belknap.

Tobias, P. V. 1967 The cranium and maxillary dentition of Australopithecus (Zinjanthropus) boisei. *Olduvai Gorge*, vol. 2. Cambridge University Press.

Tobias, P. V. 1971 *The brain in hominid evolution*. New York and London: Columbia University Press.

Tobias, P. V. 1975 Brain evolution in the Hominoidea. In *Primate functional morphology and evolution* (ed. R. H. Tuttle), pp. 353–392. The Hague: Mouton.

Tobias, P. V. 1979 'Australopithecus afarensis' and *A. africanus*: critique and an alternative hypothesis. *Palaeont. afr.* (In the press.)

Tobias, P. V. 1980 The evolution of the human brain, intellect and spirit. *First Abbie Memorial Lecture, University of Adelaide*. (In the press.)

Wallace, J. A. 1973 The dentition of the South African early hominids: a study of form and function. Ph.D. thesis, Department of Anatomy, University of the Witwatersrand, Johannesburg.

Washburn, S. L. & Benedict, B. 1979 Non-human primate culture. *Man* **14** (1), 163–164.

White, T. D. 1977 New fossil hominids from Laetolil, Tanzania. *Am. J. phys. Anthrop.* **46**, 197–230.

White, T. D. 1980 Additional fossil hominids from Laetoli, Tanzania: 1976–1979 specimens. *Am. J. phys. Anthrop.* (In the press.)

Zihlman, A. & Brunker, L. 1979 Hominid bipedalism: then and now. *Yearb. phys. Anthrop.* **22**, 132–162.

Discussion

B. Campbell (*Sedgeford Hall, Hunstanton PE36 5LT, Norfolk, U.K.*). I should like to comment on a number of points in Professor Tobias's lecture.

In making comparison between two samples, such as those of Hadar and Makapan, it is always necessary to review the total morphological pattern. A series of individual measurements, such as are listed as diagnostic criteria of *A. afarensis*, compared one by one can be of value, but do not give us all the information that we need to make an assessment of morphological difference or distance. At the same time, measurements of breadth and length of teeth are notoriously difficult to standardize and those taken by different workers are often not accurately comparable. They constitute a coarse means of morphological comparison. Multivariate analysis is the appropriate tool to make statistical comparisons of the total morphological pattern of populations.

The schematic model (figure 2), which indicates successive phases of evolution of distinct functional complexes, followed by the evolution of 'material culture', summarizes in a striking fashion the mosaic sequence of hominid evolution. We do need to remember, however, that the progress of material culture is only a weak reflection of cultural behaviour in its broadest sense. In practice it seems clear that behavioural adaptation and modification preceded anatomical change: behaviour led the way into hominization, and was presumably the motive force applying selection pressures leading to morphological changes. Material culture itself was surely a late development in the evolution of hominid culture.

Regarding the evolution of the hominid brain, it is important to realize that brain size and cranial capacity are correlated with body size and should be scaled accordingly if they are to be given the kind of meaning that is attributed to them in this Discussion. For example, the earliest *Australopithecus* hominids were small creatures, probably not much more than 3 ft (*ca.* 0.9 m) in stature. Although their brains were roughly the same size as those of African apes, being relatively smaller animals they were already significantly more highly encephalized. Similarly, the 'threefold cranial capacity increase' shown in figure 5 is partly due to increase in body size.

The form of the curve in figure 5 can be determined only by plotting every individual skull datum point without regard to taxonomic grouping. Such grouping gives a false impression of stepped cranial evolution. In particular, it completely hides the levelling out of the trend of increasing cranial capacity during the last 100 ka.

Regarding early brain growth, Professor Tobias states that during hominization natural selection favoured the evolution of 'a new brain growth' to achieve a relatively low neonatal cranial capacity. It is surely more accurate to state that the period of gestation was relatively shortened during hominization, with the result that the human baby is born with an immature brain only *ca.* 26 % of its final size.

Phil. Trans. R. Soc. Lond. B **292**, 57–64 (1981)

Printed in Great Britain

[57]

DIET AND TEETH

Dietary hypotheses and human evolution

By A. WALKER

*Department of Cell Biology and Anatomy, The Johns Hopkins University School of Medicine,
725 North Wolfe Street, Baltimore, Maryland 21205, U.S.A.*

[Plates 1 and 2]

Hypotheses concerning the diet of early hominids have played an important role in discussions on human evolution. Three investigations have helped define the extent to which dietary hypotheses may be taken and still be testable. Comparative anatomy is a fairly coarse approach, which despite convergences allows only the most specialized diets to be ruled out. A biomechanical analysis makes it clear that the changes in jaw and tooth form are subtle and outside the resolution given by present understanding of cranial function. Analysis of the microscopic tooth wear of extant species has been carried out. Major dietary types can be distinguished by their microwear. The microwear on fossil hominids appears to rule out certain diets that have been proposed for them.

INTRODUCTION

Several of the most important discussions on human evolution have been concerned with our ancestral dietary adaptations. At the simplest level, this has been caused by the preponderance of jaws and teeth in the fossil record, but more importantly it reflects the fact that the feeding habits of any species have profound consequences for many aspects of its biology. Particular dietary régimes impose constraints upon such things as body size, locomotor behaviour breeding strategy and social behaviour. They also limit a species to a geographic range, at one end of the scale, and to particular habitats, at the other. Because dietary habits so powerfully determine many aspects of a species' life style, it is not surprising that theories based on dietary models have been very important in the study of human origins.

Dart's ideas based on the notion that *Australopithecus* was a predator (Dart 1953, 1957, 1959) proved to have consequences that affected much of the thinking in the behavioural sciences and which, through popularization by the late Robert Ardrey (1961, 1976), were placed before a large general audience, Dart conceived of *Australopithecus* as

'... carnivorous creatures, that seized living quarries by violence, battered them to death, tore apart their broken bodies, disembodied them limb from limb, slaking their ravenous thirst with the hot blood of victims and greedily devouring livid writhing flesh.' (Dart 1953, p. 209).

The evidence for carnivory in *Australopithecus* included fractures in the bones of that species, an analysis of the bone collection from the Makapansgat cave deposit, and the general feeling that there was little else it could have fed on in the area at the time.

Methods, problems and evidence

There are, in fact, several ways in which we might determine the diets of extinct hominids, some of them more useful than others, but all with their own difficulties.

Among the methods that possibly can be applied to the fossil record are the following:

(1) interspecific comparisons of tooth morphology;

(2) biomechanical reconstruction;

(3) inspection of tooth microwear;

(4) carbon isotope analysis;

(5) trace element analysis;

(6) application of ecological 'rules';

(7) analysis of 'food refuse' from archaeological sites;

(8) diagnosis of cases of metabolic diseases caused by diet.

Interspecific comparisons of tooth morphology involve an understanding of dental adaptations to particular diets. If one bears in mind that mammals use their teeth for many purposes and that the teeth of mammals are only a part of the digestive system, it should be possible to make generalizations concerning dental adaptations. For instance, species that graze have, with few exceptions, hypsodont teeth in which the enamel is placed in plates or rods normal to the occlusal plane; these plates are separated by dentine or cement or both. This common, basic pattern can be found in the teeth of horses, elephants, certain rodents, and warthogs, although these groups are easily distinguishable from one another. The limits to which adaptations in different groups of mammals may converge are set in many ways, one of which involves the influence of heritage characters. For instance, the herbivorous panda bear, the carnivorous polar bear, the omnivorous grizzly bear and the termite-eating sloth bear have different tooth morphologies, but these must all function with a basic carnivore temporomandibular joint. Herbivory has not led the panda to evolve a more freely mobile mandibular condyle as it has mammalian groups long committed to herbivory. It is also apparent that the size of an animal may influence tooth shape, so that, for instance, a grazing hyrax may not develop the extremes of hypsodonty and enamel folding that are found in a horse, presumably because the smaller animal can select less abrasive grass parts while the horse must inevitably take some quantity of less desirable food with each large bite.

Examples of several mammalian dentitions are given in plate 1. Although there seem to be several examples of convergent adaptations that can be related to diet, features fundamental to each phylogenetic group impose constraints such that a grazing pig has teeth that are still recognizably pig teeth. These heritage features are the ones that make the comparative method of limited usefulness to the student of any one order of mammals. For the student of the Hominidae, it is extremely unlikely to have any useful resolving power. If, for example, a mammologist who knew nothing about hominids were asked which mammalian molars most resembled those of *Australopithecus*, the answer would probably be orang-utan molars. If asked to look outside the order Primates, the answer would probably be the molars of the sea otter (*Enhydra lutra*). This species possesses small anterior teeth, and large, broad, flat molars with thick enamel. Claims that *Ailuropoda* teeth resemble those of *Australopithecus* (see, for example, Du Brul 1977) are, I feel, not only based on a rather superficial analogy, but also depend on a *comparison* between two bear species and two *Australopithecus* species. Similarly, Jolly's (1970) model depended on a comparison between two baboon species and a hominoid/hominid pair of

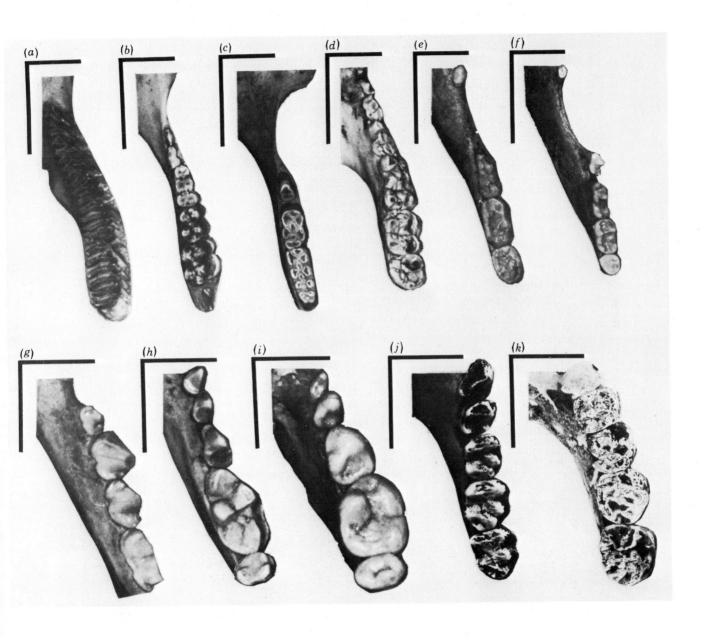

PLATE 1. Right mandibular tooth rows of selected mammals. All reduced to the same canine to third molar length.
(*a*) Capybara; (*b*) bushpig; (*c*) warthog; (*d*) giant panda; (*e*) grizzly bear; (*f*) polar bear; (*g*) spotted hyena;
(*h*) otter (*Lutra* sp.); (*i*) sea otter; (*j*) gorilla; (*k*) robust *Australopithecus*.

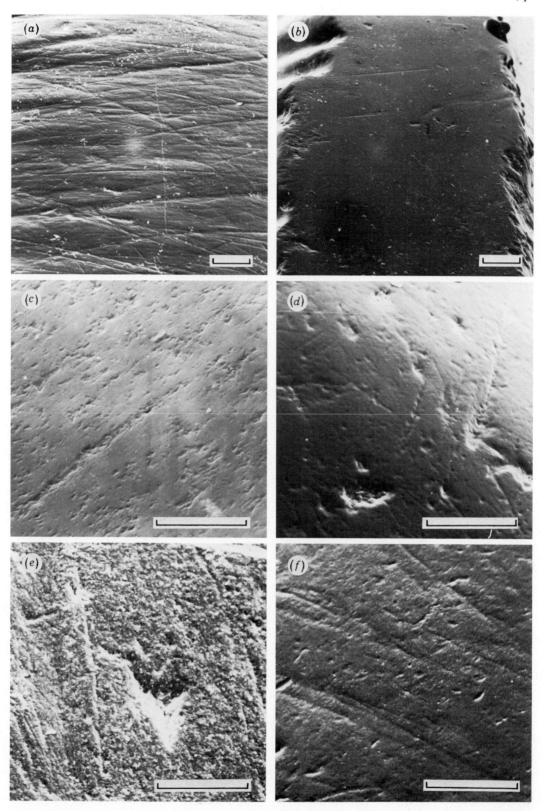

PLATE 2. Representative scanning electron micrographs of the occlusal surfaces of the teeth of selected mammals;
(*a*) white rhinoceros (grazer); (*b*) giraffe (browser); (*c*) cheetah (carnivore); (*d*) orang-utan (frugivore)
(*e*) spotted hyena (scavenger, bone eater); (*f*) robust *Australopithecus*. Scale bars: 200 μm.

species. It does not necessarily follow that, because pairs of species have *similar differences* in the morphology of their teeth and jaws, their dietary régimes are also similar. This is not to deny that similar selective pressures might have affected both pairs similarly, but the constraints of a common heritage may mean that the morphological changes that accompany a dietary change in one pair might accompany a different dietary change in the other.

Biomechanical reconstructions have some value in palaeontology. They can redefine the questions being asked and, if successful, may set limits on the mechanical characteristics of foods eaten. As with many efforts in palaeontology, the anatomy of the modern species being used for comparison is too often inadequately understood.

The first step in a biomechanical reconstruction is the choice of an appropriate modern analogue. The closest living relative is often, but not always, the best choice. To take the example of *Australopithecus robustus*, the closest living relative is *Homo sapiens*. In many respects, such as the configuration of the temporomandibular joint, the form of the teeth, and the small canines, the morphological similarities are close enough to make the analysis possible without omission of any major variable because it is found in only one of the two species. But is the modern analogue adequately understood in this instance? Our knowledge of the masticatory anatomy of *Homo sapiens* is exhaustive and years of dental research have led to an understanding of normal occlusal relationships and functions. The biomechanics of human chewing are understood in part, but not in whole, because of the peculiar nature of humans as experimental animals. Humans are suitable experimental subjects because they can respond to verbal directions to perform certain actions, yet invasive techniques can be used only rarely in humans. More is known about the forces acting on the mandible in galagos or monkeys than in people, simply because strain gauges can be applied directly to bone in living, non-human animals (Hylander 1979). Although electromyographic studies have been carried out on human volunteers (see Moller 1966), the study of bite forces can only be made under unusual circumstances (Graf 1976). However, biomechanical analyses of human biting and chewing have been made (see Walker (1978) for a review of the literature).

By modelling the muscles on a reconstructed skull of a robust *Australopithecus* (based on KNM-ER 406 and KNM-ER 729), the major lines of action of the masticatory muscles can be determined and the values for their contractile forces estimated from cross-sectional areas (figure 1). The results are somewhat surprising. Given that the skulls of *Australopithecus* and *Homo sapiens* are obviously different, it is a surprise to find that the lines of action of their muscles of mastication are very similarly arranged. Apparently, the way in which bite forces can be applied to food are the same in both, yet the muscle forces produced in *Australopithecus* were much larger than in humans. But since these bite forces are used to generate *pressures* over occlusal surfaces, the area of the loaded teeth is criticial. In the fossil hominid, the occlusal area is very much larger, maybe four or five times larger than in humans. Thus, with similar lines of muscle action, *Australopithecus* would have had to generate four or five times the bite force to create the same pressures as are recorded in modern humans. The question, then, can be rephrased. Formerly, the anatomy of robust *Australopithecus* led to the intuitive question: 'What were they eating that was so hard?' Now we see that the appropriate questions is, instead: 'What were they eating that could be masticated by modern humans as well that *Australopithecus* needed to process in greater quantities?' The answer might be a food substance that contains a large proportion of indigestible material.

Tooth microwear studies (Walker *et al.* 1978; Walker 1980) are beginning to yield results that may help to resolve the choice between major dietary types. In a study on two sympatric species of hyrax, Walker *et al.* (1978) showed that grazers and browsers could be distinguished by the microwear on their teeth. The teeth of grazers are subjected to abrasion by the siliceous phytoliths in grasses. These tiny particles (about 10 μm in diameter) cannot be avoided, and sheep, for example, ingest 10 kg of phytoliths a year (Baker *et al.* 1959). This is, of course, the

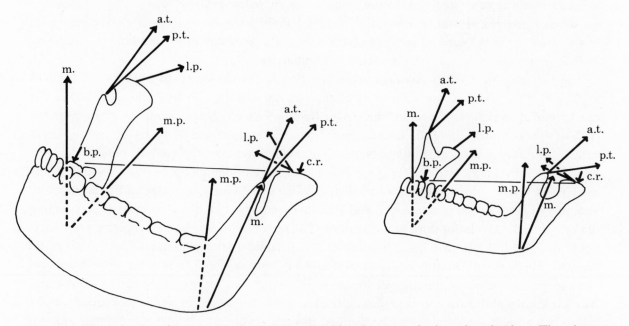

FIGURE 1. Lines of action of the muscles of mastication in modern human and robust *Australopithecus*. The orientation selected is such that the bite point (second molar) and the balancing side mandibular condyle are in the plane of the page (see Walker (1978) for details). Abbreviations: a.t., anterior temporalis; p.t., posterior temporalis; m., masseter; m.p., medial pterygoid; l.p., lateral pterygoid; b.p., bite point; c.r. condylar reaction point.

reason why the teeth of grazers are either hypsodont or continuously growing and why their enamel is orientated normal to the occlusal plane. Little by little, the teeth of grazers are ground away by phytoliths.

Other broadly defined dietary groups can also be recognized on the basis of the characteristic patterns of microwear on their teeth (plate 2). Since high quality replication methods are now available (Walker 1980), fossil specimens may be examined without either any danger to the specimen or the need to cut off small pieces that will fit in the scanning electron microscope chamber. Work is under way to document wear patterns on a series of modern mammals of known, different diets. Quantification of scratch lengths, scratch widths, scratch and pit frequencies and so on may provide a statistical basis for evaluating the probable diets of early hominids. As an example, browsing animals have about five and grazing animals 300 minute scratches per square millimetre. With the research programme at its present stage, only qualitative assessments of the microwear of extinct forms can be made. It appears that grazing (including eating husked grass seeds) and browsing can be ruled out for diet of robust *Australopithecus*. Bone crunching, suggested by Szalay (1975), can also be dismissed, since it produces characteristic wear not found in the fossil species. The dietary pattern most congruent with the observed microwear is frugivory. The microwear on molar teeth from nearly 20 robust

Australopithecus from East Africa cannot, at present, be distinguished from that found in mandrills, chimpanzees and orang-utans.

Carbon isotope analysis of bone promises to be a powerful tool in dietary studies. Laboratory studies have shown that the isotopic composition of carbon in an animal's bones is a function of the isotopic carbon in its diet (De Niro & Epstein 1978). This is true for both the carbonate and collagen fractions of bone. The ratio of ^{13}C to ^{12}C in plants eaten by herbivores depends upon the photosynthetic pathway that the plants use. Most tropical grasses have higher ^{13}C to ^{12}C ratios than most browse plants. This fact was used by De Niro & Epstein (1978) to determine the diets of the same hyrax individuals used in the microwear studies by Walker *et al.* (1978). The method discriminated accurately between individuals that were known to have been grazers and those that were known to have been browsers in a blind test. It may be possible to apply this method to fossil bones if it can be demonstrated that diagenetic changes do not affect the carbon isotope ratios.

Strontium analysis of fossil bone (Toots & Voorhies 1965) is a method that has been used with varying degrees of success to estimate past diets. Plants contain different amounts of strontium; therefore, browsing and grazing animals can be distinguished by the strontium levels in their teeth and bones. Further, although the amount of strontium lost at each trophic level is relatively small, it is significant. Thus the strontium level in herbivores is low, but it is even lower in carnivores feeding on those herbivores. Parker & Toots (1980) review the role of strontium analysis in palaeontology and assess the utility of other trace elements for dietary reconstruction. Schoeninger (1979) has shown that this method can contribute to understanding dietary differences in archaeological samples for which the only other method would be to guess the richness of diets from the accompanying grave goods and/or the burial location. The only attempt to assess the diet of *Australopithecus* by strontium analysis (Boaz & Hampel 1978) yielded uncertain results, possibly because of the taphonomic history of the sample chosen.

There are certain constraints placed upon an animal's dietary habits by its body size. These range from energetic considerations to the relative sizes of the animal and its food. Although such ecological 'rules' cannot be used to predict the diet of any particular species, they can help in setting limits on the number of possible diets to be considered. Kay & Hylander (1978) show that insectivorous and folivorous mammals differ consistently in their body size. They demonstrate that, for insectivores in which the prey are not social insects in local concentrations, the energetic cost of locating enough insects to support a large body size is too great to be practical. Most insectivores are, therefore, small, the exceptions being species that prey on colonial insects. On the other hand, mammalian folivores need to retain food in their digestive tracts for long periods of time for cellulose digestion to take place. Small mammals have short food passage times and high metabolic rates. Thus, a mere increase in body size would be a selective advantage to a folivore, and most folivores are large for this reason. Clutton-Brock & Harvey (1980) have shown that, within taxonomic families, folivores have relatively smaller brains than frugivores. Their explanation for this finding is based on the observation that leaves are an evenly distributed food source whereas fruits are very unevenly distributed in both space and time. Therefore, much more complex information is need to exploit fruit as a food resource than to exploit leaves. The larger brains in frugivores are, by this explanation, required to process this greater amount of information about the environment. Whether or not the relative brain sizes of fossil species may be subject to such analysis depends on the accuracy of body mass estimates. Unfortunately, to date we have no single individual early hominid specimen for which both the brain case and the postcranial bones are complete enough for a reliable estimate of brain size and body mass to be made.

The remains of the meals of early hominids that are found on archaeological living floors are, of course, direct evidence of diet. However, it is not at all clear in many instances that any or all of the bones were collected by hominids as food. In a discussion of the agencies that may give rise to accumulations of bones in caves, Brain (1980) concludes that several usually act together and that detailed comparative studies on single agents are needed before any particular assemblage can be attributed to hominid actions. For open sites, such as those at Olduvai Gorge (Leakey 1971), where there is an association of bone refuse and stone artefacts, the situation is much clearer. The archaeological record documents that by 2 Ma ago some early hominids were breaking and cutting animal bones for the associated meat and/or marrow (Isaac, this symposium). However, since most plant remains are never fossilized and bones often are, the record of what was eaten is obviously biased in favour of animal food. Also, since at this time robust australopithecines were contemporaries of at least one other hominid species, the question arises as to which indulged in eating animal parts. Some of the objective methods discussed in this paper may help to answer this question.

It is true that several robust bones have been found in association with living floors and it has been hinted (Bishop *et al.* 1975) that this might be taken as evidence that robust australopithecines made the tools. But if we are to take repeated association with tools as evidence of tool-making, then bovids are clearly the best candidates in the Plio-Pleistocene for tool-maker status. It can also be argued that the hominid species found on the sites must be food refuse and that those absent are the most likely tool makers. Ethnoarchaeological studies, such as those by Binford (1978) on the Nunamuit Eskimos, Yellen (1974) on the San Bushmen, and Gifford (1980) on the Dassenetch of Kenya, provide an important perspective on the process of site formation and the intuitive definition of what are called sites by archaeologists. By concentrating on the processes by which sites are formed, such studies have uncovered hidden biases that affect interpretation in archaeology. The advantage in these cases is that the remains left behind by people can be correlated with their use as observed before the site was abandoned.

As an infrequent occurrence, it might be expected that an occasional individual hominid will show signs of disease or disorders related to diet. These might range from gum disorders, affecting the alveolar bone of the jaws, to systemic metabolic diseases with nutritional causes. To follow the example used previously, robust australopithecines show little tooth and gum disease. One individual from East Turkana (KNM-ER 729) had broken the crown from a molar during life, but this episode led only to local alveolar resorption (Leakey *et al.* 1972). In contrast, some individuals of *H. erectus* (e.g. KNM-ER 730) contemporary with robust australopithecines show heavy tooth wear, alveolar resorption, and pocketing (Day & Leakey 1973).

Enamel hypoplasia, resulting from interruptions in the normal developmental process, may be caused by certain diseases or nutritive stresses. Such hypoplasia have been observed in robust australopithecine teeth (Robinson 1956; Tobias 1967; White 1978), and White (1978) has suggested that they might be related to weaning.

A single *H. erectus* skeleton, KNM-ER 1808 (Leakey & Leakey 1978), shows signs of a systemic disorder that resulted in an inflammation of the periosteum shortly before death. The diagnosis most consistent with the distribution and histological appearance of the newly formed bone and with that of the underlying bone of the skeleton is hypervitaminosis A. Further, it is very probable that this disease was of sudden onset. The underlying bone is histologically normal, but the bone resulting from the periostitis is abnormal and highly disorganized. This abnormal bone is found over all long-bone shafts and in places is up to 7 mm thick. Documented occurrences of hypervitaminosis A include many cases of children who were given overdoses of vitamin A by their mothers. These individuals show growth disturbances associated with early ossification of epiphysial cartilages. In this case, however, the individual was fully adult. Although adult examples of hypervitaminosis A are rare in the literature, cases are described in which Arctic and Antarctic explorers were forced by extreme circumstances to eat wild or domestic carnivores (Shearman 1978). The diaries make special mention of eating liver, which was often the only uncooked meat that they could chew. Because carnivore livers contain huge amounts of vitamin A, a single episode of consuming quantities of polar bear, dog, or other liver is sufficient to produce massive subperiosteal bleeding, severe bone pain, and, within a short time, extensive new bone deposition.

Although the diagnosis of a disease in a case of such antiquity cannot ever be made with certainty, the context of this case invites speculation. KNM-ER 1808, as well as being the most complete *H. erectus* skeleton known, is also among the earliest-known individual members of that species. Could it be that, before the use of fire and while butchery practices were in a formative stage, we have the remains of an individual who suffered from over-indulging in liver? Is it too unlikely that, during the transition from a more vegetarian diet to one that involved meat, dietary mistakes might be made? This case will be dealt with more fully in Walker *et al.* (1980).

Conclusions

In summary, what can we say about the diet of robust australopithecines? Based upon several lines of evidence, it now seems unlikely that they ate grass seed, leaves, or bone. It is quite likely that they maintained a form of the original hominoid diet, which was based upon a preponderance of fruit (Kay 1977). The fruits of most indigenous African plants are small, largely lacking in fleshy pulp, and are either encased in a hard external shell or pod or consist of small seeds with individual hard, protective cases. The features of the masticatory system and the microwear findings to date are consistent with bulk eating of such fruits without much preparation. By that, I mean that whole fruits (casings, pulp, seeds, and all) were probably masticated, rather than the fruit being shelled, pulped or otherwise prepared. In such a diet, the occasional harder-than-usual particle might cause the sort of microscopic damage seen on the occlusal surfaces of robust australopithecine teeth. Further, it is reasonable to assume that, once in a while, a tooth might be fractured by such a particle even though the teeth were not subjected to heavy wear by mammalian standards. By the comparative method, it was seen that the teeth of the sea otter were the most similar morphologically to robust *Australopithecus* teeth of all non-primates. Sea otters eat the flesh of molluscs, which is not abrasive in itself, but which occasionally contains a very hard fragment of shell or a pearl. The flat, broad teeth with thick enamel that characterizes these two species can be thought of as an adaptation to resist the bending and fracturing that might result from chewing such an object. Thus, although the diets of these two similarly adapted animals might not be the same, the mechanical properties of those diets might well be similar.

I thank Linda M. Perez and Pat Shipman for their help in preparing this paper. The research was supported by the National Science Foundation through grants BNS 75-16879 and BNS 78-24499.

REFERENCES (Walker)

Ardrey, R. A. 1976 *The hunting hypothesis*. New York: Atheneum.

Ardrey, R. A. 1961 *African genesis*. New York: Atheneum Press.

Baker, G., Jones, L. H. P. & Wardrop, I. D. 1959 Causes of wear on sheep's teeth. *Nature, Lond.* **104**, 1583–1585.

Binford, L. 1978 Nunamuit ethnoarcheology. New York: Academic Press.

Bishop, W. W., Pickford, M. & Hill, A. 1975 New evidence regarding the Quaternary geology, archaeology, and hominids of Chesowanja, Kenya. *Nature, Lond.* **258**, 204–208.

Boaz, N. T. & Hampel, J. 1978 Strontium content of fossil tooth enamel and diet of early hominids. *J. Paleont.* **52**, 928–933.

Brain, C. K. 1980 Some criteria for the recognition of bone collecting agencies in African caves. In *Fossils in the making* (ed. A. K. Behrensmayer & A. Hill), pp. 107–130. Chicago: University of Chicago Press.

Clutton-Brock, T. H. & Harvey, P. 1980 Primates, brains and ecology. *J. Zool.* **190**, 309–323.

Day, M. H. & Leakey, R. E. 1973 New evidence for the genus *Homo* from East Rudolf, Kenya. *Am. J. phys. Anthrop.* **39**, 341–354.

Dart, R. A. 1959 *Adventures with the missing link*. Philadelphia: The Institutes Press.

Dart, R. A. 1957 The osteodontokeratic culture of *Australopithecus prometheus*. *Transv. Mus. Mem.* no. 10.

Dart, R. A. 1953 The predatory transition from ape to man. *Int. anthrop. ling. Rev.* **1**, 201–218.

De Niro, M. & Epstein, S. 1978 Carbon isotopic evidence for different feeding habits in two hyrax species occupying the same habitat. *Science, N.Y.* **201**, 906–908.

Du Brul, E. L. 1977 Early hominid feeding mechanisms. *Am. J. phys. Anthrop.* **47**, 305–320.

Gifford, D. P. 1980 Ethnoarcheological contributions to the taphonomy of human sites. In *Fossils in the making* (ed. A. K. Behrensmeyer & A. Hill), pp. 94–107. Chicago: University of Chicago Press.

Graf, H. 1976 Occlusal forces during function. In *Occlusion: research in form and function* (ed. N. W. Rowe), pp. 90–110. Ann Arbor: University of Michigan School of Dentistry.

Hylander, W. 1979 Functional significance of primate mandibular form. *J. Morph.* **160** (2), 223–240.

Jolly, C. J. 1970 The seed-eaters: a new model of hominid differentiation based on a baboon analogy. *Man* **5**, 5–26.

Kay, R. 1977 Diets of early Miocene African hominoids. *Nature, Lond.* **268**, 628–630.

Kay, R. & Hylander, W. 1978 The dental structure of mammalian folivores with special reference to Primates and Phalangeroides (Marsupialia). In *The biology of arboreal folivores* (ed. G. G. Montgomery), pp. 173–191. Washington: Smithsonian Institutes Press.

Leakey, M. D. 1971 *Olduvai Gorge*, vol. 3. Cambridge University Press.

Leakey, M. G. & Leakey, R. E. 1978 The fossil hominids and an introduction to their context, 1968–1974. *Koobi Fora Research Project*, vol. 1. Oxford: Oxford University Press.

Leakey, R. E., Mungai, J. & Walker, A. C. 1972 New australopithecines from East Rudolf, Kenya. *Am. J. phys. Anthrop.* **35**, 175–186.

Moller, E. 1966 The chewing apparatus. *Acta physiol. scand.* **69**, 1–229.

Parker, R. & Toots, H. 1980 Trace elements in bones as paleobiological indicators. In *Fossils in the making* (ed. A. K. Behrensmeyer & A. Hill), pp. 197–207. Chicago: University of Chicago Press.

Robinson, J. T. 1956 The dentition of the Australopithecinae. *Transv. Mus. Mem.*, no. 9.

Schoeninger, M. 1979 Dietary reconstruction at Chalcatzingo, a formative period site in Morelos, Mexico. *Contrib. hum. biol. Mus. Anthrop. Univ. Michigan*, no. 2.

Shearman, D. J. C. 1978 Vitamin A and Sir Douglas Mawson. *Br. med. J.* **1**, 283–285.

Szalay, F. S. 1975 Hunting–scavenging protohominids: a model for hominid origins. *Man* (n.s.) **10**, 420–429.

Tobias, P. V. 1967 The cranium and maxillary dentition of *Zinjanthropus* (*Australopithecus*) *boisei*. *Olduvai Gorge*, volume 2. Cambridge University Press.

Toots, H. & Voorhies, M. 1965 Strontium in fossil bones and the reconstruction of food chains. *Science, N.Y* **149**, 854–855.

Walker, A. C. 1980 Functional anatomy and taphonomy. In *Fossils in the making* (ed. A. K. Behrensmeyer & A. Hill), pp. 182–196. Chicago: University of Chicago Press.

Walker, A. C. 1978 Functional anatomy of oral tissues: mastication and deglutition. In *Textbook of oral biology* (ed. J. Shaw, E. Sweeney, C. Cappuccino & S. Meller), pp. 277–296. Philadelphia and London: W. B. Saunders.

Walker, A. C., Hoeck, H. & Perez, L. M. 1978 Microwear of mammalian teeth as an indicator of diet. *Science, N.Y.* **201**, 908–910.

Walker, A. C., Zimmerman, M. & Leakey, R. E. 1980 A possible case of hypervitaminosis A in *Homo erectus*. (In preparation.)

White, T. D. 1978 Early hominid enamel hypoplasia. *Am J. phys. Anthrop.* **49**, 79–84.

Yellen, J. E. 1974 The Kung settlement pattern; an archeological perspective. Ph.D. thesis, Harvard University.

Phil. Trans. R. Soc. Lond. B **292**, 65–76 (1981) [65]
Printed in Great Britain

Tooth size and shape and their relevance to studies of hominid evolution

By B. A. Wood

Department of Anatomy, The Middlesex Hospital Medical School,
Cleveland Street, London W1P 6DB, U.K.

Teeth have the potential to provide evidence about both the patterns of diversity of fossil hominids and the functional adaptations of early hominid taxa. Comparative studies of dental function and the direct examination of wear patterns in fossil teeth are now providing data for testing hypotheses that major differences in dietary adaptations underlie lineage diversity in the early hominids.

However, this review focuses on the contributions that dental evidence can make to hominid systematic studies. Attention is drawn to the value of tooth enamel as a morphological marker and the major contribution that teeth make to the hominid fossil sample. Systematic analysis of hominid remains must start with the identification of patterns of morphological variation. Only then can the taxonomic significance of the morphological differences be assessed and attempts made to link designated taxa in a phylogenetic scheme. The preliminary results of a detailed metrical survey of early hominid premolar and molar teeth are presented. As part of this study cusp areas of first mandibular molars were measured by planimetry. Analysis of these data, without any prior assumptions about taxonomic groups, has demonstrated that the major axis of variation separates the pooled sample into morphological subgroups. These methods provide a systematic and rigorous way of identifying patterns of tooth crown morphology and will allow a more objective assessment of the affinities of individual specimens. Fossil taxa are described in terms of both absolute and relative tooth size. If canine base area and molar crown area are considered there is considerable overlap between *Australopithecus africanus* and *Australopithecus* (*Paranthropus*) *robustus* whereas there is little or no overlap between the ranges of *Australopithecus africanus* and *Australopithecus* (*Paranthropus*) *boisei*. Differences in relative tooth size among fossil taxa are taken as an example of how to attack the problem of assessing the taxonomic significance of morphological differences. Analogues from modern primates are used to derive tooth–body size relations for three relative growth models. The results suggest that increases in body size are usually accompanied by a more rapid rate of increase in canine size than in molar size. This suggests that the relatively smaller canines of the 'robust' australopithecines are not the result of simple scaling, but represent the result of selection against an allometric trend. Preliminary results of a survey of the subocclusal morphology of fossil teeth are presented to indicate the potential of radiographic studies and to demonstrate that changes in root morphology can be correlated with crown shape and relative size.

Introduction

A significant proportion of the research effort of palaeoanthropologists is occupied by the study of teeth. Indeed, some critics would claim that palaeoanthropologists are unhealthily preoccupied with the finer points of dental morphology, and their application to obscurantist taxonomic arguments. In the past criticisms such as these would have been hard to refute. For too long teeth were regarded merely as objects for description, and the views of experienced, but inevitably subjective and opinionated, observers were considered adequate judgement. Scant regard was paid to, or allowance made for, ranges of variation of tooth size and expression of morphological features, and little or no attempt was made to quantify and assess the significance of any differences. However, just as other research fields have absorbed and benefited from developments in statistical theory and method, and in particular from newer concepts of population variation and sampling, these same innovations have been incorporated into hominid palaeontological research. The image of the bespectacled professor equipped with calipers and a single fossil pronouncing authoritatively on the pattern of human evolution is long dead, but critics, and to some extent the public, will not willingly let it rest.

In the past decade or so, hominid palaeontology has seen another shift of research emphasis. There has been a move away from merely documenting the past, and a move towards understanding the broader biological context of hominid evolution. In an elegant analysis of the epistemology of hominid palaeontology, Tattersall & Eldredge (1977) have urged that, when hypotheses are made about hominid evolution, more regard should be paid to the level of complexity inherent in each hypothesis. They suggest that three levels should be recognized. At the first level are hypotheses that seek to identify morphological sets, or phena, of hominids and arrange them in a branching diagram based on the distribution of unique features. The second level develops the simpler hypotheses to include propositions about ancestor–descendant relations. The third level hypotheses they call 'scenarios'. These are complex hypotheses that attempt to explain the adaptive and functional reasons underlying evolutionary trends, and the complicated reciprocal relationships between morphology and behaviour. In summary, the two lower levels of hypotheses answer the question, how?; the third level seeks to answer the question, why?

Functional interpretations of teeth

Teeth can make their own special contribution to attempts to devise alternative evolutionary 'scenarios'. Analogues developed from studies of modern primate teeth have made it possible to use the morphology of fossil teeth to make interpretations about diet and social behaviour. In a series of reports, Kay (1975, 1978) developed a system of metrical analysis of molar teeth that differentiates between the shearing and crushing function of the tooth. Leaf-eating species tend to have relatively higher cusps, longer shearing blades and larger crushing basins for a given tooth length than have fruit-eating taxa. These features are presumably adaptations to the diet of leaves, which, because of their toughness and relatively low energy value, require more chewing and processing than fruit. Using these functional correlations, Kay (1977) has examined the diets of Miocene hominoids, but this method has yet to be applied to the study of hominid teeth.

Dietary regimes in extant primates have been correlated with tooth size as well as tooth morphology. When the crown areas of molar teeth are considered in relation to body size, frugivorous species tend to have relatively smaller teeth than do folivores or insectivores (Kay 1973, 1975). However, body size and diet are not independent variables and the relationship between tooth size and diet in primates is a complex one (Pilbeam & Gould 1974; Goldstein et al. 1978). The relative size of teeth within a dentition has also been linked with dietary preferences; frugivores are distinguished by their relatively large incisors (Hylander 1975), which they use to dehusk fruits and seeds.

Studies have also sought to relate tooth size with social behaviour. Relative canine size has been examined in relation to social organization, and Harvey et al. (1978) found that sexual dimorphism in canine size was greatest in taxa in which intragroup selection and predator pressures are significant influences.

Complementing these studies of the functional correlates of dental morphology are research programmes in which the ways that teeth are worn during life are investigated. In these studies the effects of mastication are usually examined; but examples of non-masticatory tooth use in modern human populations may also be relevant to the study of hominid teeth (Molnar 1972). Most of the literature on tooth wear relates to studies on modern human populations in which attempts have been made to correlate diet with quite gross indicators of dental wear (Molnar 1971). Macroscopic and low power microscopic studies of wear patterns in hominid teeth have also been used to examine hypotheses about dietary specialization of early hominid taxa (Wallace 1973, 1975). Scanning electronmicroscopy now allows the examination of fine details of enamel wear. These studies are still in their early stages, but preliminary results suggest that particular diets are associated with recognizable patterns of enamel microwear (Walker 1979, and this symposium).

THE PLACE OF SYSTEMATIC STUDIES

Present and future attempts to use hominid dental evidence to interpret dietary preferences and possibly even social organization are likely to make significant contributions towards our knowledge of early hominid behaviour and adaptation. However, the quite proper growth of interest in these research activities has tended to deflect interest away from, and even lead to the denigration of, studies in which teeth are used as guides to morphological groupings and phylogenetic relationships. The result is that the study of dental morphology in the context of hominid systematics is being neglected.

Hominid systematic studies seek to identify and assess patterns of morphological diversity in the hominid fossil sample. It is my contention that functional interpretations and the framing of complex hypotheses about behavioural adaptations can only proceed within a proper systematic framework. Unless workers first put forward hypotheses about the taxonomic significance of the morphological variation within the fossil record, functional interpretations can only be of the most general kind. For instance, unless one attempts to establish how many hominid taxa are represented in the fossil record, how can any differences in behaviour and adaptation of synchronic taxa be usefully discussed? Thus, even in a meeting that quite properly lays stress on attempts to reconstruct hominid behaviour, and reactionary though it may seem, I propose to examine some of the ways in which dental evidence can contribute to hominid systematic studies.

HAVE TEETH A SPECIAL CONTRIBUTION TO MAKE?

It is important that systematic studies proceed in a logical sequence (Simpson 1963; Wood 1978). The initial steps are the identification of patterns of morphology in the fossil sample and the recognition, and attempted definition of, morphological groups or 'phena'. These studies are then followed by attempts to assess the taxonomic significance of the morphological groupings and to establish any probable phylogenetic relationships among the phena. Teeth are so crucial to the survival of individuals and play such an important part in the adaptation of breeding groups to their environment that their importance in evolutionary studies is seldom questioned. However, two further properties of teeth give them additional importance. The first is a consequence of the development and structure of dental enamel, and the second relates to the contribution teeth make to the fossil record.

Although bone and tooth enamel are both mineralized tissues with a crystallite component, they differ both in their ontogenetic development and in their capacity to modify their form after maturation. Teeth develop in such a way that, after the enamel cap of the tooth crown has developed in the dental follicle, the capacity to modify crown morphology is lost. Enamel is made up of regularly orientated crystallites, which form prisms, the basic units of its structure. Enamel formation or amelogenesis starts at the boundary with the dentine and proceeds towards the eventual outer surface of the tooth crown. Before the eruption of the tooth the enamel-forming epithelial layer ceases to become active and is finally shed. Once amelogenesis has ceased, crown morphology can only be altered by the exigencies of attrition, abrasion and erosion. Thus enamel shape and size represent a faithful record of the combination of genetic and environmental influences that control and affect amelogenesis.

Bone, in contrast to enamel, does not lose its capacity to modify its size and shape. Although growth in length of long bones ceases when the cartilage forming epiphysial plates degenerates, the capacity for circumferential growth and remodelling is retained by virtue of the osteogenic potential of the periosteum. Experiments have demonstrated the capacity of bone to modify its form in response to changes in the pattern of external stresses (Washburn 1947a, b; Riesenfeld 1969, 1972, 1974; Burstein et al. 1972). Just how much of the morphology of a bone is a reflection of the loading conditions to which it was subjected during life is unknown; indeed there is debate about whether sustained submaximal stress, or infrequent, but high, loadings are the more important determinants. Thus, whereas the phenotypic plasticity of bone contributes an additional potential variable when morphological variation is being assessed, this additional factor can be discounted when assessing the significance of differences in tooth crown size and shape.

A second reason to pay special attention to patterns of dental variation is the fact that teeth are particularly well represented in the fossil record. The different rates of survival of skeletal parts during fossilization are determined by many factors. In some conditions, for example, when the skeleton is weathering by exposure to extremes of temperature and moisture, teeth tend to crack and disintegrate; this is probably related to the low tensile strength and brittleness of the enamel. However, in most phases of the process of fossilization the hardness of the inorganic materials that go to make up the structure of teeth ensure their differential survival. Enamel, which covers the tooth crown, is 96 % (by mass) mineral. It is the hardest tissue in the body, and the important surface regions are harder than the deeper layers. Enamel has a high modulus of elasticity and is particularly rigid. These characteristics, together with the compact shape of hominid tooth crowns, contribute to the particular durability of teeth in most of the depositional environments in which hominid fossils are preserved. A census of the skeletal parts found at fourteen hominid sites (Tobias 1972) showed that, at the five South African and nine east African sites examined, teeth made up respectively 75 % and 70 % of the total sample. However, by pooling the east African data, major disparities in the contribution that teeth make to the body of hominid fossil evidence at individual sites are masked. Omo and Koobi Fora are both fossil sites in the Lake Turkana Basin. However, the depositional environments at the Omo are mainly associated with the flood plain of a large perennial river system, whereas at Koobi Fora the fossils were deposited in lake margin and small ephemeral channel environments (de Heinzelin et al. 1976; Findlater 1978). In a study in which the proportions of skeletal parts preserved in fluvial and lake margin environments at Koobi Fora were compared, Behrensmeyer (1975, 1978) demonstrated that in fluvial deposits denser skeletal components, such as teeth, survived better. This effect of hydraulic sorting before sedimentation is evident when the hominid samples at Omo and Koobi Fora are compared. If each well preserved tooth is taken as an individual specimen, teeth make up nearly 90 % of the hominid sample at the Omo, whereas they constitute less than 60 % at Koobi Fora; if the proportions of specimens that are isolated teeth are compared, the disparity is even more marked. Thus, though at all sites dental remains are a major component of the hominid fossil sample, at some sites, such as Omo in Ethiopia and Laetoli in Tanzania, any deductions about the hominids represented in these samples are based almost entirely on dental evidence.

WHAT EVIDENCE DO TEETH PROVIDE?

The crown and roots of teeth potentially provide a formidable amount of morphological and metrical data. Nonetheless, discussions of the pattern and significance of variation in early hominid dental remains are often limited to relatively crude length and breadth measurements of tooth crowns (see, for example, Wolpoff 1971). In the remainder of this paper the types of dental evidence that are available are reviewed and methods for their analysis are discussed. Most of the examples cited are from comparative studies of teeth associated with 'robust' australopithecines. The theme of the review is a question: can 'robust' australopithecine teeth and dentitions be distinguished from those of other taxa? The review is not intended to be an exhaustive survey of the literature, and its emphasis on relative tooth size and the detailed analysis of canine and molar teeth reflects my particular research interests.

Crown size

The usual way to quantify the size of a tooth crown is to measure its maximum length and width, and to use either these measurements on their own, or their product, for comparative studies. Since, on the basis of such measurements, differences in length of 2 mm or less have been considered taxonomically significant (Tobias 1966), it would be prudent to examine briefly factors that affect the accuracy, reliability and descriptive utility of this type of data.

The accuracy and reproducibility of measurements are affected by both the shape of the crown and the degree of wear on the tooth. The definition of terminus points for simple crown measurements is particularly difficult for those teeth, such as upper molars, that have an irregular crown outline. Mesiodistal length of upper molars can be taken either as the 'maximum' length (Korenhof 1960) or the distance between the points of contact with neighbouring teeth. In our experience there are sometimes significant differences between these measurements on the same tooth; this point has also been noted by Tobias (1967). It is equally difficult to define terminus points for taking buccolingual breadth that give consistent results; these difficulties are increased when isolated teeth are measured. In a survey of the dental remains from Koobi Fora, repeated buccolingual measurements in the same upper molar by two experienced observers, using the same protocol, in some cases resulted in discrepancies of between 0.5 and 1 mm.

While patterns of tooth wear provide information about dental function and perhaps also taxonomic affinity (Wallace 1975), wear adversely affects the reliability of dental measurements. A particular problem is the influence of approximal wear on mediodistal crown lengths. Ideally two values should be cited, the 'actual' mesiodistal length and the 'estimated' unworn length. This estimation can be made by a combination of extrapolating the unworn parts of the occlusal surface contour and, if dentine is exposed, making an estimate of enamel thickness; corrections of about 5 % of the 'actual' mediodistal length are quite common for worn molar teeth.

The value, for comparative purposes, of crown area, when computed from simple length and breadth measurements, depends very much on the shape of the occlusal outline of the tooth. As part of a comprehensive metrical and morphological survey of Plio-Pleistocene hominid dental remains, we have prepared magnified photographs of the occlusal view of each tooth. The basal outline of the crown was defined, and the area of the crown determined by planimetry. Crown area measured directly in this way was compared to the crown area derived from the product of the buccolingual and 'estimated' mediodistal diameters by expressing it as a percentage of the derived crown area value. In mandibular first molars the crown area by planimetry was, on average, 83 % of the derived area, with a range between 74 % and 93 %; in second and third molars the range was even greater. Thus crown area computed from length and breadth measurements is a relatively unreliable estimate of the actual area of a tooth, and this point should be borne in mind when the significance of differences in derived crown area estimates in fossil samples are assessed.

One of the current problems of hominid systematics is the significance of the dental differences between the 'gracile' and 'robust' australopithecines. The hypodigm of the gracile australopithecines is usually taken to include material recovered from Member 4 at Sterkfontein and the deposits at Makapansgat and Taung; it has recently been much expanded by the addition of newly discovered specimens from Sterkfontein (Tobias 1978), but as yet no detailed data on this new material are available. The robust australopithecine sample includes the hypodigms of two taxa, *Australopithecus (Paranthropus) robustus* from South Africa, and *Australopithecus (Paranthropus) boisei* from East African sites. The derived crown areas of the canines and molars shown in figure 1 are based on data from the standard odontography of this material (Robinson 1956) and on measurements taken by the author. The ranges of canine base area and molar crown area of *Australopithecus africanus* and *Australopithecus (Paranthropus) robustus* overlap, and if these data are pooled a unimodal distribution results. Although teeth with crown areas in the non-overlapping parts of the ranges could be reliably assigned to one taxon or the other, the distribution of the values is such that many specimens could not be accurately assigned on the basis of size alone. The sample of *Australopithecus (Paranthropus) boisei* is small because it only includes teeth in mandibles or crania that have been taxonomically assigned on the basis of features other than dental ones. In molar size there is little or no overlap between *Australopithecus africanus* and *Australopithecus (Paranthropus) boisei*; similarly impressive differences in crown area are seen between teeth from the lower members of the Shungura Formation, and those in members E through to G, which have been attributed to, or closely compared with, *Australopithecus (Paranthropus) boisei*.

In addition to the sizes of individual teeth, the relative sizes of teeth within each taxa or even in individual dentitions can also be compared. Robinson (1956) pointed out that gracile and robust australopithecines from the South African sites could be distinguished on the basis of relative canine size, which is usually expressed by relating canine base area to molar crown area. While there is general acceptance that robust australopithecines do have relatively small canines, the significance of these differences is still debated. Robinson (1956) claims that differences in relative canine size indicate dietary specialization in the 'robust' taxon, whereas Brace (1967, 1972), Pilbeam & Gould (1974) and Wolpoff (1978) consider that differences in

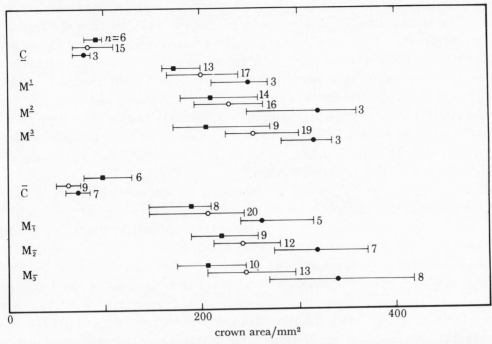

FIGURE 1. Crown base areas of canines and crown areas of molars, computed from measurements of length and breadth. Means, sample range and number of specimens (*n*) used are indicated for each taxon. Measurements for *Australopithecus africanus* (■) and *Australopithecus (Paranthropus) robustus* (○) are taken from Robinson (1956). The sample of *Australopithecus (Paranthropus) boisei* (●) comprises: Chesowanja, CHI; Peninj; OH5; KNM-ER 729, 3230; and Omo 7A-125, 74-21, F 22-1a and b.

dental proportions are simply due to the scaling effects of the larger body size of the robust form, which has been estimated to be between 10 to 25% greater than that of the gracile australopithecines. To test whether the differences in relative canine size are merely the response of allometric growth to an increase in body size, we must seek the most appropriate model for tooth–body size relations in hominid taxa. There are logical objections to generating a model from the fossil groups themselves. Allometric trends determined in this way necessarily reflect the choice of sample, and workers who then use the presence of such trends to discount any significant differences within the fossil sample are engaged in a circular argument. As an alternative tooth–body size relations in five modern primate taxa have been examined (Stack & Wood 1980). Three models of tooth–body size relations were studied: sexes of each taxon examined separately; the combined sex sample for each taxon; and the interspecific relationship between the four non-human taxa (Wood 1979). In all three models the rate of increase in canine size exceeded, or was not significantly different to, the rate of increase in molar size. Thus if gracile australopithecines, or creatures closely resembling them, are ancestral to the robust taxa (Tobias 1978; Johanson & White 1979), then there has been selection, apparently against allometric trends, for canine reduction in the larger-bodied robust australopithecines. The implication is that these differences have more taxonomic significance than if they were simply scale phenomena.

Crown shape

Relatively few comparative studies have made detailed reference to tooth crown morphology (Robinson 1956; Korenhof 1960; Frisch 1965; Tobias 1967; Sperber 1974). In those studies in which close attention has been paid to patterns of variation in mandibular molar morphology, the relative size of the cusps, the incidence of extra cusps and the presence of cingulum remnants (and the pattern of the main intercuspal fissures) have been the most commonly used distinguishing features. In a review of the differences between the gracile and robust australopithecines, Robinson (1956) acknowledges that 'morphologically the mandibular molars of *Paranthropus* and *Australopithecus* are manifestly very similar'. Nonetheless, he draws attention to several morphological features whose expression differs in the two samples; these include the presence of a protostylid and its effect on the shape of the buccal face in *Australopithecus*, the presence on $M_{\overline{1}}$ of an additional distal cusp, or C6, in *Paranthropus*, and the tendency for *Australopithecus* to have a +-shaped fissure pattern.

We were interested to try to quantify the type of differences noted by Robinson. Detailed occlusal view photographs and plaster casts were made of all available premolar and molar tooth crowns. In teeth where the course of the fissures could still be traced, the boundaries of the main cusps, any additional sixth or seventh cusps and the outline of the protostylid were defined on the photographs, and the areas of all these elements were measured by planimetry. Sperber (1974) has previously examined the cusp areas of the South African hominid molars, but he used area values derived from length and breadth measurements of each cusp. Individual cusp area data have been analysed by principal components analysis. Preliminary data on cusp areas, expressed relative to the overall size of the first mandibular molar, show that the first principal component discriminates between teeth attributed to the gracile and robust australopithecines; the cusp areas that contribute most to this separation are the protoconid and entoconid.

The results of our observations on the incidence of an accessory sixth cusp concur with those of Robinson; distal cusps are a regular feature of robust australopithecine mandibular first molars, but according to our classification no gracile australopithecine first mandibular molar has conclusive evidence of such a cusp. In modern human populations accessory cusp formation has been associated with tooth size (Dahlberg 1961; Garn *et al.* 1966). Preliminary analysis of data suggests a similar association in fossil hominid teeth, but the factors that determine whether the extra cusp should be distal or lingual are as yet unknown. Robinson's claim that the protostylid cingulum remnant is more common in gracile than robust australopithecine molars is not supported by our investigation.

In previous studies attempts have been made to analyse fissure pattern from the coordinates of defined points on the fissure system (Biggerstaff 1969, 1975; Lavelle 1978). Detailed linear, not coordinate, measurements of mandibular molar crowns have been taken on a series of living and fossil hominoids (Corruccini 1977), but this method has so far not been used to test for patterns of variability within the hominid sample. We have defined a maximum set of 26 reference points on the mandibular molar fissure pattern, each point is located by its x and y coordinates. The definitions of the reference points are such that the same system can be used to examine the teeth of Miocene hominoids and non-human primates. Analysis of these data, and also the analysis of the shapes of crown profiles, are still in progress, and the results will be reported in due course.

Subocclusal morphology

The shape and size of tooth roots are seldom referred to in surveys of early hominid dental morphology. While it is true that few isolated teeth are found with both roots and crowns

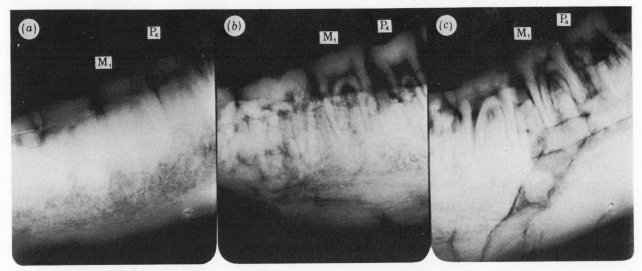

FIGURE 2. Lateral radiographs of mandibles attributed to *Australopithecus (Paranthropus) boisei*: (*a*) Peninj; (*b*) KNM-ER 3230; (*c*) KNM-ER 729. Thick lines on the grid are separated by 5 mm. Radiographs taken by Susan Abbott.

intact, information about root number can often be obtained by careful observation of the damaged alveolar borders of upper and lower jaws. Radiography also provides a means of examining roots that lie within mandibles or maxillae. Robinson (1956) and Sperber (1974) have paid particular attention to root form, and Sperber's study was the first major radiographic survey of early hominid material.

As a contribution to the analysis of the cranial remains from Koobi Fora we have undertaken a radiographic survey of the dental, mandibular and maxillary specimens from Koobi Fora, Olduvai, Peninj and Laetoli. One of the interesting findings is the range of morphology in the roots of the lower premolars. Robinson (1956) and Sperber (1974) both reported that all lower premolars in which the roots could be discerned were double-rooted, with the exception of one $P_{\overline{4}}$, which has three roots. A feature of the lower premolar crowns in the robust australopithecines is the excessive development of the talonid, with accessory cusp formation on the distal marginal ridge and a large posterior fovea (Robinson 1956; Howell 1978). This molarization' of the posterior premolar results in the $P_{\overline{4}}$ dimensions significantly exceeding those of $P_{\overline{3}}$. Radiographic images of the roots of $P_{\overline{4}}$ in KNM-ER 729, KNM-ER 3230 and the Peninj mandible are similar in shape and length to those of the molar teeth; indeed in some cases $P_{\overline{4}}$ roots are larger than those of $M_{\overline{1}}$. (figure 2). Careful assessments of comparative root lengths and inclinations, and investigations of the relationship between root size and morphology and crown size and shape have yet to be made. Nonetheless, our preliminary observations encourage us to believe that details of subocclusal morphology will make a useful contribution to the analysis of patterns of variation of early hominid tooth morphology.

CONCLUSIONS

A distinction has to be made between the ability to demonstrate differences between taxa by means of sample parameters and that to assign individual specimens to a taxon. It is clear from this review and other studies that there is sufficient overlap between the gracile and robust australopithecines in simple tooth dimensions for tooth size alone to be ineffective as an indicator of taxonomic affinity. The continuously distributed nature of morphological features, the difficulties of defining them and the generally small sample sizes also reduce the efficacy of morphological traits as taxonomic discriminators.

This review has highlighted the need for more vigorous attempts to standardize and quantify information about tooth size and shape. Simple length and breadth measurements are clearly inadequate to describe and compare a structure as complicated as a tooth. Preliminary results of an odontometric analysis of early hominid molar and premolar morphology suggest that a multivariate approach may help to establish a more rigorous definition and description of the dental characteristics of a taxon. Data such as these would provide a framework on which to test hypotheses of morphological diversity, and may also allow a more objective assessment of the affinities of individual specimens.

Research incorporated in this review has been made possible by a project grant from the Natural Environment Research Council. Charles Stack was in receipt of a Medical Research Council Intercalated Studentship. I am grateful to those institutions and to people who have allowed me to examine fossils in their care.

I would like to acknowledge the help of my research assistant, Susan Abbott, who has played a major part in the analyses cited in this paper. My thanks go to Michael Clarke, Michael Hills and Steven Graham, who have provided statistical advice.

This review was undertaken while the author was in receipt of a study grant from the Nuffield Foundation.

REFERENCES

Behrensmeyer, A. K. 1975 The taphonomy and paleoecology of Plio-Pleistocene vertebrate assemblages east of Lake Rudolf, Kenya. *Bull. Mus. comp. Zool. Harv.* **146** (10), 475–574.

Behrensmeyer, A. K. 1978 The habitat of Plio-Pleistocene hominids in East Africa: taphonomic and micro-stratigraphic evidence. In *Early hominids of Africa* (ed. C. J. Jolly), pp. 165–189. London: Duckworth.

Biggerstaff, R. H. 1969 The basal area of posterior tooth crown components: the assessment of within tooth variations of premolars and molars. *Am. J. phys. Anthrop.* **31**, 163–170.

Biggerstaff, R. H. 1975 Cusp size, sexual dimorphism and heritability of cusp size in twins. *Am. J. phys. Anthrop.* **42**, 127–140.

Brace, C. L. 1967 Environment, tooth form and size in the Pleistocene. *J. dent. Res.* **46**, 809–816.

Brace, C. L. 1972 Sexual dimorphism in human evolution *Yearb. phys. Anthrop.* **16**, 31–49.

Burstein, A. H., Currey, J., Frankel, V. H., Heiple, K. G., Lunseth, P. & Vessely, J. C. 1972 Bone strength: the effect of screw holes. *J. Bone Jt Surg.* A **54**, 1143–1156.

Corruccini, R. S. 1977 Crown component variation in hominoid lower third molars. *Z. Morph. Anthrop.* **68**, 14–25.

Dahlberg, A. A. 1961 Relationship of tooth size to cusp number and groove conformation of occlusal surface patterns of lower molar teeth. *J. dent. Res.* **40**, 34–38.

Findlater, I. C. 1978 Stratigraphy. In *The fossil hominids and an introduction to their context, 1968–1974. Koobi Fora Research Project*, vol. 1 (ed. M. G. Leakey & R. E. Leakey), pp. 14–31. Oxford: Clarendon Press.

Frisch, J. E. 1965 Trends in the evolution of the hominoid dentition. *Bibl. primatol.* **3**, 1–130.

Garn, S. M., Dahlberg, A. A., Lewis, A. B. & Kerewsky, R. S. 1966 Groove pattern, cusp number and tooth size. *J. dent. Res.* **45**, 970.

Goldstein, S., Post, D. & Melnick, D. 1978 An analysis of cercopithecoid odontometrics. I. The scaling of the maxillary dentition. *Am. J. phys. Anthrop.* **49**, 517–532.

Harvey, P., Kavanagh, K. & Clutton-Brock, T. H. 1978 Sexual dimorphism in primate teeth. *J. Zool.* **186**, 475–485.

de Heinzelin, J., Haesaerts, P. & Howell, F. C. 1976 Plio-Pleistocene formations of the Lower Omo Basin with particular reference to the Shungura Formation. In *Earliest man and environments in the Lake Rudolf Basin* (ed.

Y. Coppens, F. C. Howell, G. Ll. Isaac & R. E. F. Leakey), pp. 24–29. Chicago: University of Chicago Press.

Howell, F. C. 1978 Hominidae. In *Evolution of African mammals* (ed. V. J. Maglio & H. B. S. Cooke), pp. 154–248. Cambridge, Massachusetts: Harvard University Press.

Hylander, W. L. 1975 Incisor size and diet in anthropoids with special reference to Cercopithecidae. *Science, N.Y.* **189**, 1095–1098.

Johanson, D. C. & White, T. D. 1979 A systematic assessment of early African hominids. *Science, N.Y.* **203**, 321–330.

Kay, R. F. 1973 Mastication, molar tooth structure and diet in primates. Ph.D. thesis, Yale University.

Kay, R. F. 1975 The functional adaptations of primate molar teeth. *Am. J. phys. Anthrop.* **43**, 195–216.

Kay, R. F. 1977 Diet of early Miocene African hominoids. *Nature, Lond.* **268**, 628–630.

Kay, R. F. 1978 Molar structure and diet in extant Cercopithecidae. In *Development, function and evolution of teeth* (ed. P. M. Butler & K. A. Joysey), pp. 309–339. Academic Press: London.

Korenhof, C. A. W. 1960 *Morphogenetical aspects of the human upper molar.* Utrecht: Uitgeversmaatschappij Neerlandia.

Lavelle, C. L. B. 1978 An analysis of molar tooth form. *Acta anat.* **100**, 282–288.

Molnar, S. 1971 Human tooth wear, tooth function and cultural variability. *Am. J. phys. Anthrop.* **34**, 175–189.

Molnar, S. 1972 Tooth wear and culture: a survey of tooth functions among some prehistoric populations. *Curr. Anthrop.* **13**, 511–516.

Pilbeam, D. R. & Gould, S. J. 1974 Size and scaling in human evolution. *Science, N.Y.* **186**, 892–901.

Riesenfeld, A. 1969 The adaptive mandible: an experimental study *Acta anat.* **72**, 246–262.

Riesenfeld, A. 1972 Metatarsal robusticity in bipedal rats. *Am. J. phys. Anthrop.* **36**, 229–233.

Riesenfeld, A. 1974 Changes in metatarsal robusticity following experimental surgery. *Am. J. phys. Anthrop.* **40**, 205–212.

Robinson, J. T. 1956 The dentition of the Australopithecinae. *Transv. Mus. Mem.*, no. 9.

Simpson, G. G. 1963 The meaning of taxonomic statements. In *Classification and human evolution* (ed. S. L. Washburn), pp. 1–31. Chicago: Aldine.

Sperber, G. 1974 Morphology of the cheek teeth of early South African hominids. Ph.D. thesis, University of the Witwatersrand.

Stack, C. G. & Wood, B. A. 1980 Does allometry explain the differences between 'gracile' and 'robust' australopithecines? *Am. J. phys. Anthrop.* **52**, 55–62.

Tattersall, I. & Eldredge, N. 1977 Fact, theory and fantasy in human paleontology. *Am. Scient.* **65**, 204–211.

Tobias, P. V. 1966 The distinctiveness of *Homo habilis*. *Nature, Lond.* **209**, 953–957.

Tobias, P. V. 1967 *The cranium and maxillary dentition of Australopithecus (Zinjanthropus) boisei.* Cambridge: Cambridge University Press.

Tobias, P. V. 1972 Progress and problems in the study of early man in sub-Saharan Africa. In *The functional and evolutionary biology of primates* (ed. R. H. Tuttle), pp. 63–93. Chicago: Aldine Atherton.

Tobias, P. V. 1978 The place of *Australopithecus africanus* in hominid evolution. In *Recent advances in primatology*, vol. 3 (ed. D. J. Chivers & K. A. Joysey), pp. 373–394. London: Academic Press.

Walker, A. 1979 S.e.m. analysis of microwear and its correlation with dietary patterns. *Am. J. phys. Anthrop.* **50**, 489.

Wallace, J. A. 1973 Tooth chipping in the australopithecines. *Nature, Lond.* **244**, 117–118.

Wallace, J. A. 1975 Dietary adaptations of *Australopithecus* and early *Homo*. In *Paleoanthropology, morphology and paleoecology* (ed. R. H. Tuttle), pp. 203–223. The Hague: Mouton.

Washburn, S. L. 1947a The effect of the temporal muscle on the form of the mandible. *J. dent. Res.* **26**, 174.

Washburn, S. L. 1947b The relation of the temporal muscle to the form of the skull. *Anat. Rec.* **99**, 239–248.

Wolpoff, M. H. 1971 Metric trends in hominid dental evolution. *Stud. Anthrop.*, no. 2.

Wolpoff, M. W. 1978 Some aspects of canine size in the australopithecines. *J. hum. Evol.* **7**, 115–126.

Wood, B. A. 1978 An analysis of early hominid fossil postcranial material: principles and methods. In *Early hominids of Africa* (ed. C. J. Jolly), pp. 347–360. London: Duckworth.

Wood, B. A. 1979 Models for assessing relative canine size in fossil hominids. *J. hum. Evol.* **8**, 493–502.

LORD ZUCKERMAN, F.R.S. (*The Zoological Society of London, Regent's Park, London NW1 4RY, U.K.*). Dr Wood has told us that (to quote his own words) 'in establishing phylogenetic relationships in a systematic framework' he defines his morphological groups before assessing the significance of the differences between them. This sounds quite logical. But would he now tell us what assumptions underlie the first stage of the process?

B. A. WOOD. I had tried to make the point early in my talk that establishment of phylogenetic relationships should be the last of a number of stages in any attempted analysis of hominid fossil evidence. The first stage is to break the fossil sample into a series of subgroups based on morphological features and morphometric criteria. The criteria for these subgroups is not that there are no differences between the fossils in each group, i.e., no variation, but that the variation is more likely to be intraspecific rather than interspecific. Because we have no *a priori* knowledge of the patterns of variation in fossil taxa, I claim that we have to rely on 'models' of variation derived from appropriate modern taxa.

The second and third stages of any analysis are to establish the systematic relationships of the morphological subgroups. For example, are they conspecific or congeneric? To do this again means making subjective judgements of patterns of variation, again based on analogies drawn from extant taxa. The last stage, phylogenetic analysis, requires that we establish a series of morphoclines by trying to trace the transmission and modification of morphological features.

At all levels the analytical process is weak because it involves argument by analogy, but surely this is preferable to the circularity of making assumptions about what specimens make up fossil taxa. I stressed in my talk the importance of the results of the principal components analysis of the tooth crown data because this type of analysis makes no *a priori* assumptions about groups; as Lord Zuckerman knows it seeks major axes of variation, and in this case the major axis of variation sorts mandibular molar tooth crown morphology into groups that happen to be in agreement with the conventional taxonomic attribution of this material.

I have no defence against any accusation that decisions about classification are subjective; my aim has been to reduce the subjectivity to the lowest possible level.

Phil. Trans. R. Soc. Lond. B **292**, 77–87 (1981)   [77]
Printed in Great Britain

LOCOMOTION

Primate locomotion: some problems in analysis and interpretation

By E. H. Ashton

Department of Anatomy, Medical School, University of Birmingham, Birmingham B15 2JT, U.K.

Anatomical features biomechanically related to man's upright posture and gait are well defined. But uncertainty surrounds the evolutionary pathway leading to human bipedalism, partly because the anatomical nature of man's immediate ancestors is unknown, and partly because it is sometimes difficult to define and interpret the biomechanical significance of unique constellations of features that obtain in post-cranial remains of fossil hominoids.

In the innominate bone of *Australopithecus* the expanded iliac blade gives some appearance of similarity to that of man and has frequently been taken as indicating that *Australopithecus* had acquired a bipedal posture and gait.

Methods have been developed to define quantitatively those morphological features of the innominate bone that are functionally related to the force pattern impressed during locomotion. On the basis of multivariate comparison of these features with those of extant primate groups representing a wide range of function of the hind-limb, it has been shown: first that the australopithecine innominate bone is unique in form; secondly, that this bone is somewhat better adapted than is that of extant subhuman primates for weight transmission in a bipedal posture; thirdly, that because of a dorsal orientation of the iliac blade *Australopithecus* lacked the means of powerful abduction of the thigh. Thus, any bipedalism practised by this extinct genus must have been quite different from that characteristic of *Homo sapiens*.

Evidence from, for example, the foot, shows that it is quite possible that *Australopithecus* may have used its hindlimb in some form of arboreal locomotion, in addition to possible terrestrial bipedalism (albeit of a non-human type). It is not known whether *Australopithecus* was, or could have been, an ancestor of man. Correspondingly, whether or not such compound use of the hindlimb could have been ancestral to the human type of bipedalism is indeterminate.

INTRODUCTION

The biomechanics of the human upright posture and striding gait, long appreciated from Vesalian inference and amply confirmed by electromyographic and other modern techniques of study, are functionally correlated with aspects of form and proportion that contribute to a distinctive human complex. Many of these features affect the skeleton and, although reflected in, for instance, the curvature of the vertebral column, primarily relate to the hindlimb and pelvic girdle.

Other skeletal features, while of manifest selective significance in the context of the evolutionary emergence of *Homo sapiens*, may not necessarily have a direct biomechanical relationship to the mechanism of bipedal posture and gait. These include, for instance, the retention of free mobility of the forearm, the unique development of a mechanism, arthrological and myological, to permit true opposability of the thumb to each of the fingers in turn, and also the development of distinctive features of the shoulder that permit free mobility of the joint, especially in a plane below the horizontal.

In relation to man's evolutionary history, the biological significance of a bipedal gait and the resulting emancipation of the forelimb is axiomatic. But it is not certain how man's upright posture evolved. Such doubt stems from the fact that the fossil record of the primates is insufficient to permit detailed analysis of when the human and ape lines of descent separated. Thus the anatomical nature of man's immediate ancestors is unknown. Further uncertainty about the derivation of man's upright posture arises because it is difficult to make adequate biomechanical inferences from fossil remains, often fragmentary and of unusual morphological form.

The first of these sources of uncertainty is, and may well remain, intractable. The second is ameliorated by quantitative biomechanical and morphological study.

Bipedalism in fossil hominoids

Some human types (e.g. *Homo sapiens* from the Upper Palaeolithic together with certain remains of Neanderthal man) are well represented by postcranial skeletal parts so similar to those of living men that there is no real doubt that these now extinct groups stood and walked effectively as does extant man. Despite the remains being less complete, little real variation seems to attach to views about the posture and gait of *Homo erectus*. But earlier members of the hominoid radiation, although represented by relatively abundant postcranial remains (e.g. of *Limnopithecus, Proconsul* and *Australopithecus*), differ so much from extant apes and man as to generate doubt not only about overall posture and gait, but even about the likely locomotor use of individual skeletal parts.

In this context, much interest has centred upon the Australopithecinae. The earliest specimen of this group was discovered in 1924. Although predominantly ape-like in the form and proportions of its braincase and facial skeleton (see, for example, Zuckerman 1928), it was immediately hailed by some as a human ancestor because of presumed deviations in certain morphological features of the teeth and skull from those of the extant great apes and apparent approximations to the conditions typical of man (see, for example, Dart 1925). This view was much reiterated when extensive additional fossil material was discovered from the mid-1930s onwards (see, for example: Broom & Schepers, 1946; Le Gros Clark 1947, 1949). But others (e.g. Zuckerman 1950, 1954) repeatedly emphasized the predominantly ape-like proportions and features of the face and cranium.

From the first, claims about supposed morphological deviations of the Australopithecinae from the apes led to inferences about probable posture and gait. Initially (see, for example: Dart 1925; Le Gros Clark 1947) these were based on apparent differences in the position of the foramen magnum on the skull base from that characteristic of extant apes and on a presumed approximation to that characteristic of man. But such deviations from any extant subhuman primates were, at most, marginal and were, for three reasons, of doubtful significance. First the position of the foramen magnum of the fossils actually lay within the range of variation of e.g. *Gorilla* (Ashton & Zuckerman 1951). Secondly, such deviation as was manifest from the mean values of any extant monkeys and apes was, in scale, far less than that obtaining between extant man, on the one hand, and monkeys and apes (adult and immature), on the other. Thirdly, even these much bigger differences, although correlating with contrasts in posture and gait and in the poise of the head, from a functional viewpoint could be explained as reflections of the expansion of man's brain, together with the reduction and resiting of his facial skeleton (Ashton & Zuckerman 1952). Our conclusion was that little can thus be inferred from these features about posture in the Australopithecinae.

But the problem of locomotor pattern in the Australopithecinae was thrown into relief by the discovery (Broom & Robinson 1947) of an almost perfect innominate bone. In this, the iliac blade was broad, as in man, and, in this respect, contrasted with that of extant monkeys and apes, where it is much elongated craniocaudally. On the basis of this and of other features in which the innominate bone appeared to deviate from monkeys and apes, many workers (e.g. Le Gros Clark 1949, 1955) submittted that the morphological configuration of the bone showed that the Australopithecinae were bipeds.

But the bone was not completely like that of man, and a number of features in which it appeared to differ had been noted in certain early descriptions (see, for example, Broom *et al.* 1950). Thus, there was some doubt as to whether or not the bone was better adapted to the transmission of a pattern of forces associated with some form of bipedal gait rather than to the transmission of a force pattern characteristic of some other form of locomotion, possibly one of the types found in subhuman primates, in which the hindlimb subsumes a wide variety of functions.

By the time that this fossil innominate bone was described, an active programme of quantitative enquiry into anatomical similarities and differences between the australopithecine fossils, on the one hand, and extant apes and man on the other, was in progress in the University of Birmingham under the leadership of the then head of the Department of Anatomy, Professor S. Zuckerman. These enquiries included the innominate bone, and certain preliminary studies were made during the first half of the 1950s with, of necessity, limited material and relatively simple (univariate) statistical techniques. These analyses cited in Zuckerman (1966) gave a clear indication that, notwithstanding the relatively wide iliac blade, the proportions of the innominate bone inclined in their totality towards those of extant apes rather than towards those of extant man. It was appreciated that the studies were limited in scope, and equally it was apparent that it would be impossible ever to give a fully adequate representation of the overall morphology of a structure as complex as an innominate bone by the use of dimensions, angles and ratios. It was also realized that, although the earliest forms of electronic computer were then becoming available, it would be a long time before it would become possible to combine more than a limited number of such dimensions in multivariate statistical analysis. Equally, the biomechanical interpretation of such overall mensural complexes would be a virtual impossibility.

Consequently, it was necessary (*a*) to develop techniques to attempt to identify dimensional characters directly related to aspects of the force pattern impressed upon the pelvic girdle and thus to locomotor use of the hindlimb, (*b*) to enquire into the extent to which variation in such characters correlates with and mechanically enhances that in the impressed force pattern, and (*c*) to enquire how such a complex of defined 'locomotor' dimensions, in a fossil bone, compares with the corresponding morphological complex in extant Primates. From such comparison, the likely functional use of the hindlimb in a fossil species might be inferred.

Form and function in primate limbs and limb girdles

Any enquiry into the relationship between even limited numbers of morphological features of the innominate bone and the impressed force pattern is complex. This is because, in all primate species, and irrespective of the way in which the hindlimb is used, the shape of the bone depends upon interaction of weight bearing through the sacro-iliac and hip joints, with the forces produced by the pull of the principal muscle blocks attached to the pelvic girdle.

First it was necessary to establish that it is possible to define and quantify osteological features functionally related to the pattern of impressed forces. A supplementary enquiry was therefore undertaken on the pectoral girdle because here, apart from contact with the sternum at the sternoclavicular joint, the girdle is suspended by attached muscle blocks, which thus provide virtually the entire impressed force pattern. The impressed forces can thus be defined more easily than in the pelvic girdle, where weight bearing and muscular pull interact.

The first step in this ancillary study comprised an analysis (Ashton & Oxnard 1964*a*) of the use of the forelimb in locomotion in different groups of primates. From this, it was possible to define in each group the pattern of forces to which this region is habitually subjected. In some genera from both the Prosimii and Anthropoidea (e.g. *Lemur* and *Macaca*) the locomotor pattern is quadrupedal and the forelimb is thus normally subjected to forces of compression. In other genera of both New and Old World monkeys (e.g. *Alouatta* and *Presbytis*), the animal, while basically quadrupedal, moves on occasion by swinging from its arms, which are thus subjected to forces both of compression and of tension. At the other extreme there are genera in both the Anthropoidea (e.g. *Hylobates*) and Prosimii (e.g. *Perodicticus*) in which the pattern of movement involves a large measure of suspension from the forelimb, which is thus habitually subjected to forces of tension. Although there are definable quantitative differences between practically all primate species, the system thus forming a spectrum, it is possible to delimit not completely arbitrary subdivisions. A forelimb classification into quadrupeds, semibrachiators and brachiators in the Anthropoidea, together with the corresponding categories of quadrupeds and hangers in the Prosimii, proved to be significant in the study of the functional significance of morphological contrasts in the pectoral girdle.

The next stage of enquiry (Ashton & Oxnard 1963) comprised a quantitative study of the disposition and proportions of the major blocks of muscles attached to the shoulder girdle and of their variation between the principal locomotor groups of Prosimii and Anthropoidea as defined by forelimb function. It emerged that significant contrasts in form and proportion exist, for instance in the propulsive muscles and in those responsible for raising the arm above the head. These can be readily related to contrasts in the use of the forelimb.

On the basis of such established muscular contrasts there were defined six osteological features related to the mechanism of arm-raising. These described the extent and orientation of insertion of m. trapezius and the caudal prolongation of the scapula relating to the relative position of insertion of the radiating digitations of m. serratus magnus (this complex forming a muscular couple rotating the scapula), together with the distal extent of insertion of m. deltoideus on the humerus (this measuring the mechanical advantage of abduction of the arm).

Enquiry was first made into the pattern of variation of these quantities between the different forelimb locomotor categories (each comprising several primate genera). A simultaneous study was made of three features mechanically related to the mobility of the shoulder joint (Ashton & Oxnard 1964*b*). These comprised measures of the orientation of the glenoid cavity, of the lateral end of the clavicle and of the extent to which the shoulder projects laterally. It emerged that in all cases there was a clear-cut and progressive pattern of contrast in relation to the extent to which the forelimb was subjected to forces of tension or compression. The pattern was similar in Anthropoidea and Prosimii. Consistently, in the Anthropoidea, brachiators lay at one extreme and quadrupeds at the other, with semi-brachiators in between. Prosimian hangers corresponded with brachiators and semibrachiators, while quadrupeds in the two suborders overlay.

Man was unique in that in features relating to the facilitation of arm-raising he was like types in which the forelimb is habitually subjected to forces of tension (brachiators and hangers). In characters relating to the quadrant in which the shoulder joint is most freely mobile, he was like those in which the forelimb is habitually subjected to forces of compression (quadrupeds). In no instance did he lie in an intermediate position. The overall human complex is thus unique and can be interpreted as implying a shoulder region that gives free mobility, but especially in the quadrant below the horizontal.

Although based initially on univariate statistical comparisons, these findings were subsequently confirmed and further clarified when it became possible to compound the nine locomotor quantities by means of multivariate statistical techniques (Ashton *et al.* 1965 *a*).

An attempt was next made to define a second group of eight dimensions of the scapula that could not obviously be related to individual functions of the attached muscle blocks. These included the form of the supraspinous fossa and superior border of the scapula, the relative proportions of the supra- and infraspinous fossae, the projection and shape of the acromion, together with the orientation of the scapular spine (Ashton *et al.* 1965 *b*). When these dimensions were combined by multivariate techniques (Ashton *et al.* 1971), the separation of genera correlated to some extent with locomotor rather than taxonomic groupings of living primates. The separation was, however, less marked than for defined locomotor dimensions.

In multivariate combination the two groups of dimensions gave a locomotor separation more pronounced than was evident when either group was taken alone (Ashton *et al.* 1971).

An extension of this study to the arm (Ashton *et al.* 1976) showed that it was again possible to define functionally significant contrasts in the blocks of related skeletal muscles. Related osteological features could be designated, and these, when combined by multivariate statistical techniques, displayed a spectral arrangement of genera correlating with the pattern of locomotor use of the forelimb and thus with the force pattern to which it is subjected. Separation was not, however, so great as with dimensions of the shoulder. It was found that, in contrast to the pectoral girdle, the arm presented other dimensional characters, which, although not varying in phase with locomotor groupings, separated certain major taxonomic divisions of the primates.

In multivariate combination, the two groups of dimensions of the arm gave an overall separation of primate groups in which the major taxonomic categories were differentiated. A locomotor spectrum was apparent within each.

Conversely, when all dimensional characteristics of the shoulder and arm were combined the overall separation of primate genera was basically in accordance with locomotor function (and hence with impressed force pattern), although superimposed upon each region of this spectrum was a measure of separation into taxonomic categories.

It thus appeared that it was possible to define quantitative osteological features of the forelimb functionally related to differences of established locomotor significance in associated muscle blocks. Contrasts between forelimb locomotor groups in these osteometric features were such as to enhance the mechanical significance of contrasts resulting from differences in muscular proportion and arrangement.

We therefore proceeded to analysis of the innominate bone, with the expectation that this will also show features related to the attached muscle blocks. In addition we may expect to find other features dependent upon the direct transmission of weight through the sacro-iliac and hip joints.

Initially, as with the shoulder and arm, a quantitative analysis was made of the locomotor use of the hindlimb and pelvic girdle in different primate groups. Such hindlimb use correlates to only a relatively small extent with that of the forelimb and any attempt to provide an overall scheme of classification, based upon the total locomotor pattern of each species, seemed certain to result in an excessive number of locomotor categories. But, for biomechanical enquiry into the hindlimb and pelvic girdle, it was possible to derive a classification of purely hindlimb use, with reasonable numbers of genera within each category. An initial attempt (Ashton & Oxnard 1964a) centred upon the extent to which the hindlimb participates in leaping but proved to be too circumscribed. Later attempts (as summarized by Oxnard (e.g. 1974)) developed a concept in which, from a central core of generalized quadrupeds, there radiated specialized groups in which the hindlimb participated in a variety of types of movement (e.g. leaping, hanging, leaping and clinging, acrobatic activity). This contrasted with the concept describing forelimb use in which there was a progression from forces of compression to those of tension, but it appeared to form a working basis for biomechanical enquiry into the pelvic girdle.

As with the study of the pectoral girdle, the first stage comprised an analysis of the relative proportions and disposition of the principal blocks of muscles attached to the innominate bone (Zuckerman et al. 1973). It emerged that the most conspicuous contrasts in all muscle blocks were between man, on the one hand, and subhuman primates, on the other. Most especially, in man the abductors of the hip were more prominent than in any subhuman primate, but the extensors of the hip, despite the great development of the specialized human m. gluteus maximus, were bigger in subhuman primates.

On the basis of these muscular contrasts, a group of five bony features was initially defined (Zuckerman et al. 1973). The series was later (Ashton et al. 1981) extended to ten dimensions. These included quantities reflecting the length of the ischium, the orientation of the iliac blade, the position of the anterior superior iliac spine relative to the ventral aspect of the bone and to the centre of the acetabulum together with its lateral displacement, the orientation of the rami of the pubis, the craniocaudal dimension of the obturator foramen and the length of the inguinal ligament.

Each of these quantities gave some separation of certain locomotor groups in both Prosimii and Anthropoidea. In the Prosimii the leaper/clingers and the hangers were frequently prominent, while in the Anthropoidea the leapers (facultative and pronounced) were correspondingly conspicuous. But the biggest contrast was consistently between man and most or all subhuman primates. In each of the ten features of this group, *Australopithecus* tended to differ from man and to resemble subhuman primates, especially the great apes.

When these ten locomotor dimensions relating to muscle disposition were compounded by multivariate analysis, the differentiation of locomotor groups among subhuman primates was more complete than that which emerged in the study of any individual dimension. The contrast between man and subhuman primates was also more pronounced. Correspondingly more clear-cut was the association between *Australopithecus* and the apes together with its contrast with man.

Concurrently, a group of osteometric features of the innominate bone was selected, each feature being, so far as could be judged by biomechanical appraisal, directly related functionally to the transmission of weight from the vertebral column, through the sacro-iliac and hip joints, to the femora. There were initially four such dimensions, but the group was later extended to seven. They comprised quantities defining the positions of the acetabulum and the auricular surface of the sacro-iliac joint relative to the boundaries of the innominate bone, the relative separation of these two joints, the angulation of the iliac and ischial arms of the innominate bone, together with the craniocaudal orientation of the acetabulum.

Again, each dimension separated certain locomotor groups to some extent, the leaper/clingers and hangers from the Prosimii, together with the leapers and hindlimb acrobats from the Anthropoidea, often being individually identifiable. But, once more, the biggest contrast was consistently between man and subhuman primates. In this group of dimensions, the extent of contrast was generally greater than that obtained in the locomotor dimensions relating to the disposition of the abductors and extensors of the hip. In each of these seven features relating to the disposition of the sacro-iliac and hip joints, *Australopithecus* consistently resembled man and contrasted with subhuman extant primates.

When the seven dimensions of this group were compounded by multivariate analysis, there was again a measure of separation of locomotor groups, greater than that which resulted from the analysis of any individual dimension. Man contrasted clearly with the subhuman Primates, *Australopithecus* being, in the compound of this group of features, completely like man and thus also contrasting with all subhuman primates.

When all 17 locomotor dimensions were compounded, there was a good separation of locomotor groupings (as based on hindlimb function). This finding verified that the 17 dimensions selected were biomechanically related to locomotor use of the hindlimb and pelvic girdle. But there was effectively no differentiation of major or minor taxonomic categories. For example, quadrupeds, in this instance, from both the Prosimii and the Anthropoidea, clustered as a single group.

Man, while linking with the hindlimb acrobats of the Anthropoidea (apes), was uniquely differentiated. *Australopithecus* linked similarly with a different member of the hindlimb acrobats. It was separated to an approximately equal extent from these and from man.

In the extended study of the innominate bone (Ashton *et al.* 1981) an attempt was made, as a result of earlier findings relating to the arm (Ashton *et al.* 1976), to define a further group of features, eight in all, which, so far as could be judged, were not directly related functionally to the locomotor mechanics of the innominate bone, but which described other aspects of pelvic structure, e.g. shape of the birth canal. These comprised the length of the iliac crest, the mediolateral inclination of the iliac blade and ischiopubic rami, the dorsoventral orientation of the acetabulum, and the width and caudolateral orientation of the obturator foramen, together with the lateral displacement of the hip joints and ischial tuberosities.

Analysis of these individual 'residual' dimensions did not produce separation of locomotor groups, but certain dimensions differentiated marginally between major taxonomic categories. Man was, in the group of 'residual' dimensions, generally similar to the apes. *Australopithecus* was in some instances like both man and the apes; in others it differed from these extant Hominoidea and from all other extant primates.

When the eight residual dimensions of this group were compounded by multivariate analysis, separation of genera was broadly in accordance with the taxonomic scheme. Within the Hominoidea, *Australopithecus* and man linked independently to the apes and were again uniquely separated from each other.

When all 25 dimensions (17 locomotor plus eight residual) were combined by multivariate techniques, the principal locomotor groups of subhuman primates separated with a high degree of consistency within both Prosimii and Anthropoidea. These two suborders were well differentiated, while within each there was superimposed upon the locomotor grouping of genera some measure of separation into superfamilies within the Anthropoidea and into infraorders within the Prosimii. Man and *Australopithecus* linked independently to different extant apes and were separated from each other by a distance quite as big as that which separated either from the extant Pongidae.

Australopithecus and man thus emerged both in dimensions relating to locomotor function and in those separating taxonomic categories as differing from each other just as much as each differs from the apes. Thus, as man is unique in features relating to locomotion and to taxonomy, so is *Australopithecus* (although differently so). The fossil group is not, in any sense, intermediate in aspects of structure, as defined by these 25 dimensions, between extant apes and man.

CONCLUSION

From a purely morphological viewpoint, the definition of a unique assemblage of features of the australopithecine innominate bone, some like those of man, others like those of subhuman primates (and especially apes), with yet others differing from both, parallels findings from studies of the skull, teeth and other parts of the postcranial skeleton of this fossil group (e.g. as summarized by Ashton (1981)). Repeatedly, in some aspects of many structural and functional complexes the Australopithecinae emerge as being like man, while in other aspects they are like subhuman primates. In combination, such constellations of features differ uniquely from both those of man and those of subhuman primates and often to an extent as great as these deviate from each other. The Australopithecinae are thus quite different in their overall morphology from any hypothetical creature intermediate in form between men and apes. Such overall morphological uniqueness adds complexity to any attempt to interpret the possible position of this group in the evolution of the higher primates. Thus any conclusions, however tentative, that can be drawn from studies about probable posture and gait of the Australopithecinae do not necessarily bear upon the evolutionary pathways by which man's bipedal posture and gait evolved.

But, viewing the Australopithecinae purely as morphologically unique and thus biomechanically unusual members of the hominoid radiation, it is possible to make certain tentative inferences about their posture and gait.

In the present communication, attention has deliberately been focussed upon the innominate bone, partly because it is so well represented in the Australopithecinae, partly because, from a purely biomechanical viewpoint, it holds a most significant position in relation to posture and gait.

But already, in addition to well known studies of the innominate bone (see, for example, Le Gros Clark 1949, 1955), there have been published several other analyses of parts of the hindlimb. For instance, the proximal end of the femur of *Australopithecus* (McHenry & Corruccini 1976) has also been shown to display a unique combination of human and ape-like features, while a now-classical quantitative study of the distal end of the femur (Kern & Straus 1949) indicated an equally unique assortment of human and monkey-like characteristics.

But, notwithstanding this considerable volume of morphological study, there have persisted, throughout the 30 years following the discovery of the almost complete australopithecine innominate bone upon which the present analyses have been based, many views about the likely posture and gait of this fossil group.

On the one hand, workers, such as, for instance, Le Gros Clark (1949, 1955), regarded the group as having acquired the posture and gait distinctive of the family Hominidae, a view that was only marginally later modified (see, for example, Le Gros Clark 1967). Such views, sometimes expressed in an even more extreme form, continue to be held by certain workers. Lovejoy *et al.* (1973), for instance, were unable to find pelvic features of the Australopithecinae that 'distinguish their gait pattern from that of modern man'. Robinson (1972) also submitted that the fossil evidence supports the view that the Australopithecinae had developed a 'uniquely human method of balance control'. This, coupled with an orientation of the pelvis as in modern man, resulted, in his view, in a full development of the capacity of the Australopithecinae to stride.

On the other hand, certain other workers (e.g. Zuckerman 1954, 1966) repeatedly and forcefully expressed doubt about the possible bipedality (habitual or facultative) of the Australopithecinae.

Even among those inclining towards the view that the Australopithecinae were habitual bipeds, some (e.g. Napier 1967) pointed to features of the australopithecine pelvic girdle that would be inconsistent with the 'heel–toe' type of striding gait characteristic of *Homo sapiens*. The analysis in the present study of locomotor–related features of the innominate bone re-emphasizes such differences. When the Australopithecinae walked bipedally (as most subhuman primates sometimes do), the relative disposition of their sacro-iliac and hip joints would seem to have permitted weight to be transmitted from the trunk to the lower limb more efficiently than in any extant subhuman primate. But a human-like disposition of the sacro-iliac and hip joints does not necessarily mean that *Australopithecus* was habitually bipedal and, in fact, certain of the findings of the present study relating to the disposition of the principal blocks of the pelvic muscles could be interpreted as indicating this not to be so. For instance, the orientation of the iliac blade and the position of the anterior superior iliac spine in the fossil group are such as to make it virtually certain that the lesser gluteal muscles were not disposed as in man, where they are abductors of the hip and thus provide strong stabilizing power during the human type of striding bipedalism. In fact, when *Australopithecus* walked bipedally, its gait must have been of the rolling type that obtains when subhuman primates attempt to walk upright.

But, just as some groups of subhuman primates use their limbs in different ways when carrying out different types of locomotion (e.g. semibrachiators sometimes use their forelimb to support the body during quadrupedal locomotion and at others to suspend it during progression by arm-swinging; hindlimb acrobats sometimes use the hindlimb during quadrupedal locomotion, while at others it can take part in a wide variety of suspensory and related functions), it is possible that the hindlimb of *Australopithecus* may also have subsumed several different functions.

Such a view has been put forward by Prost (1980), who, on the basis of analysis of the intermixture of human and subhuman primate features in both the forelimb and hindlimb of *Australopithecus*, concluded that the Australopithecinae 'must have been adapted to arboreal quadrupedal vertical climbing, having the capacity, at the same time, to perform facultative terrestrial bipedalism, moving on the ground in a manner visually identical to that of humans'.

The view is even more strongly reinforced by the recent work of Oxnard & Lisowski (1980) on the foot. A detailed and highly critical appraisal of the available osteological evidence has shown, once again, many functionally significant contrasts with man, together with a total functional complex that suggests 'usage as in an arboreal species that also walks bipedally with flattened arches (like a chimpanzee or gorilla) rather than with the high arches of Man'.

Such a creature would have been very different from all living primates (human and subhuman). Whether or not its gait could have been ancestral to the human type of bipedalism remains indeterminate.

I am much indebted to Professor J. Z. Young, F.R.S., for many observations upon the typescript of this paper.

REFERENCES

Ashton, E. H. 1981 The Australopithecinae – their biometrical study. *Symp. zool. Soc. Lond.* (In the press.)

Ashton, E. H., Flinn, R. M., Moore, W. J., Oxnard, C. E. & Spence, T. F. 1981 Further quantitative features of the pelvic girdle in Primates. *J. Zool.* In the press.

Ashton, E. H., Flinn, R. M., Oxnard, C. E. & Spence, T. F. 1971 The functional and classificatory significance of combined metrical features of the primate shoulder girdle. *J. Zool.* **163**, 319–350.

Ashton, E. H., Flinn, R. M., Oxnard, C. E. & Spence, T. F. 1976 The adaptive and classificatory significance of certain quantitative features of the forelimb in Primates. *J. Zool.* **179**, 515–556.

Ashton, E. H., Healy, M. J. R., Oxnard, C. E. & Spence, T. F. 1965a The combination of locomotor features of the primate shoulder girdle by canonical analysis. *J. Zool.* **147**, 406–429.

Ashton, E. H. & Oxnard, C. E. 1963 The musculature of the primate shoulder. *Trans. zool. Soc. Lond.* **29**, 553–650.

Ashton, E. H. & Oxnard, C. E. 1964a Locomotor patterns in Primates. *Proc. zool. Soc. Lond.* **142**, 1–28.

Ashton, E. H. & Oxnard, C. E. 1964b Functional adaptations in the primate shoulder girdle. *Proc. zool. Soc. Lond.* **142**, 49–66.

Ashton, E. H., Oxnard, C. E., & Spence, T. F. 1965b Scapular shape and primate classification. *Proc. zool. Soc. Lond.* **145**, 125–142.

Ashton, E. H. & Zuckerman, S. 1951 Some cranial indices of *Plesianthropus* and other Primates. *Am. J. phys. Anthrop, new Ser.* **9**, 283–296.

Ashton, E. H. & Zuckerman, S. 1952 Age changes in the position of the occipital condyles in the chimpanzee and gorilla. *Am. J. phys. Anthrop., new Ser.* **10**, 277–288.

Broom, R. & Robinson, J. T. 1947 Further remains of the Sterkfontein ape-man, *Plesianthropus. Nature, Lond.* **160**, 430–431.

Broom, R., Robinson, J. T. & Schepers, G. W. H. 1950 Sterkfontein ape-man: *Plesianthropus. Transv. Mus. Mem.* **4**, 1–117.

Broom, R. & Schepers, G. W. H. 1946 The South African fossil ape-men: the Australopithecinae. *Transv. Mus. Mem.* **2**, 1–272.

Dart, R. A. 1925 *Australopithecus africanus*: the man-ape of South Africa. *Nature, Lond.* **115**, 195–199.

Kern, H. M. Jr & Straus Jr, W. L. 1949 The femur of *Plesianthropus transvaalensis. Am. J. phys. Anthrop., new Ser.* **7**, 53–78.

Le Gros Clark, W. E. 1947 Observations on the anatomy of the fossil Australopithecinae. *J. Anat.* **81**, 300–333.

Le Gros Clark, W. E. 1949 New palaeontological evidence bearing on the evolution of the Hominoidea. *Q. Jl geol. Soc. Lond.* **105**, 225–264.

Le Gros Clark, W. E. 1955 The os innominatum of the recent Ponginae with special reference to that of the Australopithecinae. *Am. J. phys. Anthrop., new Ser.* **13**, 19–27.

Le Gros Clark, W. E. 1967 *Man-apes or ape-men?* New York and London: Holt, Rinehart & Winston.

Lovejoy, C. O., Heiple, K. G. & Burstein, A. H. 1973 The gait of *Australopithecus. Am. J. phys. Anthrop., new Ser.* **38**, 757–779.

McHenry, H. M. & Corruccini, R. S. 1976 Fossil hominid femora and the evolution of walking. *Nature, Lond.* **259**, 657–658.

Napier, J. R. 1967 The antiquity of human walking. *Scient. Am.* **216** (4), 56–66.

Oxnard, C. E. 1974 Primate locomotor classifications for evaluating fossils: their inutility and an alternative. In *Symp. 5th Congr. Int. Primate Soc.* (ed. S. Kondo, M. Kawai, A. Ehara & S. Kawamura), pp. 269–286. Tokyo: Japan Science Press.

Oxnard, C. E. & Lisowski, F. P. 1980 Functional articulation of some hominoid foot bones: implications for the Olduvai (hominid 8) foot. *Am. J. phys. Anthrop., new Ser.* **52**, 107–117.

Prost, J. H. 1980 Origin of bipedalism. *Am. J. phys. Anthrop., new Ser.* **52**, 175–189.

Robinson, J. T. 1972 *Early hominid posture and locomotion.* Chicago and London: University of Chicago Press.

Zuckerman, S. 1928 Age changes in the chimpanzee, with special reference to growth of brain, eruption of teeth, and estimation of age; with a note on the Taungs ape. *Proc. zool. Soc. Lond.* **1928**, 1–42.

Zuckerman, S. 1950 Taxonomy and human evolution. *Biol. Rev.* **25**, 435–485.

Zuckerman, S. 1954 Correlation of change in the evolution of higher Primates. In *Evolution as a process* (ed. J. S. Huxley, A. C. Hardy & E. B. Ford), pp. 300–352. London: Allen & Unwin.

Zuckerman, S. 1966 Myths and methods in anatomy. *Jl R. Coll. Surg. Edinb.* **11**, 87–114.

Zuckerman, S., Ashton, E. H., Flinn, R. M., Oxnard, C. E. & Spence, T. F. 1973 Some locomotor features of the pelvic girdle in Primates. *Symp. zool. Soc. Lond.*, no. 33, pp. 71–165.

Phil. Trans. R. Soc. Lond. B **292**, 89–94 (1981)   [89]
Printed in Great Britain

Evolution of hominid bipedalism and prehensile capabilities

By R. H. Tuttle

Department of Anthropology and Evolutionary Biology, The University of Chicago,
1126 East 59th Street, Chicago, Illinois 60637, U.S.A.

In this paper, I present an updated version of the hylobatian model for the proximate ancestors of the Hominidae. The hylobatians are hypothesized to have been relatively small creatures that were especially adapted for vertical climbing on tree trunks and vines and for bipedalism on horizontal boughs. They were no more disposed toward suspensory behaviours than are modern chimpanzees and bonobos. According to this evolutionary scenario, bipedalism preceded the emergence of the Hominidae. The earliest hominids would be recognized as diurnally terrestrial bipeds that stood with full extension of the knee joints and walked with greater extension of the lower limbs than is common in non-human primates that are induced to walk bipedally on the ground.

The wealth of hominid fossils from the Hadar Formation, Ethiopia, and the Laetolil Formation, Tanzania, are generally compatible with the hylobatian model. They show that by *ca.* 4 Ma B.P. habitually terrestrial, bipedal hominids had evolved from arboreal ancestors. The Hadar hominids had curved fingers and toes, strong great toes and thumbs, and other features that suggest that they were rather recently derived from arboreal hominids and that they probably continued to enter trees, perhaps for night rest and some foraging.

The hominid hand bones from Hadar evince no features that are distinctly related to knuckle-walking. They relate neatly to counterparts in the hand of O.H. 7, a specimen that was found with stone tools. However, there is no evidence that the Hadar hominids of 3 Ma ago engaged in tool behaviour.

Introduction

During the century since Darwin published his revolutionary trilogy, virtually every major type of extant ape has served as a model for the physical and behavioural attributes of our early hominoid ancestors. Throughout this period, the common chimpanzee had a remarkable series of champions (Gregory 1927; Weinert 1932; Washburn 1967, 1968). Whereas the once popular gorilla (Smith 1924) has dropped out of candidacy, the bonobo (*Pan pansicus*) is gathering a notable lobby (Zihlman *et al.* 1978). Scaled-down orang-utans (Stern 1976) and certain characteristics of the lesser apes (Tuttle 1974, 1975, 1977) also have appeared in recent evolutionary models.

The field has been rife with speculation about the evolution of bipedalism because postcranial fossils are generally sparse and fragmentary, and are not always clearly associated with diagnostic cranial remains.

The Hominidae probably emerged from stem Hominoidea during the Miocene (22.5–5.0 Ma B.P.) or Pliocene (5.0–2.0 Ma B.P.) period. The best Miocene hominoid postcranial specimens are assigned to species in lineages that are collateral to the Hominidae. The forelimb and hindlimb remains of *Proconsul* and *Dendropithecus* from Kenyan Early Miocene localities are probably too early to be proximately ancestral to modern forms, and they exhibit few features that would link them clearly to the modern forms (McHenry & Temerin 1979). Kenyan and

European middle Miocene specimens (most notably *Pliopithecus vindobonensis*) are practically irrelevant to the evolutionary problem of hominid bipedalism. Late Miocene localities have also yielded little information. *Oreopithecus bambolii* is a peripheral anthropoid species (Simons 1972). The recently discovered postcranial bits from Potwar, Pakistan, are tentatively associated with craniodental specimens from the region (Pilbeam *et al.* 1977). These authors have sorted them into three groups on the basis of general size. These groupings parallel their assortment of the Potwar craniodental specimens. It is possible that some or all of the four small hominoid postcranial bits, i.e. a partial femoral head (GSP 9894), a partial talus (GSP 10785), a partial calcaneus (GSP 4664) and a juvenile radial diaphysis (GSP 7611), belong to *Ramapithecus punjabicus*, a species that has been championed as the most likely candidate for earliest Hominidae. But the specimens are too few and too incomplete for reliable functional inferences. For instance, if one presented functional morphologists with counterpart bits from a living hylobatid ape, I doubt that they could document that the beast was a part-time arboreal biped.

Thus, the earliest unequivocal evidence for hominid bipedalism comes from the Pliocene localities of Laetoli, Tanzania, and Hadar, Ethiopia. There, terrestrial bipedalism was well developed and presumably frequently practised. We can only speculate about how bipedalism was established among the ancestors of the Laetoli and Hadar hominids. Modern scenarios should be compatible with the new information from these important sites. Henceforth I will focus on one speculative model and its compatibility with the new Pliocene fossils and our experimental studies on living apes.

THE HYLOBATIAN MODEL TODAY

After rejecting the theory that humans had evolved from knuckle-walking troglodytian apes, which were closely similar to the common chimpanzee, I preferred an alternative, termed the hylobatian model (Tuttle 1969, 1974, 1975). The hypothetical hylobatians weighed between 20 and 30 lb (*ca.* 9 and 13.5 kg) and were somewhat stockier than modern hylobatid apes. Vertical climbing on tree trunks and vines and bipedalism on horizontal boughs were conspicuous components of their locomotor repertoire. They commonly stood bipedally while foraging in trees and employed bipedalism during intraspecific displays. Short bursts of bipedal running and hindlimb-propelled leaps may have been important for the manual capture of insects and small vertebrates with which they supplemented their vegetable fare.

Like the lesser apes, the hylobatians had relatively long, extensible hindlimbs powered by well developed gluteal, anterior thigh and calf muscles. The centre of gravity was low in the abdominal cavity. The lumbar spine was not foreshortened and it was capable of notable lateral flexion and rotation. The hip bones were not exceptionally elongate. They were rather wide and projected laterally. The sacrum was also wide.

The hylobatians did not have a pelvic tilt mechanism of a human sort. The deep gluteal muscles were positioned to act as extensors instead of abductors of the hip joints during bipedal locomotion. However, the tendency for the hylobatian pelvis to tilt downward on the unsupported side during the swing phases of bipedal steps could be countered somewhat by rotation and lateral flexion of the spine toward the opposite side. This was effected by special portions of the erector spinae muscles, which originated on the medial surface of the hip bone and adjacent area of the sacrum (Filler 1980), and perhaps by the quadratus lumborum and lateral abdominal muscles. Lateral flexion of the spine was also important during vertical ascents and descents on vines and tree trunks and during other climbing activities of the hylobatians. The lateral flexing mechanism and low centre of gravity were important features that enabled emergent terrestrial Hominidae to walk with more extension of the hip and knee joints than their arboreally bipedal ancestors had done.

Suspensory behaviours were probably no more common in the hylobatians than in common chimpanzees or bonobos. Arm-swinging along branches was quite rare and ricochetal arm-swinging was not practised at all. The hylobatians moved between springy supports in the peripheries of trees by hoisting, bridging, and occasionally jumping. They rarely executed long vertical drops or fed in suspensory postures.

The hylobatians' thumbs and great toes were well developed, strongly muscled, and capable of wide divergence. The chest was broader transversely than anteroposteriorly, the shoulder blades lay on the back of the chest wall, and the elongate collar bones held the shoulder joints out to the sides of the body. Mobility of the shoulder and wrist joints and extensibility and rotatory capacities of the elbow complex underpinned the hylobatians' versatile climbing, reaching and suspensory behaviour.

Compatability with fossils from Laetoli and Hadar

At Laetoli the chief evidence for hominid bipedalism is the footprints of three individuals, preserved in volcanic ash that has been dated radiometrically at *ca.* 3.6 Ma B.P. The shapes of the prints are indistinguishable from those of striding, habitually barefoot humans. They indicate that the Laetoli hominids were smaller than average *Homo sapiens* (Leakey 1979; Leakey & Hay 1979).

Several localities at Hadar (*ca.* 3.0 Ma B.P.), which are younger than the Laetolil Formation, have yielded approximately forty foot bones. One of the most informative specimens is A.L. 333–115 A–M. The 13 bones were extracted from a single lump of matrix in the Denan Dora member of the Hadar Formation. The distal ends of the left metatarsal bones and the proximal phalanges of digits I–V, the middle phalanges of digits IV and V, and the basal epiphysis of a distal phalanx are well preserved. The shafts of the proximal phalanges are markedly curved ventrally. This feature is characteristic of certain full-time and part-time arboreal apes and monkeys. The basal articular surfaces of the proximal phalanges extend dorsally as shallowly excavated and lipped structures. The heads of the metatarsal bones also have dorsal articular areas. These features would facilitate extension of the metatarsophalangeal joints. This would allow the foot to be used in plantigrade postures despite the ventral curvature of the digits. Other Hadar proximal phalanges II–V, including one from 'Lucy' (A.L. 288-ly), are like A.L. 333–115. It is difficult to imagine a foot with such markedly curved phalanges fitting neatly into the footprints at Laetoli.

In A.L. 333–115, the hallucal bones are more robust than their counterparts from the lateral toes. The base of a left hallucal matatarsal (A.L. 333–54) appears to have contacted the second metatarsal bone. In these features, the Hadar foot recalls the human condition. The broad shallow grooves on the posterior surfaces of several distal fibulae indicate that the Hadar hominids had well developed peroneal muscles. In apes, the peroneus longus muscle is a powerful flexor of the hallux; and in man, it is an evertor of the foot.

The knee joint, represented by seven distal femoral and six proximal tibial specimens, is more similar to the human condition than is the Hadar foot. The femoral condyles, popliteal groove, lateral patellar ridge and fossae for the cruciate ligaments all testify to the capacity for full extension of the knee joint during bipedal stance.

The Hadar pelvis, represented by A.L. 288–1an and 288–1ao, is a potpourri of human and non-human features. The sacrum is short and broad like human sacra. The blades of the hip bones are also broad and short. But they exhibit a greater lateral flare and orientation than do their human counterparts. Despite this resemblance to non-human anthropoid primates, the broad-beamed Hadar beast was bipedal, as attested by development of the anterior iliac and ischial spines, femoral intertrochanteric lines and other features that are hallmarks of human bipedalism.

In brief, the curved pedal phalanges, robust hallux, strongly developed peroneal muscles, broad sacrum, and the shortness and lateral orientation of the iliac blades are quite compatible with the idea that the Hadar hominids were derived rather recently from arboreal bipeds. Indeed, they too may have engaged in notable tree climbing, perhaps for night rest. Whether a human pelvic tilt mechanism or lateral flexion and rotation of the spine was predominant during their bipedal walking remains to be established.

Experimental perspectives

Electromyographic, cineradiographic and other sophisticated kinesiological techniques have not been applied extensively enough to non-human primates to provide a full basis for inter-specific comparisons of their bipedalism. However, they have underscored the uniqueness of habitual human bipedalism compared with the facultative bipedalism of monkeys and apes. *Hylobates*, the second most accomplished anthropoid biped, has not shown remarkably great similarities to *Homo* in the electromyographic pattern of their hindlimb muscles, forces applied to the ground, or details of the locomotor cycle (Tuttle & Cortright 1980). Less complete kinesiological results on pongid apes and monkeys indicate that during bipedalism their hind-limbs continue to function basically as if the subjects were moving quadrupedally. The gibbons resemble the pongid apes and monkeys more closely than the humans in this regard (Tuttle *et al.* 1979).

It is probably safe to assume that the early hylobatians shared a similar non-human kinesiological pattern. Because of the fully extended knee joints and other humanoid osteological features, many muscles in the lower limbs of the Hadar hominids probably would not have acted electromyographically like those of facultatively bipedal hominoid primates. A great challenge for evolutionary kinesiologists is to detail this novel pattern on the basis of sound biomechanical principles instead of analogies with the condition in extant forms.

COMMENT ON TOOL BEHAVIOUR

Locality FLK NN in bed I of Olduvai Gorge (dated *ca.* 1.75 Ma B.P.) and several localities in the Hadar Formation have provided considerable empirical evidence pertaining to the hands and tool behaviour of early Hominidae. It may be parsimoniously concluded that the cranial bones and 13 hand bones (Day 1976) assigned to O.H. 7 and the 12 foot bones assigned to O.H. 8 are from a single juvenile individual. Apparently, a group of hominids had come to the lake margin to forage for small vertebrates, plants and perhaps larger prey. They left behind them a number of crude stone Oldowan tools, a perhaps modified equid rib (Leakey 1971) and the body of a companion, which had fallen victim to a predator, an accident or disease.

The hand of O.H. 7 shows that its youthful possessor had a powerful grip, second to fifth fingers that were well adapted for arboreal climbing and perhaps suspensory behaviour, and fingertips and a basal thumb joint that facilitated fine manipulatory behaviour (Susman & Creel 1979). The pongid features of the fingers would not have prevented O.H. 7 from making

and using Oldowan tools. Modern great apes are quite dexterous despite the locomotor specializations of their hands (Tuttle 1970). The breadth of the fingertips in O.H. 7, particularly that
of the thumb, could have been adapted not only for precision grips but also for power grips on
sizeable, rounded objects, wherein the thumb was widely opposed to the other fingers.

The Hadar Formation has yielded no artefacts that are contemporaneous with the numerous
fossils that are assigned to *Australopithecus afarensis* (Johanson *et al.* 1978; Johanson & White
1979). About 50 hand bones are included in the hypodigm. In that there are counterparts of
O.H. 7, the Hadar hands could be lineally ancestral to it.

The proximal phalanges ($N = 15$) from adult and immature digits II–V are curved ventrally
and sport well developed lateral ridges for the fibrous flexor sheaths. Prominent tubercles and
facets on their bases document the past presence of strong palmar and collateral ligaments. The
single pollical proximal phalanx (A.L. 333–69) is quite similar to that of gracile humans.

The ventral surfaces of the middle phalanges ($N = 9$) exhibit a prominent midline ridge,
flanked by fossae for the tendons of the flexor digitorum superficialis muscle and ridges for the
fibrous flexor sheaths. There are only two distal phalanges from Hadar that are tentatively
identified as manual. They suggest a strong hand with well developed fingertips.

The Hadar Formation has produced a wealth ($N = 19$) of metacarpal specimens. Three of
them are pollical. The only complete mature pollical metacarpal bone (A.L. 333w–39) is rather
chimpanzee-like. It has a well excavated basal articular surface and a small, rounded head.
The medial metacarpal bones resemble human ones, except that the heads and bases are
relatively narrow, giving them a gracile configuration compared with human metacarpal
bones of similar length. The third metacarpal bones lack the basal styloid process. Some of the
metacarpal heads evince conspicuous markings for collateral ligaments. In some instances, the
articular surface extends dorsally onto the metacarpal heads. There are no features that suggest
knuckle-walking.

The Hadar carpal bones include two capitates, one hamate, one pisiform and one trapezium.
The pollical articular surface of the trapezium (A.L. 333–80) is rather deep, as in the chimpanzee. The gracile pisiform bone (A.L. 333–91) is elongate and rod-like, thus resembling that
of a chimpanzee. This and the robust hook on the hamate bone (A.L. 333–50) indicate that the
Hadar hominids had strong pisohamate and pisometacarpal ligaments and flexor retinacula.

The Hadar hands probably served primarily as manipulatory and climbing organs. The
generally gracile construction of the metacarpal bones and the absence of features suggesting
knuckle-walking conform well with evidence from the lower limb, which establishes that the
Hadar hominids were fundamentally terrestrial bipeds. Many features of their fingers, which
foreshadow the hand of O.H. 7, indicate that the Hadar hominids had strong power grips in
which the thumb acted conspicuously. Strong development of the ulnar wrist may be related
to climbing and other pulling actions.

I thank D. C. Johanson and D. R. Pilbeam for permission to study fossils in their keeping.
The visits to Yale University and the Cleveland Museum of National History were made
pleasant and productive by J. Barry, M. Bush, L. Dmytryk, H. French, D. Johanson, W.
Kimbel, O. Lovejoy, M. Rose and T. White. The paper was read through by D. C. Johanson,
R. G. Klein & B. Latimer. The research was supported by the Social Sciences Divisional
Research Fund and the Marian and Adolph Lichstern Fund of the University of Chicago.

References

Day, M. H. 1976 Hominid postcranial material from bed I, Olduvai Gorge. In *Human origins* (ed. G. Ll. Isaac & E. R. McCown), pp. 363–374. Menlo Park, California: W. A. Benjamin.

Filler, A. G. 1980 Anatomical evidence for the 'hylobatian' model of hominid evolution. *Am. J. phys. Anthrop.* **52**, 226.

Gregory, W. K. 1927 How near is the relationship of man to the chimpanzee-gorilla stock? *Q. Rev. Biol.* **2**, 549–560.

Johanson, D. C. & White, T. D. 1979 A systematic assessment of early African hominids. *Science, N.Y.* **203**, 321–330.

Johanson, D. C., White, T. D. & Coppens, Y. 1978 A new species of the genus *Australopithecus* (Primates, Hominidae) from the Pliocene of eastern Africa. *Kirtlandia,* no. 28, pp. 1–14.

Leakey, M. D. 1971 *Olduvai Gorge,* vol. 3. Cambridge University Press.

Leakey, M. D. 1979 Footprints in the ashes of time. *Nat. geogr. Mag.* **155**, 446–457.

Leakey, M. D. & Hay, R. L. 1979 Pliocene footprints in the Laetolil Beds at Laetoli, northern Tanzania. *Nature, Lond.* **278**, 317–323.

McHenry, H. M. & Temerin, L. A. 1979 The evolution of hominid bipedalism: evidence from the fossil record. *Yeab. phys. Anthrop.* **22**, 105–131.

Pilbeam, D., Meyer, G. E., Badgley, C., Rose, M. D., Pickford, M. H. L., Behrensmeyer, A. K. & Shah, S. M. I. 1977 New hominoid primates from the Siwaliks of Pakistan and their bearing on hominoid evolution. *Nature, Lond.* **229**, 689–695.

Simons, E. L. 1972 *Primate evolution.* New York: Macmillan.

Smith, G. E. 1924 *The evolution of man.* London: Oxford University Press.

Stern Jr, J. T. 1976 Before bipedality. *Yearb. Phys. Anthrop.* **19**, 59–68.

Susman, R. L. & Creel, N. 1979 Functional and morphological affinities of the subadult hand (O.H. 7) from Olduvai Gorge. *Am. J. phys. Anthrop.* **51**, 311–332.

Tuttle, R. H. 1969 Knuckle-walking and the problem of human origins. *Science, N.Y.* **166**, 953–961.

Tuttle, R. H. 1970 Postural, propulsive and prehensile capabilities in the cheiridia of chimpanzees and other great apes. In *The chimpanzee,* vol. 2 (ed. G. H. Bourne), pp. 167–253. Basel: Karger.

Tuttle, R. H. 1974 Darwin's apes, dental apes and the descent of man. *Curr. Anthrop.* **15**, 389–426.

Tuttle, R. H. 1975 Parallelism, brachiation and hominoid phylogeny. In *Phylogeny of the primates* (ed. W. P. Luckett & F. S. Szalay), pp. 447–480. New York: Plenum.

Tuttle, R. H. 1977 Naturalistic positional behavior of apes and models of hominid evolution, 1929–1976. In *Progress in ape research* (ed. G. H. Bourne), pp. 277–296. New York: Academic Press.

Tuttle, R. H. & Cortright, G. W. 1980 The problem of bipedalism: what do we need in order to proceed? In *Perspectives in primate biology* (ed. P. K. Seth). (In the press.)

Tuttle, R. H., Cortright, G. W. & Buxhoeveden, D. P. 1979 Anthropology on the move: progress in experimental studies of nonhuman primate positional behavior. *Yearb. phys. Anthrop.* **22**, 187–214.

Washburn, S. L. 1967 Behaviour and the origin of man. *Proc. R. Anthropol. Inst.,* pp. 21–27.

Washburn, S. L. 1968 The study of human evolution. *Condon Lectures.* Eugene: Oregon State System of Higher Education.

Weinert, H. 1932 *Ursprung der Menschheit.* Stuttgart: Enke.

Zihlman, A. L., Cronin, J. E., Cramer, D. L. & Sarich, V. M. 1978 Pygmy chimpanzee as a possible prototype for the common ancestor of humans, chimpanzees and gorillas. *Nature, Lond.,* **275**, 744–746.

Phil. Trans. R. Soc. Lond. B **292**, 95–102 (1981)   [95]
Printed in Great Britain

Tracks and tools

By MARY D. LEAKEY, F.B.A.

P.O. Box 30239, *Nairobi, Kenya, and P.O. Box,* 7, *Ngorongoro, Tanzania*

[Plate 1]

Recent discoveries in the Laetolil beds at Laetoli in northern Tanzania have revealed hominid tracks made by three individuals in a bed of cemented volcanic ash. The tracks extend for a distance of 27 m and indicate a fully upright, bipedal gait with weight distribution similar to that of modern man. A single trail proceeds alongside a dual trail in which the footsteps of the leading individual are almost exactly over-printed by the second set of tracks. Radiometric dating of an overlying tuff has yielded a figure of 3.6 Ma. Stone artefacts are unknown in the Laetolil beds, and a date of *ca.* 2 Ma for the earliest formalized tool-making is postulated on the evidence from Olduvai Gorge.

The evidence from the hominid tracks found at Laetoli will be discussed briefly in relation to the earliest well documented stone tools. This entails bridging a gap of 1.6 Ma, from 3.6 Ma B.P., the estimated date of the Laetoli tracks, to approximately 2 Ma B.P., the date of the earliest tools at Olduvai Gorge. Artefacts from the Hadar in Ethiopia (Roche & Tiercelin 1977) are claimed to belong within this intervening period, but the evidence so far put forward requires substantiation before it can be accepted unreservedly. There are also a few specimens from the Omo valley in southern Ethiopia, which appear to exceed 2 Ma age (Chavaillon 1970). But these hardly represent a stone industry in the accepted sense of the term; some are scattered finds and others are of very low technical standard (see Oakley, this symposium). This somewhat uncertain evidence will be omitted and the discussion will be restricted to the evidence from Olduvai Gorge.

Consider first the Laetoli tracks (figures 1 and 2). The site lies some 30 miles† south of Olduvai (see figure 3) and has been known for its fossils since 1935, when my husband and I visited it for the first time. Since then it has been revisited occasionally, but it was not until 1975 that the first radiometric date of 2.4 Ma B.P. was obtained and it was appreciated that the Laetoli beds considerably antedated the deposits at Olduvai Gorge (figure 4). This date was from a sample of the vogesite lava flows that overlie both the Laetolil beds and the more recent Ndolanya beds. Later the same year, G. Curtis of the University of California, Berkeley, obtained further potassium–argon dates on biotite from the Laetolil beds themselves, which gave average readings of 3.59 to 3.75 Ma B.P.

At that time two hominid mandibles, part of a maxilla, a number of teeth and various mammalian fossils had been found, but it was not until 1976 that A. Hill, palaeontologist at the National Museum, Nairobi, noticed the first fossilized tracks on the surface of a fine-grained tuff. As is so often the case, this was an accidental discovery. The first tracks to be noted were of rhinoceros, elephant, giraffe, various bovidae, carnivores and a chalicothere. Numerous small tracks, abundant at all the known sites, have proved to be of lagomorphs. To date, 15 exposures of the footprint tuff are known, mostly situated on either side of the Garusi Valley

† 1 mile ≈ 1.6 km.

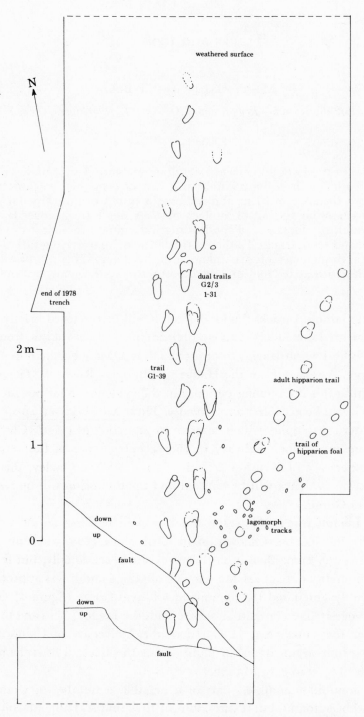

FIGURES 1 AND 2. Laetoli site G. Southern part of the hominid trails. Photograph by J. Reader, National Geographic Society.

and extending over an area of approximately 80 km². The preservation of the footprints has been reconstructed by Hay (Leakey & Hay 1979) and is due to an unusual set of circumstances, which probably occurred over a short period of time, perhaps no more than a month or so.

The footprint tuff is designated tuff 7 in the Laetolil beds and was erupted from the volcano

FIGURE 2. For description see opposite.

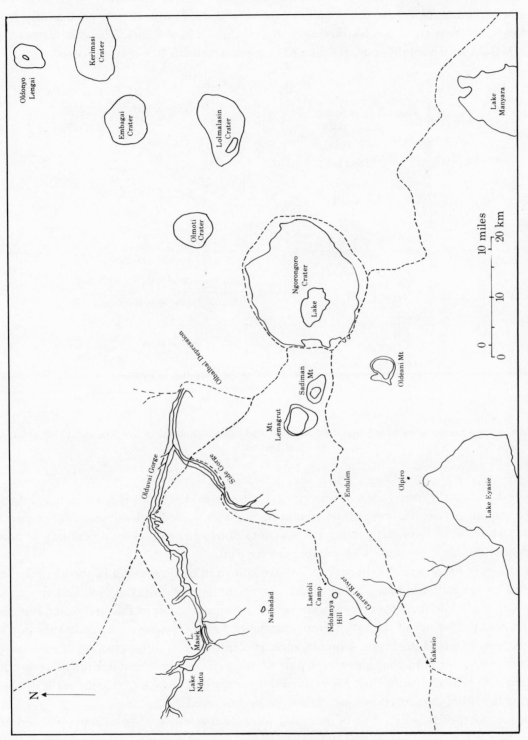

FIGURE 3. From a map compiled by the Serengeti Research Institute.

Sadiman, about 24 km to the east. It is generally 30–50 cm thick and is composed of two units. The upper part is coarse-grained, crudely bedded and contains no footprints. These are confined to the lower unit, a thinly laminated, fine-grained ash, generally $7\frac{1}{2}$ to 8 cm thick. Calcium carbonate or calcite is a major component of the footprint tuff, particularly in the lower unit, where some layers contain more calcite than lava globules. The calcite appears to fill voids from which soluble material like natrocarbonatite ash has been dissolved.

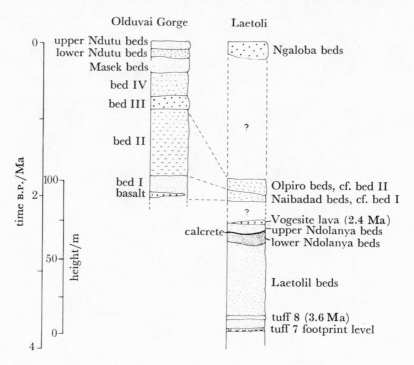

FIGURE 4. Diagrammatic sections to show the time scale and the relationships of the deposits at Olduvai Gorge and Laetoli.

The ash must have been cohesive when it first fell, to avoid erosion by wind under the semi-arid conditions in which a large proportion of the sediments are wind-worked. A close parallel can be seen today at the nearby living volcano of Oldonyo Lengai, where recent falls of natro-carbonatite ash have become quickly cemented by trona.

A number of surfaces with rain drop prints are known in the lower unit of the footprint tuff, particularly towards the base. These clearly represent light showers of rain falling on dry, dusty surfaces, while the upper levels were wetter and muddy. From this and other evidence, it seems that the history of the tuff begins near the end of a dry season and continues into the rainy season. Prints of the larger animals, such as elephant and rhinoceros, together with the hominid prints, occur in the upper, wet part of the tuff. It is noticeable that there are few superimposed prints, a factor that, taken in conjunction with the lack of erosion of the surfaces, confirms the belief that successive ash falls were buried rapidly.

The first footprints believed to be hominid were discovered in 1976. These consisted of a trail of four prints, very broad and presenting some unusual features. They are still partially infilled with matrix, so that the precise shape of the prints cannot be determined. In 1977 a far more impressive trail of hominid prints was discovered by P. Abell of the Department of

Chemistry, Rhode Island University, at a site known as G, approximately 1.6 km distant. He first noted a heel impression in which the front part of the footprint had been broken away by erosion. When overlying ash and recent soil were cleared away, a second print made by the same individual was uncovered, as well as the beginning of another trail, lying to the east. Both trails led almost due north and have now been uncovered for a distance of 27 m from the first heel print. The most southerly part, uncovered in 1979, was still partly overlain by 5–10 cm of the upper part of tuff 7, so that the footprints are completely unweathered and in a most remarkable state of preservation.

It is now evident that the trails were made by three individuals walking together. There is a single trail on the west, made by the smallest individual; the prints to the east were originally interpreted as a single trail made by a much larger individual, but are clearly double, made by two individuals walking in tandem, with the second placing his or her feet in the footsteps of the leader. All three individuals were walking in step and most likely holding one another, since any deviation in course, no matter how slight, is closely followed by all three and the stride length is virtually the same, in spite of difference in the size of the prints. At one point, towards the northern end of the trails, the smaller individual (designated G 1) appears to have paused, made a half turn to the left and then continued onwards. The dual prints to the east are weathered and rather confused in this area, so that it is difficult to determine whether these individuals also hesitated at this point.

In all, 39 prints of the small individual are preserved and 31 of the dual prints (G 2 and G 3). In these it is only possible to measure the length for the leading individual in two prints where the superimposed G 3 prints have not obliterated the heel impressions of the first.

The following measurements have been taken on the 14 prints of G 1 and 11 prints of G 2 and G 3 uncovered during 1979; they must, therefore, be regarded as provisional, pending measurements of the entire trails. The average lengths for the G 1 and G 3 prints are 18.5 and 21 cm, measured from the tip of the big toe to the centre of the heel, the two points that are generally the best defined. The lengths of the two measurable prints of G 2 are 21 and 24 cm. Prints of G 1 and G 3 are, relative to their length, narrower than those of G 2, in which four breadth measurements are possible. Measurements have been taken across the ball, and the length/breadth indices are: G 1 38 %, G 2 48 % and G 3 40 %.

Certain differences between the individual prints in each trail can be observed. In both G 1 and G 3 the average width across the toes is 83 mm, but in G 2 it is 117 mm, with deeper, broader and longer impressions of the big toe. It is evident that the toes in this individual were more splayed than in either G 1 or G 3. Gait also varies. The individual G 1 walked with feet splayed outwards with an average angle of 27° from the centre line of the trail. The angles of the prints in trail G 3 are patently not measurable, since this individual was following in the footsteps of G 2. Although the G 2 prints generally lack heel impressions it is evident that they were markedly less everted than those of G 1. Some are parallel to the midline of the trail and the average angle of eversion is 3°. In all three sets of prints the weight has been borne on the heel and lateral edge of the foot, but in G 3 the ball is relatively more deeply depressed than in G 1, in which the heel impressions are remarkably deep.

The trails are virtually in a straight line for the entire distance of 27 m. Subsequent faulting with lateral as well as vertical displacements has cut through them diagonally in several places.

Various experiments were carried out at Laetoli in an endeavour to simulate the conditions on the three trails. It was found impossible for adults of present-day stature to walk abreast as closely as did the individuals G 1 and G 2/3, in which the average distance apart for the recently discovered trails is only 17 cm. It is possible, however, for children to walk closer together.

Calculations based on the length of the foot can give an approximate estimate of stature, although even among the living races of *Homo sapiens* the recorded ratios of foot length to known stature vary from 13.4 to 16% (Pales 1976). In the Pliocene hominids the percentages may have been much greater or much less. However, with the figure of 15%, considered to be most generally acceptable, approximate estimates of stature for the two individuals in which the length of the footprints can be measured are: G 1 123 cm (4 ft 1 in) and G 3 140 cm (4 ft 7 in).

The third individual, with the broader foot, was probably rather taller than either of the other two. Even so, it seems reasonable to conclude that the stature of the three individuals was between 4 and 5 ft (*ca.* 1.2 and 1.5 m).

Interpretation of the behaviour pattern shown by the Laetoli hominid tracks can only be hypothetical and depends to a large extent on whether one considers a human or an ape-like model to be the most acceptable. If one is prepared to believe that these hominids were already on the road to man, and were not primates with a tendency to ape-like behaviour, then it is plausible to interpret the tracks as being made by a male whose foot had broad, splayed toes, closely followed by a female, with one or the other leading a juvenile. On the other hand, it seems that juvenile gorillas and chimpanzees often proceed in tandem, while at play, holding one another round the hips (Schaller 1963; A. Root, personal communication).

We have been unable to discover any evidence whatsoever for the making or using of stone tools in the Laetolil beds. A diligent search has been carried out annually and it can now be stated with some confidence that the deposits in the Laetoli area carry no imported stones; in fact, the only stones to be found are fragments of ijolite, volcanic ejecta from the volcano Sadiman.

I turn next to the evidence of the stone industries from Olduvai Gorge. The earliest industry, known as the Oldowan, is situated stratigraphically immediately above the basalt flows in bed I and is dated at 1.9 Ma B.P. This industry has been found at a number of camp sites along the shores of the former Olduvai lake. Tools, debitage and food debris occur in close association and in apparently undisturbed conditions.

The earliest tool kit contains six recognizably different tool types: choppers, polyhedrons, diskoids, subspheroids, scrapers and burins. The choppers, moreover, can be subdivided into a number of different types, such as side, pointed, two-edged and chisel-ended. Side choppers are by far the most common, both at this level and in later stages of the industry. They consist of oblong, fist-sized water-worn cobbles, crudely flaked along one of the longer sides to form a sharp, but jagged, working edge. As well as the formalized tool types, the Oldowan industry also contains numbers of sharp, unretouched flakes with chipping and evidence of wear along the edges. Although these might be regarded as waste material, knocked off when making or resharpening heavy-duty tools, the flakes are usually of quartzite, whereas the majority of heavy-duty tools is of various lavas. It seems, therefore, that they are a separate class of artefact that served a specific purpose.

The deposits of bed I above the basalt flows are believed to have lasted no more than 0.15–0.2 Ma. During this time there is little evidence of change or expansion in the Oldowan industry, although the tools from the lowest level, at site DK, tend to be rather smaller than those from the higher levels. At site FLK North, at the top of bed I, the manufacture of choppers appears to have reached its zenith. At this level, too, there is a single example of a pitted anvil, indicating, perhaps, the beginning of a bipolar technique of flaking stone, which became widely used in the upper part of the Olduvai sequence.

Even though the first hominid remains from bed I were discovered in 1959, there is still no universal agreement as to whether two or three taxa were present at Olduvai during bed I times. *Australopithecus boisei* is accepted as a robust australopithecine, but is not generally considered to have been the maker of the Oldowan tools; it seems more likely to have used natural objects for various purposes, probably adapting them to its needs with teeth and hands, but incapable of formalized tool-making to regular patterns.

The first remains of *Homo habilis*, found in the early 1960s, soon after the discovery of *Australopithecus boisei*, aroused considerable controversy, and the creation of a new species of *Homo* by Leakey et al. (1964) raised a storm of protest. Over the years, this has gradually subsided and the discovery of the cranium of '1470' by R. Leakey in 1972 seems to have brought about a general recognition that there was a stage in human evolution antecedent to *Homo erectus*, but in the direct lineage of *Homo*, to which the term *Homo habilis* could be applied.

However, some workers have now raised the question as to whether all the hominid remains from bed I and lower bed II, other than those of *Australopithecus boisei*, belong to the taxon represented by the type mandible and parietals of O.H.7 (Walker & Leakey 1978). It has been suggested that, whereas the cranial capacities of O.H.7 and '1470' are compatible, other crania from Olduvai, notably O.H.13 and O.H.24, fall below the acceptable level and may belong to another species, perhaps *Australopithecus*. But, since the extent of sexual dimorphism in *Homo habilis* is not known, it is possible that the smaller-brained crania may represent the females of *Homo habilis*. Whichever solution may eventually prove to be correct does not affect the fact that a crude but formalized stone industry existed at Olduvai approximately 2 Ma ago.

Besides the mandible and cranial parts of the *Homo habilis* type, some hand and foot bones were also discovered at the same site. From these it was deduced that the gait was fully bipedal and free-striding (Day & Napier 1964) and that the hand bones were adapted for a precision grip (Napier 1962; Susman & Creel 1979), a conclusion amply supported by the small Oldowan tools. Thus, at Olduvai, it can be shown that both free-striding bipedalism and manual dexterity existed just under 2 Ma ago. At Laetoli, there is evidence only for bipedalism, which freed the hands for purposes other than locomotion. To what extent the hands were used is unknown, but it can be accepted that manufacture of stone tools was still in the future.

In the hominid fossils recovered from the Hadar in Ethiopia (Johanson & White 1979), which are clearly related to, but perhaps later than, those from Laetoli, the cranial capacity is said to be small and has been described as 'ape-like'. Hand bones are also known and when detailed anatomical studies of this important material have been carried out they may provide a clue as to whether the brain or the hands developed first, or whether they both progressed simultaneously.

In conclusion, it can be stated that the evidence from Laetoli demonstrates that as early as 3.6–3.8 Ma ago man's ancestors had achieved a fully upright, free-standing, bipedal gait, which automatically freed the hands for purposes other than locomotion. It is not, however, until from some 1.6 Ma later, at Olduvai, that the first firmly dated and incontrovertible evidence for manufacture of formal tools is to be found. Artefacts from the Hadar, claimed to be in the region of 2.6 Ma old, may prove to fill this gap, but cannot be accepted unreservedly until the present evidence is substantiated.

During the interval between 3.8 and 2 Ma B.P. the early hominids must have progressed slowly through the stages of selecting naturally shaped objects to assist them in their activities, adapting objects by means of their hands or teeth, haphazardly breaking stones and, finally shaping stone tools to a recognizable pattern, an achievement rendered possible by the development of the precision grip and intellectual ability for conceptual thought.

Reference to the term *Australopithecus afarensis* as applied by Johanson & White (1979) to both the Laetoli and Hadar hominid material has been omitted until now, since it is largely a matter of semantics and does not affect the evidence. However, the arbitrary application of the same specific name to the hominids from the two localities, which are separated by over 1000 miles, appears to be based on insufficient proof of identity. It would have been desirable for a detailed comparison to be made of such material as is common to both sites. It is regrettable, too, that the type specimen selected for *A. afarensis* should be a worn mandible from Laetoli, when much better-preserved specimens are available from the Afar itself. Moreover, on the available evidence, it is questionable whether all the Hadar material belongs to a single species; if so, extreme sexual dimorphism must have been present. The possibility exists that two taxa are represented, as originally postulated by Johanson.

Whether the term *Australopithecus* can correctly be applied to fossils that appear to be in the direct *Homo* lineage is a matter of opinion, but the evidence at present available is capable of two interpretations: that *Australopithecus* branched off from the stock leading to *Homo* before the Laetoli and Hadar hominids and later coexisted with them, or that man's ancestors passed through an australopithecine stage of evolution. To assume tacitly, by applying the term *Australopithecus*, that the second alternative is necessarily correct, does nothing to clarify one of the most important issues in the study of man's evolution.

References (Leakey)

Chavaillon, J. 1970 Découverte d'un niveau Oldowayen dans la basse vallée de l'Omo (Ethiopie). *Bull. Soc. préhist. Fr.* **67**, 1.

Day, M. H. & Napier, J. 1964 Hominid fossils from bed I, Olduvai Gorge, Tanganyika, fossil foot bones. *Nature, Lond.* **201**, 967–70.

Johanson, D. C. & White, T. D. 1979 A systematic assessment of early African hominids. *Science, N.Y.* **202**, 321–330.

Leakey, L. S. B., Tobias, P. V. & Napier, J. R. 1964 A new species of the genus *Homo* from Olduvai Gorge. *Nature, Lond.* **202**, 7–9.

Leakey, M. D. & Hay, R. L. 1979 Pliocene footprints in the Laetolil beds, at Laetoli, N. Tanzania. *Nature, Lond.* **278**, 317–323.

Napier, J. R. 1962 Fossil hand bones from Olduvai Gorge. *Nature, Lond.* **196**, 409–411.

Pales, L. 1976 Les empreintes de pieds humains dans les cavernes. *Archs Inst. Paleont. Hum.*, mem. 36. Paris: Masson.

Roche, H. & Tiercelin, J.-J. 1977 Découverte d'une industrie lithique ancienne *in situ* dans la formation d'Hadar, Afar central, Ethiopie. *C.r. hebd. Séanc. Acad. Sci., Paris* D **284**, 1871–1874.

Schaller, G. B. 1963 *The mountain gorilla.* Chicago: Chicago University Press.

Susman, R. L. & Creel, N. 1979 Functional and morphological affinities of the subadult hand from Olduvai Gorge. *Am. J. phys. Anthrop.* **51**, 311–331.

Walker, A. & Leakey, R. E. F. 1978 The hominids of East Turkana. *Scient. Am.* **239**, 54–66.

Phil. Trans. R. Soc. Lond. B **292**, 103–107 (1981)   [103]

Printed in Great Britain

Evolution of human bipedalism: a hypothesis about where it happened†

By L. P. La Lumiere

Naval Research Laboratory, Washington, D.C. 20375, U.S.A.

A geologically plausible locality for aquatic evolutionary processes leading to bipedalism is postulated.

Introduction

Among attempts to explain the evolution of human bipedalism, the aquatic hypothesis proposed by Hardy (1960) and elaborated by Morgan (1972) and Morris (1977) suggests that, during the late Miocene or early Pliocene epochs, a group of apes was isolated by increasing desiccation of their habitat somewhere along the coast of Africa. To escape predators and to find food they entered the water, an environment for which they were poorly adapted. This radical situation resulted in heavy evolutionary pressure for morphological changes from ape to man within a relatively short span of time. The human features possibly accounted for by the aquatic hypothesis include: superior swimming ability, babies swimming at a few weeks old; relative hairlessness; hair tracts arranged for water streamlining, streamlined body compared to those of other primates; insulating layer of fat beneath the skin plus copious sweat glands; erect posture; and highly sensitive, generalized hands. Along with these, certain behavioural traits were evolved, such as fondness of aquatic activities and sea foods. At the beginning of the Pleistocene, when favourable changes permitted, the upright, hominoid descendants of these apes returned to a terrestrial existence.

So far, the aquatic hypothesis has received little acceptance because no supporting fossil evidence has been adduced (Morris 1967). In particular, no region in Africa containing marine Pliocene deposits associated with ape-like and man-like fossils has ever been found (Howells 1967; Leakey 1976).

Reflection upon the Hardy hypothesis leads to the following conclusions: (*a*) the region was a forested area inhabited by apes during the late Miocene; (*b*) the region was isolated from the rest of Africa during the Pliocene, in which period the evolution of ape-like to man-like creatures occurred; (*c*) the region was reconnected to Africa in the late Pliocene or early Pleistocene, enabling the hominoids to migrate elsewhere. Conclusion (*b*) suggests that bipedalism evolved on an island.

Evidence for the hypothetical locality

Tazieff (1972), Tazieff *et al.* (1972) and Barberi *et al.* (1972) suggest that the northern and central Afar triangle in the past was covered by sea water, with only the Danakil Alps and high volcanoes standing above water as islands. They state that the Danakil Alps are part of a horst: an uplifted crustal block that was broken off and separated from the Nubian plate to the west and the Arabian plate to the east through the action of plate tectonics and sea floor spreading.

---

† The main points of this paper were communicated to the meeting by Professor Sir Alister Hardy, F.R.S., during the general discussion.

According to Hsü *et al.* (1973), from the beginning of the Messinian (latest Miocene stage) the Mediterranean Sea was repeatedly isolated and then rejoined to the Atlantic Ocean, and was thus caused to dry up and then refill. They suggest that this cycle of drying and refilling was repeated at least eleven and perhaps as many as fourteen times. During the desiccation of the sea, massive thicknesses of salt were deposited on the bottom of the deeper parts.

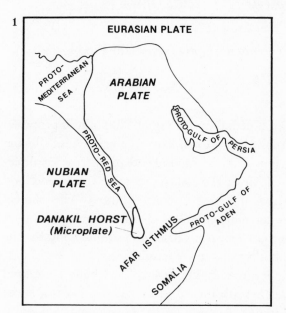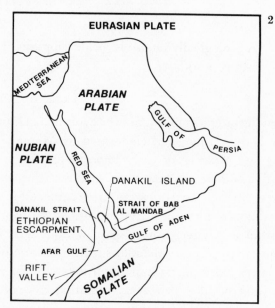

FIGURE 1. The generally supposed relation of the Nubian plate of the African continent to the Arabian plate at the time of the Late Miocene.

FIGURE 2. The configuration of the same region as shown in figure 1, but as it may have been at the beginning of the Pliocene.

Figure 1 displays the configuration of the African continent and Arabian plate as it may have been during the late Miocene. It should be noted that the proto-Red Sea and the proto-Gulf of Aden were separated by an isthmus. This land bridge, here called the Afar Isthmus, apparently existed throughout the late Miocene and was an important link in animal migrations between the continents of Africa and Eurasia (Kurten 1972; Beyth 1978; MacKinnon 1978).

The Afar Isthmus was composed of several crustal blocks. One of these, the Danakil horst, apparently acted as a 'microplate' (Le Pichon & Francheteau 1978). The horst is a mountainous region about 335 miles (540 km) long and up to 45 miles (75 km) wide (Tazieff *et al.* 1972; *Geol. Surv. Ethiopia* 1973). In figure 1, the northern end of the horst marks the southern limit of the proto-Red Sea (Frazier 1970; Barberi *et al.* 1972). It is, therefore, reasonable to suppose that the horst was occupied about 9–14 Ma ago by a group of apes that continued to live there until the forests disappeared at the end of the Miocene (Kurten 1972; MacKinnon 1978).

About the time of the Miocene–Pliocene boundary the African plate moved away from the Arabian plate, and the Danakil microplate was rotated counterclockwise (Tazieff *et al.* 1972; Le Pichon & Francheteau 1978). At the same time the Danakil microplate was tilted so that its Mesozoic sedimentary rock formations slope generally from northeast to southwest (Hutchison & Engels 1970, 1972; Beyth 1978). With the exception of volcanic peaks, the Danakil Alps today rise to a maximum of 1335 m. Finally, the microplate was detached from both the African and Arabian plates, allowing waters from the Red Sea and the Gulf of Aden to flow into the Afar triangle. Figure 2 displays the configuration of the region as it may have been at the beginning of the Pliocene. Note that the Red Sea was no longer connected to the Mediterranean Sea (Coleman 1974) as in figure 1, but was now linked to the Gulf of Aden and the Indian Ocean through two straits, one to the east of the Danakil horst (Strait of Bab al Mandab) and the other, to the west, which will be called the Danakil Strait. Thus, between 6.7 and 5.4 Ma B.P. in the latest Miocene (Messinian), a group of apes along with other animals could have been trapped on Danakil Island.

According to Barberi et al. (1972) and Mohr (1978), the central and southern Afar regions have been repeatedly covered by massive flood basalts during the Pleistocene–Holocene so that the Miocene–Pliocene history of these regions is uncertain. The several volcanoes in the middle of the Danakil horst have been intermittently active from the late Miocene – early Pliocene to the present. About the time of the Miocene–Pliocene boundary the Danakil horst apparently was surrounded by water to the east, the north and the west, while the southern end was covered by extensive flood basalts. The Danakil horst initially may not have been a geographical island, but under the conditions described above, for many land animals, it would have been a biological island.

A SCENARIO FOR THE EVOLUTION OF GENUS *HOMO*

Forests probably covered most of Danakil Island at the beginning of the Pliocene, but these must have soon died. Those near sea level and the coast would have been the first to disappear, while those at higher, cooler elevations in the mountains would have remained longer. The dwindling forest would have produced exactly the environmental conditions required by the Hardy hypothesis: those apes near the coast, losing their forest, gradually would have been forced into water to find both food and protection from predators. Increasing dryness would probably have destroyed much vegetation, and thus reduced the population of both herbivores and carnivores.

Those apes living along the coast would probably have searched for food by wading in the shallow water, a behaviour often compelling upright bipedal movement. (Their cousins along the Ethiopian escarpment and elsewhere undoubtedly retreated with the dwindling forests.) Thus, the island coastal apes, forced to live under unusual conditions, would have rapidly evolved into the upright, hairless hominids described by Hardy and by Morgan.

Sporadic and episodic volcanism within the Afar triangle has been a feature since the early Miocene (Barberi et al. 1972; Gass 1974). Intermittently, the Danakil Strait has been closed and bridged by lava flows as it is today (Frazier 1970; Hutchison & Engels 1972; Lowell & Genik 1971). Eustatic sea level fluctuations combined with erosion probably reopened the strait within a short time. However, during the short time that the island was connected to the mainland, migration of animals must have occurred with the hominids among them. These hominids had evolved in and near the water, and, as they wandered over the lava bridge to the Ethiopian escarpment and then elsewhere, they stayed near water for two reasons: (1) water was their protection against predators; and (2) water provided them with food and drink.

In their meandering search for food, the hominids drifted southward along the western shores of the Afar Gulf. Whenever possible, they explored the rivers and streams that emptied into the embayment from the African Rift Valley.

The foregoing suggests that the aquatically evolving apes were isolated on Danakil Island for at least 1½ Ma and perhaps as long as 3 Ma before returning to the mainstream of African life.

Suggested locality for exploration

There is much tectonic activity within the Afar triangle (Tazieff 1972). Much of the region is covered by flood or plateau basalts (*Geol. Surv. Ethiopia* 1973), and exposed continental basement is limited. Quaternary and Recent deposits are more extensive and cover both basement and

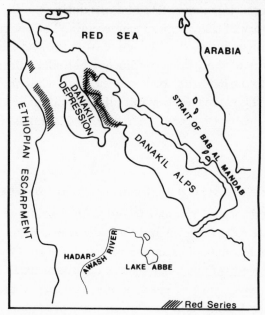

FIGURE 3. The location of the Tertiary deposits known as the Red Series which should yield fossil hominids if the hypothesis here put forward is correct.

basalts, especially along the Ethiopian and Somalian escarpments and the coast between the Danakil Alps and the Red Sea. The Red Series are Tertiary deposits that contain Miocene fossils (Frazier 1970; Hutchison & Engels 1970; Beyth 1978). The radiometric age of the series ranges from 5.4 to 24.0 Ma B.P. (Barberi *et al.* 1972). Deposits occur along the foothills of the western edge of the northern section of the Danakil Alps and east of the Danakil Depression. They also occur along the foothills of the Ethiopian escarpment west of the depression. The location of the Red Series is indicated in figure 3. If this hypothesis is correct, fossils of our ape-like and man-like ancestors should be found in them and in Quaternary formations.

Conclusions

This hypothesis combined with those of Hardy and Morgan suggests some answers, implicitly as well as explicitly, to many questions posed by students of human evolution. The main points are as follows.

1. A geologically plausible locality where aquatic evolutionary processes could have occurred is postulated.
2. A time zone for these processes is suggested, filling a hiatus in current theory.
3. A geological formation likely to contain hominoid as well as hominid fossils is identified.

The author extends his thanks for assistance with articles and manuscripts, comments, criticisms and suggestions to N. Z. Cherkis, R. H. Feden, H. S. Fleming, R. S. Perry, P. R. Vogt, and A. C. Hardy. He thanks E. J. Andersen and C. S. Fruik for drawing the accompanying figures.

REFERENCES (La Lumiere)

Barberi, F., Borsi, S., Ferrara, G., Marinelli, G., Santacroce, R., Tazieff, H. & Varet, J. 1972 Evolution of the Danakil depression (Afar, Ethopia) in light of radiometric age determinations. *J. Geol.* **80**, 720–729.

Beyth, M. 1978 A comparative study of the sedimentary fills of the Danakil depression (Ethiopia) and Dead-Sea rift (Israel). *Tectonophysics* **46** (3/4), 357–367.

Coleman, R. G. 1974 Geologic background of the Red Sea. In *The geology of continental margins* (ed. C. A. Burk & C. L. Drake), pp. 743–751. New York: Springer-Verlag.

Frazier, S. B. 1970 Adjacent structures of Ethiopia: that portion of the Red Sea coast including Dahlak Kebir Island and the Gulf of Zula. *Phil. Trans. R. Soc. Lond.* A **267**, 131–141.

Gass, I. 1974 Complexities of the Afar triple junction. *Nature, Lond.* **249**, 309–310.

Geol. Surv. Ethiopia 1973 *Geological map of Ethiopa.*

Hardy, A. C. 1960 Was man more aquatic in the past? *New Scient.* **7**, 642–645.

Howells, W. W. 1967 *Mankind in the making.* Garden City, New York: Doubleday.

Hsü, K. J., Cita, M. B. & Ryan, W. B. F. 1973 The origin of the Mediterranean evaporites. In *Initial reports of the Deep Sea Drilling Project* (ed. W. B. F. Ryan *et al.*), vol. 13, no. 2, pp. 1203–1231. Washington: U.S. Government Printing Office.

Hutchison, R. W. & Engels, G. G. 1970 Tectonic significance of regional geology and evaporite lithofacies in northeastern Ethiopia. *Phil. Trans. R. Soc. Lond.* A **267**, 313–329.

Hutchison, R. W. & Engels, G. G. 1972 Tectonic evolution in the southern Red Sea and its possible significance to older rifted continental margins. *Bull. geol. Soc. Am.* **83**, 2989–3002.

Kurten, B. 1972 *The age of mammals.* New York: Columbia University Press.

Leakey, R. E. F. 1976 Hominids in Africa. *Am. Scient.* **64**, 174–178.

Le Pichon, X. & Francheteau, J. 1978 A plate-tectonic analysis of the Red Sea – Gulf of Aden area. *Tectonophysics* **46**, 369–406.

Lowell, J. D. & Genik, G. J. 1971 Sea-floor spreading and structural evolution of southern Red Sea. *Bull. Am. Ass. Petrol. Geol.* **56** (2), 247–259.

MacKinnon, J. 1978 *The ape within us.* New York: Holt, Rinehart & Winston.

Mohr, P. A. 1978 Afar. *Rev. Earth. planet. Sci.* **6**, 145–172.

Morgan, E. 1972 *The descent of woman.* New York: Stein & Day.

Morris, D. 1967 *The naked ape.* New York: McGraw-Hill.

Morris, D. 1977 *Manwatching.* New York: Abrams.

Tazieff, H. 1972 The Afar triangle. In *Continents adrift*, pp. 133–141. San Francisco: W. H. Freeman & Co.

Tazieff, H., Varet, J., Barberi, F. & Giglia, F. 1972 Tectonic significance of the Afar (or Danakil) depression. *Nature, Lond.* **125**, 144–147.

Phil. Trans. R. Soc. Lond. B **292**, 109–119 (1981)   [109]
Printed in Great Britain

GENETIC CONSIDERATIONS

The major histocompatibility complex of primates: evolutionary aspects and comparative histogenetics

By H. Balner

Primate Center T.N.O., P.O. box 5815, Rijswijk, The Netherlands

All mammalian species investigated have a chromosomal region designated as the major histocompatibility complex or m.h.c. The biological significance of the m.h.c. goes far beyond controlling the most important histocompatibility or transplantation antigens; the capacity to respond immunologically, the susceptibility to disease (including cancer), the serum level of several complement factors and numerous other biological traits are regulated by genetic systems closely linked within that chromosomal region.

While the basic structure of the m.h.c. seems to be rather similar for all mammalian species, the similarities among the m.h.c. of human and non-human primates are particularly impressive. In this communication, m.h.c. gene products of rhesus monkey, chimpanzee and man are compared and reviewed. Evolutionary aspects of the persistence of the m.h.c. region or 'supergene' throughout the animal kingdom are discussed.

A symposium dealing with evolution is hardly the right forum for a discussion of primate tissue antigens, since only a very limited number of primate species have been investigated and studies on these were not really aimed at trying to solve evolutionary problems. Nevertheless, when serological methods were used to compare m.h.c.-controlled tissue antigens of man, the chimpanzee and the rhesus monkey (also with those of several other primate species), observations were made that permit certain cautious conclusions concerning the probable phylogenetic relations among those species.

In view of the multidisciplinary nature of this symposium, it might be appropriate to start with a brief introduction to the major histocompatibility complex (m.h.c.), its organization, biological significance and some of its evolutionary aspects.

The concept of an m.h.c. was first introduced by Snell in the early 1950s. Working with in-bred strains of mice, he made the distinction between genes associated with acute and with chronic rejection of allografts (transplants exchanged among individuals of the same species). Acute rejections were assumed to be due to disparity for products of an m.h.c., slow rejection to disparities for products of multiple 'minor' histocompatibility genes (Snell *et al.* 1953). Today we know that, in nearly all species investigated, there is a cluster of closely linked highly polymorphic genes designated as the m.h.c. Broadly speaking, the m.h.c. is involved in cellular recognition and differentiation phenomena and in the regulation of immune responses (for details, see Götze (1977)).

For practical purposes, the m.h.c. can be divided into three parts that delineate regions related by their genetic origin and/or function (Klein 1977). Class I genes code for molecules that are target antigens in transplantation reactions and play a role in the recognition of virus-infected cells; class II genes are involved in cellular proliferation, cell to cell interactions and immune responsiveness; class III genes control complement components or receptors for complement.

The evolutionary aspects of the m.h.c. have been the subject of numerous investigations and speculations. Here we will address ourselves to three questions only. (1) Which classes of organisms have a demonstrable m.h.c.? (2) How can the absence or presence of an m.h.c. in different species be explained in terms of evolutionary development? (3) How similar are m.h.c. products of various species and what are the implications of such similarities in terms of evolution?

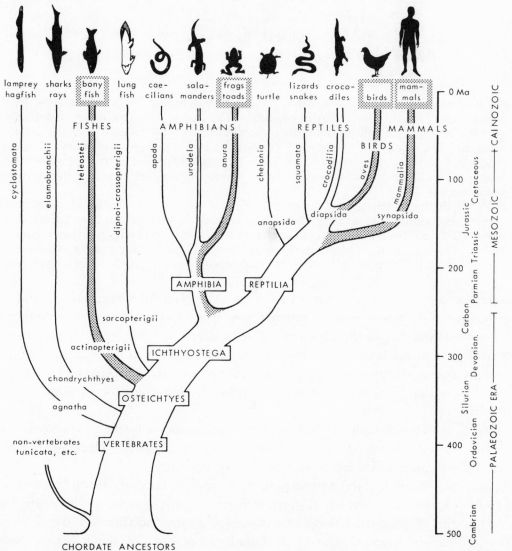

FIGURE 1. Convergent evolution of the major histocompatibility complex (m.h.c.) among vertebrates. The presence of a 'genuine' m.h.c. as defined by the capacity to mount an acute allograft reaction is indicated by a shaded branch of the evolutionary tree. Note that the emergence of this type of m.h.c. did not proceed in a straight evolutionary line. Solid black symbols at the top indicate that relevant data are available for at least some members of that class; no data are available for dipnoi (e.g. lung fish). The figure is modified after Klein (1977, fig. 10.2).

An answer to the first question obviously depends on the criteria applied. If the criterion is an organism's capacity to effect an acute allograft rejection, then such a 'true m.h.c.' cannot be demonstrated in invertebrates. Among the vertebrate species, a true m.h.c. is present in some bony fishes, some amphibia and all birds and mammals investigated so far. This is schematically depicted in figure 1. If we accept this information, the emergence of the m.h.c. did not proceed in a straight evolutionary line, since some relatively young phyla such as reptiles lack a genuine m.h.c. while older ones (like bony fish) seem to have it. There are even differences among closely related phyla, since some amphibia (anura) have a typical m.h.c. while others do not. Likewise, birds and reptiles that are rather closely related phylogenetically do not show the same development with regard to an m.h.c.

What is the evolutionary explanation for such 'erratic' development (question (2))? Most investigators regard the occurrence of the m.h.c. as a typical example of convergent evolution. To quote Ohno (1970): 'divergent species maintain ancestral [m.h.c.] genes; natural selection independently favours similar types of tolerable mutations to cope with demands by similar environments'. Thus, while all vertebrates have the ancestral m.h.c. gene, it evolves into a functional m.h.c. only when there is a need for it and at different stages of evolution. Cohen (1979) agrees with the principle of convergent evolution. However, he also believes that an ancestral gene that did not develop into a genuine m.h.c. (in invertebrates and some vertebrates) may have evolved into that species' predominant minor histocompatibility locus.

The third and last question deals with similarities observed for m.h.c. products of different species. There are various methods of comparison. One of the more sophisticated ones is the determination of amino acid sequences of the m.h.c. products. When data for sequences of class I antigens of the murine H-2 complex became available, it appeared that the similarity among the allelic products of the K or the D locus was about 80%. When the products of those two linked loci were compared, the similarities were slightly less outstanding but still 60–80%. Similar studies of the A- and B-locus antigens of HLA revealed 90% similarity among the allelic antigens and 80–90% similarity between the products of the two loci. The observation that closely linked loci such as HLA-A and -B code for products that are biochemically nearly identical certainly suggests that an original single locus was duplicated, probably to maintain the advantage of heterozygosity even when in-breeding occurs (Ohno 1970). Finally, a striking similarity with regard to amino acid sequences of the N terminal of the class I molecules was also found when antigens of mouse and man were compared (Klein 1977). Such interspecies similarity between the products of homologous loci in phylogenetically rather distant mammalian species again favours the hypothesis that the modern mammalian m.h.c. developed from a common ancestral gene.

RhLA, THE MAJOR HISTOCOMPATIBILITY COMPLEX OF RHESUS MONKEYS

In the mid-1960s, the increasing activity in clinical organ transplantation led to a major interest in human tissue typing and a search for optimal animal models for preclinical transplantation research. For the latter purpose, the rhesus monkey was a particularly suitable candidate because of its phylogenetic closeness to man and the availability of much biological background information. Thus, around 1965, two teams of investigators (one in Holland, one in the U.S.A.) began studying the tissue antigens of rhesus monkeys. Domestic breeding was initiated and, by 1970, a number of pedigreed families was available to facilitate genetic studies of the m.h.c. and its products. In the context of this review, the RhLA story will be told in a very cursory fashion only. As before, we will subdivide the m.h.c. into three classes of genes.

The class I or SD antigens of RhLA were the first to be identified. The closely linked, highly polymorphic A and B loci were established in 1970 (Balner et al. 1971). SD antigens are identifiable with alloantisera, i.e. sera raised by cross immunization of individuals of the same species, and by the use of a complement-dependent cytotoxicity test. About 25 *A*- and *B*-locus antigens are now identifiable; their characteristics and biological significance are fully described elsewhere (Vreeswijk *et al.* 1977). Three categories of class II products of RhLA have also been studied: the *D* or m.l.c. determinants, the Ia or B-cell specific antigens and the *Ir* genes. The *D* or major m.l.c. locus of rhesus was established in 1973 (Balner & Toth 1973). Products of the *D*

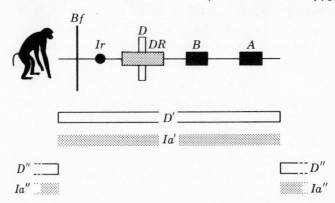

FIGURE 2. Tentative model of RhLA, the major histocompatibility complex of the rhesus monkey. An explanation for the symbols used and for the suggested mapping positions of the proposed genes and loci is given in Balner (1980*b*).

locus have an overriding influence on reactivity in mixed lymphocyte culture (m.l.c.). Disparity for D antigens evokes a proliferative response, which is measurable *in vitro*, by means of the incorporation of radiolabelled thymidine. The *D*-locus antigens can be identified by a cellular method with 'homozygous typing cells'. Evidence has been recently obtained that loci other than *D* can also exert an influence on m.l.c. reactivity (for details, see Es & Balner (1979)). The Ia or B-cell specific antigens of rhesus have been known since 1974 (Balner & Vreeswijk 1975). They are the homologues of the murine Ia antigens, and like SD antigens, are identifiable with alloantisera. However, tissue distribution, chemical characteristics and biological properties of Ia antigens are different from those of SD antigens. Initially, there was evidence for only one major locus controlling the Ia antigens of primates, the *DR* locus, which defines Ia antigens highly associated (possibly identical) with the D antigens mentioned earlier. More recently, non-DR Ia antigens of rhesus monkeys have been identified, some being controlled by RhLA, others not (for details, see Es & Balner (1979)). Finally, there are m.h.c.-controlled *Ir* genes. In mice and in rhesus monkeys, *Ir* genes have been identified by determining the capacity to respond immunologically to certain synthetic antigens. The nature of the *Ir* gene product is not known; it may be a 'T-cell receptor', a structure by which T lymphocytes recognize foreign antigens and subsequently help other cells to mount an effective immune response (for details regarding *Ir* genes of rhesus, see Dorf *et al.* (1975)). Some class III gene products of rhesus monkeys have also been investigated. Thus, Bf, the proactivator of complement factor C3, was found to be controlled by the m.h.c. (Ziegler *et al.* 1975), as it is in man and the chimpanzee.

Figure 2 schematically illustrates the current knowledge of the approximate mapping positions of some of the loci of RhLA. Details, also with regard to the biological function of the depicted loci, are presented elsewhere (Balner 1980*a*, *b*). It should also be mentioned that cell hybridization studies by Garver *et al.* (1980) have revealed that the m.h.c. of the rhesus monkey is located on that species' homologue of the human chromosome no. 6, which carries the HLA complex. Garver's studies also showed that some of the enzyme systems syntenic with HLA in man are syntenic with the m.h.c. also in rhesus monkeys and in chimpanzees (see below).

ChLA, THE MAJOR HISTOCOMPATIBILITY COMPLEX OF CHIMPANZEES

Tissue antigens of chimpanzees have been investigated less extensively than those of man or the rhesus monkey. Yet the availability of a chimpanzee breeding colony at the Primate Center T.N.O. made it attractive also to study the tissue antigens of a primate species very closely related to man phylogenetically. In this section we will briefly summarize the current knowledge of the m.h.c. of chimpanzees. Again, the ChLA region will be subdivided into the three classes of genes proposed by Klein (1977).

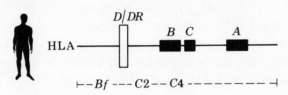

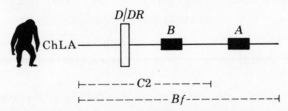

FIGURE 3. Current state of genetic mapping of the ChLA system and comparison with the human HLA system. An explanation for the symbols used and for the suggested mapping positions of the proposed genes and loci, is given in the text and in Balner (1980a) and Jonker & Balner (1980a, b).

Class I or SD antigens of the chimpanzee were first reported in 1967 (reviewed in Götze (1977)). Because of the paucity of available typing reagents and related animals for segregation studies, the progress in tissue typing of chimpanzees lagged behind that for man and the rhesus monkey. It was not until 1973 that two linked series of class I antigens were established and shown to be markers of the chimpanzee's m.h.c., designated as ChLA (Balner et al. 1974). The A- and B-locus products of chimpanzees were clearly the homologous of the products of the A and B loci of man and rhesus monkeys (see following section). (For details regarding serological techniques, genetic analysis etc., see Balner et al. (1978).) The class II determinants of ChLA were more difficult to identify than their counterparts in class I. A major m.l.c. or D locus was tentatively reported in 1973 (Seigler et al. 1974). But it was not until recently that the ChLA-linked D locus was firmly established and some of its determinants were defined (Jonker & Balner 1980b). Only little information is available on Ia or DR antigens of chimpanzees. The close phylogenetic relation with man permitted the use of human anti-DR typing reagents in attempts to demonstrate DR antigens in chimpanzees. Such 'cross-species typing' (see below) revealed that chimpanzees probably carry DR antigens similar to those of man (Balner 1980a). Immune response genes have not yet been demonstrated in chimpanzees. With regard to class

III determinants, two complement factors, C2 and Bf, were shown to be ChLA-linked also in chimpanzees (Raum *et al.* 1980); the genetic control of factor C4, which is also m.h.c.-linked in man, is the subject of current investigations. Finally, Garver, Pearson and their coworkers were able to prove synteny of ChLA with the enzyme systems SOD2, GLO-1, ME-1 and PGM3, all on chimpanzee chromosome 5, the homologue of human chromosome 6 (Garver *et al.* 1980).

Figure 3 schematically depicts the current state of provisional genetic mapping of the identifiable loci of the ChLA system and a comparison with some of the known loci of the human HLA system. The position of the chimp's *A* and *B* loci is unquestionably identical to that of the *A* and *B* loci of HLA. Linkage of the *D* locus with ChLA is now firmly established.† There is also evidence that C2 and Bf are linked to ChLA (see above). When the segregation of C2 in chimp families, was studied, an aberrant segregation pattern was observed in a single offspring, suggesting a recombinational event. Since that particular offspring appeared to be a recombinant also for the *D* locus product (Jonker & Balner 1980a), C2 as well as *D* can be provisionally mapped 'to the left' of the ChLA-*A* locus.‡ Thus, if *D* is placed outside the *A–B* region (which is reasonable in view of the firm data for the homologous loci of man and rhesus monkey), the most reasonable mapping positions are those depicted in the figure 3.

SIMILARITIES AMONG M.H.C.-CONTROLLED TISSUE ANTIGENS OF DIFFERENT PRIMATE SPECIES

In this last section, we will briefly review what has been done so far to compare m.h.c.-controlled antigens among several primate species by serological means and the conclusions that can be cautiously drawn.

Comparing primate characteristics by cross-species typing is certainly not as accurate as comparing chromosomal banding patterns (Dutrillaux *et al.* 1973; Mitchell & Gosden 1978), gene mapping by various kinds of hybridization (Finaz *et al.* 1975; Pardue & Gall 1970), biochemical analysis (Jeffreys & Barrie, this symposium; King & Wilson 1975) and data obtained with monoclonal antibodies (Brodsky *et al.* 1979). Nevertheless, cross-species typing as described here can also reveal similarities and dissimilarities that may be revelant to phylogeny and evolution.

Let us now discuss briefly the principle of cross-species typing. Let us first take chimpanzee and man; as indicated, *A*- and *B*-locus antigens of chimpanzees are most readily identified with antisera raised by alloimmunization of chimpanzees. Likewise, selected human allo-antisera will identify *A*- and *B*-locus antigens of humans. To compare the SD antigens of the two species, a simple approach would be: (*a*) to test chimp cells with human typing reagents; (*b*) to test human cells with chimp typing reagents; and (*c*) to absorb the antisera of both species with cells of either species and subsequently retest the absorbed reagents with cells of both species (there are of course refinements of cross-species typing which have been described elsewhere (Balner 1980a)). However, when performing these kinds of serological tests, one is often

---

† Although the data for the chimp's *DR* or *D*-related Ia antigens are scanty and based on cross-species typing only, it is fair to predict that the position of *DR* in relation to *D* will be similar to that in man and rhesus monkey (for details Jonker & Balner (1980a)).

‡ Since the relevant parent of the recombinant offspring in question was homozygous for a *B*-locus antigen, C2 and *D/DR* can be mapped to the left of the *A* locus and their mapping position with regard to the ChLA *B* locus are not yet known (although *D/DR* is very likely located outside the *A–B* region (Jonker & Balner 1980a).

faced with problems and uncertainties. Therefore, it was necessary to establish rules according to which the degree of similarity between cell membrane antigens of related species can be assumed. The criteria that we have used are shown in table 1. Thus, when cross-species typing between the chimpanzee and man was done in both directions (chimp to man and man to chimp), 'meaningful' serological patterns were obtained, i.e. some human HLA antigens are probably very similar to corresponding ChLA antigens. Moreover, A-locus antigens of the one species

TABLE 1. CRITERIA FOR ASSUMING THE PRESENCE OF HLA-LIKE ANTIGENS ON CHIMPANZEE CELLS

serological conditions that apply	likelihood that HLA-like antigen is present on chimp cells
1. a single HLA serum shows polymorphism, by one technique	unlikely
2. several HLA sera show concordant typing results { with one technique	unlikely
with several techniques	possible
3. HLA reactivity removed by absorption with chimp cells (retesting on human cells)	probable
4. 'meaningful' results obtained in absorption and elution studies on cells and sera of both species (see text for explanation)	very likely
5. alloimmunization of chimpanzees yields antibody of same HLA specificity in man	very likely

corresponded only to A-locus antigens of the other and the same so for the B locus products of both species. This is schematically shown in figure 4. Some of the similarities indicated in the figure could be shown to be 'near-identities' when detailed studies were performed along the lines of points 4 and 5 of table 1 (e.g. ChLA-A108 and HLA-A11 (Balner 1980a)).

This 'game' of cross-species typing can of course also be played to compare D and DR antigens (class II) of the two species. Thus, highly concordant results were obtained when human sera defining certain human DR antigens were tested with suspensions of chimpanzee B lymphocytes (Balner 1980a). Therefore, according to the rules of table 1, we can cautiously predict that chimpanzees carry DR antigens similar to those of man. However, absorption studies and the reverse typing (i.e. using chimpanzee anti-DR sera for the typing of human B cells) have not yet been done. Likewise, conventional cellular methods for identifying D-locus antigens were employed to compare the D or m.l.c. antigens of the chimp and man. Provisional data reveal that it is indeed possible to type chimpanzees with human typing cells†; likewise, typing cells of chimpanzees have shown some meaningful reactions when tested with human cells (Jonker & Balner 1980a). Thus, it can be cautiously concluded that D- and DR-locus products of chimpanzees resemble the homologous m.h.c. products of man.

Cross-species typing has also been performed with the panel of antisera that define the RhLA-A and -B locus antigens of rhesus monkeys. The sera were first tested with cells from two cercopithecoid species, the Asian stumptail (M. arctoides) and an African baboon species

† 'Typing cells' homozygous for D-locus antigens are traditionally used to determine D antigens in man, the chimpanzee, the rhesus monkey and dogs (for details see Jonker & Balner (1980a)).

(*P. cynocephalus*). The methods were the same as those used for chimp–human typing and the criteria used for assuming similarities were again those shown in table 1. The results revealed that, of the 15 RhLA antigens identifiable at that time (1972), stumptails and baboons seemed to carry six or seven antigens presumably similar to those of rhesus monkeys (RhLA 1, 6, 9, 19, 11 and 14 for stumptails; RhLA 1, 5, 6, 19, 2, 11 and 13 for baboons). Here, the evidence for

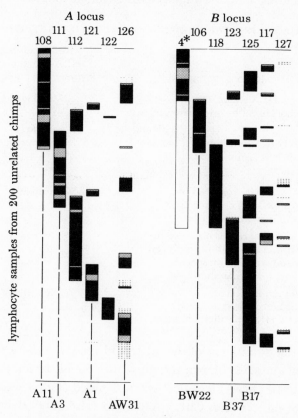

FIGURE 4. ChLA antigens of chimpanzees. Distribution of antigens controlled by the *A* and *B* loci of ChLA in 200 unrelated chimpanzees. The vertical columns indicate lymphocytotoxicity patterns of groups of antisera (group numbers at the top). An antigen was assigned if the majority or all sera of a group reacted strongly positive (black horizontal bars); shaded horizontal bars indicate variable, mostly weak serological reactions and uncertainty about the presence of an antigen; blanks are negative reactions and interrupted horizontal lines indicate that an animal was not typed for a particular antigen. The cell samples depicted in the left part of the figure were arranged for an optimal display of *A*-locus antigens, those in the right part for *B*-locus antigens. Symbols at the bottom of the figure stand for human HLA antigens 'associated' with certain ChLA antigens of chimpanzees; associations are based on results of typing part of the chimp population with human HLA sera (from Balner *et al.* 1978).

similarity was somewhat weaker than in the chimp–human comparison, since the reverse pattern of testing could not be performed (reliable alloantisera defining class I antigens of stumptails or baboons are not available).

From the standpoint of phylogeny, an important question is whether meaningful serological results can be obtained when cross-species typing is performed among less closely related primate species, e.g. when comparing hominids with simians. This kind of work has been carried out and the results are depicted in figure 5 in a highly schematic fashion. In the course of these studies, it appeared, that groups of sera defining RhLA antigens never showed meaningful concordant results when tested against panels of human and chimpanzee cells, although many individual sera displayed polymorphic patterns (i.e. positive and negative lymphocytotoxic reactions). Such results were difficult to interpret, also because absorption or elution studies had not been performed. Nevertheless, it was interesting that RhLA sera, which showed a particular reactivity pattern against chimpanzee cells (only negative, only positive or clearly polymorphic reactions), usually displayed a similar reactivity pattern when tested against human cells. But

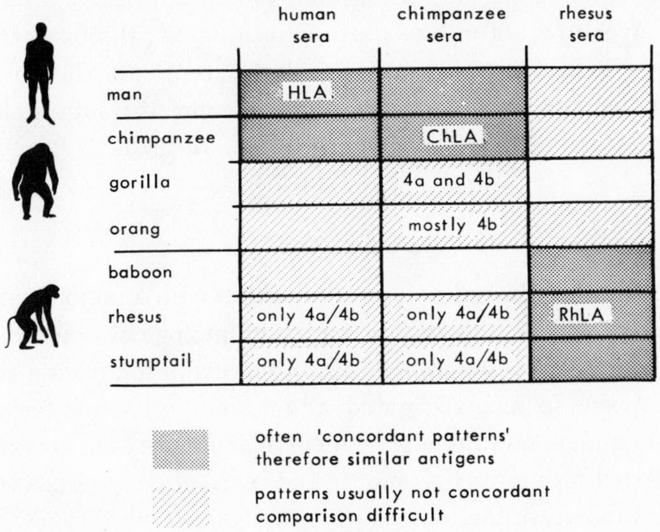

	human sera	chimpanzee sera	rhesus sera
man	HLA		
chimpanzee		ChLA	
gorilla		4a and 4b	
orang		mostly 4b	
baboon			
rhesus	only 4a/4b	only 4a/4b	RhLA
stumptail	only 4a/4b	only 4a/4b	

often 'concordant patterns' therefore similar antigens

patterns usually not concordant comparison difficult

FIGURE 5. Sharing of tissue antigens between several primate species. Schematic presentation of conclusions drawn from results obtained in direct cross-species typing. Human, chimpanzee and rhesus alloantisera that define m.h.c.-controlled antigens were screened for cytotoxic reactivity against lymphocytes from the other species shown in the figure. For details and a further explanation of symbols and abbreviations, see text and Balner (1980a).

when the same sera were tested against orang-utan lymphocytes, reactivity patterns were erratic, with no resemblance whatsoever to the patterns observed in chimp and man.† Likewise, when testing human and chimpanzee alloantisera with cells from rhesus monkeys or other cercopithecoids, uninterpretable reactivity patterns were obtained. Only sera with anti-4a or anti-4b reactivity‡ showed interesting patterns. If we accept the results summarized in figure 5, also for combinations for which no absorption and elution experiments had been done, then the following, very tentative conclusions can be drawn. (a) Man and the chimpanzee 'share' a fairly large number of m.h.c.-controlled class I antigens, possibly also some of the class II antigens. However, no such similarities were found between man and the chimp on the one hand and gorilla and orang-utan on the other. A tentative conclusion would be that chimpanzees are closest to man phylogenetically, an opinion also held by a number of investigators who base their conclusions on cytogenetic, biochemical or other experimental approaches (Bodmer & Bodmer 1978). (b) Rhesus monkeys share class I m.h.c.-controlled antigens with other cerco-

† When testing RhLA sera against dog cells and cells from numerous mouse strains, the results were also erratic and uninterpretable. In those combinations, however, pre-existent heteroantibodies may interfere more strongly than in interprimate tissue typing.

‡ Antigens 4a and 4b are so-called supertypic HLA antigens first reported by Rood & Leeuwen (1963). They are present on chimpanzee and rhesus monkey cells and are considered to be a 'basic substance' of certain m.h.c. products of primates, and possibly of all mammalian species (Balner et al. 1974).

pithecoid simians. Surprisingly, the 'degree of sharing' was rather similar for rhesus and the Asian stumptail macaque, as for rhesus and an African baboon species. However, by means of this serological approach, RhLA-like antigens could not be detected on cells of man or apes. The genetic distance between hominoids and cercopithecoids is likely to be the reason for this difference. (c) The so-called supertypic tissue antigens 4a and 4b (Rood & Leeuwen 1963) seem to be shared by all primate species so far investigated. This observation would be in accord with data obtained recently by Bodmer's group using monoclonal antibodies directed against some of the 'basic molecular structures' of m.h.c.-controlled antigens; those supertypic specificities were also widely distributed among primate species. Both sets of data (Bodmer's data obtained with monoclonal antibodies and ours with regard to 4a and 4b) support the concept of a common ancestral gene as the origin of the modern m.h.c. antigens.

SUMMARY

The m.h.c. is a cluster of closely linked polymorphic genes with a major impact on cell to cell recognition, morphogenesis, cell differentiation and immunological defences. Its presence in many, but not all, vertebrate species suggests a convergent evolution from a common ancestral gene. In all mammalian species so far investigated, a 'genuine' m.h.c. has been found. The very similar organization of the m.h.c. and the biochemical near-identity of certain m.h.c. products, even among remotely related species such as mouse and man, also suggests a common ancestral gene as the origin of the modern m.h.c.

The m.h.cs of three primate species (man, the rhesus monkey and the chimpanzee) have been studied and compared. As expected, the organization of the m.h.c. in the three species is virtually identical. Results of so-called serological cross-species typing among those three and a few other primate species suggest a rather high degree of sharing of antigens between chimpanzee and man and also among the cercopithecoid simians investigated. However, there was little sharing of m.h.c. antigens between the hominoids on the one hand and the cercopithecoids on the other. The only exceptions were the supertypic antigens 4a and 4b, which may represent a 'basic molecular structure' shared by so-called private m.h.c. antigens of each species. Further, it appeared that the genetic distance among the hominoid species investigated is smallest between man and chimpanzee.

The work was supported by the ZWO-Fungo Organization and the Commission of the European Communities (contribution no. 1649 of the Biology – Medical Research Division). The author is a member of the Biology – Medical Research Division of the European Communities.

REFERENCES

Balner, H. 1980a *The major histocompatibility complex of primates.* Lyon: Fondation Mérieux. (In the press.)
Balner, H. 1980b The DR system of rhesus monkeys; a brief review of serology, genetics and relevance to transplantation. *Transplantn Proc.* **12** (3), 502–512.
Balner, H., Gabb, B. W., D'Amaro, J., Vreeswijk, W. van & Visser, T. P. 1974 Evidence for two linked loci controlling the serologically defined leukocyte antigens of chimpanzees (ChLA). *Tiss. Antigens* **4**, 313–238.
Balner, H., Gabb, B. W., Dersjant, H., Vreeswijk, W. van & Rood, J. J. van 1971 Major histocompatibility locus of rhesus monkeys (RhLA). *Nature, Lond.* **230**, 177–180.
Balner, H. & Toth, E. K. 1973 The histocompatibility complex of rhesus monkeys. II. A major locus controlling reactivity in mixed lymphocyte cultures. *Tiss. Antigens* **3** (4), 273–290.

Balner, H. & Vreeswijk, W. van 1975 The major histocompatibility complex of rhesus monkeys (RhLA). V. Attempts at serological identification of MLR determinants and postulation of an I region in the RhLA complex. *Transplantn Proc.* **7** (1), 13–20.

Balner, H., Vreeswijk, W. van, Roger, J. H. & D'Amaro, J. 1978 The major histocompatibility complex of chimpanzees: identification of several new antigens controlled by the A and B loci of ChLA. *Tiss. Antigens* **12**, 1–18.

Bodmer, W. F. & Bodmer, J. G. 1978 Evolution and function of the HLA system. *Br. Med. Bull.* **34**, 309–316.

Brodsky, F. M., Parham, P., Barnstable, C. J., Crumpton, M. J. & Bodmer, W. F. 1979 Monoclonal antibodies for analysis of the HLA system. *Immun. Rev.* **47**, 3–61.

Cohen, N. 1979 Evolution of the major histocompatibility complex in vertebrates: a saga of convergent gene evolution? *Transplantn Proc.* **11**, 1118–1122.

Dorf, M. E., Balner, H. & Benacerraf, B. 1975 Mapping of the immune response genes in the major histocompatibility complex of the rhesus monkey. *J. exp. Med.* **142**, 673–693.

Dutrillaux, B., Rethoré, M., Prieur, M. & Lejeune, J. 1973 Analyse de la structure fine des chromosomes du gorilla (*Gorilla gorilla*). Comparisons avec *Homo sapiens* et *Pan troglodytes*. *Humangenetik* **20**, 343–354.

Es, A. A. van & Balner, H. 1979 Effect of pretransplant transfusions on kidney allograft survival. *Transplantn Proc.* **11** (1), 127–137.

Finaz, C., Cochet, C., de Grouchy, J., Van Cong, N., Rebourcet, R. & Frezal, J. 1975 Localization géniques chez le chimpanze (*Pan troglodytes*) comparaison avec le carte factorielle de l'homme (*Homo sapiens*). *Annls Génét.* **18**, 169–177.

Garver, J., Estop, A., Meera Khan, P., Balner, H. & Pearson, P. 1980 Evidence of similar organization of the MHC chromosome in man and other primates. *Cytogenet. Cell. Genet.* (In the press.)

Götze, D. (ed.) 1977 *The major histocompatibility system in man and animals* New York: Springer-Verlag.

Jonker, M. & Balner, H. 1980a Current knowledge of the D/DR region of the major histocompatibility complex of rhesus monkeys and chimpanzees. *Hum. Immun.* (In the press.)

Jonker, M. & Balner, H. 1980b Mixed lymphocyte reactivity in chimpanzees. II. Family studies and identification of D locus antigens. *Tiss. Antigens.* (In the press.)

King, M. & Wilson, A. 1975 Evolution at two levels in humans and chimpanzees. *Science, N.Y.* **188**, 107–116.

Klein, J. 1977 Evolution and function of the major histocompatibility system; facts and speculations. In *The major histocompatibility system in man and animals* (ed. D. Götze), pp. 339–378. New York: Springer-Verlag.

Mitchell, A. R. & Gosden, J. R. 1978 Evolutionary relationships between man and the great apes. *Sci. Prog., Oxf.* **65**, 273–294.

Ohno, S. 1970 *Evolution by gene duplication.* New York: Springer-Verlag.

Pardue, M. & Gall, J. 1970 Chromosomal localization of mouse satellite DNA. *Science, N.Y.* **168**, 1356–1358.

Raum, D., Balner, H., Petersen, B. H. & Alper, Ch. A. 1980 Genetic polymorphism of serum complement components in the chimpanzee. *Immunogenetics* **10**, 455–468.

Rood, J. J. van. & Leeuwen, A. van. 1963 Leukocyte grouping. A method and its application. *J. clin. Invest.* **42** 1382–1390.

Seigler, H. F., Ward, F. E., Metzgar, R. S., Stulting, S. M., Phaup, M. B. & Adams, B. J. 1974 Mixed-lymphocyte-culture responses in chimpanzee families. *Transplantn Proc.* **6** (2), 135–139.

Snell, G. D., Smith, P. & Gabrielson, F. 1953 Analysis of the histocompatibility-2 locus in the mouse. *J. natn. Cancer Inst.* **14**, 457–480.

Vreeswijk, W. van., Roger, J. H., D'Amaro, J. & Balner, H. 1977 The major histocompatibility complex of rhesus monkeys RhLA. VII. Identification of five new serologically defined antigens. *Tis. Antigens* **9**, 17–30.

Ziegler, J. B., Alper, Ch., A. & Balner, H. 1975 Properdin factor B and histocompatibility loci linked in the rhesus monkey. *Nature, Lond.* **254**, 609–611.

Phil. Trans. R. Soc. Lond. B **292**, 121–131 (1981)   [121]
Printed in Great Britain

The emergence of man: information from protein systems

By E. M. Jope, F.B.A.
Archaeology Department, The Queen's University of Belfast, Belfast BT7 1NN,
Northern Ireland

Protein amino acid sequences are not directly very informative about the emergence of man from his immediate primate ancestry. But this could be because too little attention has been given to protein systems most relevant to the progress of hominization, those that, through their cell-surface action or enzymatic control of biosynthesis of other key proteins or hormones, can modulate the course of cell and tissue development, and so determine changes in tooth architecture, bone and tissue structure, brain and nerve cell development, etc. There are also the histones and other proteins associated with DNA in the genetic material, which have some modulating influence on gene expression. The whole process of carrying information from the genetic material to a species-reproducible morphology is through a cascade of multiple interlocking systems involving proteins at every turn. It is through changes in balance within these systems, and subsequent selection pressures, that the modulations of primate morphology and behaviour that constitute hominization have proceeded, and the process must be understood in terms of cytobiochemistry to give a fully detailed definition of the evolving human genome.

Human protein data in terms of amino acid sequences† reveal little about the emergence of man from his immediate primate ancestry. They suggest that man and apes are genetically very similar (Nei & Roychoudhury 1974; Nei 1975; King & Wilson 1975; Manueledis & Wu 1978; Bruce & Ayala 1978). Yet different they certainly are in morphology and behaviour patterns. However much the selective pressures have been at work on the polymorphic systems (Bodmer & Cavalli-Sforza 1976), the prime determinants underlying these heritable evolutionary differences must be sought at molecular level, coded in the DNA–protein complexes that make up the genetic material, the genes grouped in the chromatin of the chromosomes. This information is processed through RNA systems into intricate networks of protein and metabolic pathways (figure 1) to emerge as a heritable morphology and behaviour pattern with nuances of variance but astonishing overall species reproducibility (note some forward thinking in Needham (1942)). In this process many protein systems exercise a modulating control. These protein systems must therefore be fully understood, in terms of changes in molecular structure and of biological behaviour, and also in relation to DNA and RNA sequences, if the cumulative processes of hominization are to be defined.

Recent studies of base-pair sequences in DNA (Jeffreys & Barrie, this symposium) have provided a method of inferring protein amino acid sequences, and this has tended to discourage direct protein sequenation. But protein sequencing is still sometimes necessary. First, some amino acid residues of the primary sequence undergo post-biosynthetic modifications that profoundly affect their biological properties, as occurs with post-synthetic modifications of histones (Isenberg 1979) and hydroxylation of many prolines and lysines in the collagens (see

---

† These data are for many protein systems only available by gel electrophoretic methods, which only reveal about 40 % of the amino acid differences (Ferguson 1970), but this does not greatly alter the above conclusion.

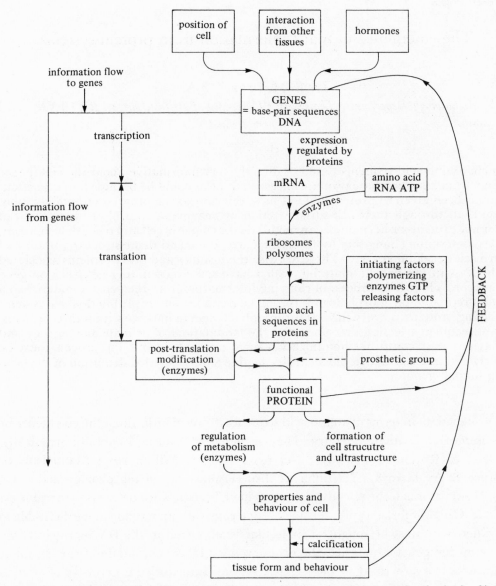

FIGURE 1. The molecular basis of morphogenesis. Summary diagram showing the molecular basis of information
flow from the genome DNA, through functional proteins, to cell development and tissue form.

below). Secondly, direct sequencing is necessary with fossil protein material, in which molecular structures can survive even from the distant past (Wyckoff 1972; Jope 1980; cf. below), the DNA material being less fully preserved (Jeffreys 1980).

Study of protein systems is thus an indispensable complement to DNA constitution in tracing the emergence of the hominid genome. There are the proteins of both histone and non-histone type closely associated with the DNA in the primary genetic material, the chromatin of the chromosomes (Bonner *et al.* 1968; Elgin & Weintraub 1975; Kedes 1979). These proteins exercise a strong and cell-type-specific control over the parts of the genome that are transcribed as mRNA (Truman 1974). The simple view that the histones have been invariant through eukaryote evolution is now being subjected to considerable modification (Isenberg 1979). It is becoming clear that specific subunits in the histone molecules are significant, and some mechanisms that can influence growth are beginning to emerge, such as the post-biosynthetic phosphorylation of specific serine and threonine residues (Isenberg 1979).

The RNAs are themselves complex entities, with some polymorphisms (Newrock *et al.* 1977; Kedes 1979), and have a close and potentially modulating relation with protein molecular units (Harwood 1979; Kedes 1979). Their mechanism of operation with RNA may sometimes be by binding to specific membrane surfaces (Harwood 1979). RNA data have their own contribution to make to genetic distance assessment (Grantham & Gantier 1980).

Beyond these primary molecular stages of transcription and translation of genetic instructions at molecular level, a mammalian organism develops through the embryonic stages (gastrulation, etc.), and the complexities of cell differentiation and growth, with backfeeding interactions, resulting in specialized tissue formation (always involving proteins), into adult life (Wessells 1977). These processes operate through networks of interacting metabolic systems, largely involving proteins (figure 1), each protein itself needing many other preformed molecules (protein–enzyme transferase systems and hormones) to complete its biosynthesis. The human genome contains at least 10^5 (and probably nearer 10^6) genes coding for biosynthesis of proteins (Bodmer & Cavalli-Sforza 1976). Only by isolating and defining each specific protein can its function in the organism be assessed, and the parts of the genetic material that determine its biosynthesis and control its operation located in the genome.

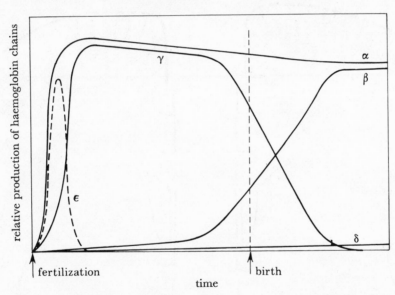

FIGURE 2. The polymorphic forms of human haemoglobin α, β, γ, δ, ϵ: their place in the development of the living system, from the embryo into adult life. (Adapted from Zuckerkandl (1965)).

In living organisms many proteins are in the form of molecular families of homologous constitution with a graded range of properties. This protein *polymorphism* probably reflects DNA mutations, deletions, gene duplications, and analogous processes in the genetic material. With the genes potentially operable but switched on or repressed by various mechanisms (Ochoa & de Haro 1979) these polymorphisms provide within a population a cumulative heritable reserve of adaptability to varying conditions and constraints, as in environment or the transition from embryonic to adult life, and are the basis of evolution by selective pressure. The haemoglobin family (figure 2) provides an excellent example of the range of variability while still retaining the basic biological function of oxygen transport (Zuckerkandl 1965).

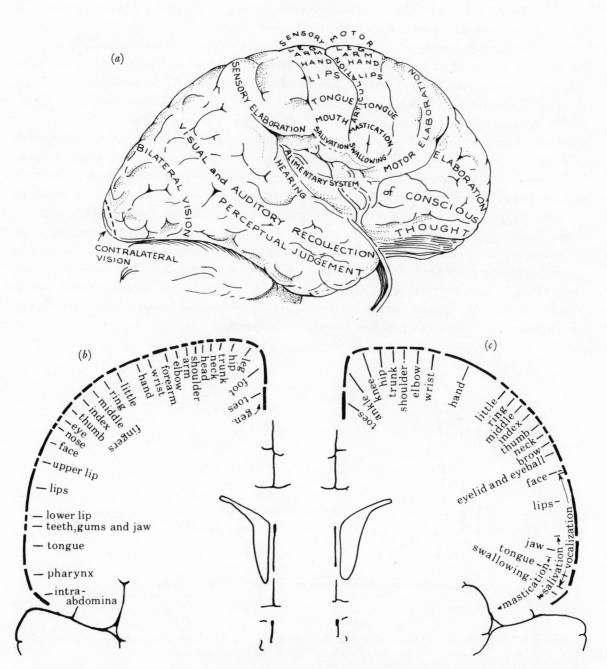

FIGURE 3. Diagram of the lateral aspect of a right human cerebral hemisphere (from Penfield & Rasmussen (1950)). The regions from which somato-sensory and somato-motor responses are evoked by electrical stimulation are shown diagramatically in transverse section in (b) and (c) respectively. In (a) the localization of electrically evoked visual ('vision') and auditory ('hearing') responses are also indicated. The remaining entries in (a) are entirely hypothetical and are based on Penfield's interpretations concerning the possible functions of the remaining areas. The functions of speech (see R. E. Passingham, this symposium) are most commonly represented in the left hemisphere. This diagram directs attention to areas of cells particularly apt for detailed cytochemical study.

One reason why protein data have so far been uninformative about the emergence of man may be because the potentially more informative protein systems in relation to morphogenesis and behaviour have been comparatively little studied. Many of the distinctive hominizing features, such as postnatal increase in brain size, reduction in tooth size, differentiation of power and precision grip, muscular control over nuances of facial expression, sequencing of images, and speech, are concerned with particular cells of the tissues, brain and nervous system, some in specific restricted regions of the cerebral cortex (figure 3). It is the protein systems of these groups of cells that need intensive cytochemical study, especially concerning mitosis induction or inhibition (Thornley & Lawrence 1975), in differentiation processes, and in tissue formation, with all the cell-to-cell surface interactions involved. The microtechniques necessary for identifying and localizing the significant molecules in, on and around the cell are gradually becoming available (see, for example: Elliott & Gardner 1980; Barer & Jope 1950).

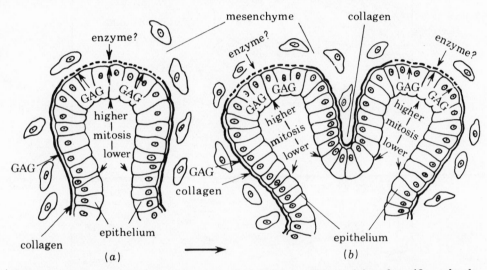

FIGURE 4. Schematic diagram illustrating the localized surface activity of specific molecular species (GAG, collagen) during lobe formation. (Adapted from Wessells (1977).)

The collagen family (and their associated post-translational enzymes, so essential in re-modelling) give an instructive example of protein molecules through which some genetic control seems to be exercised, during embryonic and at later stages, over cellular development, group-ing and remodelling, thus regulating the tissue architecture and function (such as is discussed below for the brain), that is, morphogenesis. The collagens are a varied polymorphic family of homologous structures (e.g. the closely packed helical domains of repeated -Gly-Pro-X-). Collagens are very versatile in function, the result of long cumulative gene duplication (Miller 1977; Tanzer 1978). Their monomers assemble outside the cell into trimers, and then into microfibrils and fibrils, to give a fibrous tensile structure to a tissue (skin, tendon, bone, etc.); they can also provide a necessary firm matrix (e.g. basal lamina) for differentiated cell and tissue development (Wessells 1977). Yet internally the collagen molecular structure is in a continually dynamic state of 'breathing' (Torchia & Vander Hart 1976; Piez & Trus 1978). Collagen mol-ecules have many active sites on the surface, and through these are involved in interactions with other molecular complexes, such as the proteoglycans (made up of glycosaminoglycan (GAG) and some protein), to give an immense diversity of macromolecular structures (Wessells 1977;

Hascall & Heinegard 1974; Scott 1980). The GAGs (polymers of acetylated aminosugars and uronic acids, often sulphated) are themselves vital factors in determining the progress of complex tissue growth, such as lobe formation (figure 4), being removable by hyaluronidases in remodelling. The proteoglycan GAG complexes appear to be a necessary factor at the outermost actively growing part of a lobe in cleft formation, whereas the collagens provide fibre formation for binding within the inner folds of a cleft; each is removable enzymatically in remodelling where no longer required (figure 4; Smith *et al.* 1975; Wessells 1977). These complex heterogeneous polysaccharides (GAG) illustrate the way in which a class of substances of the utmost importance in controlling morphogenesis can lurk unrecognized for a long time (Wessells 1977; Bernfield *et al.* 1973; Bannerjee *et al.* 1977; Cohn *et al.* 1977).

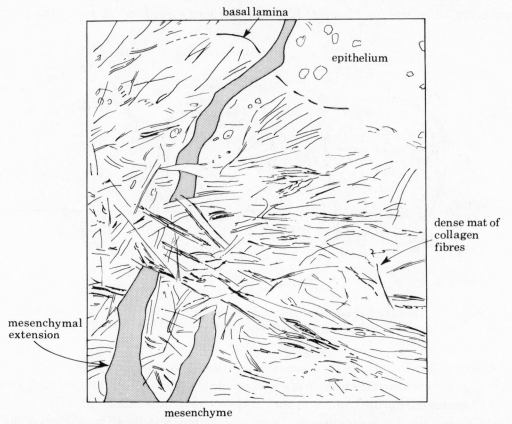

FIGURE 5. Diagram drawn from an electronmicrograph of a developing tooth germ. The shaded area shows a mesenchymal cell extension penetrating through the mat of collagen fibres and the basal lamina, to make the contact that is needed for the development and growth of the tooth itself. The cytobiochemistry of this diagram underlies the determination of dental architecture. (Adapted from Slavkin & Bringas (1976) and Wessells (1977).)

A matrix to hold cells, during cell grouping and remodelling, is a necessary background to tissue formation. Collagens (type IV) are very active in basement membrane surfaces lying at the interface between the extracellular matrix and the cell plasma membrane (Harwood 1979). In some basal laminae, however, there proves to be comparatively little collagen. More work is still needed on the great variety of tissue types and organs, and it is clear that the precise locations of many of these proteins and protein-like substances (whose biosynthesis is largely genetically controlled) can exert a strong influence on the progress of tissue formation. It is this precise directing and location of these molecules that underlies morphogenesis, and protein molecules play a role at every turn.

Collagens provide also the complex layered substance of teeth (Volpin & Veis 1973). The reduction in size of canines and other teeth is another significant hominizing trend, progressing around 5–2 Ma ago. This can be seen against the molecular background of odontological cytodifferentiation, in which collagen has played a considerable part. Tooth architecture is already being determined with the development of tooth germs at the embryonic stage (figure 5; Slavkin & Bringas 1976). These tooth germs are extrusions of mesenchyme cells, some of which manage to penetrate a dense mass of collagen fibres to make contact with the epidermal cells (figure 5), which stimulates the actual tooth formation. This selective penetration may be due to selective proteolysis of the collagenous fibres, controlled perhaps by cell–cell or tissue–tissue interactions, and must be a main determinant for dental architecture. Tooth architecture can be a sensitive marker in following the emergence of man, and even revealing distinctions among the living races of man (Turner 1976).

Collagenous polypeptides are sometimes involved in enzymic activity, as, most significantly, when they form subunits of an acetylcholinesterase in synaptic membranes of electric fish (Lwebuga-Mukasa et al. 1976), and they are found in other unexpected contexts, such as part of a link protein in a protease of the complement system, which is a vital protector of the life of the individual animal and so of the continuation of the species (Porter 1980).

Collagens provide the main fossil protein material that is relevant to the emergence of man, as their molecular structures can survive fairly well (Jope 1980). Too little is yet known of the sequences of their amino acid chains 1055 residues in length (Hulmes et al. 1973; Piez & Trus 1978), but they must have only limited evolutionary substitutions as the functional requirements impose a structural conservatism. Immunological distinctions among primate collagen appear to be possible, but until more is known of the molecular structural basis of such sensitive discriminations they cannot be fully interpreted (Furthmayr & Timpl 1976). It has been noted that the immunological recognitions occur largely in the non-helical teleopeptide tails (Bornstein & Hesse 1970). Herein, however, lies a paradox; in collagen all the tyrosine is found in these non-helical teleopeptides (Hulmes et al. 1973) and it is tyrosine that is most readily lost in fossil bone material, indicating degradation in these tails (Jope 1976). More data on the molecular mechanisms of these immunological observations is clearly needed.

Blood groups, histocompatibility complexes, and other immune reaction systems are sensitive phylogenetic markers at subspecies level and should be informative in charting the emergence of man. The HLA system, for instance, clearly distinguishes between man and apes (Balner, this symposium), and the blood groupings (A, B, O and Lewis) give useful classifications among the races of man (Nei & Roychoudhury 1974). Their evolutionary significance, however, still remains uncertain (Bodmer & Cavalli-Sforza 1976), though they do provide a containing barrier for population groupings, even within the species. The molecular mechanisms by which they operate are only partially understood, though it is clear that protein molecules are widely involved; they are now being investigated by biophysical techniques (Dwek et al. 1977; Amzel & Poliak 1979). The molecular background of the A, B, O and some other blood group systems is now reasonably worked out (Watkins 1972; Crumpton 1979; Porter 1979). In the A, B, O groups the operative determinant group is polysaccharide, carried on a protein–branched-chain polysaccharide supramolecule, with the small key determinant groups N-acetylgalactosamine or galactosamine attached to a specific position by specific protein–enzyme transferase systems (protein enzymes) (figure 6; Crumpton 1979). These complexes are heritable and should therefore be detectable as small changes in the genome DNA sequence. Each complex depends upon a chain of interacting protein systems, and once again the underlying protein biochemistry has to be fully explored to define the developing human genome.

Postnatal increase in brain size and in functional integration in specific regions is distinctive to man; how did these changes actually come about in molecular terms? Tobias (this symposium) has discussed the anatomy and timing of the hominizing brain size increase; we must now examine the cytomolecular processes involved. The trend could have been due to selection of slight modifications within the metabolic systems controlling the processes of mitosis, cell differentiation, cell cloning and cell-to-cell surface interactions in specific parts of the cerebral neocortex (figure 3; see above) in the postnatal regime (giving longer continuing mitosis, yielding larger clones of brain cells of the same type (cf. Truman 1974), with a more complex convoluted topology). These processes are better understood for other organs, such as kidney (cf. Wessels 1976). These cellular events could have been brought about by changes in balance between stimulation and restriction of production of particular enzyme or other protein or hormone systems, and have become stabilized in morphological evolution due to selection pressures, size being sometimes advantageous (cf. Pilbeam & Gould 1974). With this cellular modulation must also have been linked the corresponding modulation of control of postnatal bone growth to give a more capacious cranium.

For this increasing trend in brain size and the heightened organization to be heritable there must have been genomic variety in the DNA base-pair arrays through the population, controlling a change of balance in amounts of various proteins assembled at particular points in the metabolic cascade (Tsuboi *et al.* 1979). These would hardly be detectable (as between apes and man) at molecular level except in base-pair sequences, but the significant lengths can only be localized in the genome from a full basic knowledge of the cytochemistry of the brain cells involved. For this reason we await with great interest the expansions of the primate DNA sequencing work and correlations with the human genome reported by Jeffreys (this symposium).

The problems of defining the hominizing of the brain, however, must lie ultimately in studying the increasing synaptic organization of the multiple connections of the diverse cortical neurons; it is precisely these that are most difficult to systematize (Shepherd 1979). Recent work stresses the role of the hippocampus in learning processes and is beginning to reveal morphological changes in the dendritic spines (Shepherd 1979). The molecular basis of functioning of these highly specialized cell groupings now needs to be defined. It is not so much with the molecular neurotransmitters (nearly all small molecules that can penetrate membranes e.g. γ-amino-butyric acid, GABA) that we are concerned here, but with the processes of molecular, cell and tissue organization that can lead to the marshalling of neurosynaptic connections. These operations must be programmed by biomolecular systems, in which proteins will play a leading part (Krnjevic 1974; Shepherd 1979). Their detailed study in these tissues could be significant in mapping the emergence of the human genome.

The effects of *hormones* in the hominizing process must not be neglected; once again their biosynthesis is intimately dependent upon protein systems. The peptide hormones are particularly instructive. Neurohypophysial peptide hormones *vasopressin* and *oxytocin* are active in regulating memory consolidation and retrieval (de Wied 1980), and comparatively small modifications in their production rate in specific cerebral cell groups could have contributed to heightened ability to set and retain the image of given items in a particular sequence; this ability is stressed by Brown (this symposium) as a major higher hominizing capability. The evolution of such peptide molecules as vasopressin or oxytocin has proceeded by a complex series of interactions between the processes of precursor biosynthesis, with intermediate stages of modification, and proteolytic enzymes producing the final active hormone from the precursors. Duplication (with or without fusion) may also have been a strong influence in giving the necessary small required modulation to some protein operative in the system (Acher 1980). In such interplay between multiple systems small changes at one point could have had profound effects, giving evolutionary consolidation through selective pressures.

Professor Young (this symposium) draws attention to the long period of pre-puberty as a characteristic of man and its importance in giving a long childhood for learning. He then notes the possibly vital role of the pineal gland, and one of its hormone products, melatonin, is now known to regulate the onset of puberty (Niv *et al.* 1978). Production of melatonin (4-acetoxy-tryptamine) is controlled by specific protein systems.

We return once more to the higher activities of the human brain, which mark off man from other primates. Of these, the capability for sequential thought, and perhaps the fine nuances of muscular control that give the communicative potential of speech and of facial expression, are perhaps the most significant. Enhanced integration of signals, and particularly the ordered seriation and storage of responses, integrated with an equally efficient signal retrieval system, must underlie the processes of sequential thought. It is the detail of cellular and molecular processes through which these operate that we must try to understand. Twenty years ago Humphrey & Coxon (1963) wrote a book entitled *The chemistry of thinking*, and many of the problems there described still remain.. But it is the avowed aim of the neurosciences to provide a coherent account of the total performance and behaviour of an animal or man in cellular and molecular terms (McGeer & Eccles 1978). Enhanced integration of signals and particularly the ordered storage of responses and integrated retrieval are the facilities of the versatile brain capable of sequential thought. These must operate through an increasingly ordered synaptic neuron connections network. The biochemistry of the synaptic neuron connections will be basically the same; all the more highly marshalled grouping of responses and retrieval at will must operate ultimately through molecular processes. This could be through local surface concentration patterns of significant active substances (de Weid 1980), which could control cell-to-cell recognition. It is perhaps such cloned molecular groupings that should be sought in pursuing the molecular biology of sequential thought.

This overview of some aspects of the biochemistry of hominization, particularly stressing the role of proteins, is intended to suggest new lines of enquiry worth more concentrated attention in programming future research in human palaeobiology.

I wish to thank the following for particularly helpful discussions during the preparation of this paper: Dr R. J. Elliott, Professor D. T. Elmore, Dr A. Ferguson, Dr P. R. Laming, Professor L. T. Threadgold, Dr G. B. Wisdom (Belfast), Dr A. J. Jeffreys (Leicester), Professor C. G. Phillips (Oxford), Professor J. E. Scott (Manchester), Professor V. P. Whittaker (Göttingen), Professor J. Z. Young (London).

REFERENCES (Jope)

Acher, R. 1980 Molecular evolution of biologically active peptides. *Proc. R. Soc. Lond.* B **210**, 21–42.

Amzel, L. M. & Poljak, J. 1979 The three-dimensional structure of immunoglobulins. *A. Rev. Biochem.* **48**, 961–997.

Ayala, F. J. (ed.) 1976 *Molecular evolution.* Sunderland, Massachusetts: Sinnauer.

Barer, R, Holiday, E. R. & Jope, E. M. 1950 The technique of ultraviolet absorption spectroscopy with the Burch reflecting microscope. *Biochem. biophys. Acta* **6**, 123–134.

Bannerjee, S. D., Cohn, R. H. & Bernfield, M. R. 1977 Basal lamina of embryonic salivary epithelia: production by epithelium and role in maintaining lobular morphology. *J. Cell Biol.* **73**, 445–463.

Bernfield, M. R., Cohn, R. H. & Bannerjee, S. D. 1973 Glycosaminoglycans and epithelial organ formation. *Am. Zool.* **13**, 1067–1083.

Bodmer, W. F. & Cavalli-Sforza, L. L. 1976 *Genetics, evolution and man.* San Francisco: Freeman.

Bonner, J., Dahmus, M. E., Farnborough, D., Huang, R-C. C., Marushige, K. & Tuan, D. Y. H. 1968 The biology of isolated chromatin. *Science, N.Y.* **159**, 47–56.

Bornstein, P. & Nesse, R. 1970 The comparative biochemistry of collagens: the structure of rabbit skin collagen and its relevance to immunological studies of collagen. *Arch. Biochem. Biophys.* **138**, 143–150.

Bruce, E. J. & Ayala, F. J. 1978 Humans and apes are genetically very similar. *Nature, Lond.* **276**, 264–265.

Cohn, R. H., Bannerjee, S. D. & Bernfield, M. R. 1977 Basal lamina of embryonic salivary epithelia; nature of glycosaminoglycan and organization of extracellular materials. *J. Cell Biol.* **73**, 464–478.

Crumpton, J. R. 1979 Antigenicity and immunogenicity. In *Defence and recognition* (ed. R. R. Porter), pp. 143–155. Baltimore.

Cuetrecasas, P., Hillenberg, M. D., Chang, K.-J. & Bennet, V. 1975 Hormone receptor complexes and their modulation of membrane function. *Rec. Prog. Hormone Res.* **31**, 37.

Dwek, R. A., Wain-Hobson, S., Dower, S., Gettins, P., Sutton, R., Perkins, S. J. & Givol, D. 1977 Structure of an antibody-combining site by magnetic resonance. *Nature, Lond.* **266**, 31–37.

Elgin, S. C. R. & Weintraub, H. 1975 Chromosomal proteins and chromatin structure. *A. Rev. Biochem.* **22**, 725–774.

Elliott, R. J. & Gardner, D. I. 1980 Cartilage glycosaminoglycans; extraction, fractionation and measurement from 10 μm thick, layers. *Ann. rheum. Dis.* **39**, 100–102.

Ferguson, A. 1980 *Biochemical systematics and evolution.* Glasgow: Blackie.

Furthmayr, H. & Timpl, R. 1976 Immuno chemistry of collagens and procollagens. *Int. Rev. connect. Tiss. Res.* **7**, 61–101.

Gay, S. & Miller, E. J. 1978 *Collagen in the physiology and pathology of connect. Tiss. Res.* **8**, 159–226.

Grantham, R. & Gantier, C. 1980 Genetic distances from m-RNA sequences. *Naturwissenschaften* **67**, 93–94.

Hascall, U. C. & Heinegård, D. 1974 Aggregation of cartilage collagens. I. The role of hyaluronic acid. *J. Biol. Chem.* **249**, 4232–4244.

Harwood, R. 1979 Collagen polymorphism and messenger RNA. *Int. Rev. connect. Tiss. Res.* **8**, 159–226.

Hulmes, D. J. S., Miller, A., Parry, D. A. D., Piez, K. A. & Woodhead-Galloway, J. 1973 Analysis of the primary structure of collagen for the origin of molecular packing. *J. molec. Biol.* **79**, 137–148.

Humphrey, G. & Coxon, R. V. 1963 *The chemistry of thinking.* Illinois: Springfield.

Isenberg, I. 1979 Histones. *A. Rev. Biochem.* **48**, 159–191.

Jeffreys, A. J. 1980 Personal communication.

Jope, E. M. 1976 The evolutions of plants and animals under domestication: the contribution of studies at molecular level. *Phil. Trans. R. Soc. Lond.* B **275**, 99–116.

Jope, E. M. 1980 Ancient bone and plant proteins: the molecular state of preservation. In *Biogeochemistry of amino acids* (ed. D. E. Hare, T. C. Hoering & K. King), pp. 23–31. New York: Wiley.

Kedes, L. H. 1979 Histone genes and histone messengers. *A. Rev. Biochem.* **48**, 837–870.

King, M. C. & Wilson, C. A. 1975 Evolution at two levels in humans and chimpanzees. *Science, N.Y.* **188**, 107.

Krnjevic, K. 1974 Chemical nature of synaptic transmission in vertebrates. *Physiol. Rev.* **54**, 418–540.

Lwebuga-Mukasa, J. S., Lappi. S. & Taylor, P. 1976 Molecular forms of acetylcholinesterase from *Torpedo californica*: their relationship to synaptic membranes. *Biochemistry, Wash.* **15**, 1425.

McGeer, P. L. & Eccles, J. C. 1978 *The molecular neurobiology of the mammalian brain.* New York: Plenum Press.

Manuelidis, L. & Wu, J. C. 1978 Homology between human and simian repeated DNA. *Nature, Lond.* **276**, 92–94.

Miller, E. J. 1977 Biochemical characteristics and biological significance of the genetically distinct collagens. *Molec. cell. Biochem.* **13**, 165–192.

Moscana, A. A. (ed.) 1974 *The cell surface in development.* New York: Wiley.

Needham, J. 1942 *Biochemistry and morphogenesis.* Cambridge University Press.

Nei, M. 1975 *Molecular population genetics and evolution.* Amsterdam: North Holland.

Nei, M. & Roychoudhury, A. K. 1974 Genetic variations within and between the three major races of man. *Am. J. hum. Genet.* **26**, 421–448.

Newrock, K. M., Alfagema, C. R., Nardi, R. V. & Cohen, L. H. 1977 *Cold Spring Harb. Symp. quant. Biol.* **42**, 421–431.

Niv, I., Reiter, R. J. & Wurtman, R. J. (eds) 1978 Physiological control of melatonin synthesis and secretion. *J. neur. Transmiss.* **13** (suppl.), 59–70.

Ochoa, S. & de Haro, C. 1979 Regulation of protein synthesis in eukaryotes. *A. Rev. Biochem.* **48**, 549–580.

Penfield, W. & Rasmussen, F. 1950 *The cerebral cortex of man.* New York: Macmillan.

Piez, K. A. & Trus, B. L. 1978 Sequence regularities and packing of collagen molecules. *J. molec. Biol.* **122**, 419–432.

Pilbeam, D. & Gould, S. J. 1974 Scaling and size in human evolution. *Science, N.Y.* **186**, 892–901.

Porter, R. R. (ed.) 1979 *Defense and recognition.* M.P.T. int. Rev. Sci. Baltimore: University Park Press.

Porter, R. R. 1980 The complex proteins of the complement system. *Proc. R. Soc. Lond.* B **210**, 477–498.

Rakic, P. 1974 Neurons in the rhesus monkey visual cortex: relation between time of origin and eventual disposition. *Science, N.Y.* **183**, 425–427.

Scott, J. E. 1980 Hierarchical structures in connective tissues. *Connect. Tiss.* **11**, 111–120.

Shepherd, G. M. 1979 *The synaptic organization of the brain.* Oxford University Press.

Slavkin, H. C. & Bringas, P. 1976 Epithelial–mesenchyme interactions during odontogenesis. IV. Morphological evidence for direct heterotypic cell-cell contacts *Dvl Biol.* **50**, 428–442.

Smith, G. N., Toole, B. P. & Gross, J. 1975 Hyaluronidase activity and glycosaminoglycans synthesis in the amputated newt limb. *Devl Biol.* **43**, 221–232.

Tanzer, M. L. 1978 The biological diversity of collagenous proteins. *Trends biochem. Sci.* B **3** 15–17.

Thornley, A. C. & Lawrence, E. D. 1975 Chalones; glycoprotein mitosis inhibitors. *Int. J. Biochem.* **6**, 313.

Torchia, D. A. & Vanderhart, D. L. 1976 ^{13}C magnetic resonance evidence for anisotropic molecular motion in collagen fibrils. *J. molec. Biol.* **104**, 315–321.

Truman, D. E. S. 1974 *The biochemistry of cytodifferentiation.* Oxford: Blackwell.

Tsuboi, S. 1979 Glucocorticoid binding proteins, feedback control of ACTH secretion. *Brain Res.* **179**, 181–185.

Turner, C. G. 1976 Dental evidence on the origins of the Ainu and the Japanese. *Science, N.Y.* **181**, 911–913.

Volpin, D. & Veis, A. 1973 Cyanogen bromide peptides from insoluble skin and dentine bovine collagens. *Biochemistry, Wash.* **12**, 1452–1464.

Watkins, W. M. 1972 In *Glycoproteins* (ed. A. Gottschalk), ch. 7. Amsterdam: Elsevier.

Wessells, N. K. 1977 *Tissue interactions and development.* Menlo Park, California: Benjamin.

de Wied, D. 1980 Behavioural actions of neurohypophysial peptides. *Proc. R. Soc. Lond.* B **210**, 183–195.

Wyckoff, R. W. G. 1972 *The biochemistry of animal fossils.* Bristol: Scientechimica.

Zuckerkandl 1965 Evolution of hemoglobin. *Scient. Am.* **212**, 110–118.

Phil. Trans. R. Soc. Lond. B **292**, 133–142 (1981)   [**133**]
Printed in Great Britain

Sequence variation and evolution of nuclear DNA in man and the primates

By A. J. Jeffreys and P. A. Barrie

*Genetics Department, University of Leicester, University Road, Leicester LE*1 7*RH, U.K.*

Recent advances in nucleic acid technology have facilitated the detection and detailed structural analysis of a wide variety of genes in higher organisms, including those in man. This in turn has opened the way to an examination of the evolution of structural genes and their surrounding and intervening sequences. In a study of the evolution of haemoglobin genes and neighbouring sequences in man and the primates, we have investigated gene arrangement and DNA sequence divergence both within and between species ranging from Old World monkeys to man. This analysis is beginning to reveal the evolutionary constraints that have acted on this region of the genome during primate evolution. Furthermore, DNA sequence variation, both within and between species, provides, in principle, a novel and powerful method for determining interspecific phylogenetic distances and also for analysing the structure of present-day human populations. Application of this new branch of molecular biology to other areas of the human genome should prove important in unravelling the history of genetic changes that have occurred during the evolution of man.

Introduction

The biochemical, physiological, morphological and behavioural characteristics of any organism are largely determined by the precise nature of the genetic information inherited from its parents. Ultimately, this information can be specified as a set of nucleotide base pair sequences that together define the DNA sequence of the organism's entire genome. Once these sequences have been experimentally determined, it should be possible, at least in principle, to decipher them in terms of stretches of DNA coding for various RNAs and proteins, that is, structural genes, interspersed with additional DNA elements, whose role, in part or in whole, might be to modulate the expression of these genes. The precise DNA sequence of a given animal's genome depends on its particular parentage and ultimately on the detailed evolutionary history of the species. A comparison of DNA sequences between related species should therefore reveal the rates and detailed characteristics of genomic evolution at the molecular level.

In this paper we shall describe the various approaches to studying molecular evolution in primates, and show how new methods in nucleic acid technology, in particular the use of recombinant DNA, have provided a way to a detailed comparative study of nuclear DNA, both within human populations and between man and the primates.

Approaches to analysing genetic variation at the molecular level

All genetic variation, both within and between species, is ultimately due to variation in nucleotide sequences, primarily in the nuclear DNA. Intraspecific variation, between, for example, different human races, can give important clues to the relationship between racial groups and hence to the recent evolutionary history of man. Similarly, interspecific differences between man and primates can reveal rates of evolution, recent major events in the evolution of the human genome and possible genomic sequences of human ancestors. While neither approach can ever enable us to specify the detailed nucleotide sequence of a hominid ancestor, we should at least be able to define a constrained series of possible sequence types. Whether or not such possible ancestral sequences can ever be interpreted in terms of overall phenotypic effect will require an ability, as yet non-existent, to recognize control sequences in the genomic DNA of higher organisms and to understand their effect at the cellular and organismal level.

Since it has only very recently become possible to examine nuclear DNA sequences in detail, most work to date has centred on amino acid sequences of proteins, which in turn are specified by only a very limited fraction of total nuclear DNA. Comparisons of proteins in different humans by various electrophoretic and immunological techniques have revealed considerable genetic variation in amino acid sequence in many different proteins (Harris & Hopkinson 1972) and has contributed to our understanding of genetic variation between human races (Bodmer 1975). At the interspecific level, amino acid sequence comparisons of homologous proteins in man and the primates have shown a considerable similarity within the primates, as expected from their evolutionary relatedness (Dayhoff 1972). These similarities make it difficult to use such data to construct detailed molecular phylogenies of recent primate evolution. In an attempt to increase the resolving power of protein divergence, Sarich & Wilson (1968) have used microcomplement fixation assays to estimate immunological distances between complex sets of presumably homologous proteins isolated from various primates, and have used these distances to produce molecular phylogenies and to estimate divergence times of various primate groups in recent evolution.

Evidence is accumulating that non-coding nuclear DNA sequences have evolved more rapidly than structural gene sequences coding for proteins, perhaps as a result of the preferential elimination by selection of structural gene nucleotide substitutions that unfavourably alter the amino acid sequence of a protein (Gummerson & Williamson 1974; Van Ooyen et al. 1979; Konkel et al. 1979). It therefore follows that any attempt to examine evolution by comparing amino acid sequences will ignore what is probably the major reservoir of genetic variability between species, namely non-coding DNA. Furthermore, these regions are likely to contain control elements that modulate gene activity, and genetic variation within these elements might be crucial in generating altered gene regulation patterns that could result in profound phenotypic variation (King & Wilson 1975; Bruce & Ayala 1978).

There have been various approaches to studying primate evolution at the DNA level. Comparative karyotypic analyses of man and the primates have shown an evolutionary conservatism in gross chromosome organization, although interspecific differences, revealed particularly by chromosome banding techniques, have given useful phylogenetic information (De Grouchy et al. 1978). To study the molecular evolution of nuclear DNA sequences, Kohne (1970) has compared the relative sequence homologies of total nuclear DNA isolated from various primates. Nuclear DNAs from two different species were denatured, and the resulting single-stranded DNA preparations were mixed and annealed to produce interspecific hybrid duplex DNA. The reduction in melting point (ΔT_m) of these heteroduplexes, compared with perfectly matched double-stranded DNA isolated from one species, gave a measure of the reduced homology and therefore sequence divergence between nuclear DNAs from two species. It was found that related species had closely homologous DNAs, and that the overall degree of sequence divergence between two species varied in a phylogenetically consistent fashion. From such measurements, a molecular phylogeny of primate evolution could be constructed.

Both DNA ΔT_{m} analysis and estimates of immunological distance of proteins by micro-complement fixation revealed, surprisingly, what appeared to be a reduced rate of molecular divergence in recent primate evolution. This has been interpreted as evidence that macro-molecular sequences do not evolve in a clock-like mode, and that for some reason the rate of occurrence and/or fixation of genetic variation has indeed declined in recent primate evolution. Alternatively, it is possible that divergence times for various primate subgroups have been estimated incorrectly from palaeontological evidence, and that the evolutionary clock rate has been constant within primate species, which have diverged in evolution much more recently than has hitherto been supposed (Simons 1969; Wilson *et al.* 1978).

Estimation of homologies between primate DNAs by interspecific nucleic acid reannealing (Kohne 1970) gives no information about the detailed character of sequence divergence between related genomes. To overcome this problem, simple subfractions of cellular DNA have been compared in detail among various primates. Brown *et al.* (1979) have mapped the cleavage sites for 11 different restriction endonucleases in mitochondrial DNA isolated from man and from various Old World monkeys. They find clear interspecific homologies between the maps of this simple (16 400 base pairs) circular organelle DNA, and deduce that no gross rearrange-ments of the mitochondrial genome have occurred within the group of species examined. They use cleavage site map differences to calculate the overall degree of DNA sequence divergence and find that the interspecific differences in mitochondrial DNA sequences are considerably greater (4–17-fold) than in nuclear DNA. Why mitochondrial DNA should evolve so rapidly is unknown, and therefore the use of mitochondrial DNA as a model for nuclear DNA evolution should be treated with caution. Furthermore, the observed interspecific divergence of this DNA appears to be relatively insensitive to phylogenetic distance.

To date, the only comparisons of specific nuclear DNA sequences between various primates have been made on simple, highly repetitive DNAs (Manuelidis & Wu 1978; Donehower & Gillespie 1979; Singer & Donehower 1979). These enigmatic tandem repetitive elements show considerable variation between primate species and can also vary within a single block of tandem repeats in one species. Since mechanisms probably exist that enable such sequence families to expand and contract rapidly in evolution, these repetitive elements are unlikely to be suitable models for overall nuclear DNA evolution.

ANALYSIS OF SINGLE COPY STRUCTURAL GENES IN HUMAN DNA

The enormous complexity of human DNA, with a haploid genome size of 3×10^9 base pairs, has until recently precluded any analysis of structural genes present in one copy per haploid genome. However, recent advances in recombinant DNA technology have enabled us to examine in detail small selected parts of the human genome and to begin to characterize both structural genes and the DNA sequences that separate them.

To date, the best characterized set of human genes are those that code for the globin poly-peptides of haemoglobin. In the human foetus, the major species of haemoglobin is HbF (a mixture of $\alpha_2^G \gamma_2$ and $\alpha_2^A \gamma_2$ tetramers). At birth, HbF is replaced by adult haemoglobin (HbA, $\alpha_2 \beta_2$, plus a low level of HbA$_2$, $\alpha_2 \delta_2$). These various related haemoglobins are encoded by corresponding α-, β-, γ- and δ-globin genes. The α-globin genes remain expressed throughout foetal and adult life; in contrast, there is a switch from $^G\gamma$- and $^A\gamma$- to β- and δ-globin gene expression towards the end of gestation (see Weatherall & Clegg 1979).

Messenger RNAs for α-, β- and γ-globins have been isolated from foetal and adult reticulocytes and have been copied into double-stranded complementary DNA (cDNA) by means of reverse transcriptase. These globin cDNAs have been inserted into plasmid vectors and cloned to provide recombinant globin cDNAs, each plasmid containing a totally pure DNA copy of α-, β- or γ-globin messenger RNA (Little *et al.* 1978). Since a globin cDNA sequence is homologous with its corresponding structural gene, these cloned cDNAs have been of enormous use in the detection of human globin genes.

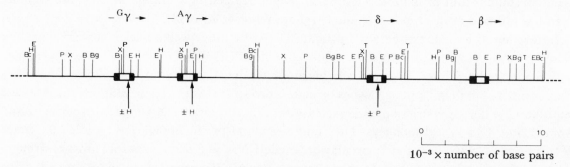

FIGURE 1. A physical map of restriction endonuclease cleavage sites around the human γ-, δ- and β-globin genes. Data for this map were taken from Flavell *et al.* (1978), Little *et al.* (1979), Bernards *et al.* (1979) and Jeffreys (1979). The positions of coding sequences are indicated by closed boxes, and those of major intervening sequences by open boxes. The direction of transcription is shown by horizontal arrows. Cleavage sites that show no polymorphic variation in northern Europeans are shown above the map for restriction endonucleases *Bam* HI (B), *Bcl* I (Bc), *Bgl* II (Bg), *Eco* RI (E), *Hind* III (H), *Pst* I (P), *Taq* YI (T) and *Xba* I (X). Endonuclease *Taq* YI cleavage sites near the ᴳγ- and ᴬγ-globin genes have not yet been mapped. It should be stressed that this map was deduced from Southern blot analyses of globin DNA fragments present in restriction endonuclease digests of total human DNA, and therefore only cleavage sites that generate fragments containing globin genes are shown here. Additional cleavage sites that show a presence/absence of polymorphic variation in northern Europeans are indicated by vertical arrows (Jeffreys 1979).

Globin genes can be detected in total human DNA by means of cloned cDNAs as nucleic acid hybridization probes. Human DNA is cleaved with a restriction endonuclease and denatured, and the complex series of digest products are fractionated according to size by electrophoresis through an agarose gel. DNA fragments are transferred from the gel to a nitrocellulose filter by blotting (Southern 1975) and the filter is hybridized with ³²P-labelled cloned globin cDNA. The probe binds only to the corresponding structural gene sequence, and the restriction endonuclease fragment of human DNA that contains this globin gene can be detected by subsequent autoradiography of the filter. By means of this approach, a cloned β-globin cDNA is found to detect human DNA fragments containing the closely homologous β- and δ-globin genes. Similarly, γ-globin cDNA detects ᴳγ- and ᴬγ-globin gene fragments. Comparison of these fragments in human DNA digested with various combinations of different restriction endonucleases enables us to arrange these fragments into a physical map of cleavage sites around these non-α-globin genes (Flavell *et al.* 1978; Little *et al.* 1979; Bernards *et al.* 1979).

Figure 1 shows the physical map of the human ᴳγ-, ᴬγ-, δ- and β-globin genes. All four genes are closely linked to each other and each is interrupted by at least one intervening sequence. There are also substantial tracts of DNA separating these genes; the function of this intergenic DNA is unknown, although it seems likely that these sequences, in part or in whole, will be involved in globin gene expression and regulation of, for example, the γ to β switch at birth (Fritsch *et al.* 1979).

This arrangement of the human γ- and β-globin genes has been confirmed by examining cloned genomic DNA. Human DNA cleaved with a restriction endonuclease has been inserted into a λ bacteriophage vector. Subsequent growth in *Escherichia coli* of a sufficient number of different λ–human DNA recombinants gives a 'library' of cloned human DNA fragments covering most of the human genome. The library can then be screened for bacteriophage containing the human DNA sequence of interest. By this approach, fragments of human DNA containing β-related globin genes have been purified (Lawn *et al.* 1978). This purification opens the way to a detailed fine-structure analysis of this small region of the human genome.

VARIATIONS IN DNA SEQUENCE BETWEEN INDIVIDUALS

As already noted, virtually all genetic variation within a population can ultimately be traced back to individual variation of nuclear DNA sequences. It is therefore important to establish just how much individual variation occurs at this fundamental level. This could be determined by cloning β-globin genes from various individuals and directly comparing their sequences, at the moment an exceedingly onerous task. Alternatively we could screen for DNA sequence variants that by chance create or destroy restriction endonuclease cleavage sites near globin genes; such variants would cause an alteration of globin restriction fragment size, which could be detected in a restriction endonuclease digest of total human DNA, with cloned globin cDNAs as probes for globin genes. An extensive screening of 60 unrelated individuals, mainly northern Europeans, showed that almost all the restriction endonuclease cleavage sites round the β-related globin genes shown in figure 1 are invariant (Jeffreys 1979). Of 52–54 different cleavage sites examined, only three showed a presence/absence polymorphic variation in northern Europeans. Curiously, all three variant sites were within intervening sequences (figure 1), suggesting that genetic variation might be accumulating preferentially in these sections of the genome.

This survey indicated that, on average, approximately one base pair in every 100 in this region of the genome varies polymorphically in the population screened, although few of these variants will create or destroy a detectable restriction enzyme site. Also, the actual level of sequence divergence between two randomly selected chromosomes will be less than one base pair per 100, since both chromosomes will possess identical alleles at the majority of variable loci.

These variant restriction endonuclease cleavage sites provide a major new type of human genetic marker. This type of screening analysis could be repeated for any section of single copy human DNA, with random cloned fragments of human DNA, even those of completely unknown function, as probes. This approach would provide enormous numbers of variant sequence markers in all parts of the human genome. We are currently investigating racial variation in gene frequencies of the globin markers; it is likely that, as with proteins, gene frequencies will be markedly race-dependent and will provide important clues to the relationships between various human races, and their origins.

GLOBIN GENES AND SURROUNDING SEQUENCES IN PRIMATES

The β-globin genes of man have now been well characterized, both in terms of gene structure and organization and in terms of genetic variability within man (albeit to date only within northern Europeans). We were therefore interested in comparing this area of the human genome with the homologous region of primate DNAs.

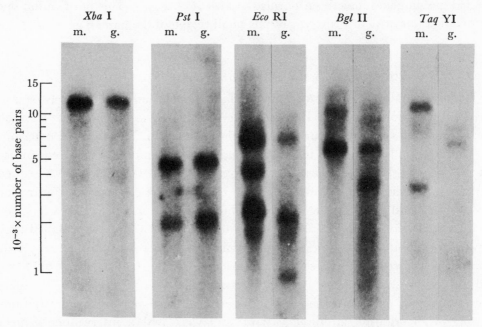

FIGURE 2. A comparison of β- and δ-globin DNA fragments produced by restriction endonuclease cleavage of human and gorilla DNA. Samples (15 μg) of human (m.) and western lowland gorilla (*Gorilla gorilla gorilla*) (g.) white blood cell DNA were cleaved with the indicated restriction endonucleases, alkali-denatured and electrophoresed through a 1 % (by mass) agarose gel; DNA fragments were then transferred, by blotting, to a nitrocellulose filter. Fragments containing the β- and δ-globin genes were labelled by hybridizing the filter with ³²P-labelled cloned human β-globin cDNA (plasmid pHβG1; Little *et al.* 1978) and labelled fragments were detected by autoradiography (see Jeffreys (1979) for experimental details).

We first compared human and gorilla globin genes. Total human and gorilla DNAs were cleaved with a restriction endonuclease, DNA fragments were separated by agarose gel electrophoresis and blotted onto a nitrocellulose filter. Fragments of β- and δ-globin DNA were detected by hybridization with ³²P-labelled cloned human β-globin cDNA (figure 2). Certain restriction endonucleases (*Xba* I, *Pst* I) gave patterns of β- and δ-globin DNA fragments that were indistinguishable between man and gorilla. This immediately shows that the gorilla also has one β- and one δ-globin gene, and that the arrangement of these genes is, within the resolution of the system, identical in the two species. Other restriction enzymes generate patterns of β- and δ-globin DNA fragments that differ to a greater or lesser extent between man and gorilla. This is evidence of sequence divergence accumulating between the two species' DNA, sufficient to create or destroy a fraction of the restriction endonuclease cleavage sites. Detailed mapping of gorilla β-globin genes gives the physical map shown in figure 4. As can be seen, sufficient divergence has occurred to cause about 16 % of cleavage sites to differ between the two species (table 1).

We extended this analysis to the yellow baboon, a representative of the Old World monkeys.

We were concerned that human and baboon DNAs have diverged so far that human β-globin cDNA would fail to detect the homologous baboon genes in total baboon DNA. Figure 3 shows that human and baboon β-globin DNA sequences have in fact been well conserved. By subjecting filters to post-hybridization washes of increased stringency (by progressively lowering the ionic strength of the washing solution), we can examine the stability of DNA hybrids made

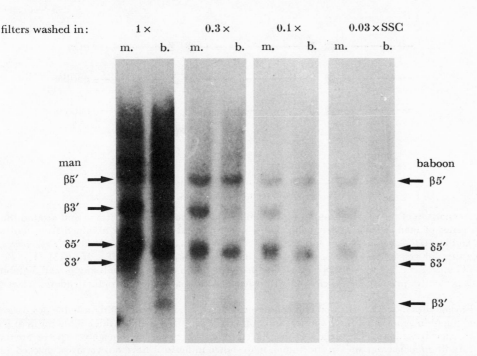

FIGURE 3. Detection of β-globin DNA fragments in restriction endonuclease digests of baboon DNA. DNA samples prepared from man and from a yellow baboon (*Papio cynocephalus*) were digested with restriction endonuclease *Eco* RI. Human (m.) and baboon (b.) digests were alkali-denatured, electrophoresed through a 1 % (by mass) agarose gel and transferred to a nitrocellulose filter. The filter was hybridized with ^{32}P-labelled pHβG1 DNA at 65 °C in 3 × SSC (1 × SSC = saline sodium citrate: 0.15 M NaCl, 15 mM trisodium citrate (pH 7.0)). Unbound label was then removed by washing in 1 × SSC at 65 °C. Identical filters were given a subsequent higher stringency wash in 1 ×, 0.3 ×, 0.1 × or 0.03 × SSC at 65 °C and remaining labelled globin DNA fragments were detected by autoradiography. Since endonuclease *Eco* RI cleaves within both the δ- and β-globin gene, each gene gives rise to two hybridizable fragments (see figure 1). The autoradiographic positions of the resultant δ5', δ3', β5' and β3' globin DNA fragments are indicated; all fragments except the β3' fragment appear identical in the two species (see figure 4).

between baboon globin genes and the human β-globin cDNA probe. Only at the highest stringency (0.03 × SSC at 65 °C, see figure 3) is there preferential loss of heterologous man–baboon DNA hybrids; at lower stringencies the human probe is capable of detecting specifically the baboon genes. At the lowest stringency (1 × SSC at 65 °C) additional human and baboon DNA fragments become labelled; these fragments contain ^{G}γ- and ^{A}γ-globin genes which show partial homology to β-globin cDNA.

All β-globin DNA fragments detected in baboon and human DNA cleaved with *Eco* RI are identical except for one. This again establishes that the baboon contains both a β- and a δ-globin gene. Detailed mapping of baboon DNA shows that these genes are arranged as in man and gorilla, but that a substantial divergence of cleavage sites has occurred between the baboon and gorilla/man (figure 4; table 1). Extension of this analysis to the ^{G}γ- and ^{A}γ-globin

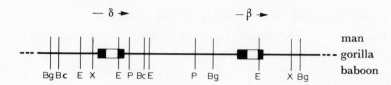

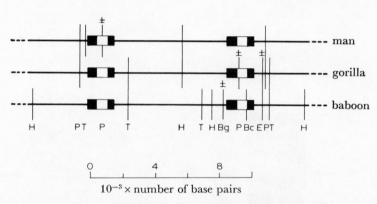

$10^{-3} \times$ number of base pairs

FIGURE 4. A comparison of the physical maps of restriction endonuclease cleavage sites in and around the δ- and β-globin genes of man, gorilla and baboon. DNA was prepared from blood obtained from four western lowland gorillas (*Gorilla gorilla gorilla*) and from liver removed from a single yellow baboon (*Papio cynocephalus*). Cleavage sites for restriction endonucleases *Bcl* I (Bc), *Bgl* II (Bg), *Eco* RI (E), *Hind* III (H), *Pst* I (P), *Taq* YI (T) and *Xba* I (X) were mapped near the β- and δ-globin genes, by analysing β- and δ-globin DNA fragments present in primate DNAs cleaved with various combinations of restriction endonucleases (figures 2, 3).

The cleavage sites shown are divided into conserved sites, which map to indistinguishable positions around the δ- and β-globin genes in all three species, and non-conserved sites, each of which is absent in at least one of the three species examined. Cleavage sites that have been shown to vary within a given species are indicated thus: ± . Additional cleavage sites in the human map shown in figure 1 have not yet been checked across all three species, and are therefore omitted.

TABLE 1. DNA SEQUENCE DIVERGENCE IN THE β-GLOBIN LOCI OF VARIOUS PRIMATES

	percentage difference in:			
	β- and δ-globin genes		total genome:	
	cleavage sites †	DNA sequence‡	DNA sequence §	
man–man‖	3	< 1	—	
man–gorilla	16	3	2.6	man–chimpanzee
man–baboon	44	10	10.5	man–green monkey
gorilla–baboon	33	7	10.8	chimpanzee–green monkey

† Percentage difference in cleavage sites taken from figures 1 and 4. A polymorphic site is scored as a half difference.

‡ Calculated from the cleavage site variation by the method of Upholt (1977).

§ Total genomic DNA sequence divergence of corresponding man–great ape–Old World monkey pairs derived from ΔT_m measurements (data taken from Kohne (1970)).

‖ Cleavage site and DNA sequence variation found within man (northern European) (Jeffreys 1979), scoring polymorphic sites as half differences.

genes has shown that the entire topology of the β-related globin gene region shown in figure 1 is indistinguishable between man, gorilla and baboon.

Despite the small number of primate individuals examined, intraspecific variant cleavage sites have been detected (figure 4), including a *Pst* I cleavage site within the major intervening sequence of the β-globin gene in gorilla. There is a curious polymorphism in gorilla for the presence/absence of an *Eco* RI cleavage site to the 3' side of the β-globin gene. This site is present in all species of Old World monkey so far examined, but is absent in man. The gorilla would thus appear to represent a species in some way intermediate for this site between monkeys and man.

The degree of cleavage site divergence can be used to calculate an approximate extent of overall sequence divergence between two species (table 1). As seen, the degree of interspecific divergence is considerably greater than that seen within a human population and seems to vary in a phylogenetically consistent fashion; thus man and gorilla show a greater map homology than does either species compared with baboon. Furthermore, the divergence of sequence homology near the β- and δ-globin genes is similar to overall genomic DNA sequence divergence calculated from ΔT_m measurements (Kohne 1970). The β-globin DNA region of the primates seems therefore to have evolved at a rate similar to that of the entire genome.

THE FUTURE

This comparison of primate β-globin genes has shown a region of DNA whose topology has remained invariant over tens of millions of years, yet has accumulated genetic divergence that should prove useful in estimating phylogenetic distances. This analysis could be repeated with any single copy region of the genome to produce refined and testable divergence estimates for primate phylogenies. We are also extending this analysis further back to prosimians, to search for events such as gene duplication that have been crucial in moulding the contemporary arrangement of these genes.

The advantage of studying DNA over proteins is already apparent: the amino acid sequences of primate globin polypeptides show little variation, yet by analysing globin DNA, we can detect genetic variation within and between genes that is probably never expressed at the protein level. We should stress, however, that the phenotypic significance of these interspecies variants is not clear; it is possible that these variants have become fixed in evolution by chance and do not contribute to the phenotypic difference between two species. Current DNA technology makes it at least theoretically possible to sequence, for example, the entire human and gorilla genomes. Within the two sequences will be differences that are instrumental in determining the characteristics of a man or a great ape. Whether we could ever be able to recognize such sequences would require an understanding of DNA sequences that we do not yet possess. Ultimately, it might be possible to test for important sequence differences by introducing selected human DNA sequences into a great ape zygote and observing the effects of this genetic alteration on the phenotype of the offspring; however, such an approach is likely to be precluded on both technical and ethical grounds.

P. A. B. is the recipient of a research scholarship from the University of Leicester.

REFERENCES

Bernards, R., Little, P. F. R., Annison, G., Williamson, R. & Flavell, R. A. 1979 Structure of the human $^G\gamma$- $^A\gamma$- δ -β-globin gene locus. *Proc. natn. Acad. Sci. U.S.A.* **76**, 4827–4831.

Bodmer, W. F. 1975 Genetic markers, evolution and selection. In *Transfusion and Immunology Plenary Session Lectures of the Fourteenth Congress of the International Society of Blood Transfusion and the Tenth Congress of the World Federation of Hemophilia* (ed. E. E. Ikkala & A. Nykanen), pp. 35–46. Helsinki: Vammala.

Brown, W. M., George, M. & Wilson, A. C. 1979 Rapid evolution of animal mitochondrial DNA. *Proc. natn. Acad. Sci. U.S.A.* **76**, 1967–1971.

Bruce, E. J. & Ayala, F. J. 1978 Humans and apes are genetically very similar. *Nature, Lond.* **276**, 264–265.

Dayhoff, M. O. (ed.) 1972 *Atlas of protein sequence and structure*, vol. 5. Silver Spring, Maryland: National Biomedical Research Foundation.

De Grouchy, J., Turleau, C. & Finaz, C. 1978 Chromosome phylogeny of the primates. *A. Rev. Genet.* **12**, 289–328.

Donehower, L. & Gillespie, D. 1979 Restriction site periodicities in highly repetitive DNA of primates. *J. molec. Biol.* **134**, 805–834.

Flavell, R. A., Kooter, J. M., De Boer, E., Little, P. F. R. & Williamson, R. 1978 Analysis of the β-δ-globin gene loci in normal and Hb Lepore DNA: direct determination of gene linkage and intergene distance. *Cell* **15**, 25–41.

Fritsch, E. F., Lawn, R. M. & Maniatis, T. 1979 Characterisation of deletions which affect the expression of fetal globin genes in man. *Nature, Lond.* **279**, 598–603.

Gummerson, K. S. & Williamson, R. 1974 Sequence divergence of mammalian globin messenger RNA. *Nature, Lond.* **247**, 265–267.

Harris, H. & Hopkinson, D. A. 1972 Average heterozygosity per locus in man: an estimate based on the incidence of enzyme polymorphisms. *Ann. hum. Genet.* **36**, 9–19.

Jeffreys, A. J. 1979 DNA sequence variants in the $^G\gamma$-, $^A\gamma$-, δ- and β-globin genes of man. *Cell* **18**, 1–10.

King, M. C. & Wilson, A. C. 1975 Evolution at two levels in humans and chimpanzees. *Science, N.Y.* **188**, 107–116.

Kohne, D. E. 1970 Evolution of higher-organism DNA. *Q. Rev. Biophys.* **3**, 327–375.

Konkel, A. D., Maizel, J. V. & Leder, P. 1979 The evolution and sequence comparison of two recently diverged mouse chromosomal β-globin genes. *Cell* **18**, 865–873.

Lawn, R. M., Fritsch, E. F., Parker, R. C., Blake, G. & Maniatis, T. 1978 The isolation and characterization of linked δ- and β-globin genes from a cloned library of human DNA. *Cell* **15**, 25–41.

Little, P. F. R., Curtis, P., Coutelle, C., Van Den Berg, J., Dalgleish, R., Malcolm, S., Courtney, M., Westaway, D. & Williamson, R. 1978 Isolation and partial sequence of recombinant plasmids containing human α-, β- and γ-globin cDNA fragments. *Nature, Lond.* **273**, 640–643.

Little, P. F. R., Flavell, R. A., Kooter, J. M., Annison, G. & Williamson, R. 1979 Structure of the human foetal globin gene locus. *Nature, Lond.* **278**, 227–231.

Manuelidis, L. & Wu, J. C. 1978 Homology between human and simian repeated DNA. *Nature, Lond.* **276**, 92–94.

Sarich, V. M. & Wilson, A. C. 1968 Immunological time scale for hominid evolution. *Science, N.Y.* **158**, 1200–1202.

Simons, E. L. 1969 The origin and radiation of the primates. *Ann. N.Y. Acad. Sci.* **167**, 319–331.

Singer, D. & Donehower, L. 1979 Highly repeated DNA of the baboon: organization of sequences homologous to highly repeated DNA of the African green monkey. *J. molec. Biol.* **134**, 835–842.

Southern, E. M. 1975 Detection of specific sequences among DNA fragments separated by gel electrophoresis. *J. molec. Biol.* **93**, 503–517.

Upholt, W. B. 1977 Estimation of DNA sequence divergence from comparison of restriction endonuclease digests. *Nucl. Acids Res.* **4**, 1257–1265.

Van Ooyen, A., Van Den Berg, J., Mantei, N. & Weissmann, C. 1979 Comparison of total sequence of a cloned rabbit β-globin gene and its flanking regions with a homologous mouse sequence. *Science, N.Y.* **206**, 337–344.

Weatherall, D. J. & Clegg, J. B. 1979 Recent developments in the molecular genetics of human hemoglobin. *Cell* **16**, 467–479.

Wilson, A. C., Carlson, S. S. & White, T. J. 1978 Biochemical evolution. *A. Rev. Biochem.* **48**, 573–639.

Phil. Trans. R. Soc. Lond. B **292**, 143–149 (1981)   [143]
Printed in Great Britain

Immunological reactions from fossil material

By J. M. Lowenstein

122 *MR2, University of California School of Medicine, Department of Medicine,
San Francisco, California* 94143, *U.S.A.*

Genetic relations among living species can be deduced from biochemical as well as morphological similarities, but our understanding of fossil species has depended entirely on their morphology. Residual proteins in fossils might provide genetic information, but their small quantity and chemical alterations due to time and environmental agents have prevented the obtaining of species-specific analysis. This report describes a radioimmunoassay capable of detecting extremely small amounts of fossil proteins, such as collagen and albumin. Species-specific proteins have been identified in a frozen Siberian mammoth, a Pleistocene bison, and a series of human fossils that includes Neanderthal, *Homo erectus* and *Australopithecus robustus*. This technique promises to provide molecular data on the genetic affinities of fossil and living species.

Introduction

Study of organic evolution by means of the comparative anatomy of fossil and living species is limited in its precision by at least two factors: the unavoidably subjective element in anatomical interpretation, and the varying rates of morphological change in different lineages. Biochemical comparison of different species minimizes the subjective factor, for base or amino acid sequences, or immunological reactions, can be replicated in many laboratories. Furthermore, there is increasing evidence that, unlike morphological change, the rate of DNA base substitutions, and hence of amino acid substitutions in proteins, is a fairly constant function of time, so that the number of differences in the comparable DNA or proteins of two species is a measure of their time of divergence from a common ancestor (Wilson *et al.* 1977). Frogs, for example, have changed morphologically relatively little in the past 100 Ma in comparison to all the placental mammals, in particular the primates. Yet frog proteins have undergone as much change during this interval as those of mammals (Wilson *et al.* 1977).

Phylogenetic trees constructed from the biochemical similarities of homologous DNA and proteins have helped to clarify the evolutionary relations of living species (Ayala 1976), but our understanding of fossil species has continued to depend almost exclusively on their anatomical characteristics. In some cases, the conclusions drawn from biochemical and anatomical data are irreconcilable, as in the question of the phyletic status of the Miocene hominoid *Ramapithecus*, considered by many anthropologists to be a hominid (Simons 1977). Analysis of DNA and 40 different proteins shows 99 % identity between humans and chimpanzees (King & Wilson 1975). Sarich & Cronin (1976) find equal closeness between human, chimpanzee and gorilla proteins, based on the immunological cross reactions of the albumins and transferrins, and conclude that the three species diverged from a common ancestor about 5 Ma ago. If this is correct, then *Ramapithecus*, which lived some 8–20 Ma ago, could not have been 'human' (Zihlman & Lowenstein 1979). The issue continues to be disputed whether DNA and proteins, or fossil jaws and teeth, are the best criteria for phyletic status.

This controversy, like many others in evolution, might be clarified if one could make biochemical as well as morphological comparisons between the fossil and the living species. Biochemical analyses of fossils, consisting mostly of amino acid abundances, have not yielded species-specific information due to the small quantity of residual proteins and the chemical changes that they have undergone (Wyckoff 1972). When I began this project about three years ago, I hoped to overcome both the quantitative and the qualitative problem by developing a radioimmunoassay for fossil collagen. With radioimmunoassay it is possible to measure even tiny amounts (nanograms or picograms) of proteins, and I reasoned that even broken down proteins might retain some of their original species-specific sequences. Collagen is the principal protein of bone (about 20 % of fresh bone) and is so tough and insoluble that collagen fibrils have been seen by electron microscopy in dinosaurs 200 Ma old (Wyckoff 1972). While testing fossils for collagen, I used antisera to albumin as a control and discovered, to my surprise, that serum factors as well as collagen may survive in fossils for millions of years.

MATERIAL AND METHODS

A solid phase radioimmunoassay was developed for collagen, albumin and other proteins (Lowenstein 1980). First, the fossil extract or protein solution is pipetted into the cups of a polyvinyl microtitre plate, allowed to remain for 1 h at room temperature, then washed out. Secondly, rabbit antibody to the specific protein is pipetted into the cup, allowed to remain for 24 h, then washed out. Finally, ^{125}I-labelled goat anti-rabbit gamma globulin (GARGG) is placed in the cups, allowed to remain for 24 h, then washed out. The cups are cut from the plate and the radioactivity measured in a scintillation counter. In this double antibody assay, radioactivity increases with the amount of the target protein in the cup. First, some of the protein binds irreversibly to the plastic. Secondly, some of the rabbit antibody binds to the protein. Finally, the radioactive goat antibody binds to the rabbit antibody.

Collagen was extracted from the skin of various species by acetic acid 0.5 M and purified by repeated salt precipitation. Antibodies were raised in rabbits by intramuscular injection of 5 mg of type I collagen dissolved in 1 ml of acetic acid (0.05 M), emulsified with Freund's complete adjuvant. After 3 weeks, a second intraperitoneal injection of 5 mg of collagen without adjuvant was given, and the rabbits were bled 2–3 weeks later. Antibodies to mummy and *Homo erectus* fossil bone were made by injecting rabbits with a mixture of fossil extracts and insoluble residue. The albumins and anti-albumins, as well as the mammoth muscle extract and anti-mammoth serum were obtained from Dr V. M. Sarich, Dr E. M. Prager and Dr A. C. Wilson, Biochemistry Department, University of California, Berkeley. Fossil bone fragments were ground to a fine powder and extracted for 1 week at room temperature with EDTA (0.2 M, pH 7.4), to decalcify. The residue was further extracted for 1 week with acetic acid, 0.5 M. The EDTA and acetic acid extracts were tested by radioimmunoassay for collagen and albumin.

RESULTS

First it was necessary to establish that collagen evolution follows a pattern similar to that of other proteins. Collagen, the main structural protein of metazoans, from sponges to man, is a triple helix with approximately 1000 amino acids in each helix and with extensive homology between species (Balazs 1970). Every third amino acid is glycine and 10–15 % are hydroxyproline. Mammalian collagens differ among themselves in amino acid composition by only about 5% (Fietzek & Kuhn 1976). In looking for species differences, the immunological approach has advantages over direct sequencing, in that the rabbit makes antibodies mostly against those determinants that differ from its own collagen and so amplifies the differences while minimizing the homology (Furthmayr & Timpl 1976).

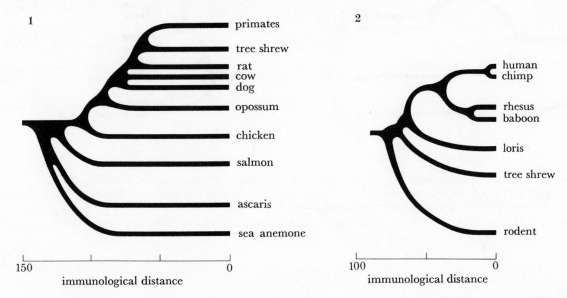

FIGURE 1. Collagen phylogeny constructed from immunological cross reactions (l.c.). Immunological distance, $D_1 = -100 \lg C_1$, where C_1 is a measure of cross reaction between two species, by radioimmunoassay; cross reactions between mammals and invertebrates are detectable.

FIGURE 2. Primate collagen phylogeny. As is true for many other proteins, human and chimpanzee collagens are nearly identical.

As has been done with many other proteins, I have constructed a collagen phylogeny (figures 1, 2) based on cross reactions between species, ranging from sea anemone to primates. For comparison, the albumin phylogeny, determined by the same radioimmunoassay technique, is shown in figure 3 and 4. Both agree as to the near identity of the proteins of humans and African apes. These results differ from previous immunological phylogenies only in that the standard methods, immunodiffusion and complement fixation, fail to give cross reactions when the divergence times of two species are greater than *ca.* 100 Ma. The sensitivity of the radioimmunoassay makes it possible to detect cross reactions between protein species that have been evolving separately for hundreds of millions of years. In figure 5, the immunological distances (defined in the legend to figure 1) are calibrated against time for those species having reasonably good geological dating. The primates, the most disputed group, are interpolated. Values for the last 100 Ma, for collagen and albumin, are nearly identical. The collagen curve tends toward its asymptotic limit sooner than the albumin curve does, because of the relative weakness of anti-collagen antibodies (Furthmayr & Timpl 1976). Nevertheless, cross reactions between human and invertebrate collagens can be detected. In principle, a fossil species might be placed on one of the phylogenetic trees by its relative distance from the living species. Before this can be done in practice, however, more needs to be known about the effects on apparent immunological distances due to degenerative changes in fossil proteins.

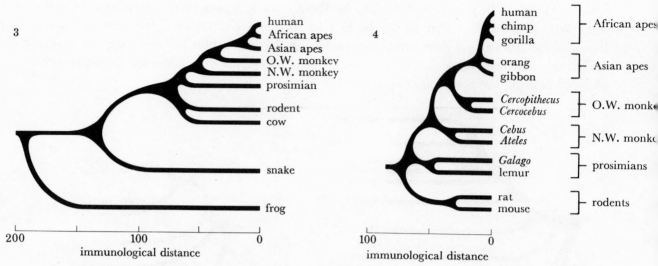

FIGURE 3. Albumin phylogeny constructed from radioimmunoassay data. This is similar to albumin trees generated from other immunological techniques, with the difference that radioimmunoassay detects cross reactions between species that diverged more than 100 Ma ago.

FIGURE 4. Primate albumin phylogeny, very similar to the collagen phylogeny. Again the human protein groups are nearly identical to the protein group of the African apes.

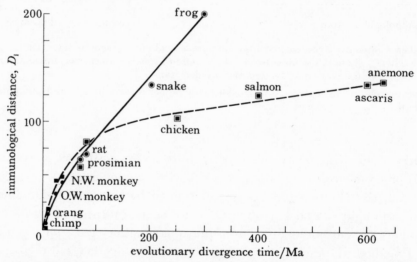

FIGURE 5. Time calibration of immunological distance (from human): ◉, ▣, geological divergence times; ●, ——, albumin; ■, ----, collagen. Values up to about 100 Ma are nearly identical for collagen and albumin. Anti-collagen antibodies are weaker and so approach their asymptotic limit earlier.

I have applied this radioimmunoassay to the detection of residual proteins in a variety of fossils. The most likely fossil in which to find albumin would be a frozen mammoth, for the soft tissues as well as the bones are preserved at a temperature that minimizes protein breakdown. The baby mammoth known as Dima was discovered near Magadan, U.S.S.R., in 1977, and refrigerated immediately. The Evolutionary Biochemistry Group at the University of California, Berkeley, obtained a piece of muscle from this mammoth and attempted to identify albumin by micro-complement fixation and immunodiffusion. Though these efforts were initially unsuccessful, homogenized muscle injected into rabbits evoked antibodies that reacted with elephant albumin, indicating that mammoth albumin was present in small amounts. Using the

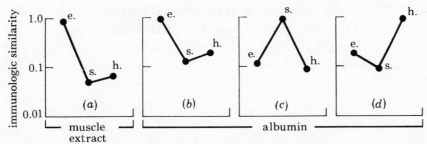

FIGURE 6. Immunological similarity of mammoth and elephant albumin: Muscle extracts from the frozen baby mammoth Dima (*a*), ^{14}C date 44 ka B.P., has anti-albumin reactions nearly identical with those of elephant albumin (*b*) and quite different from those of the sea cow (*c*) (a distant relative of the elephant) and human (*d*) albumin. A value of 1.0 indicates immunological identity, 0 indicates no cross reaction.

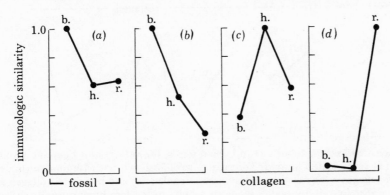

FIGURE 7. Immunological similarity of fossil bison and bovine collagen. (*a*) A North American bison bone fragment of Pleistocene age was tested as an 'unknown' and found to have strong reaction with bovine anti-collagen. Reactions of bovine (*b*), human (*c*) and rat (*d*) collagen are shown for comparison.

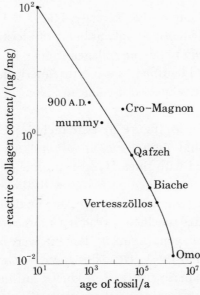

FIGURE 8. Immunologically reactive collagen in extracts of human fossil bones (nanograms of collagen per milligram of bone). The point on the ordinate is derived from a fresh femur removed at surgery; A.D. 900 (Hungarian burial); mummy (Egyptian, 800 B.C.): Cro-Magnon (from Musée de l'Homme, Paris); Qafzeh (Neanderthal, Israel); Biache (*Homo erectus*, France); Verteszöllos (*Homo erectus*, Hungary); Omo (*Australopithecus robustus*, Ethiopia).

radioimmunoassay method, I demonstrated both by directed reaction and by inhibition that the muscle extract contained the equivalent of 3 µg of elephant albumin per millilitre (Prager *et al.* 1980). This material reacted strongly with antibody to elephant albumin and weakly with other mammalian anti-albumins (figure 6). The ^{14}C date for this mammoth is 44 ka.

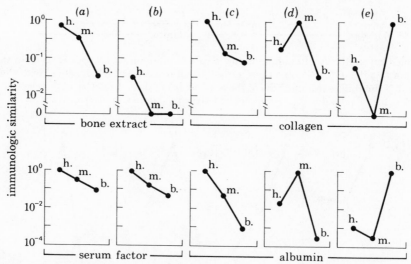

FIGURE 9. Reactive collagen and serum factor in two human fossils, (*a*) radius of an Egyptian mummy 3 ka old and (*b*) mandible of *Homo erectus* 0.5 Ma old. Top: reactions of fossil extracts with human (h.), monkey (m.) and bovine (b.) anti-collagens; the reactions of human (*c*), monkey (*d*) and bovine (*e*) collagen are shown for comparison. Bottom: reactions of antibodies made in rabbits to the two human fossils, with human (h.), monkey (m.) and bovine (b.) serum. Reactions of human, monkey and bovine anti-albumins are shown for comparison. The anti-fossil antibodies did not, however, react with pure albumin, which implies that the immunogen is another serum factor.

Professor F. Jenkins, Museum of Comparative Zoology, Harvard University, provided me with three sets of fossil bone fragments identified only as being of Pleistocene age. When tested, one gave a strong reaction with antibody to bovine collagen (figure 7), the others gave no reaction. The reacting specimen was then identified as a North American bison; the others were horse and mastodon, for which I had no related anti-collagens. None of the three gave reactions with specific anti-albumins.

I have tested a range of human fossils (figure 8) that includes Egyptian mummy, Cro-Magnon, Neanderthal, *Homo erectus* and *Australopithecus robustus*. All gave positive collagen reactions, though the amount decreased with time. Hydroxyproline determination, a measure of collagen, revealed that the amount of collagen decreased with the age of the fossil and also there was a decrease in reactivity of the remaining collagen, due no doubt to chemical changes. The collagen remaining retained species specificity, reacting more strongly with antibody to human collagen than with other anti-collagens (figure 9). Rabbits were immunized with extracts from two human fossils, the mummy and the Verteszöllos *Homo erectus* (the only two of which there was sufficient quantity for this experiment) and produced antibodies that reacted more strongly with human serum than with the serum of other species (figure 9). Though these antibodies reacted with serum in a pattern similar to that of anti-albumins, they did not react with purified albumin; therefore, it appears that some unidentified serum factor other than albumin has survived in these fossils.

DISCUSSION

While one might expect to find identifiable proteins in a frozen Siberian mammoth, it is perhaps surprising that collagen, albumin and other serum factors survive in fossil bones that have been subjected to ambient temperatures and to the effects of water, chemical and bacterial action for thousands or millions of years. One clue to this survival comes from my control studies on human bone ash. Bone powder was heated at a temperature of 850 °C until the nitrogen content was reduced to a negligible amount. Yet an EDTA extract of this material consistently gave radioimmunoassay evidence of small but definite amounts of surviving human collagen and albumin. From this, and from the fossil results, it seems that the calcium apatite matrix in which the proteins are embedded provides considerable protection against the destructive effects of temperature and chemical agents. Furthermore, proteins need not survive intact to account for these reactions, as most immunological determinants consist of a few adjacent amino acids, so that fragments could retain immunological reactivity. The mammoth albumin was shown by Sephadex chromatography to be mostly in an aggregated form, yet it reacted nearly identically to elephant albumin.

Obviously, a great deal more systematic work needs to be done before phylogenetic interpretations can confidently be made from fossil immunological data. Nevertheless, these early results offer the hope that we may be able to obtain useful molecular genetic information from many fossils.

This research was supported by the L.S.B. Leakey Foundation, the Wenner-Gren Foundation for Anthropological Research, and the Research Committee of the University of California, San Francisco. I thank Adrienne L. Zihlman for primate material, D. Michaeli and S. Gay for purified collagens, V. M. Sarich, J. E. Cronin, E. M. Prager and A. C. Wilson for albumins, antisera and mammoth material, P. E. Hare, F. Jenkins, I. Lengyel, Y. Coppens and B. Vandermeersch for fossil material, and Sherwood Washburn for advice and encouragement.

REFERENCES (Lowenstein)

Ayala, F. J. (ed.) 1976 *Molecular evolution.* Sunderland, Massachusetts: Sinauer.

Balazs, E. A. (ed.) 1970 *Chemistry and molecular biology of the intercellular matrix,* vol. 1. New York: Academic Press.

Fietzek, P. P. & Kuhn, K. 1976 The primary structure of collagen. *Int. Rev. connect. Tiss. Res.* **7**, 1–60.

Furthmayr, H. Timpl, R. 1976 Immunochemistry of collagens and procollagens. *Int. Rev. connect. Tiss. Res.* **7**, 61–101.

King, M. & Wilson, A. C. 1975 Evolution at two levels in humans and chimpanzees. *Science, N.Y.* **188**, 107–116.

Lowenstein, J. M. 1980 Immunospecificity of fossil collagens. In *The biochemistry of amino acids* (ed. P. E. Hare). New York: John Wiley and Sons.

Prager, E. M., Wilson, A. C., Lowenstein, J. M. & Sarich, V. M. 1980 Mammoth albumin. *Science, N.Y.* **209**, 287–289.

Simons, E. L. 1977 Ramapithecus. *Scient. Am.* **236** (5), 28–35.

Sarich, V. M. & Cronin, J. E. 1976 Molecular systematics of the primates. In *Molecular anthropology* (ed. M. Goodman & R. Tashian. New York: Plenum.

Wilson, A. C., Carlson, S. S. & White, T. J. 1977 Biochemical evolution. *A. Rev. Biochem.* **46**, 573–639.

Wyckoff, R. W. G. 1972 *The biochemistry of animal fossils.* Baltimore: Williams and Wilkins.

Zihlman, A. L. & Lowenstein, J. M. 1979 False start of the human parade. *Nat. Hist., N.Y.* **88**, 86–91.

Phil. Trans. R. Soc. Lond. B **292**, 151–153 (1981)   [151]

Printed in Great Britain

THE HUMAN BRAIN

Chairman's introduction

By C. G. Phillips, F.R.S.

Department of Human Anatomy, South Parks Road,
Oxford OX1 3QX, U.K.

Much has been said at the symposium about the pre-eminent role of the brain in the continuing emergence of man. Tobias has spoken of its explosive enlargement during the last 1 Ma, and how much of its enlargement in individual ontogeny is postnatal. We are born before our brains are fully grown and 'wired up'. During our long adolescence we build up internal models of the outside world and of the relations of parts of our bodies to it and to one another. Neurons that are present at birth spread their dendrites and project axons which acquire their myelin sheaths, and establish innumerable contacts with other neurons, over the years. New connections are formed; genetically endowed ones are stamped in or blanked off. People born without arms may grow up to use their toes in skills that are normally manual. Tobias, Darlington and others have stressed the enormous survival value of adaptive behaviour and the 'positive feedback' relation between biological and cultural evolution. The latter, the unique product of the unprecedentedly rapid biological evolution of big brains, advances on a time scale unknown to biological evolution.

Sherrington wrote that most animal life is mindless, but that the behaviour is purposeful in the sense used in J. Z. Young's introductory remarks, of adaptation for survival to reproduce and to protect the brood. At some level in the evolution of higher animals, and at some stage in the ontogeny of the individuals, there emerge signs of what Sherrington called 'recognizable mind'. Darwin, before him, devoted two chapters of the *Descent of man* to anecdotal evidence of this emergence in wild, captive and domesticated animals.

Brain size is in part related to body size, but the enlargement of the human brain has not gone along with any proportionate enlargement of the body. Big brains have given to the primates the general advantages for survival that attach to adaptive behaviour which is less 'stimulus-bound' than that of lower animals: exploratory drives; internal trial-and-error; orientation to what may be happening beyond the range of sight, smell and hearing; and knowledge of the consequences of particular actions, as in copulation, sowing and harvesting. All this creates selection pressures for yet bigger brains. Enlargement, however, has been local as well as general: of particular areas in relation to specific abilities. Refined geometric analysis of endocranial casts from the skulls of living primates is calibrating the accuracy of measurements of areas of cortex by matching the casts against the fresh brains. Measurements of casts from dated fossil skulls will then be able to tell us over what evolutionary periods the specific enlargements occurred. The method cannot measure the volume of cortex buried in the walls of deep sulci. We still, however, have to look beyond gross morphology, to the increasing intricacy of the intrinsic neuronal microarchitecture that characterizes each area and to the extrinsic connections that link the areas with one another, with their related thalamic nuclei, and with other levels of the central nervous system. This can be done only by comparative research on the series of living primates.

Elliot Smith thought that the correlation of skilled movements with foveal and stereoscopic vision was a leading factor in primate evolution. Arboreal life 'tended to develop the motor cortex itself, trained the tactile and kinaesthetic senses and linked up their cortical areas in bonds of more intimate associations with the visual cortex'. Hands of primitive pentadactyl structure, whose prehensile function was at first limited to arboreal locomotion, came to replace the muzzle in tactile exploration and manipulation, with differentiation of precision patterns and grips from power grips. Neurological research on Old World primates is filling in the details in Elliot Smith's outline by unravelling the organization of the enlarged visual areas (in front of, as well as behind, the lunate sulcus); of the enlarged peri-Rolandic somaes-thetic and motor areas; and of the enlarged association cortex that lies between. Tuttle has stressed that structural adaptations of the hands of modern apes for arboreal locomotion have not compromised the continuing neurological differentiation of precision patterns and grips. Though incapable of full pulp-to-pulp opposition of thumb and index on account of the relative shortness of the thumb, 'every chimpanzee', according to A. H. Schultz, 'can extract a thorn out of its skin, and this more dextrously than most of us'. Enlargement of hand cortex and differentiation of hand function considerably antedated bipedalism. It has advanced still further in skilled man. A century ago, Hughlings Jackson remarked 'the more movements, the more grey matter'.

Language is unique to the genus *Homo*. A taxonomist visitor from another planet might well write *Homo loquax*. Every human infant with healthy brain and hearing, and exposed to human speech, will learn to speak. Fewer are exposed to reading and writing. We are not yet quite certain if the hemisphere that is dominant for language shows selective enlargement in the region of Wernicke's and Broca's areas, and we know little of their intrinsic neural networks for the analysis and production of elaborate patterns of sound. Specialized organ-ization, however, there must be. With a brain about the size of a chimpanzee's, a microcephalic human can speak more than, for example, the Hayes's 'Viki', who joined their family at the age of three days and after $6\frac{1}{2}$ years could only whisper 'mama', 'papa' and 'cup', often with fingers on lips in the way she had been taught. The brain, not the vocal tract, would be the limiting factor: a whisper is acceptable as speech, and people who have suffered laryngectomy can produce oesophageal speech. The much smaller brain of the parrot evidently contains neural apparatus of a kind that man possesses and chimpanzee lacks. In 1879 the Guy's neurologist, Samuel Wilks, published, in the *Journal of mental science*, 'Notes from the history of my parrot, in reference to the nature of language'. He taught the bird by frequent initial repetition. 'After a few hours it is heard attempting to say the phrase, or, I should say, trying to learn it. It evidently has the phrase somewhere in store, for eventually this is uttered perfectly.' It would repeat the first two or three words, then add 'another and another word', working for hour after hour before becoming word-perfect after some days had elapsed. In forgetting, the last words were lost while the first two or three were retained. 'The result of my observations in respect to the parrot's faculty for acquiring language is – that it has a vocal apparatus of a most perfect kind, that it can gather through its ear the most delicate intonations of the human voice, that it can imitate these perfectly by continued labour, and finally hold them in its memory; also, that it associates these words with certain persons who have uttered them.'

Man's big brain has had enormous survival value in the context of limited social groupings with limited spatial and temporal horizons. Until recently, rare individuals only have ever reckoned with events in distant lands, or beyond the time span of a few agricultural cycles, one session of a parliament, or even a human lifetime. Always there has been intra-species predation on other groups. Sherrington hoped that in the further course of evolution, altruism would replace predatoriness as a leading human characteristic. The apparatus of predation has come far since the Stone Age. Altruism within limited communities has led to local and global overpopulation. There may not be time for the big brain to undergo further biological evolution. Only if cultural evolution can surmount our present crisis will our descendants be entitled to claim that *Homo loquax predatorius* has given place to *Homo sapiens sapiens*.

Phil. Trans. R. Soc. Lond. B **292**, 155–166 (1981)   [155]
Printed in Great Britain

Exploring the dorsal surface of hominoid brain endocasts by stereoplotter and discriminant analysis

By R. L. Holloway

Department of Anthropology, Columbia University, New York 10027, U.S.A.

One of the more vexing problems with hominoid endocasts has been to secure reliable information that goes beyond their volumes. One method is explored here, where a large number ($N = 171$) of radial distances from a homologous internal central point to the dorsal endocast surface are measured in a polar coordinate system. From two pilot studies, one with a hominoid sample of $N = 64$, and the other with an enlarged sample of $N = 92$, the following results can be mentioned tentatively: (1) there are residual data that differ taxonomically in different cortical regions once overall endocast size is corrected in allometric fashion; (2) the major cortical regions where these differences appear most strongly are in the lower parietal lobule, anterior occipital zone, and the dorsoanterior region of the frontal lobe; (3) the method shows excellent promise in objectively and quantitatively depicting taxa-specific shape differences in functionally understood cortical regions through multivariate statistical analyses.

INTRODUCTION

Brain endocasts, whether 'natural', as found in some of the South African australopithecine sites, or as produced from latex moulds of cranial interiors, are the closest empirical 'windows' to the evolution of the hominid brain that we possess. Apart from their size, however, little if any definitive information has been gleaned from them without considerable speculation. The unfaithfulness of replication of gyral and sulcal relief patterns, at least on hominoid endocasts, is infamous, with but a few minor exceptions. In addition, brain endocasts are very difficult to measure in any meaningful sense. Traditional caliper measurements can be applied to landmarks left by the internal bony table of the cranium, but these have no functional relevance to the underlying brain. Measurements such as length, width, height, whether in chords or arcs, only describe space, and even the measurements or indices devised by Kochetkova (1978) to measure brain lobes are probabilistic guesses, without clear empirical tests, and further run into the abyss of allometric correction.

At the risk of appearing in a Panglossian role, my current research on a large sample of hominoid endocasts ($N = 92$) is suggesting that more information resides in (on) an endocast than its volume and a few morphological features of varying value, such as meningeal patterns, sinus variations, petalial asymmetries, or selected gyral and sulcal patterns such as the lunate sulcus or Broca's 'cap'.

This paper is an updated preliminary and exploratory report on pilot studies that show very considerable promise, objectively and quantitatively, in depicting regional morphological changes that might later be related to our functional knowledge of neurological structure, and which also may provide information useful in taxonomic assignments within the Hominoidea.

MATERIALS AND METHODS

Table 1 is a list of the hominoid endocasts used in the current sample ($N = 92$). Each endocast, with the exception of many of the fossil hominids, was made of latex rubber, as described by Holloway (1978).

TABLE 1. HOMINOID SAMPLE BREAKDOWN

species or specimen	number	volume/ml
1. *Pan paniscus*	16	327–439
2. *Pan troglodytes*	15	385–449
3. *Gorilla gorilla*	16	422–615
4. *Homo sapiens*	13	1166–1659
5. australopithecines		
(*a*) 'gracile'	4	404–485
1. Taung		404
2. STS 5		485
3. STS 60		436
4. OMO 338		427
(*b*) 'robust'	3	506–530
1. SK 1585		530
2. OH 5		530
3. KNM-ER 732		506
6. *Homo erectus*		
(*a*) *Indonesian*	5	813–1059
(*b*) *Chinese*	4	890–1220
7. Solo	5	1013–1250
8. Neanderthal	4	1350–1641 (La Chapelle, La Ferrassie, La Quina, Neanderthal)
9. unclassified	7	KNM-ER 1470, 1813, 1805, 3733, 3883, OH 9, Rhodesian (S15-1285)
total	92	

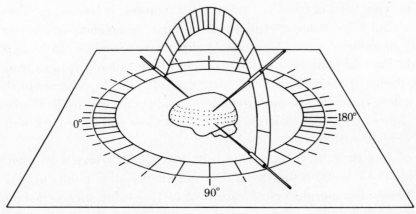

FIGURE 1. Schematic drawing of the stereoplotting apparatus, originally devised by A. Walker and D. Oyen. (The inner circular element rotates through 360°. The pointer on the vertical arch sweeps 180°.) Measurements are taken to the nearest millimetre.

The measuring device is a coordinate stereoplotter (figure 1), designed by Oyen & Walker (1977), which provides a critical 'localness' of homologous points on the endocast surface that can be initially specified in a polar coordinate system, e.g. two angles and a radial distance. This system permits accurate and replicable measurements to be taken, and provides a large matrix of data, which can be treated in a variety of multivariate statistical ways. This system has the further advantage of graphic depiction in relation to neuroanatomical and neuro-physiological maps.

Each endocast is placed in the apparatus such that: (1) the midsagittal plane is aligned along the 0–180° horizontal axis; and (2) a homologous centrepoint 'within' the endocast is defined as that point exactly midway between frontal and occipital poles, which in hominoids, at least, are homologous structures. The endocasts are then measured every 10° in both horizontal and vertical directions, yielding a total of 171 data points (radial distances from the

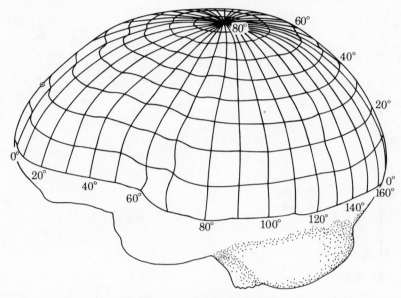

FIGURE 2. Stereoplot 'net' cast over an endocast shape. Each intersection is a point where a radial distance from the surface to a homologous centre point is taken in millimetres.

surface of the endocast to a homologous centre point) *for each side*. In these preliminary studies, only the *left side* of each endocast was measured, except in those obvious cases, such as Taung, SK 1585 etc., where only right-sided endocasts exist, or in those, e.g. Solo, where the right side was less distorted than the left.

Each measurement was first placed on a map of coordinate intersections, and then punched onto data cards, the specimens being arranged according to taxa in a subfile list. Thus, for each endocast, there would be 19 radial distances, one measured every 10° anterior and posterior, for each of the 10° vertical transects between 0° (horizontal) and the 80° level. Figure 2 shows an 'endocast net', as it were, where each intersection represents a coordinate of a radial distance.

For convenient statistical reasons, the original pilot analyses were conducted on a series of individual vertical transects at 20° intervals from anterior to posterior. Thus two sets of data 'decks' were analysed, one called 'evens', composed of a horizontal transect, beginning at the midsagittal plane and containing values at 20° intervals, giving a total of 10 values for each specimen in each of the horizontal transects, and a second set, called 'odds', composed of the intervening 9 values at 20° intervals for each horizontal transect.

The reasons for this division were as follows: (1) the total number of specimens in any one taxonomic group, e.g. *Pan paniscus*, was *less* than 19; (2) there are only ten taxonomic groups, not counting 'unknowns'. Since discriminant analysis was anticipated as a useful preliminary way of exploring the data, it was decided to keep the number of variables to a minimum in terms of the constraints known for discriminant analysis, e.g. not having more variables than either groups or specimens within groups. Alas, even this was an impossible task, given the low sample sizes of some of the hominid groups. Later analyses were based on selecting the highest univariate F-ratios, and choosing only *that* number of variables below the specimen number in the taxonomic group with the lowest number of specimens, e.g. 4 for Neanderthal.

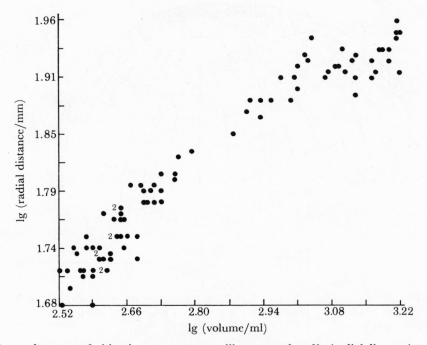

FIGURE 3. A sample output of a bivariate scattergram to illustrate a plot of lg (radial distance) against lg (endocast volume) for 92 hominoid endocasts.

Statistical procedures

It should be apparent that a radial distance from a centre point to the dorsal endocast surface will depend on the size of the endocast, and that, if additional information (shape?) to size is expected, some method of allometric correction must be used.

By the use of a scattergram routine from SPSS, each radial distance and endocranial volume was converted to its logarithmic equivalent, and the same coordinate point for all 92 cases was plotted against volume, yielding a straight-line regression equation of form lg (radial distance) $= k + \alpha$ lg (volume), or radial distance $= k$ (volume)$^{\alpha}$. This was done for each point, generating 171 equations in total, or ten or nine equations for each 'even' or 'odd' transect. These equations were then used to calculate the *expected* value of radial distances for each point, as if they had fallen exactly on the equation line. In other words, each point was considered as an independent variable in the early phase of the analysis.

These *expected* values were next subtracted from the *actual* radial distances, yielding a residual, called DIFF 1, DIFF 2... DIFF 10, etc., depending on its angular location. In other words, the DIFFs are the residual values of the allometric corrections, and each 'even' deck gives ten DIFFs at 20° intervals, and each 'odd' deck nine DIFFs at 20° intervals. Thus for one side of an endocast there result 171 DIFFs.

The correlation coefficients were all high, but varied in different locations on the dorsal endocast surface, ranging from 0.93 to 0.98. All were significant at the 10^{-5} level. The exponents (slopes, α) also varied, from about 0.28 to 0.50, again depending on the particular point and angular transect. The overall average was about 0.33, as would be expected from geometrical considerations (i.e. the cube of the radius would approximate volume).

The DIFFs, as described above, thus became the variables analysed by means of a variety of statistical techniques, mainly (1) ANOVA, (2) discriminant analysis, and (3) factor analysis.

HYPOTHESIS AND PRELIMINARY RESULTS

Two basic questions were being asked of the data: (1) if allometric corrections were made, would the residual information pattern itself in a meaningful way?; and (2) would it be possible to translate this (these) pattern(s) into one(s) having functional meaning neurologically?

The first test was to ascertain that the DIFFs, or residuals, were related to taxonomic groups *and not to volumes*. Thus the ANOVA procedure was used, in which each DIFF was the dependent variable, with the taxonomic groups as independent variable, and lg (volume) a covariate. The resulting F-ratios (between-group-to-within-group variance ratio), after allowance for covariance between the DIFFs and lg (volume), were all high and significant, indicating that no further significant relation between the DIFFs and lg (volume) existed, and that the patterns of DIFFs were explainable by their taxonomic group.† Furthermore, the values of the F-ratios varied considerably depending on the location of the points on the endocast. In other words, it was possible to map the univariate F-ratios for all 171 locations and study the placement of highest and lowest values. By and large, the highest F-ratios were in locations of considerable neuro-anatomical interest, such as the inferior parietal–anterior occipital zone, the superior parietal zone and a small portion of the frontal lobe. These findings will be described in greater detail in the discussion section of this paper.

Discriminant analyses were performed, again by means of the SPSS package, for each horizontal transect, 'even', and 'odd'. The explicit hypothesis tested was: if there was no further relevant information after allometric correction, the DIFFs (residuals) should *not* show any meaningful taxonomic classification results: i.e. the percentage of classifications correct should be random, or approximately 50. In fact, the classification scores varied for each transect, depending on the transect and on whether nine or ten DIFFs were being used. Classification results were higher when ten rather than nine variables were used. The classification results were *also* very dependent upon the combinations of taxonomic groups used.‡

---

† This was particularly true when ANOVA was used on all groups. No significant variation was found that could be related to the base 10 logarithm of the endocast volume. A warning here is in order. For other group combinations, e.g. extant only or fossils only, the relations of the DIFFs to volume do change, and some of the ANOVA results suggest that some of the DIFFs are related to the covariate as well as to the taxonomic group. The statistical tables are misleading, however. When the DIFFs for the extant group are plotted against (volume) there are two large clusters: one for pongids, and one for *Homo sapiens*, with a huge gap in between. This amounts to plotting a line with only two points (or centroids): there are no such relations within the pongid or *Homo* groups. Nevertheless, some of the DIFFs do show weak, but sometimes significant, correlations with lg (volume).

‡ If all the decks are combined, and data points linearly arranged, one can select those coordinates where F-ratios are highest. While not reported here, these runs have yielded higher classification scores for all three of the group combinations discussed, and permit one to avoid non-singular covariance matrices.

Table 2 indicates the variability of classification scores for each transect, when different groups are used. 'Unknown' specimens such as KNM-ER 1813, 1805, 1470, 3733, 3883, OH9, and the Rhodesian endocast were not classified on the trial runs but were retained as a group for later predictions.

TABLE 2. DISCRIMINANT ANALYSIS† CLASSIFICATION RESULTS (PERCENTAGE CORRECT)

Grouping A: all subfiles, extant + fossil.
Grouping B: extant species only (*Pan paniscus, Pan troglodytes, Gorilla, Homo sapiens*).
Grouping C: fossil hominids only (Indonesian + Chinese *Homo erectus*, Solo, australopiths, Neanderthal).
Parenthesized values are for the stepwise method, based on the method of Wilks (A).)

transect	grouping A	grouping B	grouping C
0° horiz.	89 (87)	92 (87)	100 (96)
10° even	73 (63)	73 (68)	88 (80)
10° odd	62 (62)	67 (65)	96 (80)
20° even	74 (69)	73 (72)	100 (92)
20° odd	65 (66)	75 (70)	84 (76)
30° even	67 (62)	73 (70)	88 (84)
30° odd	56 (49)	63 (65)	84 (80)
40° even	58 (59)	80 (73)	80 (64)
40° odd	63 (62)	80 (78)	80 (84)
50° even	75 (68)	83 (85)	84 (64)
50° odd	56 (49)	67 (65)	92 (72)
60° even	61 (60)	68 (70)	92 (92)
60° odd	52 (45)	71 (69)	88 (84)
70° even	56 (43)	63 (55)	96 (76)
70° odd	46 (39)	60 (52)	84 (64)
80° even	51 (46)	62 (53)	80 (72)
80° odd	36 (33)	55 (58)	84 (72)

† Based on direct method.

It should be mentioned that the discriminant analyses were done in two ways: (1) direct method, in which all nine or ten DIFFs were entered; (2) the stepwise method, in which only several were selected for inclusion, depending on their F-values and the results of their inclusion on lowering the Wilks A value at each step.‡ As table 2 suggests, the classifications are highest in the lower transects, i.e. 0 (horizontal, 19 values), 10, 20, 30, and the highest univariate. F-ratios are in the posterior coordinates. *Most* of the misclassifications occur between *Pan paniscus* and *Pan troglodytes*, or between *Homo erectus* (Java) and *Homo erectus* (China). Curiously, the classifications between *Australopithecus africanus* and *Australopithecus robustus* are often very high, e.g. 100%. However, the sample sizes for these taxa are very low ($N = 4, 3$, respectively) and their covariance matrices are non-singular, and so considerable caution must be exercised in interpreting these results as truly significant (see also table 3).

Space forbids a full discussion of the factor analytic explorations. The point in trying these techniques was to reduce the data to some number of factor scores lower than the number of specimens in any one taxonomic group (i.e. $N = 4$). Discriminant analyses were tried on the

‡ I have hesitated to go beyond the very shallow analyses offered here because I am not yet comfortable with the statistical methods employed. If the MAHAL method (also stepwise) is used, the classification results vary slightly, and the SPSS (Nie *et al.* 1975) set of options, provides a great number of different routines. For example, if individual group covariance matrices are used for classification, rather than a pooled-with-group matrix, the classifications improve slightly, although the discriminant functions and scores do not change. Classifications will also change depending on the *a priori* probabilities assigned for each group. In the data provided in this paper, all groups have been given *equal* probabilities, and have not been weighted by group sizes. I assume that this is a more robust test.

factor scores, and, in general, there was a loss of information, which reduced the classification scores. (Factoring was done by the PA1 principal components technique of SPSS, with Varimax rotation.)

DISCUSSION

I must stress that these results are only preliminary and of a tentative nature. I believe that they are encouraging and show considerable promise, provided that our sample sizes for certain taxonomic groups improve and that further statistical refinements are made.

Hopefully, the choice of the central point as a 'homologous centre' is reasonable, as all evidence points to both frontal and occipital poles being homologous points in both a structural and functional sense, between pongids and hominids.†

Some of the difficulties of these studies, however, should be explicitly stated. The underlying assumption is that the shape differences between the various taxa are due to evolutionary changes of the brain rather than other adaptive processes such as craniobasal flexion, postural adjustments, masticatory functions etc. At the moment, I do not know how to test this assumption, nor how to weight the various possibilities. It depends very much on our basic understanding of such postural-masticatory influences on the cerebrum, rather than on exocranial structure. My own belief is that those influences are minimal.

Another area of uncertainty is the method of using residual (DIFFs) information from allometric corrections based on log–log regressions. It should be immediately evident that there is a certain *relativity* in this method, as the corrections depend on the construction of the base line. Certain taxonomic groups heavily weight the regressions, such as two species of *Pan, Gorilla* and *Homo sapiens*. One can argue that, after all, 92 examples give a very good representation of the hominoids; on the other hand, one could argue that the inclusion of values *to be tested* is not maximally appropriate. Still, it is the best base line that we have.

The relativity question must be given serious consideration, since classification scores *and* F-ratios change considerably depending on the groups compared. Figures 4–6 show the mappings of univariate F-ratios in three different combinations of taxonomic groups: (1) all groups ($N = 10$) without 'unknowns'; (2) only extant species, *Pan paniscus, Pan troglodytes, Gorilla* and *Homo sapiens*; (3) fossil groups only, where Indonesian and Chinese *Homo erectus* are combined, Solo is separate, australopithecines are combined and neanderthals are separate ($N = 4$). Table 3 shows the different classifications possibilities depending on such selections of groups. In these cases, there are no non-singular matrices.

I have included two additional diagrams to illustrate some of the depictional possibilities of these methods. Figure 7 is a map of the probabilities from t-tests on each coordinate between *Homo erectus* and *Homo sapiens*, with all p-values lower than 0.05 encircled. It is intriguing that the major differences are in those regions of the endocast that we normally associate with posterior and inferior parietal lobe (Wernicke's area, in part?), and the dorsal anterior part of the frontal lobe. My point here, I must stress, is not that these values are correct or proof of significant cerebral neurological differences between the two groups, as the sample sizes are pathetically small. Rather, it represents an interesting depictional possibility. Similarly, figure 8 is a Cartesian, and thus distorted, rendition of Brodmann's areas, as applied to a human

† Some effort has been made to check the internal 'centre' point, to see if its location is also homologous. Unfortunately, precise stereographic atlases do not exist for most primates. Median sagittal sections of both human and chimpanzee brains, as illustrated in a variety of anatomy books, indicate that the centre point does consistently fall in the thalamus zone, just anterior to the posterior commissure.

TABLE 3. SOME SAMPLE DISCRIMINANT ANALYSIS CLASSIFICATIONS (PERCENTAGE† CORRECT) FOR VARIOUS TAXONOMIC COMBINATIONS, BASED ON SELECTING HIGHEST F-RATIO VALUES‡

grouping	direct	stepwise
Panp, Pant, Gorilla§	95.7	85.1
Panp+, Pant, Gorilla	100.0	97.9
Pith+Sina, Solo, Aust+Robt, Nean	64.0	84.0
Panp, Pant, Gorilla, Homo§	78.3	75.0
Panp+Pant+Gorilla, Aust+Robt	96.3	94.4
Panp+Pant, Gorilla, Aust+Robt	83.3	77.8
Pith+Sina, Solo, Nean	72.2	100.0
Homo sapiens, Nean	100.0	100.0
Pith+Sina, Aust+Robt	100.0	100.0

† The percentage values are for both direct and stepwise solutions, by the methods of Wilks (Λ).

‡ Each grouping yields its own univariate F-ratios for each 171 points. These are ordered according to rank, and the highest ratios are selected for discriminant analysis. In these runs, there were no non-singular covariance matrices, as the number of variables selected was always $N-1$, the lowest number of specimens within a taxonomic group.

§ Almost all misclassifications occur between *Pan paniscus* and *Pan troglodytes*.

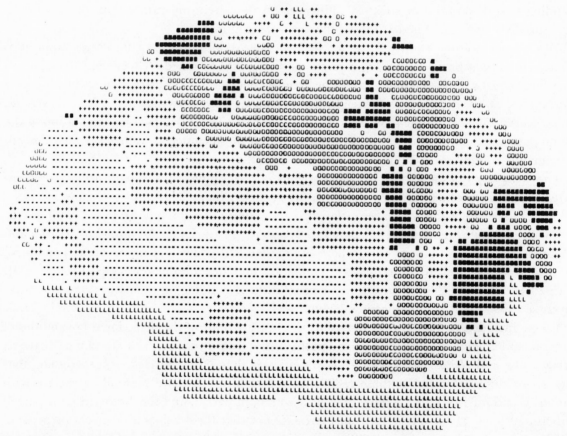

FIGURE 4. A SYNMAP of 171 univariate F-ratios plotted within an endocast shape. The darkest areas have the highest F-ratio values, ranging from 8.5 to 12.7, and significant at less than the 10^{-5} level. This map is for all groups combined, i.e. fossil and extant species

The SYNMAP symbols have been chosen such that L represents non-significant F-ratios, and the five gradations, of darkness represent increasingly significant F-ratios, roughly at the 5×10^{-2} to 10^{-2}, 10^{-3}, 10^{-4} and 10^{-5} levels. The outline of the endocast is only approximate, based on the figure 2 'net' shape. In reality, there are no data points *below* the horizontal plane passing through frontal and occipital poles.

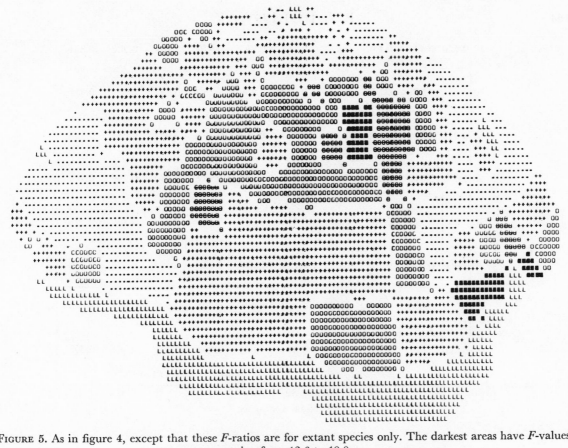

FIGURE 5. As in figure 4, except that these *F*-ratios are for extant species only. The darkest areas have *F*-values ranging from 12.6 to 18.0.

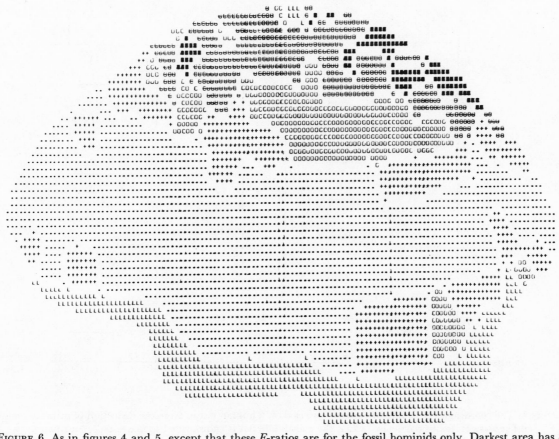

FIGURE 6. As in figures 4 and 5, except that these *F*-ratios are for the fossil hominids only. Darkest area has *F*-values ranging from 15.0 to 21.3.

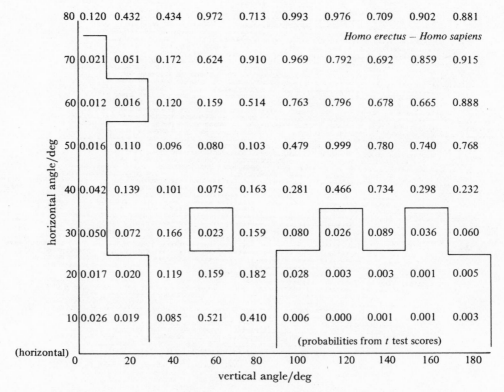

FIGURE 7. A tentative plot, every 20°, of the *p*-values associated with 'student' *t*-tests of the DIFFS between *Homo erectus* and *Homo sapiens* (for depictional purposes only).

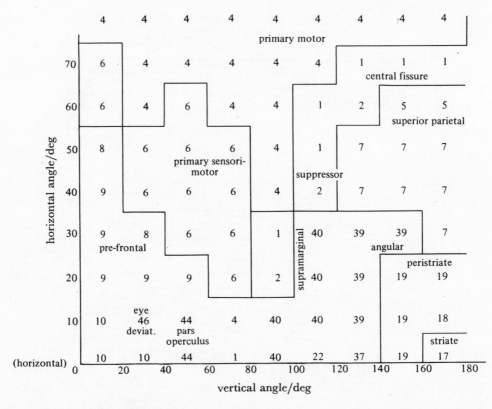

FIGURE 8. The coordinates of Brodmann's areas as based on a human brain. Note the distortion of primary motor and sensory cortex in particular, when the coordinate net is transformed to Cartesian coordinates.

brain (not endocast) cast. More work is needed on actual brain casts to ascertain the locational variation of gyral and sulcal patterns.

Space forbids adequate discussion of the meaning of these results. While the first size correction leaves DIFFs with useful information, it does *not* mean that size has been totally disregarded. In fact, if for certain taxonomic groups the DIFFs with the highest F-ratios are plotted against lg (volume), there are clear trends, with multiple R of about 12 to 20%. I interpret these findings to mean that certain regions show size differentials above and below the expected allometric-corrected values. These are, however, only *relative* to those particular groups being compared. It is too early to be certain that this interpretation is correct, but it does appear to be the most promising and reasonable explanation to date. Thus, with reference to figure 4, the highest F-ratios are distributed mainly in those areas of Brodmann's that are 'peristriate', i.e. 19, 37, and 8, which is prefrontal, and in areas 5 and 7, which is the superior parietal region. Given the complex composition of groups (i.e. all extant *and* fossil groups as separate samples), no evolutionary interpretation should be made. It should be remembered that the F-ratios are only a measure of between-group-to-within-group variances.

With regard to figure 5, extant species only, the F-ratios are highest in areas 19–37 and 17–19 (striate and peristriate). If the DIFFs for the highest F-ratios are plotted against $\log_{10}$ (volume) the highest multiple R (R^2) is about 0.22, with most values being between 0.05 and 0.10, and non-significant. In this case, the sample sizes are $N = 13$ or greater for each species, and the tentative conclusion that I would draw is that the inferior parietal region shows the most significant variations once 'size' is removed.

Figure 6, which depicts the distribution of F-ratios for the fossil hominids only, suggests that the greatest degree of change has occurred in areas 5, 7 and 4, the first two being the superior parietal region. In this case, however, plotting the DIFFs against lg (volume) gives R^2 values of approximately 0.65, with negative correlations, and all significant. These results suggest, tentatively, that the major changes in endocast surface morphology since the australopithecines have been in the superior parietal region and that, furthermore, the increments have been somewhat *less* than would be expected on a purely allometric basis. This, in obverse terms, would mean that significant changes from apes to hominids have been directed towards enlargement of the superior parietal lobule. Indeed, if F-ratios are plotted for pongids (each group separate) and australopithecines only, areas 5 and 7 show the highest values. If *Pan paniscus* and *P. troglodytes* are combined, *Gorilla* being kept as a separate taxon, the F-ratios show that areas 8, 9, 6 and 19–37 score highest, the latter moiety representing inferior parietal lobule.

Unfortunately, it is beyond the scope of this paper to discuss all combinations of groups adequately, and in particular the patterns of classifications for the 'unknowns' listed in table 1. For those interested, KNM-ER 1470 is most frequently classified as an australopith, as are 1805 and 1813. KNM-ER 3733 and 3883, and OH9 are classified as *Homo erectus*, and the Rhodesian endocast as a Neanderthal. These results are wholly tentative, of course, and are based on small samples. They are found without *a priori* probability weighting of group membership, that is, each 'unknown' has an initial equal probability of being classified in any of the fossil groups. This is a very robust 'test', and the results are admittedly gratifying, but they should be taken with extreme caution until the sample sizes are enlarged and the statistical procedures are refined.

In summary, stereoplotting of the dorsal endocast surface of hominoids is showing considerable promise in objectively and quantitatively delineating those regions of the cerebral surface that have undergone differential expansion during the course of hominid evolution.

In the course of this research, I have had the support of N.S.F. grants GS92231x, Soc-74-20149, BNS78-05651, BNS79-11235, and a Guggenheim Fellowship, for which I am most grateful. In the task of collecting so many data points, I am indebted to my students: Barry Cerf, Tim Wolfe, Joel Wallman, Jacqueline Goodman, Michael Billig and Alan Barstow. I am especially grateful to Ms Christine de Lacoste for her help in constructing and using the SYNMAP programs for visual presentation. I especially thank Ms Jan Engebretsen and Ms Joan Witkin for their help in correcting errors and in putting all of the separate transects together. Finally, my thanks go to Mr John Gurche for his artistic talents, and to my colleagues who made it possible for me to endocast so many of the hominoid materials: Mr Carlos Medina, Dr J. Schwartz, Ms Theya Molleson, Dr Thys van Audenaarde, Dr Richard Thorington, Dr R. van Gelder, Dr Yves Coppens, Dr Roger Saban, Dr Alan Walker, Dr F. Clark Howell, Dr Phillip Tobias, Mr Alan Hughes, Dr Bob Brain, Dr Mary Leakey, the late Dr L. S. B. Leakey, Mr Richard Leakey, Dr Teuku Jacob, Dr G. Sartono, and Dr G. H. R. von Koenigswald. Dr David Post and Dr Frank Findlow have patiently provided me with advice on statistical matters, but any errors are entirely my own.

REFERENCES (Holloway)

Dudik, E. E. 1972 *Synmap; user's reference manual.* Cambridge: Laboratory for Computer Graphics and Spatial Analysis (Harvard University).

Holloway, R. L. 1978 The relevance of endocasts for studying primate brain evolution. In *Sensory systems in primates* (ed. C. R. Noback), pp. 181–200. New York: Academic Press.

Kochetkova, V. I. 1978 *Paleoneurology.* Washington, D.C.: J. H. Winston. New York: John Wiley.

Nie, H. N., Hull, C. H., Jenkins, J. G., Steinbrenner, K. & Bent, D. H. 1975 SPSS. *Statistical package for the social sciences.* New York: McGraw-Hill.

Oyen, O. J. & Walker, A. 1977 Stereometric craniometry. *Am. J. phys. Anthrop.* **46**, 177–182.

Phil. Trans. R. Soc. Lond. B **292**, 167–175 (1981)   [167]
Printed in Great Britain

Broca's area and the origins of human vocal skill

By R. E. Passingham
*Department of Experimental Psychology, University of Oxford, South Parks Road,
Oxford OX1 3UD, U.K.*

Chimpanzees appear to be unable to learn to speak. It is usual to attribute their lack of vocal skill to limitations of their vocal tract, and to the absence in their neocortex of any area corresponding to Broca's area in the human brain. The first signs of Broca's area in hominid endocasts are therefore taken to represent an evolutionary development of great significance. There are two outstanding questions. First, what exactly does Broca's area do? Secondly, why does Broca's area in one hemisphere play a much greater role in controlling speech than does the corresponding area in the other hemisphere?

The following answers are proposed. (1) Broca's area seems to be concerned not with the production of individual sounds but with the regulation of sequences of sounds. Chimpanzees have no need for such an area because their natural calls are not made up by varying the sequential order of elementary units. (2) Cerebral dominance for speech may result from the fact that the vocal cords are innervated in the same way as other central organs, such as the tongue. Each hemisphere sends a projection, and the two projections overlap extensively so that either hemisphere can assume full control. It is argued that it is most efficient for a single hemisphere to dominate where a complex sequence of movements must be programmed. This re-organization has occurred for the production of song in some songbirds and for the control of the vocal cords in human speech.

Chimpanzees ape but they do not parrot. If a chimpanzee is brought up in a human household it copies some of the actions of its caretakers (Hayes & Hayes 1952); but it does not imitate their speech (Kellogg 1968). Even with extensive coaching the highest achievement of a chimpanzee has been to say 'mama', 'papa', 'cup' and 'up', and these with poor articulation (Hayes & Nissen 1971). The ape repeats what it sees but not what it hears.

The failure of apes to speak is partly accounted for by the limitations of their vocal tract. In man the back of the tongue forms the front wall of the superpharyngeal cavity, and the shape of this cavity can thus be altered by movements of the tongue. This is not so in the chimpanzee, and they are therefore able to produce only a restricted range of vowels (Lieberman 1975). But the ability of man to speak depends not only on the configuration of the vocal tract but also on the neurological mechanisms controlling the movements of the vocal cords. We may reasonably wonder whether similar mechanisms are lacking in the brains of apes.

In man speech is partly under the control of 'Broca's area', which lies on the opercular surface of the third frontal convolution (Bailey & von Bonin 1951). Damage to this region leads to a poverty of speech and a loss of fluency (Benson 1967; Mohr 1976). It is understandable that there should have been great interest in whether this region can be identified on the endocasts of early hominids, because its presence might be taken to be a mark of the advent of the ability to speak (Holloway 1972, 1978).

Whereas we have no access to the actual brains of the early hominids the brains of monkeys and apes are there for us to examine. But the microscopic study of the cell layers of frontal cortex has not yet settled the issue. In the human brain Broca's area can be differentiated on cytoarchitectonic criteria and it has been labelled area FCBm (von Economo 1929). In their early studies von Bonin & Bailey believed that they could identify an area with a similar microscopic structure in the brains of the rhesus monkey and chimpanzee (von Bonin & Bailey 1947; von Bonin 1948; Bailey *et al.* 1950). But on reconsidering the material they were less confident that they could make out a special subregion of area FC that they could reasonably label FCBm (von Bonin & Bailey 1961). There the matter must rest until further studies are undertaken, perhaps with the newer pigment stain that has proved valuable in distinguishing between the superior temporal cortex of man and monkey (Braak 1978).

There are other ways of attacking the question (Passingham 1979). The area of the neocortex that directly controls the vocal cords can be identified in patients during surgical operations. Vowel sounds can be evoked by electrically stimulating the inferior part of frontal motor cortex, and movements of the lips and jaws can be elicited from much the same area (Penfield & Rasmussen 1950; Penfield & Roberts 1959). In chimpanzees stimulation of this same region of motor cortex produces movements of the larynx (Bailey *et al.* 1950). That movements of the vocal cords themselves can be elicited in this way has been directly demonstrated in rhesus monkeys (Hast *et al.* 1974). By recording from the muscles of the larynx it was shown that the intrinsic muscles are controlled by sites anterior to those directing the extrinsic muscles, as in swallowing, and that both sites lie within the area tentatively designated FCBm (von Bonin & Bailey 1947). But this very demonstration casts doubt on the suggestion that this area in the rhesus monkey is functionally similar to Broca's area in man, for electrical stimulation of Broca's area does not give rise to movements of the vocal cords as indicated by vocalization; in the human brain Broca's area lies anterior to the region of frontal cortex that directly controls the vocal cords (Penfield & Roberts 1959). In other words if there is an area analogous to Broca's area in the chimpanzee or monkey brain it must lie in front of the region initially proposed and labelled FCBm (Jürgens 1979).

Whether there is in fact such a region is best judged from the effects of cortical damage on vocalization. Incomplete removals of the area directly controlling the larynx in monkeys have no discernible effect on the animals' spontaneous calls, and the monkeys can still make a call when given a signal as they have been taught to do before the operation (Sutton *et al.* 1974; Sutton 1979). More complete removals, including the area representing the face, do impair the monkey's ability to call; the voice is feeble and low-pitched (Green & Walker 1938). But it is not clear to what extent the general facial paralysis contributes to the animal's problem.

Even if we could be confident that the effect was the direct result of interference with the mechanisms controlling the vocal cords it would be analogous to the syndrome produced in patients by damage to the motor mechanisms of vocalization rather than the speech mechanisms of Broca's area. The speech disorder of patients with lesions of Broca's area alone is not to be accounted for by an elementary problem with articulation or phonation (Mohr 1976). A better parallel for the loss of fluency in such cases is provided by the marked decrease in spontaneous calling that follows the removal of prefrontal cortex in monkeys, that is of the area in front of premotor cortex (Myers 1976). But the symptom is most effectively produced in monkeys by damage to the orbital prefrontal cortex (Ervin *et al.* 1975), which also changes them emotionally (Butter & Snyder 1972; Kling & Mass 1974). It is possible that the change in vocalization is secondary to an alteration in temperament. For the moment, then, we can find no very promising candidate for the role of Broca's area in the monkey brain. The brain of apes has yet to be explored.

Let us suppose that Broca's area is indeed uniquely human. We are left with two outstanding questions. First, what exactly does Broca's area do, and how did an area with this function evolve? Secondly, why does Broca's area in one hemisphere play a much greater role in directing speech than does the same part of the brain in the other hemisphere?

Function

To answer the first question we must consider the functional organization of motor and premotor cortex in monkeys. In the primary motor area, MI, the body is represented in an inverted position; if a stimulating electrode is moved up the cortex in front of the central sulcus, movements will be elicited first of the face, then of the arm, the leg and finally the tail (Woolsey *et al.* 1952). This somatotopic map is crudely preserved in premotor cortex. The face area of MI is reciprocally connected via fibres to the larynx area of ventral premotor cortex; and the arm and face areas are reciprocally connected to the central and dorsal premotor cortex, the leg being represented above the arm (Kunzle 1978*a*; Matsumara & Kubota 1979; Muakkassa & Strick 1979). We may assume, without knowing it to be true, that in the human brain Broca's area is reciprocally connected to the larynx area.

We have supposed that the monkey brain lacks a region analogous to Broca's area, that is a higher centre directing the larynx area. But there are mechanisms in premotor cortex for the higher regulation of actions as carried out by the limbs. If we understood the influence of these areas on the movements of the limbs we might be in a better position to appreciate the nature of the influence of Broca's area on the movements of the vocal cords.

The motor area is particularly concerned with the production of the discrete and independent movements that are essential for skilled performance. It influences the muscles most directly through the fibres of the pyramidal tract. In primates this tract contains over $1\frac{1}{2}$ times as many fibres as in carnivores and rodents, after allowance is made for differences in body size, and over $3\frac{1}{2}$ times as many as in ungulates (Passingham 1981). In other words the size of the tract correlates with the degree of independence with which the digits can be moved, being greatest in animals with a hand, less in those with a paw, and least in animals with hooves.

The importance of motor cortex for skilled movements is more directly demonstrated by examining monkeys in which the pyramidal tract has been sectioned or in which motor cortex has been removed. In either case rhesus monkeys can still climb and leap, and can reach out and grasp objects with the whole hand; but they are unable to pick up small objects between thumb and forefinger in a fine precision grip (Lawrence & Kuypers 1968; Passingham *et al.* 1978). That the animal is unable to make discrete finger movements can be shown by requiring it to put its forefinger through a small hole so as to push a piece of food off a shelf. After removal of motor cortex and somatosensory cortex on one side rhesus monkeys are unable to do this with the affected hand (Passingham & Perry 1981).

Just as the sensory areas of the neocortex are primarily concerned with the analysis of fine detail, so the motor area appears to have an especial interest in the generation of refined movements. We might expect to find the larynx area to share a similar concern. As we have already noted we know nothing of the contribution of this area in monkeys and apes. In the squirrel monkey the repertoire of cackles, chirps, shrieks and so on can be elicited by electrically stimulating structures other than the neocortex (Jürgens & Ploog 1970). The chimpanzee vocabulary consists essentially of variations on a series of grunts, barks, screams and hoots (Marler 1969), and one might wonder whether the neocortex would be necessary for the production of such poorly articulated vowel sounds. In man, by comparison, the larynx area clearly contributes to the production and articulation of the very many discrete sounds used in human speech. Electrical stimulation of this area disrupts articulation (Penfield & Roberts 1959), and damage disrupts the execution of the many refined movements involved in vocal skill (Mohr 1976).

To return to the control of the limbs, we have now to consider the influence exerted by higher centres in premotor cortex. A monkey's ability to perform acts in a correct sequence can be tested by requiring it to carry out a series of manipulations. For example it can be arranged that a box containing food can only be opened if three catches are operated in the correct order. Monkeys in which an area including dorsal premotor cortex has been removed are poor at this task (Deuel 1977). Yet they have no problems in operating each of the latches on its own. Their problem lies in the ordering of the three movements.

The brain must programme not only the order in which a series of acts must be performed but also how many there are to be in the sequence. Monkeys can be trained to count by requiring them to press a button once or five times depending on some previous instruction. They are poor at this task if dorsal prefrontal cortex is removed (Passingham 1978). This area lies in front of dorsal premotor cortex and is linked to it by anatomical connections (Kunzle 1978b).

By analogy with dorsal premotor cortex it is tempting to suggest that the primary function of Broca's area is to direct the sequencing of the basic movements, in this case the movements of the vocal cords. Meaning is conveyed in speech by the serial ordering of the phonemes and morphemes, and a high order of vocal skill is demanded (MacNeilage 1970). Patients with large anterior cerebral lesions may suffer some loss of verbal fluency (Benson 1967); but they also have difficulties in sequencing sounds. In one study such patients were found to be able to say 'ba-ba-ba', but unable to repeat the sequence 'ba-da-ga' (Mateer & Kimura 1977). The lesions encroach on tissue controlling movements of the face, since the same patients have difficulties with copying simple facial movements or with repeating sequences such as retracting the lips, putting out the tongue and biting the lower lip (Mateer & Kimura 1977). It is possible to demonstrate a defect in reproducing the sequence without a corresponding difficulty in copying each oral movement on its own. This has been done by electrically stimulating anterior points in the left cerebral hemisphere of patients undergoing neurosurgery under local anaesthesia. On three occasions stimulation of inferior frontal sites well forward of the motor area has rendered the patient unable to copy a sequence of oral movements although the ability to copy each one on its own was preserved (Ojemann & Mateer 1979).

If it is accepted that Broca's area plays some role in the sequencing of speech sounds then the apparent lack of such an area in the brains of other primates may have a simple explanation. The calls of these animals are not constructed by the sequencing of elements to form the message; they can be treated rather as single elements, the equivalent of the basic phoneme. These primates have no need of a cortical area regulating the serial order of sounds.

Birds compose their songs in a quite different way. The basic elements are the notes and glissandi, and these are ordered into syllables and then into phrases. Some birds have relatively simple stereotyped songs, but others, such as the robin, rock wren and canary, sing long songs and possess a very large repertoire of song variants (Bremond 1968; Kroodsma 1975; Nottebohm 1977; Jellis 1977). In their structure, though not in their content, these songs are more like human speech than are the calls of other primates.

Dominance

The brains of some song birds also offer a clue as to the answer to the second question that we posed. Why is Broca's area in the left hemisphere more important for speech than the corresponding area in the right hemisphere? Speech is controlled by the left hemisphere in 96% of right-handed but only 70% of left-handed or ambidextrous subjects, by the right hemisphere in 15% of non-right-handed but only 4% of right-handed people, and by both hemispheres in 15% of non-right-handed people but in none of those who are right-handed (Milner 1975). The link with handedness makes it tempting to suggest that the left hemisphere is specialized for both manual and vocal skills, and that handedness may hold the key to the evolutionary origin of cerebral dominance for speech (Kimura 1976, 1979).

But cerebral dominance for vocalization can be present without handedness, as is shown by the existence of some birds in which there is an asymmetry in the neural control of song. In canaries, chaffinches and white-crowned sparrows, section of the nerve innervating the left syrinx markedly impairs singing, whereas section of the nerve innervating the right syrinx has little or no effect (Nottebohm 1977). Left dominance has also been demonstrated in canaries for the central controlling area, the hyperstriatum ventrale pars caudale; the number of syllables of song that the bird loses is much greater if lesions are made on the left rather than on the right (Nottebohm 1977).

This example suggests that there may be reasons why cerebral dominance is of advantage for the production of sounds. Perhaps the key to dominance lies not in handedness but in the way in which the brain innervates the vocal cords. The hand is controlled mainly by the contralateral hemisphere. If the motor area of that hemisphere is damaged the ipsilateral motor cortex is unable to direct the normal range of movements of that hand. This is true in monkeys even if the damage occurs very early in life (Passingham *et al.* 1978). The arrangement is quite different for central organs of the body, such as the tongue and jaw. If the motor cortex is electrically stimulated in man the limb that moves is always the one opposite the hemisphere stimulated; but movements of the tongue and jaw can be elicited from either hemisphere (Penfield & Roberts 1959). If the hypoglossal nerve, which innervates the tongue, is cut on one side in the monkey, stimulation of the motor area on the other side still elicits most tongue movements (Walker & Green 1938). This indicates that there are paths from each hemisphere to both sides of the tongue. If, therefore, the motor area is removed in one hemisphere, a monkey can still rotate and deviate its tongue to either side; and it remains able to rotate its tongue either way even if the hypoglossal nerve is sectioned ipsilateral to the cortical lesion (Green & Walker 1938).

It has been demonstrated in monkeys that the vocal cords also receive a bilateral innervation from the neocortex; the cords can be excited by electrical stimulation of either cortical larynx area (Hast *et al.* 1974). Vocalization can be induced in patients by stimulating the left or the right hemisphere (Penfield & Roberts 1959). This bilateral organization permits considerable recovery of function. It has traditionally been believed that lesions of Broca's area in people give rise to a long-lasting aphasia, but more careful analysis indicates that where the lesion can be shown to be confined to Broca's area and the adjacent larynx area the patients recover their speech remarkably well (Mohr 1976; Mohr *et al.* 1978). It is reasonable to suppose that this improvement occurs in part because the corresponding areas in the contralateral hemisphere can take over the relevant function.

It does not necessarily follow that because an organ can be controlled by either hemisphere it would be most efficient for one hemisphere to assume the dominant role. The movements of the tongue, for example, are relatively simple, and there is no reason why the relevant cortical areas cannot coordinate their instructions without loss of proficiency. But such an arrangement would not be optimal for the execution of complex sequences of movement, as in the production of speech. In such a case we would surely expect the highest skill to be achieved if the sequence was directed by one central programme, located in a single hemisphere, rather than by two separate programmes which must use the long commissural pathways to coordinate their instructions. The same reasoning applies to the production of intricate songs by those birds that, like canaries, learn a new song each season (Nottebohm 1977, 1979).

This is not to say that the right hemisphere normally makes no contribution to speech, even in people who are fully right-handed. This can be shown by using the amount of blood flowing to any cortical area as a measure of the metabolic requirements and therefore of the activity of that region. When a person talks there is an increase in the blood supply to Broca's area, but there is also a similar increase to the corresponding region of the right frontal lobe (Lassen *et al.* 1978). But, whatever the contribution of the right hemisphere under normal circumstances, the left hemisphere can direct speech efficiently on its own. In right-handed people damage to the inferior frontal region of the right hemisphere only rarely gives rise to the gross symptoms of aphasia (Hécaen & Albert 1978).

If there is an advantage in programming speech from one area rather than two it follows that those people in whom speech is controlled by both hemispheres should be at a disadvantage. There is suggestive evidence that this may be so, in particular that cerebral lateralization of speech may be less firmly established in some people who stutter. One method for investigating cerebral dominance for language is the dichotic listening technique. Different digits or words are played simultaneously to the two ears; the subject reports the words he hears, and if he gives mainly the words played to the right ear it is assumed that his left hemisphere is dominant for speech. In one study stutterers were found to differ from other subjects in reporting fewer of the words played to their right ear and more of those to the left; 55 % of the stutterers actually reported more words presented to their left than to their right ear (Curry & Gregory 1969). The most plausible interpretation of these results is that in these stutterers speech was less firmly represented in the left hemisphere, even though they were all right-handed.

The diagnosis of dominance made on the basis of the dichotic listening test usually agrees well with the results obtained by a more direct procedure, the sodium amytal test (Milner 1975). Sodium amytal is injected into the blood supply of one hemisphere; in this way the activity of a hemisphere can be temporarily inhibited. If speech is controlled only by the left hemisphere it will be disrupted by left-sided but not by right-sided injections. If injections into the blood supply of either hemisphere produce dysphasic symptoms we know that speech is represented in both hemispheres.

The sodium amytal test has been performed on very few stutterers. Of the seven right-handed tested two have shown evidence of bilateral representation of speech (Jones 1966; Andrews *et al.* 1972; Luessenhop *et al.* 1973). Speech was found to be controlled by both hemispheres in three of the four subjects who were ambidextrous or left-handed, and there was a suggestion that this might also be so in the fourth (Jones 1966; Luessenhop *et al.* 1973). The sample is small, but the results are as expected from the data on dichotic listening.

An objection immediately presents itself. On the sodium amytal test speech has been shown to be bilaterally represented in 18 out of the 122 patients who were ambidextrous or left-handed, and had not suffered any early brain injury (Milner 1975). We are not told whether any of these patients stuttered, but we may assume that they did not all do so, as the fact would surely have been noted. But the objection rests on an assumption: this is that in these patients the sequencing of speech was carried out by both hemispheres, and without a penalty. This assumption is not justified. Certainly speech was disrupted by injection of sodium amytal into the blood supply of either hemisphere, but the type of speech problem often differed for the two hemispheres (Rasmussen & Milner 1975). In 43 % of the patients with bilateral representation, errors of sequencing followed injection on one side and errors of naming the other. Errors of programming a sequence were detected on simple tasks requiring counting, enumerating the days of the week or the months of the year, and going through the alphabet. At least in these patients the production of such series was controlled by only one hemisphere.

For the moment we may reasonably entertain the notion that where complex sequences must be programmed it will be more efficient to set up one programme rather than two. We do not know whether it is the learning or the production of such sequences that imposes the constraint. The general view proposed here is distinct from the idea put forward by Levy (1977) to account for cerebral dominance. Her suggestion is not that any function will be carried out more effectively if it is controlled by a single hemisphere. Instead she points out that the capacity of the brain might be better used if particular functions are carried out by only one hemisphere instead of two. She argues that to duplicate programmes would be needless; it is argued here that to do so would be counter-productive.

I wish to thank Professor L. Weiskrantz and Dr A. Cowey for their comments on the manuscript.

References (Passingham)

Andrews, G., Quinn, P. T. & Sorly, W. A. 1972 Stuttering: an investigation into cerebral dominance for speech. *J. Neurol. Neurosurg. Psychiat.* **35**, 414–418.

Bailey, P. & von Bonin, G. 1951 *The isocortex of man.* Urbana: University of Illinois Press.

Bailey, P., von Bonin, G. & McCullogh, W. S. 1950 *The isocortex of the chimpanzee.* Urbana: University of Illinois Press.

Benson, F. D. 1967 Fluency in aphasia: correlation with radioactive scan localization. *Cortex* **3**, 373–394.

Braak, H. 1978 On magnopyramidal temporal fields in the human brain–probable morphological counterpart of Wernicke's sensory speech region. *Anat. Embryol.* **152**, 141–169.

Bremond, J. C. 1968 Recherches sur la sémantique et les éléments vecteurs d'information dans les signaux acoustiques du rouge-gorge (*Erithacus Rubecula* L.). *La terrie et la vie* **22**, 109–220.

Butter, C. M. & Snyder, D. R. 1972 Alterations in aversive and aggressive behaviors following orbital frontal lesions in rhesus monkeys. *Acta Neurobiol. Exper.* **32**, 525–565.

Curry, F. & Gregory, H. 1969 The performance of stutterers on dichotic listening tasks thought to reflect cerebral dominance. *J. Speech Hear. Res.* **12**, 73–82.

Deuel, R. K. 1977 Loss of motor habits after cortical lesions. *Neuropsychologia* **15**, 205–215.

Ervin, F. R., Raleigh, M. & Steklis, H. D. 1975 The orbital frontal cortex and monkey social behavior. *Abstr. Soc. Neurosci.* **1975** (1), 554.

Green, H. D. & Walker, A. E. 1938 The effects of ablation of the cortical face area in monkeys. *J. Neurophysiol.* **1**, 262–280.

Hast, M. H., Fischer, J. M., Wetzela, B. & Thompson, V. E. 1974 Cortical motor representation of the laryngeal muscles in *Macaca mulatta*. *Brain Res.* **73**, 229–240.

Hayes, K. J. & Hayes, C. 1952 Imitation in a home-raised chimpanzee. *J. comp. Physiol. Psychol.* **45**, 450–459.

Hayes, K. J. & Nissen, C. H. 1971 Higher mental functions of a home-raised chimpanzee. In *Behavior of non-human primates* (ed. A. M. Schrier & F. Stollnitz), pp. 59–115. New York: Academic Press.

Hécaen, H. & Albert, M. L. 1978 *Human neuropsychology.* New York: Wiley.

Holloway, R. L. 1972 New australopithecine endocast, SK 1585, from Swartkrans, South Africa. *Am. J. phys. Anthrop.* **37**, 173–186.

Holloway, R. L. 1978 Problems of brain endocast interpretation and African hominid evolution. In *Early hominids from Africa* (ed. C. Jolly), pp. 379–401. London: Duckworth.

Jellis, R. 1977 *Bird songs and their meaning.* London: B.B.C. publications.

Jones, R. K. 1966 Observations on stammering after localized cerebral injury. *J. Neurol. Neurosurg. Psychiat.* **29**, 192–195.

Jürgens, U. 1979 Neural control of vocalization in non-human primates. In *Neurobiology of social communication in primates* (ed. H. D. Steklis & M. J. Raleigh), pp. 11–44. New York: Academic Press.

Jürgens, U. & Ploog, D. 1970 Cerebral representation of vocalization in the squirrel monkey. *Expl Brain Res.* **10**, 532–554.

Kellogg, W. N. 1968 Chimpanzees in experimental homes. *Psychol. Rec.* **18**, 489–498.

Kimura, D. 1976 The neural basis of language qua gesture. In *Studies in neurolinguistics*, vol. 2 (ed. H. Whitaker & H. A. Whitaker), pp. 145–156. New York: Academic Press.

Kimura, D. 1979 Neuromotor mechanisms in the evolution of human communication. In *Neurobiology of social communication in primates* (ed. H. D. Steklis & M. J. Raleigh), pp. 197–219. New York: Academic Press.

Kling, A. & Mass, R. 1974 Alterations of social behaviour with neural lesions in nonhuman primates. In *Primate aggression, territoriality and xenophobia* (ed. R. L. Holloway), pp. 361–386 New York: Academic Press.

Kroodsma, D. E. 1975 Song patterning in the rock Wren. *Condor* **77**, 294–303.

Kunzle, H. 1978*a* Cortico-cortical efferents of primary motor and somatosensorty regions of the cerebral cortex in *Macaca fascicularis*. *Neuroscience* **3**, 25–39.

Kunzle, H. 1978*b* An autoradiographic analysis of the efferent connections from premotor and adjacent prefrontal regions (areas 6 and 9) in *Macaca fascicularis*. *Brain Behav. Evol.* **15**, 185–234.

Lawrence, D. G. & Kuypers, H. G. J. M. 1968 The functional organization of the motor system in monkeys. I. The effects of bilateral pyramidal lesions. *Brain* **91**, 1–14.

Lassen, N. A., Ingvaar, D. A. & Skinhøj, E. 1978 Brain function and blood flow. *Scient. Am.* **239**, 50–59.

Levy, J. 1977 The mammalian brain and the adaptive advantage of cerebral asymmetry. *Ann. N.Y. Acad. Sci.* **299**, 264–272.

Lieberman, P. 1975 *On the origins of language.* New York: Macmillan.

Luessenhop, A. J., Boggs, J. S., Laborwit, T. L. J. & Walle, E. L. 1973 Cerebral dominance in stutterers determined by Wada testing. *Neurology, Minneap.* **23**, 1190–1192.

MacNeilage, P. F. 1970 Motor control of serial ordering of speech. *Psychol. Rev.* **77**, 182–196.

Marler, P. 1969 Vocalizations of wild chimpanzees. *Proc. 2nd Congr. Primatol.*, vol. 1, pp. 94–100. Basel: Karger.

Mateer, C. & Kimura, D. 1977 Impairment of nonverbal oral movements in aphasia. *Brain Lang.* **4**, 262–276.

Matsumura, M. & Kubota, K. 1979 Cortical projection to hand–arm motor area from post-arcuate area in macaque monkeys. *Neurosci. Lett.* **11**, 241–246.

Milner, B. 1975 Psychological aspects of focal epilepsy and its neurological management. *Adv. Neurol.* **8**, 299–321.

Mohr, J. P. 1976 Broca's area and Broca's aphasia. In *Studies in neurolinguistics*, vol. 1 (ed. H. Whitaker & H. A. Whitaker), pp. 202–235. New York: Academic Press.

Mohr, J. P., Pessin, M. S., Finkelstein, S., Funckenstein, W. H. H., Duncan, G. W. & Davis, K. R. 1978 Broca's aphasia–pathologic and clinical. *Neurology, Minneap.* **28**, 311–324.

Muakkassa, K. F. & Strick, P. L. 1979 Frontal lobe inputs to primate motor cortex: evidence for four somatotopically organized 'premotor areas'. *Brain Res.* **177**, 176–182.

Myers, R. E. 1976 Comparative neurology of vocalization and speech. Proof of a dichotomy. *Ann. N.Y. Acad. Sci.* **280**, 745–757.

Nottebohm, F. 1977 Asymmetries in neural control of vocalization in the canary. In *Lateralization in the nervous system* (ed. S. Harnad, R. Doty, L. Goldstein, J. Jaynes & G. Krauthamer), pp. 23–44. New York: Academic Press.

Nottebohm, F. 1979 Origins and mechanisms in the establishment of cerebral dominance. In *Handbook of behavioral neurology*, vol. 2 (ed. M. S. Gazzaniga), pp. 295–344. New York: Plenum Press.

Ojemann, G. & Mateer, C. 1979 Human language cortex: localization of memory, syntax, and sequential motor-phoneme identification system. *Science, N.Y.* **205**, 1401–1403.

Passingham, R. E. 1978 Information about movements in monkeys (*Macaca mulatta*) with lesions of dorsal prefrontal cortex. *Brain Res.* **152**, 313–328.

Passingham, R. E. 1979 Specialization and the language area. In *Neurobiology of social communication in primates* (ed. H. D. Steklis & M. J. Raleigh), pp. 221–256. New York: Academic Press.

Passingham, R. E. 1981 Primate specialization in brain and intelligence. *symp. zool. Soc. Lond.*

Passingham, R. E. & Perry, V. H. 1980. In preparation.

Passingham, R. E., Perry, V. H. & Wilkinson, F. 1978 Failure to develop a precision grip in monkeys with unilateral cortical lesions made in infancy. *Brain Res.* **145**, 410–414.

Penfield, W. & Rasmussen, T. 1950 *The cerebral cortex of man.* New York: Macmillan.

Penfield, W. & Roberts, L. 1959 *Speech and brain mechanisms.* Princeton University Press.

Rasmussen, T. & Milner, B. 1975 Clinical and surgical studies of the cerebral speech area in man. In *Otfrid Foerster symposium on cerebral localization* (ed. K. J. Zülch, O. Creutzfeldt & G. C. Galbraith), pp. 238–255. Berlin: Springer.

Sutton, D., Larson, C. & Lindeman, R. C. 1974 Neocortical and limbic lesion effects on primate phonation. *Brain Res.* **71**, 61–75.

Sutton, D. 1979 Mechanisms underlying vocal control in non-human primates. In *Neurobiology of social communication* (ed. H. D. Steklis & M. J. Raleigh), pp. 45–67. New York: Academic Press.

Von Bonin, G. 1948 The frontal lobes of primates: cytoarchitectural studies. *Ass. Res. nerv. ment. Dis.* **27**, 67–83.

Von Bonin, G. & Bailey, P. 1947 *The neocortex of Macaca mulatta*. Urbana: University of Illinois Press.

Von Bonin, G. & Bailey, P. 1961 Pattern of the cerebral isocortex. *Primatologia* **2** (suppl. 10), 1–42.

Von Economo, C. 1929 *The cytoarchitecture of the human cerebral cortex*. London: Oxford University Press.

Walker, A. E. & Green, H. D. 1938 Electrical excitability of the motor face area: a comparative study in primates. *J. Neurophysiol.* **1**, 152–165.

Woolsey, C. N., Settlage, P. H., Meyer, D. R., Sencer, W., Pinto Hamuy, T. & Travis, M. 1952 Pattern of localization in precentral and 'supplementary' motor areas and their relation to the concept of a premotor area. *Ass. Res. nerv. ment. Dis.* **30**, 238–264.

Phil. Trans. R. Soc. Lond. B **292**, 177–188 (1981)   [177]

Printed in Great Britain

EMERGENCE OF HUMAN BEHAVIOUR PATTERNS

Archaeological tests of alternative models of early hominid behaviour: excavation and experiments

By G. L. Isaac

Anthropology Department, University of California, Berkeley, California 94720, U.S.A.

Several rival hypotheses have been advanced regarding behavioural innovations, which may have put important selection pressures towards the development of cognitive faculties and expanded brain functions. These hypothesized changes in behaviour include increased dependence on tool-making, intensification of hunting as a subsistence activity and social patterns involving food-sharing. Archaeology constitutes one of the principal sources of evidence against which such hypotheses can be tested and the paper reports on research that has been undertaken in recent years to make the tests clear and explicit. In addition to excavation, the work reported includes experimental studies of bone fracture, experiments in the manufacture and use of stone tools and experiments on processes of site formation.

Investigators of human evolution and cultural development tend implicitly to base their interpretation on the principle of uniformitarianism. That is to say they tend to explain as many features of early hominid adaptation as possible by constructing their models from some combination of the characteristics of modern apes and the characteristics of modern humans. This mode of procedure is surely the most convenient one to adopt in the initial stages of enquiry. However, it is very important also that its limitations be recognized. As Lancaster (1968), Freeman (1968) and others have pointed out, a major part of the fascination of the study of the early antecedents of the human way of life is that we are investigating systems that have no living counterparts. Since there are no proto-humans alive today and there are no societies with proto-languages we clearly need to bear in mind the possibility that some, perhaps many, features of early hominid adaptive systems were distinctive and original.

Since the behavioural systems of early hominids would have had profound influence on brain evolution, the topic, while fraught with difficulties, is one of considerable importance. This paper offers a preliminary report on research that is designed to make the interpretation of early archaeological data on hominid behaviour more rigorous by subjecting sets of rival hypotheses to carefully devised tests. The work is being done by a team for which I am co-ordinator and spokesman.

Figure 1 presents a time table that indicates the first known appearance in the geological record of anatomical innovations that are a part of the human adaptive complex as we now know it. The figure presents, in a highly simplified fashion, minimum ages for important *anatomical shifts* in the human direction. What can be said about *behavioural* changes? For this, very largely we have to turn to archaeological evidence.

The ability of archaeologists to make a specific contribution to knowledge of early hominid patterns of life hinges on, but is not limited to, one particular innovation, namely hominid involvement in the making of recognizable implements from durable materials, most particularly stone. Once artefacts of stone began to be made they became markers for the movements and activities of their makers and archaeological inference can go beyond technology.

The upper half of figure 1 provides a time table of archaeological evidence for a series of significant technological, economic and cultural innovations.

The earliest known well documented and securely dated stone tools are those excavated by H. Merrick and J. Chavaillon from member F of the Shungura Formation at the Omo. These are almost exactly 2 Ma old. Stone artefacts that may well be about $2\frac{1}{2}$ Ma old have been reported by Roche & Tiercellin (1977) from the Hadar, but we await further work for confirmation of the geological relationship and hence the age. The best studied and most informative set of very early archaeological occurrences are those of bed I at Olduvai (Leakey 1971), which

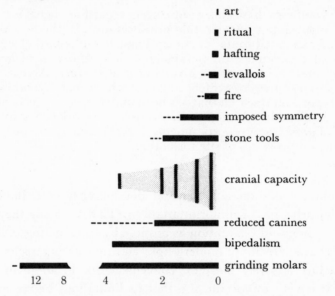

FIGURE 1. A time table showing the first known geological records of the appearance of human anatomical and behavioural traits. There is an almost complete gap in the record between 8 and 4 Ma ago.

are between 1.9 and 1.6 Ma old. Major features of the configuration discovered by M. Leakey are as follows: (1) stone tools were made; (2) the behaviour of the tool makers was such that they discarded a scattering of artefacts here and there over the landscape, but also such that concentrated patches of artefacts formed in some places called sites by archaeologists; (3) some of these patches contain artefacts only, but others also contain quantities of the broken-up bones of a variety of animals, and in two cases the patch of artefacts coincides with the skeletal remains of the carcass of a single large animal. Subsequent research at Koobi Fora, Melka Kunturé, Chesowanja and Gadeb has shown that this configuration is not peculiar to Olduvai (see, for example: Isaac 1978; Harris 1978; Chavaillon 1976; Bishop *et al.* 1978).

The question then arises: what does this configuration mean? Can archaeological investigations of these material remains inform us about the adaptive patterns of early tool-making hominids? The first round of research revealed the configuration, the second is attempting to probe its evolutionary meaning.

The overall time table allows us to identify two grand puzzles that demand attention as we grope towards an understanding of the dynamics of human evolution. The first is the question of the circumstances surrounding the adoption of bipedal stance and locomotion and the second the nature of the selection pressures leading to a sustained trend towards brain enlarge-ment and reorganization. From the time table it can be seen that the archaeological record as we now have it can do little or nothing to eludicate the circumstances of the shift to bipedalism, which took place at least $1\frac{1}{2}$ to 2 Ma before the date of the oldest recognizable tools yet found. On the other hand the known record of marked brain expansion and the known archaeological record coincide rather closely and it has long seemed reasonable to suggest that these two phenomena were related. That is to say, it is widely believed that some of the novel behavioural ingredients that caused the archaeological record to start forming were also significant deter-minants of the trend towards brain enlargement.

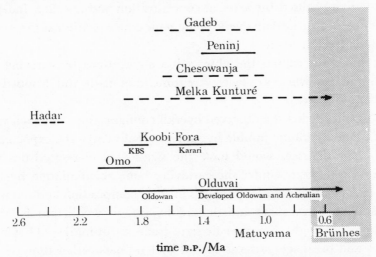

FIGURE 2. The approximate time relations among localities in east Africa yielding early archaeological evidence. Dotted lines denote less certain age determinations.

BEHAVIOURAL INTERPRETATION: HYPOTHESES AND TESTS

At first glance the configuration just indicated seems familiar and readily interpretable. Where we see artefacts among the bones of a large animal, we quickly conclude that this is a fossil butchery site indicative of meat-eating on a large scale (Leakey 1971; Isaac 1971, 1978). Equally, the clusters of artefacts and broken bones from many different animals seem obvious to us as living sites (Leakey 1971) or home bases (Isaac 1969, 1978). But one should ask, as critics have indeed begun to ask (see, for example, Binford 1977), whether these are the only possible explanations. In adopting them without further question might we not be guilty of simply projecting familiar human-ness backwards 2 Ma? As I will briefly indicate at the end of the paper, the butchery, meat-eating, and home base interpretations are apt to get incor-porated as components of far-reaching interpretations of the dynamics of human evolution. It surely behoves us to test these interpretations, to destruction if possible, before too much higher order theory is based on them.

As E. O. Wilson (1975) has pointed out, writers on human evolution have tended to be passionate advocates of one particular explanation or interpretation. However, in recent years the style has been changing in favour of the formulation of alternative or rival hypotheses, each with its own test implications that can serve to guide research. This not only turns out to be a constructive move, but also it is fun! What follows is a hasty portrait of how our research group is attempting to apply this approach. I will pose a series of problems as questions, then indicate two or more possible answers or rival hypotheses plus the predictions that follow from the hypotheses. Then I will indicate the kinds of research being done to test the extent to which the predictions are met. In most instances the research is still in progress by others and so I can only whet your appetites while you await fuller reports from the investigators themselves.

(a) How did the clusters of artefacts and bones form?

Some possible explanations that have occurred to various people are as follows.

(i) These are hydraulic jumbles in which artefacts and bones have been washed together by water currents.

(ii) Hominid activity caused the artefact concentration and another, independent, agency, such as carnivore-feeding formed an overlapping bone concentration at some common amenity, for instance a shade tree, or a water hole.

(iii) That the hominids caused the observed configurations by carrying both stones and bones to particular places, where artefacts were sometimes made and dropped and where bones were broken up and discarded.

Each of these would predict the observed overall configuration, but each would predict differences in detail. The hydraulic jumble hypothesis would carry the expectation that the concentrations and their matrices would have the size-sorted characteristics and sedimentary fabric of a water-lain deposit. Under the carnivore bone accumulation hypothesis the bones would resemble carnivore-chewed assemblages in their composition and damage patterns. The hominid stone and bone transport and discard hypothesis would predict that among other things some of the bones might show specific signs (such as cut marks) of having been processed with stone knives and breakage patterns caused by hammers rather than by jaws.

All of these suggested explanations need to be taken seriously, and it should be recognized that they are not mutually exclusive. Combinations may have acted to form individual sites. Almost all archaeological horizons in east Africa were covered over and preserved by sediments deposited from moving water, albeit in some cases very gently moving water which laid down only silts and clays. This means that, even where it seems highly improbable that the concentration of materials could have been caused by hydraulic forces, it is necessary to assess the extent to which the material has been moved about before interpreting the details of arrangement.

One member of the team with which I work, K. Schick, has embarked on a programme of experimental work designed to help archaeologists assess the degree to which an excavated assemblage has been transported, winnowed or rearranged. Her work involves a wide variety of controlled observations on the processes by which material accumulates and on the effects of geological and other agencies that could cause the materials to become stratified. The results of these experiments will be used to guide interpretation of archaeologically observed configurations.

The bone assemblages from a series of sites at Koobi Fora and Olduvai have been carefully studied by H. Bunn and those from Olduvai have also been studied by R. Potts. Both have independently looked for distinctive hammer breakage patterns and for modifications such as cut marks. At some sites the results of these searches have been positive and reports on these important new findings, which meet the predictions for hominid involvement with the bones, and which effectively falsify hydraulic or carnivore causation alone, will shortly be published.

Another new finding, which helps to distinguish the three rival hypotheses under discussion, has been the discovery by N. Toth, E. Kroll and K. Schick that at several sites numbers of stone artefacts and bones can be fitted back together again.

Preliminary plans by Kroll, who is doing detailed analyses of arrangement patterns, allow us to see that fitting pieces of stone and bone tend to be clustered in a way that would not be predicted if the artefacts and bones had simply been washed together.

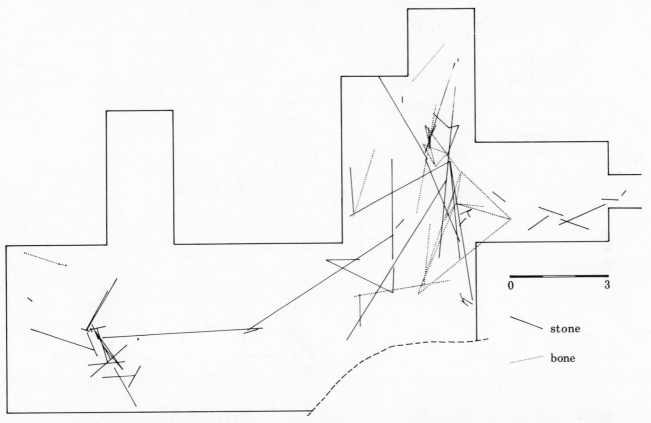

FIGURE 3. A plan of the excavated area at an early site (FxJj 50) in the Koobi Fora area. The lines join up the find places of artefact and bone pieces that fit back together. The configuration strongly implies that the hydraulic jumble hypothesis should be rejected.

(b) What kinds of hominid behaviour patterns resulted in the formation of sites?

Given the working hypothesis that the site concentrations formed through active hominid manipulation of stones and bones, the question arises, what were the hominids doing at these places?

Many of the sites are located in stoneless terrain and it is very clear that stones were carried to the locality and flaked there. As the study of conjoining pieces shows, some artefacts were removed from the immediate vicinity in which they were made. However, the accumulation of bones is not so clearly attributable to proto-human transport, since bones, while in live animals, are independently mobile! Alternative hypotheses again need to be considered.

(i) Artefacts were made and discarded at places where a variety of animal carcasses were periodically available for butchery and for breaking of bones, for instance the margin of a water hole, where animals recurrently died, or a bend in a river, where drifting carcasses washed up.

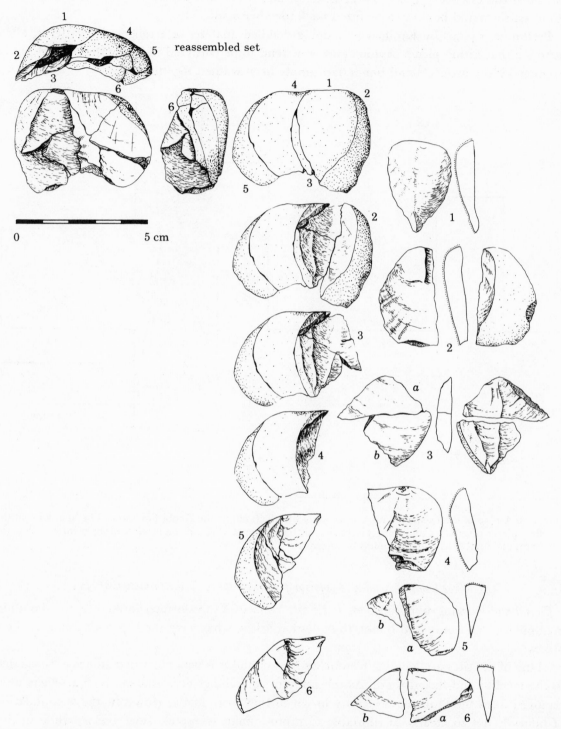

FIGURE 4. An example of a set of flakes from site FxJj 50 that fit back together. The reassembled set is shown at the top and successive stages of disassembly are set out below. The flakes can be seen to have been struck from the margin of a water-rounded cobble. After the striking of the flakes, the cobble would have had the form of a chopper, but this had been removed from the vicinity where the flaking was done.

(ii) Bones and meat from many different carcasses were carried to a central locality at which the manufacture of stone artefacts was also carried out.

At the present time I cannot offer decisive evidence to prove false either of these alternatives. However, given the considerable diversity of species at some of the sites, and given their varied physiographic settings, such as flood plains on the shores of lakes for the Olduvai FLK Zinj site, and flood plains on channel banks for FxJj 50, one is inclined to regard the first explanation as less credible.

If the second hypothesis is adopted, then this implies the transport of food, a behaviour common in birds and bees but rare among mammals and almost unknown in primates other

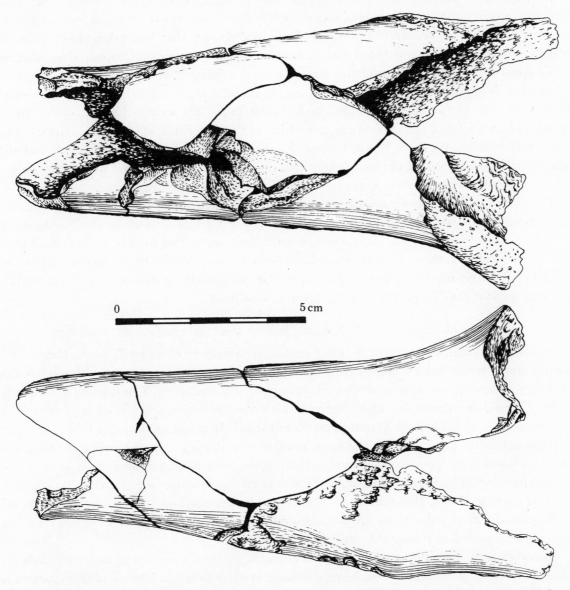

0   5 cm

FIGURE 5. An example of pieces of bone that fit back together. The reassembled set has been identified by H. Bunn as a humerus shaft from a large alcelaphine antelope. Experimental evidence strongly suggests that the fracture of the shaft was induced by a hammer blow. Part of what is almost certainly the articular end of this same bone was also found at the site and this has scored lines on it that seem to be cut marks inflicted by the sharp edge of a stone tool.

than humans. Whether the food was transported for sharing among an entire social group or simply for the feeding of the young would be an important follow up question, to which we can as yet offer no answer, or even any potential tests.

Another important question that arises as we pursue this chain of investigation is the matter of the amount of time and the number of site usage episodes that formed early sites. Were the assemblages of artefacts and bones at such living sites as the Olduvai FLK Zinj site or FxJj 50 and FxJj 20 at Koobi Fora deposited as refuse during a single sustained period of occupancy or did they accumulate as a result of a long drawn-out series of short return visits, with each visit leading to the discard of an increment of refuse?

We know of no simple measures of duration and recurrence of occupancy, but patient work may help to put limits on the mode of accumulation. For instance, the degree of preburial bone weathering would allow one to distinguish bone assemblages that had taken many years to accumulate. H. Bunn has concluded that, at least at some of the early sites, subaerial weathering is not apparent on most bones, probably implying accumulation over no more than a year or so.

Another line of attack follows deductive logic. If at the majority of early hominid sites usage bouts were brief and short, there might also be many 'mini-sites' scattered about, places where activities lasted a few hours or a day or so and led to the deposition of just a few artefacts and other refuse items. We have begun to look for these and have indeed found some, but the sample areas searched and the series excavated need to be much enlarged before any judgement of the relative frequency of mini- and maxi-sites can be reached.

The early sites have been variously called occupation sites, living sites, home bases etc. All these are loaded terms that involve many tacit backward projections of the familiar forms of modern *Homo sapiens* patterns. For instance, even if food was carried to these places and if tools were made and used there, they need not have been sleeping places. In her spatial analysis of the sites, E. Kroll is seeking to formulate questions such as these and to seek discriminants between various possible modes of site usage and formation.

(c) *What do the early stone tools themselves teach us about the organisms that made them?*

Within our team this problem is being studied in a variety of ways. J. W. K. Harris and I are testing for correlations between the characteristics of assemblages and the characteristics of the environmental context in which each variant set was discarded. This is being done in the hope of identifying distinctive habitat-specific activities. We have also looked for evidence of change through time (Isaac & Harris 1978; Harris 1978). In pursuing this work it became clear that we needed to know whether the early artefact assemblages represent opportunistic least-effort solutions to the problem of obtaining sharp edges from stone, or whether, as in most late prehistoric and modern assemblages, there was a fairly elaborate set of culturally defined, arbitrary artefact forms. Different archaeologists can look at the same assemblage and come up with quite different judgements on this question. Approaches other than laboratory sorting were clearly needed to resolve this uncertainty.

In addition we realized, as did many other workers, that if we are to move towards an understanding of the adaptive significance of tools in early hominid life, we need to ascertain first the uses to which they *can* be put, and secondly to seek evidence of how they actually *were* used.

Both the complexity of design problem and the problem of function called for a combination of experiments and close scrutiny of the sets of excavated ancient artefacts. A start on this large and important task has been made for the project by N. Toth, who has learned to replicate all of the artefact forms so far recovered from the early sites at Koobi Fora using the same raw materials as were used between 1¼ and 2 Ma ago. He will be reporting his specific findings elsewhere, but it appears that the features of the early stone artefact assemblages can be accounted for as the application of an opportunistic, least-effort strategy applied to locally available forms of stone. Even such apparently fancy forms as the Karari scraper need be no more than this.

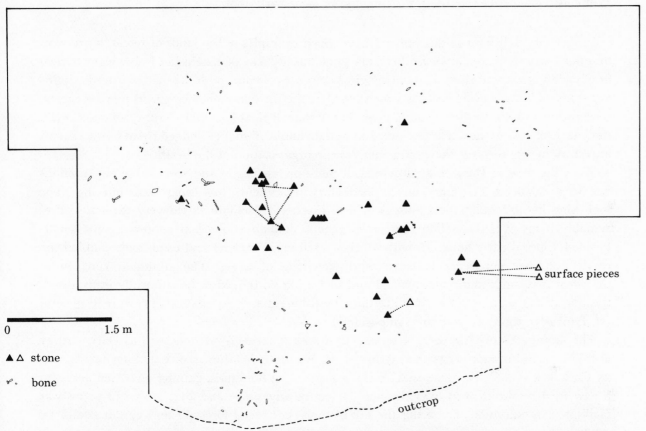

FIGURE 6. An example of the disposition of finds at a mini-site of the kind that our research group is now searching out and excavating. At this one (FxJj 64), stone flakes, derived from the knapping of just three or four stones, form a cluster superimposed on a scatter of bone fragments. Such sites have the advantage that they may represent a single bout of activity during one visit to the locale, lasting from between an hour or so to a day or so. This example was found by A. K. Behrensmeyer and excavated by F. Marshall.

In the investigation of function, Toth and other members of our group have demonstrated that by means of simple flakes and core tools it is perfectly possible to perform all the most basic functions that in ethnography and later prehistory are necessary to the human way of life: branches can be chopped off and then sharpened so as to form a digging stick or spear; a simple carrying device such as a bark tray can be prepared; and animals, even very large pachyderms over which the non-human carnivores have great difficulty, can be cut up.

These experiments, together with those done by P. Jones and the late L. Leakey (Jones, this symposium) and by others, go a long way to confirm the view that the discovery of how to obtain sharp-edged tools had great potential adaptive significance. Among others, they facilitate access to energy-rich food types such as meat and deep tubers.

However, what early tools might have been used for and what they actually were used for are not necessarily the same things. N. Toth has tackled this also, working with L. Keeley, a pioneer researcher on the distinctive wear patterns that are induced on stone by contact with such materials as wood, bone, hide, meat and plant tissues of various kinds. As Keeley and Toth will report in due course, preliminary examinations seem to imply that several different varieties of use wear are evident on chert flakes from the Koobi Fora Formation.

The finding, by H. Bunn and R. Potts, of cut marks on bones represents still another important class of evidence regarding the function of some early tools.

In the preceding part of this paper I have given examples of the kinds of research question that our research group, among others, are pursuing. By way of conclusion I now want to deal briefly with how these kinds of archaeological enquiries connect with the overall interdisciplinary study of human evolution. As I mentioned in the introduction, two grand puzzles can be recognized, and it is to the second of these that archaeological data seem most relevant, namely the puzzle of how natural selection acted to initiate and sustain a prolonged trend in the human ancestral lineage towards the enlargement and reorganization of the brain.

Since the time of Darwin, a succession of more or less vague and speculative explanations has been advanced. Two stand out as particularly prominent, 'tool-using' and 'hunting'. The tool-using line of explanation, though widely invoked, is seldom stated very explicitly. Presumably it involves the notion that novel genetic configurations that endowed some small-brained, bipedal early hominids with superior abilities in making and using tools enabled the carriers of these genotypes to leave more surviving offspring. The argument runs on to the effect that, since many tool making and tool-using skills need to be culturally transmitted, the adaptive importance of tools led to the establishment and elaboration of culture in general (cf. Lancaster 1968; Tobias, this symposium).

The hunting theory has been recounted in dramatic terms by writers such as Dart, Ardrey and Morris and in more restrained terms by, for example, Washburn & Lancaster (1968) and by Campbell (1966). It argues that, for savannah-living hominids, gaining increased access to a new food resource, meat, was the main selective advantage and that successful access was facilitated by mutations favouring the use of tools, enhanced foresight and cunning, and by mutations favouring communication and cooperation, especially among males.

Very recently, various workers, including myself (Washburn 1965; Hewes 1961; Lee 1979; Lancaster 1978; Isaac 1978), have been involved in making explicit yet another line of explanation, food-sharing. This subsumes tools and hunting, adds some other components and then goes on to argue that it was the adoption of a whole integrated complex of behavioural innovations that in each generation gave individuals, or perhaps kin groups, with somewhat more versatile brains, a crucial advantage over their contemporaries.

The investigations outlined in the body of this paper are all aimed at helping to distinguish the relative credibility of these and other rival large-scale overarching theories of the evolutionary dynamics of human brain enlargement. The information that we now have does not make it seem that the earlier approximations, 'tool-using' and 'hunting' are wrong, only that they are seriously incomplete. For instance, use of stone tools could only have become important as a part of a whole series of social, reproductive and dietary changes (cf. Parker & Gibson 1979).

Archaeological research has shown that many early artefacts occur jumbled up among the broken bones of edible animals. Does this circumstantial evidence really imply that the early hominids were hunting in a serious way? I have already indicated the existence of new evidence that tends to sustain the hypothesis that the tool-making hominids were eating meat and marrow. However, there are more ways of obtaining flesh and bone than by hunting and killing. We need to consider scavenging as an alternative. There are aspects of the bone assemblages associated with early artefacts that would be more plausibly predicted under the scavenging hypothesis than under the hunting hypothesis (cf. Vrba 1975; Schaller & Lowther 1969). Most tropical modern human gatherer–hunters catch and consume quantities of medium to smallish animals, which size range it is unusual to obtain by scavenging. However, the archaeological bone assemblages from Olduvai (Leakey 1971) and from Koobi Fora (H. Bunn, personal communication) are dominated by bones from medium to large animals, precisely the size range of carcasses that do provide scavenging opportunities (Vrba 1975). The relative importance of these two alternatives remains to be explored in further research.

However, even if meat-eating and hunting are adopted as reasonably well documented components of early hominid behaviour, the hunting hypothesis remains far from satisfactory as a comprehensive explanation of the basis for the evolution of the human brain–mind–culture complex. For instance, what were the females and children doing while males hunted?

The food-sharing hypothesis would predict the following as having been important: tools, transport of food, meat-eating, gathered plant foods, division of labour and the existence of places at which members of a social group would reconvene at least every day or so and at which discarded artefacts and food refuse would accumulate. The archaeological configuration observed at Olduvai and at Koobi Fora fits many of these predictions.

This line of explanation has important potential for helping us to understand the complex dynamics of the last 2 or 3 Ma of human evolution. It has already been adopted in such widely read popular books as *Origins*, written by Leakey & Lewin (1977). However, it is a hypothesis, not an established truth. This is why our research group has systematically sought to test it by attempting to prove its predictions false. However, there are important gaps: we assume that plant foods were the dominant source of energy and nutrition for the early Pleistocene hominids, but, beyond the preliminary findings of A. Walker in his studies of tooth wear (this symposium), we have few ways to test that assumption or to ascertain when gathering with postponed consumption of plant foods began. One member of our group, J. Sept, intends to attack an aspect of the problem by studying the feeding opportunities that are represented in modern analogues of the situations in which field evidence shows that early hominids lived, made tools and died.

Once the food-sharing system had been established the theory predicts that it would have produced steady selection pressure in favour of capabilities for developing social systems based on reciprocity. There are clear potential cross ties here between this theory and the recently enunciated theories of the evolution of social tendencies through the mechanism of kin selection (Hamilton 1964; Trivers 1971; Wilson 1975).

The food-sharing line of explanation is not an entirely new suggestion, but until recently it was implicit rather than explicit. In 1975 I sought to rectify this by stating clearly the thesis that the early tool-making hominids lived in social groups that manifested division of labour and practised food-sharing at home bases (Isaac 1976). Many people took this to mean that the early hominids must have been relatively placid, cooperative, gentle creatures who lived essentially human lives, less a few trappings of cultural elaboration. This does not necessarily follow, and I return to the point made at the outset: there are no living counterparts of the early hominids and we should expect that, as we refine our information about them, more and more distinctive and unexpected features may appear. To illustrate this let me close by pointing out that recent research on finger bones (Susman *et al.* 1979) and shoulder joint (Vrba 1979) strongly imply that the hominids of 2 Ma ago, though adapted to bipedal locomotion, were also well adapted for tree climbing. It is entirely possible that they did not sleep at their so-called home bases but that they slept in trees.

REFERENCES (Isaac)

Bishop, W. W., Hill, A. & Pickford, M. 1978 Chesowanja: a revised geological interpretation. In *Geological background to fossil man* (ed. W. W. Bishop), pp. 309–327. Edinburgh: Scottish Academic Press.

Binford, L. 1977 Olorgesailie deserves more than the usual book review. *J. anthrop. Res.* **33**, 493–502.

Campbell, B. G. 1966 *Human evolution.* Chicago: Aldine.

Chavaillon, J. 1976 Evidence for the technical practices of Early Pleistocene hominids: Shungura Formation, lower Omo valley, Ethiopia. In *Earliest man and end environments in the Lake Rudolf Basin* (ed. Y. Coppens, F. C. Howell, G. Ll. Isaac & R. E. F. Leakey), pp. 565–573. Chicago: University of Chicago Press.

Freeman, L. G. 1968 A theoretical framework for interpreting archaeological materials. In *Man the hunter* (ed. R. B. Lee & I. DeVore), pp. 262–267. Chicago: Aldine.

Hamilton, W. D. 1964 The genetical evolution of social behaviour II. *J. theor. Biol.* **7**, 17–52.

Harris, J. W. K. 1978 The Karari Industry: its place in East African prehistory. Ph.D. thesis. University of California, Berkeley.

Hewes, G. W. 1961 Food transport and the origins of hominid bipedalism. *Am. Anthrop.* **63**, 687–710.

Isaac, G. Ll. 1969 Studies of early culture in East Africa. *Wld Archaeol.* **1**, 1–28.

Isaac, G. Ll. 1971 The diet of early man. *Wld Archaeol.* **2**, 278–299.

Isaac, G. Ll. 1976 East Africa as a source of fossil evidence for human evolution. In *Human origins: Louis Leakey and the east African evidence* (ed. G. Ll. Isaac & E. R. McCown), pp. 121–137. Menlo Park: W. A. Benjamin.

Isaac, G. Ll. 1978 The food-sharing behaviour of protohuman hominids. *Scient. Am.* **238**, 90–108.

Isaac, G. Ll. & Harris, J. W. K. 1978 Archaeology. In *Koobi Fora research project*, vol. 1 (ed. M. G. Leakey & R. E. Leakey), pp. 64–85. Oxford: Clarendon Press.

Lancaster, J. B. 1968 On the evolution of tool-using behaviour. *Am. Anthrop.* **70**, 56–66.

Lancaster, J. B. 1978 Carrying and sharing in human evolution. *Hum. Nature* **1** (2), 82–89.

Leakey, M. D. 1971 Excavations in Beds I and II, 1960–1963. *Olduvai Gorge*, vol. 3. Cambridge University Press.

Leakey, R. E. F. & Lewin, R. 1977 *Origins.* New York: E. P. Dutton.

Lee, R. B. 1979 *The !Kung San.* Cambridge University Press.

Parker, S. T. & Gibson, R. 1979 A developmental model for the evolution of language and intelligence in early hominids. In *The behavioural and brain sciences*, vol. 2, pp. 367–408. Cambridge University Press.

Roche, H. & Tiercellin, J. J. 1977 Discovery of an old lithic industry *in situ* in the Hadar Formation, Central Afar, Ethiopia. *C. r. hebd. Séanc. Acad. Sci. Paris* D **284**, 1871–1874.

Schaller, G. B. & Lowther, G. R. 1969 The relevance of carnivore behaviour to the study of early hominids. *SWest. J. Anthrop.* **25**, 307–340.

Susman, R. L. & Creel, N. 1979 Functional and morphological affinities of the subadult hand (O.H. 7) from Olduvai Gorge. *Am. J. phys. Anthrop.* **51**, 311–331.

Trivers, R. L. 1971 The evolution of reciprocal altruism. *Q. Rev. Biol.* **46**, 35–57.

Vrba, E. 1975 Some evidence of chronology and palaeoecology of Sterkfontein, Swartkrans and Kromdraii from the fossil Bovidae. *Nature, Lond.* **254**, 301–304.

Vrba, E. S. 1979 New study of the scapula of *Australopithecus africanus* from Sterkfontein. *Am. J. phys. Anthrop.* **51**, 117–130.

Washburn, S. L. 1965 An apes-eye view of human evolution. In *The origin of man* (ed. P. DeVore), pp. 89–107. New York: Wenner Gren Foundation.

Washburn, S. L. & Lancaster, C. S. 1968 The evolution of hunting. In *Man the hunter* (ed. R. B. Lee & I. De Vore), pp. 293–303. Chicago: Aldine.

Wilson, E. O. 1975 *Sociobiology: the new synthesis.* Harvard: Belknap.

Phil. Trans. R. Soc. Lond. B **292**, 189–195 (1981)   [189]
Printed in Great Britain

Experimental implement manufacture and use; a case study from Olduvai Gorge, Tanzania

By P. R. Jones

Donald Baden-Powell Quaternary Research Centre, University of Oxford,
60 Banbury Road, Oxford OX2 6PN, U.K.

[Plates 1 and 2]

Experiments involving the manufacture and use of stone tools are described. The original tools that served as models came from two sites in upper bed IV at Olduvai Gorge, Tanzania. The following conclusions are drawn. Widespread use of terms such as 'crude' or 'refined' in describing stone tools tells us nothing of the technical level achieved by the makers of the assemblages. The different qualities of the available raw materials, the forms in which they occur and how they function when used may have influenced the tool maker's designs and the morphology of the tools. The experiments suggest uses for the tools that are relevant to our understanding of what is found on some archaeological sites.

Introduction

The terminology that the Palaeolithic archaeologist uses owes a great deal to the recent experimental manufacture and use of stone tools. Without experimental work we would not be able to suggest what tools might or might not have been used for. This experimental work is particularly important when we consider that virtually all our evidence for the technology and material culture of early hominids for about $1\frac{1}{2}$ Ma consists of stone tools and their *debitage* of manufacture.

Several 'common sense' rules have been set out by Coles (1973, pp. 15–18) that experimental work must follow if results are to provide useful information. These experiments, though they can never provide definitive evidence (except in conjunction with microwear analysis (see, for example, Keeley & Newcomer 1977), do suggest the possibilities or impracticalities of any given method of manufacture or suggested use of a tool, and provide a framework of suggestions within which the archaeologist can view his material.

In this paper it is assumed that efficiencies noted by myself during tool manufacture and use apply also to early tool makers. It seems reasonable to suggest that early tool makers must have 'balanced' their industry with raw material availability, time, and required tool performance, in short, that they arrived at some equilibrium with their environment (see Spier 1970). We already know how lithic industries can reflect a scarcity or abundance of raw materials by exhibiting 'wasteful' methods or intensive use and reuse of materials. They must reflect not only the stages in between these extremes, but other factors as well. A wasteful or inefficient approach that did not reach some equilibrium with its resources would presumably not have lasted very long. In looking at the archaeological record we inevitably see most clearly the long-lasting successes. The Developed Oldowan and Acheulean industrial complexes, for example, must have been efficient in this sense and in equilibrium with their environments, i.e. 'successful', to have lasted as long as they did.

Here I will describe some of my experiments involving tool replication and use. The original tools that served as models come from two sites in upper bed IV at Olduvai Gorge, Tanzania. The raw materials used (phonolite and basalt) were collected from the same sources as those used by early tool makers and, after much experimental work, the general 'style' of hand axes from each site was duplicated. All of the flaking to be discussed was carried out by direct free-hand percussion with a hammer stone. Drawing on the results obtained, I show several things: first, that the widespread use of terms such as 'crude' or 'refined' in describing stone tools tells us nothing of the technical level achieved by the makers of the assemblages; secondly, that the different qualities of the available raw materials, the forms in which they occur, and how they function when used, may have influenced the tool makers' designs and thus the morphology of the tools; thirdly, that the experimental work that I carried out suggests uses for these tools that are relevant to our understanding of what is found on some archaeological sites.

Figures 1 and 2, plate 1, show edge and side views of hand axes from WK and HEB in upper bed IV. The two specimens have very different basic morphologies: the tool from HEB is large, symmetrical, with straight edges, and shows flat flaking on each face. The WK hand axe has an unretouched primary flake edge, little secondary retouch of the main flake blank, and deep flake scars. A large number of the hand axes from WK incorporate primary flake edges in the finished tool. Secondary retouch of the tool blank (generally large flakes) is minimal and an average scar count for the WK sample is 10.5 per specimen (Leakey 1975). The HEB hand axes show extensive invasive secondary flaking and an average scar count for these tools is 20 (Leakey 1976). The WK hand axes are thicker in relation to their breadth and generally shorter than those from HEB.

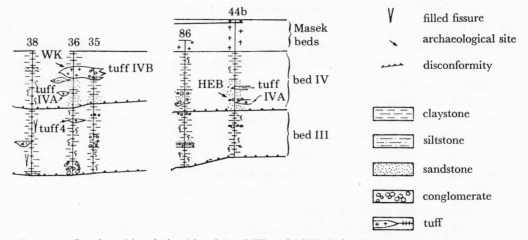

FIGURE 5. Stratigraphic relationship of sites WK and HEB. (After Hay (1976, fig. 41).

In short, the HEB tools appear more 'refined' than those from WK. Had they occurred in unstratified surroundings, the small basalt tools would almost certainly be considered the older on the basis of a general technical simplicity or 'primitiveness' that they seem to represent. In fact, as figure 5 shows, the HEB site occurs stratigraphically lower in the section than WK and is therefore the older of the two. I suggest that the thickness:breadth ratios, scar counts, retouched edges, and flat flaking are more a reflection of the qualities of the raw materials from which the tools are made than indicators of technological sophistication (Jones 1979).

In the course of my experimental work at Olduvai I duplicated the WK and HEB types of hand axe and used them for various activities. The following paragraphs discuss the differences between phonolite and basalt, both in their occurrence and their flaking properties, and show how these differences might have affected the tool makers' approach to each.

FIGURE 1. Edge views of two hand axes from bed IV, Olduvai Gorge. The one on the left is made of basalt and from WK (total length 12 cm). The tool on the right is from HEB and made of phonolite.

FIGURE 2. The same two tools shown in plan view. Note the flat flaking on the phonolite tool on the right.

Phil. Trans. R. Soc. Lond. B, volume 292

Jones, plate 2

FIGURE 3. A basalt hand axe about 13 cm long, shown with the *debitage* of manufacture.

FIGURE 4. A phonolite hand axe made on a large flake shown with the *debitage* of manufacture. The tool is about 18 cm long.

Occurrence of basalt and phonolite in the Olduvai area

Phonolite occurs on the surface at Engelosin (see figure 6 and Hay (1976)) in large blocks and slabs. Early tool makers generally made their tools on selected slabs or large flakes struck from blocks. The material is fine-grained, brittle and relatively easy to work.

Basalt was found by early tool makers in the form of large boulders and cobbles, from which flakes had to be struck as blanks for tool manufacture. These cobbles and boulders occur in seasonal river beds (figure 5), where the material has been deposited by river action as the waters came down from the volcanoes Lemagrut and Sadiman, south of the present gorge (Hay 1976). Although WK is very close to one of these channels, the tool makers would have had to go a considerable distance upstream to obtain boulders of the required size (R. Hay, personal communication).

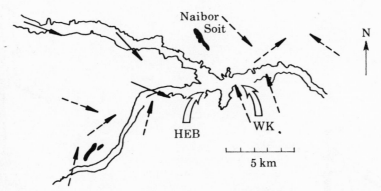

FIGURE 6. Map showing raw material sources and the drainage that brought basalt into the Olduvai area from the south. (After Hay (1976, fig. 64).) ——► Based on channel measurements; ---► inferred on other grounds.

The removal of flakes from smooth, water-rounded cobbles is not easy and it took me a little more than a month to duplicate the results of the WK tool makers. The material is tough and the secondary hand axe trimming flakes are detached by large, swinging, follow-through blows.

Since the size and shape of these raw materials varies considerably at their sources and since the materials have very different mechanical properties, different techniques are required to make tools from them. Figures 3 and 4, plate 2, show experimental tools, together with *debitage* in each of these materials.

Further experimental work involved the use of the replicated tools for specific tasks. I have used tools of this type for wood-cutting and chopping and found that the cutting edges in both of these materials sustain so much damage in such a short time that I consider this an unlikely use for them. After some experimentation it became apparent that the main work for which these tools are suited is butchery. I have therefore concentrated most of my experimental work on this.

Butchery experiments

A more detailed account of my butchery methods and experiments has been published elsewhere (Jones 1980). Here I will briefly summarize the relative efficiencies of phonolite and basalt tools. Most of the butchery experiments were carried out on goats. Figures 7–9 illustrate some stages of the butchery experiments. My procedure was modelled on the traditional butchery methods used by the Wakamba workers at Olduvai. The various stages of goat butchery provide a good test of several of the qualities required of a butchery tool. These stages are: skin incision, skin cutting, skin removal, disjointing legs at the tops of the metatarsals and metacarpals, removal of intestines by sawing through ribs near the sternum and cutting belly muscle, and the final disjointing of limbs at shoulder and pelvis.

While using phonolite flake tools for butchery I found that the primary unretouched edges were sharp, brittle, and easily blunted. The retouched edge was stronger and a lot more work could be carried out with it. The phonolite biface of the HEB design could easily be resharpened by simply removing a second series of flakes from its edges.

The basalt primary flake edges are sharp, strong and not so easily blunted as phonolite. Basalt hand axes made in the style of those found at WK are small and difficult to resharpen. They are made on relatively small flakes and the retouched edges are not so efficient as those in phonolite.

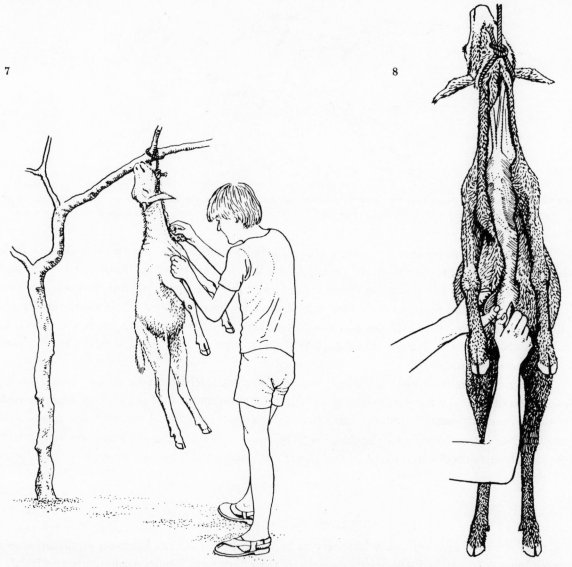

7   8

FIGURE 7. Experimental butchery followed the procedure used by the Wakamba workers at Olduvai (who use metal tools). The initial incision has been made with a flake and the skin is now being cut with a biface.

FIGURE 8. Showing the throat-to-tail cut that is the first stage of skin removal.

In general it was found that hand axes have several advantages over the simple flake. In butchering a goat (let alone an elephant) many flakes are required, each having to be tightly gripped between thumb and forefinger (figure 10). The short cutting edge of a flake limits the amount that can be cut at each stroke. The hand axe, however, with its weight and bulk is easily held in the hand and requires less effort to use over a long working period (1–2 h).

Using basalt and phonolite tools of different designs for butchery gives us some practical reasons for designing a different type of tool in each of these materials. After extensive replication of WK type tools in basalt I found that making a hand axe from a flake would generally take less than 2 min; sometimes as little as 50 s. I also found that if I used a large flake as the tool blank it was possible to make a relatively thin, straight-edged hand axe, but then the manufacture time was increased to about 15 min and the result of this work was scarcely more useful, for butchery, than the 1 min product.

When working with phonolite it is not difficult to make a tool of the WK type, but we have already noted that the primary flake edges are quickly blunted when used for butchery and, if the tool has not been designed in the correct way, resharpening is not easily accomplished. It

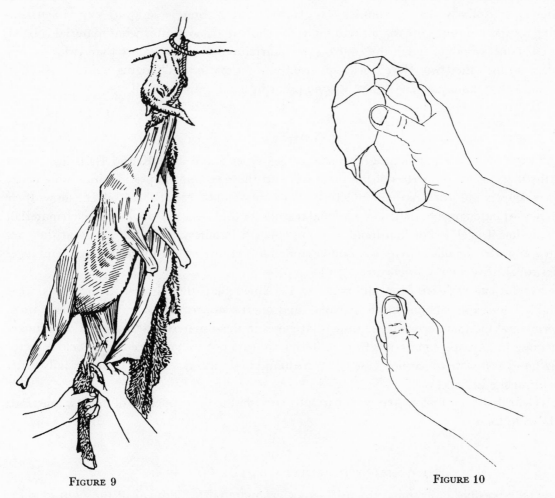

FIGURE 9   FIGURE 10

FIGURE 9. The skin is almost completely removed. Note how the lower parts of the limbs are removed with the skin.

FIGURE 10. Illustrating the ways in which a hand axe and a flake are held while being used for butchery. The hand axe has a longer edge and is more easily held than the flake.

seems to me that a short manufacture time is being used at WK for the practical reason that tool efficiency can hardly be increased by spending more time on manufacture, the 'law of diminishing returns'. At HEB, where phonolite was used, the retouched edge is considerably more useful than the primary flake edge; resharpening is easily carried out, and it is therefore worth while to make a large tool of this design. In my experimental work, a tool of this type required about 5 min to make.

Thus we have two different raw materials with different mechanical flaking properties, different edge strengths, and that function differently when used. It seems that the early tool makers were making their tools accordingly.

The third major raw material that was used for hand axe manufacture at Olduvai was quartzite. At Naibor Soit (figure 6) this material occurs in slabs from which tools can easily be made. Fine retouch is not easy and flakes often shatter when struck. Quartzite is a versatile material and takes different stone-working techniques without difficulty. It is interesting to note that, whereas bifaces occur in many different raw materials in bed IV assemblages, small tools such as scrapers always occur in either quartzite or chert. The chert is strong, fine-grained and flint-like, but was of limited use to early tool makers because it occurs in small (10–15 cm diameter), irregularly shaped nodules (Hay 1976, p. 184). Simple scraping experiments involving scrapers of phonolite, basalt and quartzite show that, no matter what material is being scraped (bone, wood, or hide), the edge on the quartzite tool will last more than twice as long as edges on the other two. Here it was apparently not a matter of changing the tool design in materials other than quartzite; there was no point in making them at all.

Summary

The experimental manufacture of bifaces of the types found at WK and HEB has shown that the mechanical properties of the materials and the sizes and shapes in which they occur at their sources influence tool manufacture. The experimental use of these bifaces shows their efficiency for butchery and indicates practical reasons for the biface morphology in each material. Not only has it been found that hand axes are efficient butchery tools, but also that they are altogether better for this activity than other stone tools occurring within the same assemblages (Jones 1980). (See Clarke & Haynes 1970.)

Archaeological evidence from Olduvai bed IV shows that, though several materials were available for scraper manufacture, quartzite and chert were regularly and consistently used. Experimental manufacture and use show that edges in these materials last a great deal longer than those in any other material. Raw material appears not to have been so critical a factor where hand axes were concerned, since they are found in several raw materials at virtually every Acheulean site in bed IV.

It is clear that early tool makers were carefully considering the properties of the raw materials available to them.

Discussion: implications for Olduvai

It is now possible to examine the archaeological material at Olduvai in the light of these practical experiments. The developed Oldowan and Acheulean industrial complexes are seen to coexist at Olduvai for some 0.75 Ma. Various interpretations have been made: it has been suggested that the industries represent various seasonal activities of one cultural group in which different activities required different tool kits (Isaac 1976). Another view is that they represent two totally distinct cultural groups (Leakey 1975). In either case, I would suggest, on the basis of my experiments, that the assemblages classed as Acheulean are better equipped to carry out fast, efficient butchery of large animals. Indeed, on the understanding that these bifaces, made on large flakes, mark the most significant difference between the two industries (Leakey 1975), the activity that they seem to represent, heavy-duty butchery, may be suggested as the main activity difference. In Olduvai bed II the stratigraphy is sufficiently clear to enable R. L. Hay to observe: 'the known Acheulean and Developed Oldowan B sites appear to differ in their palaeogeographic distribution. Sites of the Acheulean industry, as defined by the percentage of bifaces, lie more than 1 km inland from the margin of the lake, whereas contemporaneous Developed Oldowan B sites tend to lie within 1 km. of the lake margin' (Hay 1976, p. 181). This could represent the different seasonal activities of one cultural group moving close to and then away from the lake at different times of the year. There are modern ethnographic examples of just this kind of seasonal movement, for example the Hadza, who live east of Lake Eyasi in Tanzania, generally remain within one small drainage basin but live in dispersed groups during the rainy season and regroup to live near the few water holes during the dry season (L. Smith, personal communication).

The evidence is also consistent with the two culture groups theory, each of them exploiting different parts of their environment. The 'Acheulean' groups, staying by rivers leading into the lake where shelter, water and associated vegetable foods are available, would also be near what were presumably open plains where large animal carcasses could be sighted and scavenged.

The geographical area with which we are dealing is small (a few kilometres squared) and presumably well within the daily range of early hominids. My experimental tool manufacture provides some other interesting information that helps to put the archaeological material into perspective: an Acheulean site such as WK with 146 bifaces (hand axes and cleavers) could easily represent the products of three tool makers working for a day.

I would like to thank Dr Mary Leakey for her encouragement and support while I was at Olduvai, Paul Sila, Kavevo Kimeu and Mwongela Mwoka for their assistance with my butchery experiments, D. Bygott for the drawings of goat skinning, and the Boise Fund of Oxford for financial assistance. The photographs in figures 1–4 were taken by J. Reader.

References (Jones)

Clark, J. D. & C. Vance Haynes 1970 An elephant butchery site at Mwangandas Village, Karonga, Malawi, and its relevance for Paleolithic archaeology. *World Archaeol.* **1** (2), 390–411.

Coles, J. 1973 *Archaeology by experiment*. London.

Hay, R. L. 1976 *Geology of the Olduvai Gorge*. Berkeley: University of California Press.

Isaac, G. 1976 The activities of early African hominids. In *Human origins* (ed. G. Ll. Isaac & E. R. McCowan), p. 496.

Jones, P. R. 1979 Effects of raw materials on biface manufacture. *Science, N.Y.* **204**, 835–836.

Jones, P. R. 1980 Experimental butchery with modern stone tools and its relevance for palaeolithic archaeology. *World Archaeol.* **12** (2), 153–165.

Keeley, L. & M. Newcomer 1977 Microwear analysis of experimental flint tools: a test case. *J. archaeol. Sci.* **4**, 29–62.

Leakey, M. D. 1971 *Olduvai Gorge*, vol. 3. Cambridge University Press.

Leakey, M. D. 1975 Cultural patterns in the Olduvai Sequence. In *After the australopithicines* (ed. K. W. Butzer & G. Ll. Isaac), pp. 477–493. The Hague: Mouton.

Leakey, M. D. 1976 The early stone industries of Olduvai Gorge. In *The earlier industries of Africa* (ed. J. D. Clark) & G. L. Isaac), pp. 14–41. U.I.S.P.P. Congress (Nice), colloquium no. 5.

Spier, R. E. G. 1970 *From the hand of man*. Boston: Houghton Mifflin.

Phil. Trans. R. Soc. Lond. B **292**, 197–204 (1981)   [197]
Printed in Great Britain

Symbolic and syntactic capacities

By R. W. Brown

Department of Psychology and Social Relations, Harvard University, William James Hall,
33 Kirkland Street, Cambridge, Massachusetts 02138, U.S.A.

Three kinds of information invite renewed speculation about the origin of language. Studies of manual signing in chimpanzee have now shown that this species has a rudimentary symbolic capacity, but they have not shown that chimpanzee has any syntactic capacity. Diverse instances of something like language invention in historic times converge on the conclusion that iconicity is the primary principle of symbol invention, and the iconic possibilities are far greater with manual symbols than with vocal symbols. The study of fossil endocasts may eventually show when, in the fossil record, the hominid brain became organized in ways associated with linguistic capacities in present-day *Homo sapiens*, but it is unlikely ever to be able to distinguish the brain substrate for manual language from the substrate for vocal language. These several pieces of evidence suggest that the symbolic capacity developed before any syntactic capacity and was at first manifest in manual iconic form.

My title is, I think, an imperfect disguise for the fact that this is another paper on the slightly eccentric subject of the origin of language. Human beings will not let that hopeless problem rest. Fragments of new information can still entice us into trying once again, and I have three new things in mind: (1) experiments that attempt to teach a sign language to a great ape, about a dozen chimpanzees and one gorilla to date (Fouts 1973; Gardner & Gardner 1978; Patterson 1978; Terrace 1979); (2) instances of something like language invention occurring in the present day; (3) new thoughts and findings from archaeology, palaeoneurology and palaeoanthropology.

Signing in apes

The controversy concerning the nature of the capacities that have been demonstrated in studies of language-like behaviour in the great apes is especially heated just now. The rise in temperature results from the publication of a book and several papers by Terrace (1979) of Columbia University and his associates (Terrace *et al.* 1979) reporting the results of their four-year effort to teach a sign form of English to the male chimpanzee that they call Nim. Terrace's surprised conclusion from his own study is that there is no evidence that chimpanzee can create a sentence though there is evidence that chimpanzee can learn words. This is also my present opinion, but I prefer to speak of syntax rather than the sentence and symbol rather than word.

I will use symbol to mean a token or vehicle that is associated with and represents a referent on the basis of arbitrary convention (after C. S. Pierce and many others). Syntactic capacity means to me the ability to put symbols in construction so as to express compositionally meanings that are other than the sum of the meanings of the individual symbols. A simple paradigm for English is the contrast between *dog chase cat* and *cat chase dog*.

The studies of signing in the great apes have all been developmental, and my way of trying to understand their results is by comparison with what appear to be invariant features in the early stages of development of spoken and sign language in present-day *Homo sapiens*. The data base for *Homo sapiens* is, of course, far from adequate. It includes studies of a large number of historically unrelated spoken languages, Finnish, Japanese, Samoan, Luo and Mayan Cakchiquel among others (see, for example: Bloom 1970; Blount 1969; Bowerman 1973; Brown 1978; Tolbert 1978), but the studies of sign language are all of the American Sign Language (A.S.L.) (see, for example: Ashbrook 1977; Bellugi & Klima 1972; Hoffmeister 1977; Lacy 1972 *a, b*; McIntire 1977). There are three differences between child language and ape sign language that lead me to think that young children have a syntactic capacity and that young apes do not.

Syntactic capacity

(i) *Mean length of utterance (m.l.u.)*

The m.l.u. in morphemes for a sample of child speech or of child sign language is calculated in a standardized way, and this index of linguistic development rises steadily with age for several years for all normal children (Brown 1973). Terrace has calculated m.l.u. values for Nim, and they do not rise at all but hold steady at values between 1.1 and 1.6. M.l.u. most directly reflects the complexity of construction that the child's brain is able to accomplish, and its steady rise probably results both from the maturation of the brain and the accumulation of linguistic information. A failure to increase suggests that the symbol combinations being produced are not in construction at all but are only strings of single symbols. In young children, for several years, the longest construction produced in a sample is closely related to the mean length of construction and is not much above the mean. Terrace reports for Nim that the upper bound or longest unbroken string is unrelated to the m.l.u. and may assume very large values when the m.l.u. is not greater than 2.0. This fact suggests that utterance length does not reflect complexity and so reinforces the impression that Nim's strings were only strings and not constructions. Nim's longest string was made of 16 signs and reads in English: 'Give orange me give eat orange me eat orange give me eat orange give me you'. There is no evidence in this string or in the other long strings reported for any great ape that the information transmitted increases with the length of string.

(ii) *Symbol sequencing*

In many languages, word order has syntactic significance and children learning such languages, from the time when they first begin combining words, follow the ordering rules of the model language. Probably sequencing is the first syntactic device that children can utilize, and it is largely because they utilize it that the constructions of child speech are roughly intelligible from the start (Brown 1970, 1973). It is fair to look at sign sequencing in Nim and all the other non-human primates for evidence of syntactic construction as opposed to symbol stringing because all of them were taught a kind of pidgin signed English that preserves English word order (Terrace *et al.* 1979). This simplest fair summary is that chimpanzees tend to produce their multi-sign combinations in all possible orders, and that suggests the absence of syntax (Brown 1970; Terrace 1979).

(iii) *Prompting and imitation*

A number of sessions between Nim and one or another teacher were put on videotape. A frame-by-frame examination of these permanent records revealed to Terrace that Nim had seldom signed spontaneously, on his own initiative, but almost always required human prompting to sign at all, and when he signed with a teacher the signs that he produced were very often complete or partial imitations of those produced by his teacher. Child speech, by contrast, is characteristically spontaneous rather than responsive, and imitations constitute a small proportion of all utterances, a proportion that rapidly approaches zero. As far as prompted imitation accounts for multi-sign combinations, there is, of course, no reason to invoke creative syntax.

In this rapid review of three reasons for believing that the great apes have not yet demonstrated a capacity for syntax, apes have been represented primarily by one chimpanzee, Terrace's Nim. It might reasonably be contended that Nim is unrepresentative by reason of training method, individual intelligence or whatever. Such is, in fact, the position of the trainers of other apes using sign language, including A. and B. Gardner, F. Patterson and R. Fouts. They may be correct, but none of them has as yet published m.l.u. data different from Terrace's nor has any published different sequencing data or data on prompting or imitation that are different from Terrace's. For the most part, they have simply not made full reports on these matters. Looking at the reported data in studies earlier than Terrace's rather than at interpretations of data, I find no reason to believe that Terrace's findings are essentially different from those of anyone else.

Symbolic capacity

It is perfectly clear that the chimpanzee and gorilla are able to make recognizable approximations to manual responses that, in the hands of humans, function as symbols. We must, however, not make much of response topography. It was excessive attention to topography that led earlier generations of psychologists and primatologists (see, for example: Hayes & Hayes 1951; Kellogg & Kellogg 1933) to concentrate on vocalization in their search for language-like behaviour. This was just the wrong place to look since vocalization in apes and monkeys is neurologically and functionally closer to vocalization in lower mammals than it is to human verbalization (Myers 1976). Superficial topography cannot establish certain manual responses as symbolic; only evidence that they are associated with, and representative of, referents can do that.

There is completely convincing evidence, both experimental and naturalistic, that all the apes so far studied associate manual signs with referents (see, for example: Gardner & Gardner 1971; Terrace 1979). The ability of apes to maintain a sizeable repertoire of conventional signs and to use them to name referents on sight and also apparently to request them when out of reach seems to me to constitute an at least rudimentary symbolic capacity, and that is the most solid new thing that these studies have taught us.

I qualify the symbolic capacity demonstrated as rudimentary because there are some kinds of evidence of representation of a referent that one always obtains from children which seem to be missing from apes. For example, a child, having looked out of the window and seen his father's car draw up, will go to his mother in the next room and announce *Daddy*, which seems to be a report. The single-word utterances of children are also used to name the agent of an action, the owner of an object or the location of something sought, and in several other ways (Greenfield & Smith 1976). It seems clear that a symbolic capacity of this sort would have far more selection value than a capacity that does not go beyond naming and requesting. As soon as a report is possible, one individual can benefit from the experience of another, and the process of making experience cumulative across individuals and across time, which is the essence of cultural evolution, can begin.

LANGUAGE INVENTION IN THE PRESENT

Six congenitally deaf children, born to hearing parents who would not sign to their offspring because experts on the education of the deaf advised against it, proceeded to invent their own sign language. A group (Feldman *et al.* 1978) at the University of Pennsylvania has studied the development of this language over an age range from 17 months to 54 months. The number of signs in construction increased with age, and rules of sequencing constituted the first syntax. The principal point of present interest is the fact that the invented signs were not ever arbitrary but were always iconic; that is, such as to suggest the nature of their referents. To sign *hammer* one child pounded the air, and to sign *jar* another child twisted his hand as if to remove a lid.

On the Polynesian island of Rennell, the anthropological linguist Kuschel (1973) found a congenitally deaf man, Kangobai by name, who was said to be the first deaf person born on that island in 24 generations. Kangobai had, all his life, the necessity of communicating with people whose language he could not learn. He invented a large number of signs but not, as far as Kuschel noticed, a syntax. Kangobai's signs were all iconic. To sign *drink*, he raised his cupped hand to his mouth.

Writing is language in a form that leaves an enduring trace, and, since the first writing systems were independent of speech, they constitute a record of a kind of invented language. All early writing systems known to me are stongly iconic. For instance, in the Zapotec hieroglyphs from 660 B.C. (Marcus 1980), one can still easily tell the hill-with-two-peaks glyph from the hill-of-the-puma glyph, the latter having a lion's head on top.

All naturally evolved communal sign languages have a clear strain of iconicity that is much stronger than the trickle of onomatopoeia in spoken languages (Mandel 1977; Schlesinger & Namir 1978). Manual icons do not always mime actions performed on referents; they sometimes approximate referent appearance. The two hands half-open with palms upward constitute the sign for *book* in many sign languages, and the two hands hooked at the thumbs with the fingers spread and fluttering like wings are often used to mean *butterfly*. Experiments have shown that normal hearing children, mute autistic children and adults with no knowledge of any sign language are able to learn iconic signs much more easily than non-iconic signs (Brown 1978; Konstantareas *et al.* 1978).

To say that there is always a clear iconic strain in sign languages proper is not to deny that in most respects they operate with arbitrary conventions. The evidence is clear that iconicity plays little or no role in the learning of these languages by deaf children in early childhood and that it plays no role in the processing of these languages in highly fluent adults (Klima & Bellugi 1979; Wilbur 1979). Where it does operate is in the invention of new signs (Schlesinger & Namir 1978). While this process is in many ways governed by conventional rules (allowable hand configurations, allowable locations in the signing space, etc.), there is also often a clear iconic element.

While the definition, by Pierce and myself, of the symbol specify that it must be related to its referent by purely arbitrary convention, the evidence from Gleitman's deaf children, from Kangobai, from hieroglyphs and pictograms and modern sign languages is that the primary principle of symbol invention is iconicity, a certain kind of non-arbitrariness. However, the point of the stipulation of arbitrary convention in definition of the symbol, by Pierce and every-one else, is not primarily to exclude invented icons but rather to exclude indices that are naturally related to referents in the manner of smoke to fire and a scream to a wound. There is a secondary intent to specify arbitrary convention because only this kind of association allows for an infinite variety of symbols. Iconicity is somewhat limiting but, very much to my present point, it is far less limiting when the organs of response are the hands than when they are the vocal cords and articulators.

ARCHAEOLOGY, PALAEONEUROLOGY AND PALAEOANTHROPOLOGY

In the majority of right-handed hearing adults, the left cerebral hemisphere seems to be specialized for language processing. A lesion in Broca's area, just above the Sylvian fissure in the anterior frontal lobe, results in some degree of expressive aphasia, and a lesion in Wernicke's area, at the posterior end of the Sylvian fissure, results in receptive aphasia. If and where sign language skills are localized in the cortex is still not known for the congenitally deaf fluent user of sign language (Kimura 1979). There does seem to be good evidence (Hécaen 1975; Zangwill 1975) that ideomotor apraxia, which entails the inability to create gestural icons that might represent an object, and also ideational apraxia, which entails difficulty in integrating the components of complex motor skills such as are required for the use of some tools and the construction of most, are lateralized and in areas close to and possibly overlapping the speech areas. If we could know when in prehistoric times the hominid brain developed the areas in the left hemisphere that are in man today functionally specific to language, we might hope to know when and in what form language originated. However, the brain is software and does not fossilize. From fossil skulls much can be learned about brain size and shape, but, it was long supposed, nothing at all about the kind of functional organization represented by the two major speech areas.

Until about 10 years ago, it was the prevailing view of neurologists that the functional asym-metries of the human brain could not be correlated with anatomical asymmetries and, indeed, that there were no anatomical asymeties of consequence. It is now clear that there are anatomi-cal differences between the hemispheres, and the most striking and consistently present of these are in the region of the posterior end of the Sylvian fissure (Geschwind & Levitsky 1968; Gallaburda *et al.* 1978). The posterior area of the planum temporale that forms part of Wer-nicke's area is generally larger on the left side. The gross asymmetry in size of the left and right planum temporale is associated with an asymmetry of cellular organization. A difference on the cytoarchitectonic level suggests that the hemispheral asymmetry in area size may be functionally associated with language processing. Is there any way that this anatomical dif-ference could be detected in fossil skulls?

The pressure of the brain on the inner table of the skull vault during the life of the individual causes an impression to be formed that preserves some of the local variations of contour. For fossil skulls casts have been made of the endocranium, and these endocasts have been studied for indications of anatomical asymmetry of the cerebral hemispheres. Holloway wrote in 1976 that, with the possible exception of the Neanderthal fossil, La Chapelle-aux-Saints, he knew of no hominid brain endocast studied to date that unambiguously demonstrated an asymmetry between the hemispheres in a region regarded as involved in language ability. LeMay (LeMay & Culebras 1972; LeMay 1976) believes that the Sylvian fissures can be seen on the La

Chapelle-aux-Saints skull and that the posterior end is higher on the right as it is in most modern right-handed persons. She believes that there is, less clearly, a hint of the same asymmetry in an endocast of Peking *H. erectus*.

Even if LeMay's observations are correct, it is not possible to infer from Sylvian asymmetries alone anything about functional language areas. From asymmetries of the fissure, asymmetries of hemispheral size do not necessarily follow; nor, of course, do asymmetries of cell architecture. Furthermore, these anatomical differences have not yet been proved to be the structural substrate for language. The great apes have the Sylvian asymmetry but certainly no spoken language, and probably only a rudimentary language capacity of any sort, and they have not been shown to have any definitive functional asymmetries at all (Geschwind 1979). So, as yet, hominid brain endocasts teach us nothing unambiguous about the origin of language, but it has been a fascinating surprise to me that they could come at all close to doing so, and, as Holloway's paper at this meeting testifies, the story is not over.

Stone tools are almost as potent as fossil skulls in attracting speculation about the origin of language. There are reasons to think that the cognitive operations involved in tool construction and in language use are similar. Tools made to standardized forms imply manual dexterity and, it can be argued, a level of social consensus that could only be attained through language (Holloway 1976). Tools and weapons give some evidence of a non-random distribution of handedness as early as Pleistocene *Australopithecus* and from handedness an inference to cerebral dominance and language is often made (Steklis & Harnad 1976). I cannot critically evaluate the many ingenious arguments. What strikes me about stone tools in the context of the other data that I have reviewed is that they are, incidentally, icons, icons that appear long before the carved statuettes and cave paintings of the Upper Palaeolithic (Marshack 1976).

A tool is in part conventional but in part, of course, suited to a purpose and so able to suggest that purpose as well as a way of life in which that purpose has a place. At any rate, we today, or the archaeologists and palaeoanthropologists among us, treat tools as icons, as not entirely conventional symbols, as chips from a very remote referent, which, surviving into the present, are able to convey a kind of report. In their own time, when transported from one context into another, they may also have functioned in this way.

Perhaps the iconic principle that appears so clearly in the invention of manual signs today first operated incidentally and unintentionally when stones were shaped to fit a function. Perhaps what will eventually seem to us most consequential in the experiments on language-like behaviour in the great apes will not be the accomplishments of Nim, Washoe and the other users of sign language, but an observation made by Premack (1976), who has used arbitrary plastic tokens in most of his work, a brief observation, preliminary to the work with arbitrary tokens. Premack found that icons resembling various fruit referents were learned more easily and better retained than were arbitrary tokens. The ability to detect resemblance where man detects it and to benefit from such resemblance in associating a symbol with a referent could be the ability most directly relevant to the origin of language.

References (Brown)

Ashbrook, E. 1977 Development of semantic relations in the acquisition of American Sign Language. Manuscript, Salk Institute for Biological Studies, La Jolla, California.

Bellugi, U. & Klima, E. 1972 The roots of language in the sign talk of the deaf. *Psychology Today* **76**, 61–64.

Bloom, L. 1970 *Language development: form and function in emerging grammars.* Cambridge, Massachusetts: M.I.T. Press.

Blount, B. G. 1969 Acquisition of language by Luo children. Ph.D. thesis, University of California, Berkeley.

Bowerman, M. 1973 *Early syntactic development: a cross-linguistic study with special reference to Finnish.* Cambridge University Press.

Brown, R. 1970 The first sentences of child and chimpanzee. In *Psycholinguistics* (ed. R. Brown), pp. 208–231. New York: The Free Press.

Brown, R. 1973 *A first language.* Cambridge, Massachusetts: Harvard University Press.

Brown, R. 1978 Why are signed languages easier to learn than spoken languages? II. *Bull. Am. Acad. Arts Sci.* **32**, 25–44.

Feldman, H., Goldin-Meadow, S. & Gleitman, L. 1978 Beyond Herodotus: the creation of language by linguistically deprived deaf children. In *Action, gesture, and symbol* (ed. A. Lock), pp. 351–414. London: Academic Press.

Fouts, R. S. 1973 Acquisition and testing of gestural signs in four young chimpanzees. *Science, N.Y.* **180**, 978–980.

Gallaburda, A. M., LeMay, M., Kemper, T. L. & Geschwind, N. 1978 Right–left asymmetries in the brain *Science, N.Y.* **199**, 852–856.

Gardner, B. T. & Gardner, R. A. 1971 Two-way communication with an infant chimpanzee. In *Behavior of nonhuman primates* (ed. A. Schrier & F. Stollnitz), vol. 4. New York: Academic Press.

Gardner, R. A. & Gardner, B. T. 1978 Comparative psychology and language acquisition. In Psychology: the state of the art (ed. K. Salzinger & F. Denmark). *Ann. N.Y. Acad. Sci.* **309**, 37–76.

Geschwind, N. 1979 Specializations of the human brain. *Scient. Am.* **241**, 180–199.

Geschwind, N. & Levitsky, W. 1968 Human brain: left–right asymmetries in temporal speech region. *Science, N.Y.* **161**, 186–187.

Greenfield, P. M. & Smith, J. H. 1976 *The structure of communication in early language development.* New York: Academic Press.

Hayes, K. H. & Hayes, C. 1951 Intellectual development of a home-raised chimpanzee. *Proc. Am. phil. Soc.* **95**, 105.

Hécaen, H. 1975 The relationship between aphasia and disturbances of gesture and perception. In *Foundations of language development* (ed. E. H. Lenneberg & E. Lenneberg), pp. 117–133. New York: Academic Press.

Hoffmeister, R. 1977 The acquisition of American Sign Language by deaf children of deaf parents: the development of the demonstrative pronouns, locatives, and personal pronouns. Ph.D. thesis, University of Minnesota, Minneapolis.

Holloway, R. L. 1976 Paleoneurological evidence for language origins. In Origins and evolution of language and speech (ed. S. R. Harnad, H. D. Steklis & J. Lancaster). *Ann. N.Y. Acad. Sci.* **280**, 330–348.

Kellogg, W. N. & Kellogg, L. A. 1933 *The ape and the child.* New York: McGraw-Hill.

Kimura, D. 1979 Cases of 'aphasia' in the deaf. *Recent developments in language and cognition: sign language research.* Copenhagen: NATO Advanced Study Institute.

Klima, E. S. & Bellugi, U. 1979 *The signs of language.* Cambridge, Massachusetts: Harvard University Press.

Konstantareas, M., Oxman, J. & Webster, C. 1978 Iconicity: effects on the acquisition of sign language by autistic and other severely dysfunctional children. In *Understanding language through sign language research* (ed. P. Siple) pp. 213–237. New York: Academic Press.

Kuschel, R. 1973 The silent inventor: the creation of a sign language by the only deaf–mute on a Polynesian island. *Sign Lang. Stud.* **3**, 1–28.

Lacy, R. 1972a Development of Pola's questions. Manuscript, Salk Institute for Biological Studies, La Jolla, California.

Lacy, R. 1972b Development of Sonia's negations. Manuscript, Salk Institute for Biological Studies, La Jolla, California.

LeMay, M. 1976 Morphological cerebral asymmetries of modern man, fossil man, and nonhuman primate. In Origins and evolution of language and speech (ed. S. R. Harnad, H. D. Steklis & J. Lancaster). *Ann. N.Y. Acad. Sci.* **280**, 349–366.

LeMay, M. & Culebras, A. 1972 Human brain morphologic differences in the hemispheres demonstrable by carotid angiography. *New Engl. J. Med.* **287**, 168–170.

McIntire, M. 1977 The acquisition of American Sign Language hand configurations. *Sign Lang. Stud.* **16**, 247–266.

Mandel, M. 1977 Iconic devices in American Sign Language. In *On the other hand: new perspectives in American Sign Language* (ed. L. Friedman), pp. 57–107. New York: Academic Press.

Marcus, J. 1980 Zapotec writing. *Scient. Am.* **242**, 50–64.

Marshack, A. 1976 Some implications of the Paleolithic symbolic evidence for the origin of language. In Origins and evolution of language and speech (ed. S. R. Harnad, H. D. Steklis & J. Lancaster). *Ann. N.Y. Acad. Sci.* **280**, 330–348.

Myers, R. E. 1976 Comparative neurology of vocalization and speech: proof of a dichotomy. In Origins and evolution of language and speech (ed. S. R. Harnad, H. D. Steklis & J. Lancaster). *Ann. N.Y. Acad. Sci.* **280**, 745–757.

Patterson, F. G. 1978 The gestures of a gorilla: sign language acquisition in another pongid species. *Brain Lang.* **5**, 72–97.

Premack, D. 1976 *Intelligence in ape and man.* Hillsdale, New Jersey: Erlbaum.

Schlesinger, I. M. & Namir, L. (eds) 1978 *Sign language of the deaf.* New York: Academic Press.

Steklis, H. D. & Harnad, S. R. 1976 From hand to mouth: some critical stages in the evolution of language. In Origins and evolution of language and speech (ed. S. R. Harnad, H. D. Steklis & J. Lancaster). *Ann. N.Y. Acad. Sci.* **280**, 445–455.

Terrace, H. S. 1979 *Nim.* New York: Knopf.

Terrace, H. S., Petitto, L. A., Sanders, R. G. & Bever, T. G. 1979 Can an ape create a sentence? *Science, N.Y.* **206**, 891–902.

Tolbert, M. K. 1978 The acquisition of grammatical morphemes: a cross-linguistic study with reference to Mayan (Cakchiquel) and Spanish. Ph.D. thesis, Harvard University.

Wilbur, R. B. 1979 *American Sign Language and sign systems.* Baltimore: University Park Press.

Zangwill, O. L. 1975 The relation of nonverbal cognitive functions to aphasia. In *Foundations of language development* (ed. E. H. Lenneberg & E. Lenneberg), pp. 95–106. New York: Academic Press.

LORD ZUCKERMAN, F.R.S. (*The Zoological Society of London, Regent's Park, London NW1 4RY, UK.*). I should like to say how much I admired Professor Brown's critical exposition of a subject that has usually been dealt with in a theatrical manner. I have followed most of the work of recent years on the capacity of chimpanzees to learn American Sign Language, and have been privileged to be kept informed by H. S. Terrace of his progress in the disproof of the idea that, in using or stringing, apes are demonstrating a syntactic and semantic capacity. I was surprised, however, that R. Brown made no reference to the recent work showing that pigeons can do much of what the ape is supposed to do.

Terrace's work has re-emphasized the part that cues play in experiments of the kind that Brown has described. Some recent writings almost take us back to the days of Clever Hans, the horse that could tap out the cube root of sequences of, I believe, nine numbers. I have experience of the speed with which monkeys can learn tricks, and I am very aware of the artificial circumstances out of which far-reaching conclusions are drawn. We heard (this symposium) of chimpanzees using twigs to winkle ants from a hole. Forty years ago a chimpanzee called Sally manicured my nails with a straw almost every second day. But I did not draw the conclusion that this was normal behaviour. We had a chimpanzee that painted abstracts during the period that D. Morris was our curator of mammals. Soon after, a chimpanzee in Baltimore started doing the same. I have one of his works. But since Dr Morris left the Zoo no further ape Rembrandts have turned up in our colony.

Phil. Trans. R. Soc. Lond. B **292**, 205–211 (1981)   [205]

Printed in Great Britain

Emergence of higher thought 3.0–0.2 Ma B.P.

By K. P. Oakley, F.B.A.

Department of Anthropology, University College London,
London WC1E 6BT, U.K.

The oldest known probable manuport is the dark reddish jasperite pebble from a layer with *Australopithecus* at Makapansgat, Transvaal (*ca.* 3 Ma).

There are indications at two earliest Acheulian sites in east Africa that *Homo erectus* of *ca.* 1.5 Ma B.P. was interested in red mineral pigment. At Terra Amata, near Nice, 75 shaped pieces of red ochre were found with the earliest European Acheulian industry (*ca.* 0.3 Ma B.P.). This occurrence indicates that to an Acheulian society red mineral pigment had great symbolic value.

Several flint and chert artefacts from Acheulian sites in Britain are described on account of embedded fossils, evidently regarded as symbolic, with a visual pattern stimulating to an aesthetic impulse in the minds of men who selected the material in preference to the more readily available plain flint. Most remarkable are two humanly struck flakes of coral-bearing chert found in the Swanscombe Gravels (0.2 Ma B.P.). This starry stone, it is inferred, was a manuport carried about 120 miles (*ca.* 193 km) from an outcrop of Jurassic (Portlandian) rock at Tisbury in Wiltshire.

Possibly the oldest known piece of evidence bearing on the predilections of the Late Pliocene hominids is the reddish cobble†, with presumably weathered-out features making it resemble a humanoid face, that was found in 1925 by W. I. Eitzman at the site that became known as the Limeworks Quarry, Makapansgat, in the Transvaal (Dart 1974). It was recovered from a pink stony breccia, later identified by T. C. Partridge (unpublished, 1980) as member 4 in his terminology, overlying the main level with *Australopithecus* remains (the grey breccia, member 3), and dated on the basis of palaeomagnetic readings (McFadden *et al.* 1979) at 3 Ma B.P. The cobble weighs *ca.* 260 g. It is jasperite, or banded ironstone of Precambrian age. The banded character reflects varying proportions of iron and silica in the make-up of the rock. The more deeply weathered layers are probably relatively rich in iron, while the more indurated ones are richer in silica (I. G. Stanistreet, unpublished, 1980). Banded ironstones outcropping about 3 miles (4.8 km) NNE of the limeworks were the probable source of the rock fragment (B. Maguire, unpublished, 1980) that was eroded to form this large pebble or cobble. It is obviously very water-worn, as though subjected to fluviatile action, and may first have come to rest in the gravel of a river bed.

The means by which it was eventually transported from, say, a river bed to a cave breccia is a matter for speculation. On the principle of Occam's razor, it seems reasonable to accept Dart's hypothesis (see below), based on the remarkable fact that this reddish cobble was unique, quite foreign to the layer of pink stony breccia in which it was found. J. W. Kitching recalls that when he first saw the specimen it still had some of the pink breccia adhering to it

---

† It is preserved in the Bernard Price Institute for Palaeontology, University of the Witwatersrand, Johannesburg; catalogue number L1713.

(B. Maguire, unpublished, 1980). Dart suggests that one of the australopithecine hominids noticed this reddish head-like cobble (I say, perhaps at a river margin), picked it up and carried it as a treasured object to their temporary dwelling place in one of the Makapansgat rock shelters. To my mind, the colour of the cobble was a very significant aspect. According to Sir James Fraser, in a number of creation myths the first men were modelled out of red clay or earth. Red is the colour most attractive to the Hominoidea, i.e. apes and men. Anyone who doubts this should try offering a tray of boiled sweets, each of a single colour, to a group of children, and the marked preference in favour of selecting the red ones will soon become evident.

While D. Morris was carrying out his intensive painting experiments with the young male chimpanzee Congo, when this ape showed signs of becoming tired of the activity, Morris found that, on offering him a brush that had been dipped in red paint, Congo showed a slight but definite preference for this colour, and continued painting for a further spell, as though this colour supplied a boosting effect that the colour blue, for example, did not.

We all know about the extensive use of red ochre by the Upper Palaeolithic cave artists, mainly 30–12 ka ago; we also know that Neanderthal man (with Mousterian culture, Middle Palaeolithic) made some use of red ochre and occasionally pieces of the black pigment, manganese dioxide. However, it came as a surprise when de Lumley, in his excavations of the coastal rock shelter at Terra Amata, near Nice, found in association with the earliest known European Acheulian culture 75 shaped pieces of red ochre (de Lumley 1978). The deposits at Terra Amata are considered to be of late Mindel age (0.3 Ma B.P.). One might say the hunt is now on for earlier evidence of hominid interest in pigments, particularly red mineral pigments, because the use of such material is unlikely to have had any value other than symbolic. The power of this symbolism may be gauged by the lengths to which Australian aborigines will go to obtain red ochre for use in their rituals. Sollas (1924, p. 278) says:

> Howitt tells us of one tribe (Dieri) that at certain times of the year dispatched an expedition of 70 or 80 picked men under experienced leaders, who, if necessary, fought their way across country to the 'mines', some 300 miles off...The ochre is dug out of the 'mine' and kneaded into large cakes weighing, when dry, from 70 to 80 lbs[†]. The men carry this away on their heads.

One might say that to the 'stone age mind' red ochre played a role not unlike that played by gold in the civilized world of today.

As the base of Acheulian culture is probably a diachronic horizon it is highly likely that the use of red ochre occurred in Africa considerably earlier than that represented at Terra Amata. In this connection the words published by Clark & Kurashina (1979) are worth quoting. They were describing the oldest known Acheulian hand axe occupation site at Gadeb on the South-East Plateau of Ethiopia. 'The occupation floor...yielded several fragments of heavily weathered basalt which, when rubbed, give a red pigment. None of the pieces show unquestionable evidence of rubbing, but the possibility should not be ignored'. Later they concluded: '*Homo erectus*, even at this unusually early time (1.5 Ma ago) may have been experimenting with pigment'. In dealing with incipient use of red pigment, one should not confine one's attention to red ochre. Leakey (1958) recorded that in excavation of the Chellean I (now regarded as Early Acheulian) occupation site at BK in Olduvai Bed II he found two 'lumps of

† 1 lb (pound) ≈ 0.45 kg.

red ochre which clearly were brought to the site by man, thus suggesting that even in Chellean I times man was interested in colouring matter'. After subsequent mineralogical examination the two lumps proved to be reddened volcanic tuff, and not red ochre, and consequently I believe that an important discovery has since been overlooked. Was not Leakey's discovery in fact comparable with the finding by Clark & Kurashina on the floor at Gadeb of weathered basalt that on being rubbed gave a red pigment?

The probability is that interest in mineral-red pigment marked an important threshold in the hierarchy of evolving human minds. Did it perhaps coincide with speech and the beginnings of social organization in the cultural evolution of *Homo* (Wreschner 1976)? Unendowed with natural ornamentation apart from the glories of head hair, man may well have turned to artificial colouring of his skin and apparel as soon as tribes, moieties and family groups were formed and required to be distinguished when sighted at a distance.

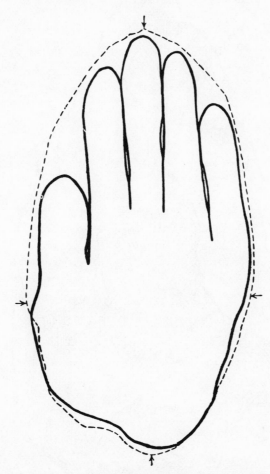

FIGURE 1. Outline of long-ovate Acheulian flint hand axe 20.4 cm long, overlain by outline of adult human hand. After R. R. Schmidt (1936).

Apart from the use of red mineral pigments in Acheulian times, there are other indications of the use of symbols (cf. Edwards 1978) and symbolic thought over this long hand-axe period, which eventually included the transition from *Homo erectus* to hominids belonging to a primitive subspecies of *Homo sapiens* (e.g. Swanscombe man). One only has to consider the conceptual nature of the bifacial hand axes, characteristic of the Acheulian culture, and compare them with the tool kit of the Oldowan culture that preceded them, to realize at once that the introduction of the Acheulian biface hand axe was a major innovation. The Acheulian hand axe was a general purpose tool widely used in Africa, southwest Asia and Europe for hundreds of thousands of years, and was evidently designed by means of a sort of symbolic logic. Schmidt (1936) showed that the bifacial hand axe was based on the human hand as model (figure 1). With the onset of symbolic thought, a bifacial hand axe was perhaps subconsciously visualized as representing a third hand, a hand that unlike the flesh-and-blood original had the capability to cut and skin the carcasses of the animals scavenged or hunted.

There are a few exceptional Acheulian artefacts that, through an adventitious element in the stone of which they were made, served the artistic mind's eye to distinguish them in the way that a blazon does on a sword hilt.

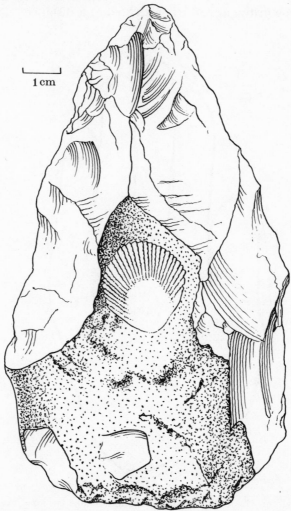

FIGURE 2. Pointed Acheulian hand axe of flint showing one valve of embedded shell of Upper Cretaceous bivalve mollusc, *Spondylus spinosus* (J. Sowerby). West Tofts, Norfolk (length 13.5 cm). By courtesy of the Curator, University Museum of Archaeology and Ethnology, Cambridge; *del.* M. O. Miller.

In the first example (figure 2) a fossil bivalve mollusc shell in the flint served as a blazon unique to the owner. This hand axe was found at West Tofts, Norfolk. The important fact emerged from examining the hand axe that the fossil was on a weathered portion of the block of flint out of which the tool was fashioned. We may infer that the fossil in its exposed state was noticed before the block of flint was selected, and also that as the toolmaker worked this block into the pointed biface he deliberately took care to avoid flaking the area that bore the fossil, thus leaving it to occupy a central position on one face of the completed hand axe. This specimen was called to my attention by R. J. MacRae of Oxford, who had noted it while going through the collections of hand axes in the University Museum of Archaeology and Ethnology, Cambridge, U.K. A note on and an illustration of this hand axe appear in Oakley (1973).

Following the publication of the note on the West Tofts hand axe I received a letter from D. Downes of the City of Liverpool Museums† informing me that in their Archaeological Collections there was an Acheulian flint hand axe from the Middle Gravels at Swanscombe that had a conspicuous fossil echinoid of the type commonly known as a shepherd's crown embedded in the flint (figure 3). The fossil echinoid, a flint mould, is remarkably large in relation to the size of the implement, measuring 37 mm in diameter, which is nearly two-fifths of the length of the whole implement. Although the fossil has been slightly chipped along the left margin, it was evidently intended to be the central feature of the tool. It is difficult to speculate on what significance this fossil had in the mind of the toolmaker who fashioned the implement about 0.2 Ma ago. Perhaps the most striking aspect of the fossil was its five-fold symmetry, marked by five pairs of grooves (the ambulacral areas) that intersect at the centre to form a star. Archaeological findings and folklore indicate clearly that in the Celtic Iron Age and probably earlier flint shepherd's crowns were regarded as thunder stones, supposedly hurled down from the sky by a god such as Thor of the Norse mythology. Flint moulds of echinoids are most often seen on field surfaces when soil derived from the Chalk has been washed by a heavy rainstorm; so it is not improbable that the idea that these objects had fallen from the sky readily sprang to the mind of the untutored finder, particularly when the storm had been accompanied by lightning and the consequent thunder.

Perhaps the most strange example of stone with fossil structures that attracted Acheulian man takes us again to the gravels at Swanscombe that yielded the three bones of the fossil skull now referred to *Homo sapiens steinheimensis*. Alvan Marston, who discovered the first two bones of that skull, also found in the same Middle Gravels two pieces of chert containing a fossil compound coral of a kind usually found in calcareous rocks of Jurassic age. Both flakes have an ochreous stain, like many of the flints in the Swanscombe Gravels. They show conchoidal fractures of a kind indicating that they had been struck from the parent chert by man. No outcrops of such coral-bearing chert are known to occur in the catchment area of the Lower Thames, which deposited the Swanscombe Gravels. We can only infer that these flakes were manuports, that is to say, they had been transported by Acheulian hunters from a distant source. Evidently this exotic chert, wherever it outcropped, was valued by the Acheulian hunters as precious stones would be today. When the macroscopic characters of the fossil coral in these flakes were first examined they were identified as those of *Isastraea oblonga*. When thin sections of them were studied microscopically by the Polish authority on Jurassic corals E. Roniewicz, she confirmed that one of the flakes did belong to that species, although she referred it to a new genus *Pseudodiplocaenia* (figure 4). The second and larger flake Oakley 1971, p. 582, pl. IA) showed features unrecorded in any known Jurassic coral. At first she intended to use this Acheulian flake as the holotype of a new genus and species, but on more detailed study she found that certain critical structures were too imperfectly preserved to justify this course of action. She did find, however, that the mineralization of the two flakes was the same, and so she had no doubt that they had all come from the same source.

† Now known as Merseyside County Museums (p. 6).

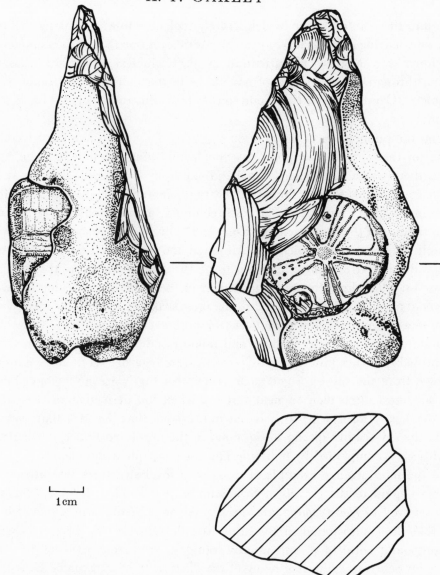

1 cm

FIGURE 3. Pointed Acheulian hand axe of flint with an embedded Upper Cretaceous echinoid, *Conulus* sp. *Left*, right edge of hand axe showing side of echinoid; *right*, hand axe viewed from above, with oral surface of echinoid exposed (mouth central, anus marginal half-left); *below*, cross section of hand axe. Middle Gravels, Swanscombe, Kent (length 9.5 cm). By courtesy of the Director, Merseyside County Museums. Reg. no 42.17.237. *del*. M. H. R. Cook.

5 mm

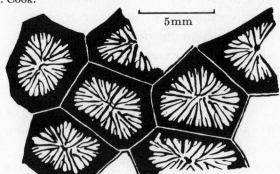

FIGURE 4. Transverse section of the Upper Jurassic coral *Pseudodiplocaenia oblonga* (Fleming). Drawing based on silicified corallum in pale grey chert from Portlandian beds, Tisbury, Wiltshire. Reproduced by courtesy of E. Roniewicz.

There is only one location in Britain where coral-bearing chert containing *Pseudodiplocaenia oblonga* is known to occur, namely the Portlandian beds outcropping at Tisbury in Wiltshire, about 120 miles (193 km) from Swanscombe.

As regards numeracy in the thought of Acheulian man, it may be worth noting that on the average the corallites in *P. oblonga* are five-sided polygons. What could the pattern presented by these corals have symbolized in the thoughts of Swanscombe man? The only possible clue that we have is in the widespread folk name for fossil compound corals of this kind; they are known as starry stones. Is it conceivable that even 0.2 Ma ago they called to mind the night sky?

SUMMARY

If the reddish, face-featured pebble of jasperite from Makapansgat, Transvaal, is accepted as a manuport, the roots of art can be assessed as going back at least 3 Ma. In east Africa at the stage of the earliest Acheulian hand-axe culture, 1.5 Ma B.P., *Homo erectus* had developed an interest in red mineral pigments. At the same cultural stage, but in the Riviera, 0.3 Ma B.P., true red ochre was regularly used by *H. erectus*, possibly for body decoration (rock art is unknown before 0.03 Ma B.P.). English examples of Middle Acheulian flint hand axes, 0.2 Ma B.P., are described in which an ornate fossil in the raw material has been preserved as a feature of the finished tool. Flakes of chert containing a starry fossil structure appear to have been transported 120 miles (193 km) by the Middle Acheulian men of Swanscombe. It is inferred that in the transition from *H. erectus* to early *H. sapiens* 'art as a human behaviour' (Dissanayake 1980) was emerging.

I would like to record my thanks to Dr E. K. Brain, Mrs Jill Cook, Mr Rupert Cook, Miss C. Eckert, Dr R. P. S. Jefferies, Mr Brian Maguire, Dr T. C. Partridge, Mrs Willow Pierce, Professor M. A. Raath, Dr I. G. Stanistreet, Professor Phillip Tobias and Margaret Warhurnt for their generous help in the preparation of this paper.

REFERENCES (Oakley)

Clark, J. D. & Kurashina, H. 1979 Hominid occupation of the east-central highlands of Ethiopia in the Plio-Pleistocene. *Nature, Lond.* **282**, 33–39.

Dart, R. A. 1974 The waterworn australopithecine pebble of many faces from Makapansgat. *S. Afr. J. Sci.* **70**, 167–169.

Dissanayake, E. 1980 Art as a human behavior: towards an ethological definition of art. *J. Aesthetics Art Criticism* **38**(4), 397–406.

Edwards, S. W. 1978 Nonutilitarian activities in the Lower Palaeolithic: a look at the two kinds of evidence. *Curr. Anthrop.* **19**, 135–137.

Frazer, J. G. 1923 *Folklore in the Old Testament* (abridged). London: McMillan.

Leakey, L. S. B. 1958 Recent discoveries at Olduvai Gorge, Tanganyika. *Nature, Lond.* **181**, 1099–1103.

Lumley, H. de 1978 Les fouilles de Terra Amata à Nice. Premiers résultats. *Bull. Mus. Anthrop. préhist. Monaco* **13**, 29–51.

McFadden, P. L., Brock, A. & Partridge, T. C. 1979 Palaeomagnetism and the age of the Makapansgat hominid site. *Earth planet. Sci. Lett.* **44**, 373–382.

Morris, D. 1962 *The biology of art.* London: Methuen.

Oakley, K. P. 1971 Fossils collected by the earlier palaeolithic men. In *Mélanges de préhistoire, d'archéocivilization et d'ethnologie offerts à André Varagnac*, pp. 581–584. Paris: Serpen.

Oakley, K. P. 1973 Fossil shell observed by Acheulian man. *Antiquity* **47**, 59–60.

Schmidt, R. R. 1936 *The dawn of the human mind.* London: Sidgwick & Jackson. (Transl. R. A. S. Macalister from R. R. Schmidt, *Der Geist der Vorzeit.*)

Sollas, W. J. 1924 *Ancient hunters and their modern representatives* (3rd edn). London: Macmillan.

Wreschner, E. E. 1976 The red hunters: further thoughts on the evolution of speech. *Curr. Anthrop.* **17**, 717–719.

Phil. Trans. R. Soc. Lond. B **292**, 213–216 (1981)   [213]

Printed in Great Britain

Some tentative conclusions

By J. Z. Young, F.R.S.

The Wellcome Institute for the History of Medicine, 183 Euston Road, London NW1 2BP, U.K.

Perhaps it was too much to hope that we should get very far with answers to the questions:
What is man?; where, when and why did he begin? But with a sound basis of chronology, such
as was provided by Curtis, the dates by which several important stages had been reached can
now be fixed more definitely than before. Evidence such as that of Tuttle and Leakey establishes that some hominids were certainly walking bipedally before 3.0 Ma ago. But as Simons
asked 'How long before?' The conditions for bipedalism may have first arisen after the marked
cooling *ca.* 14 Ma ago that led to formation of an Antarctic ice cap, producing a fall in sea levels
and drier conditions generally (Kennet 1977). Much forest was then replaced by open prairie
and many cursorial herbivores and carnivores appeared. Such circumstances would have
favoured development of the earliest terrestrial anthropoids, who were probably still partly
climbers, as indicated by the curved phalanges.

Unfortunately there is almost no evidence about the state of man's ancestors between the
large fossil jaws of *Ramapithecus* about 15–8 Ma ago and the bipedal creatures living in Africa
between 4 and 3 Ma ago. Apparently they were not yet using implements at that later period.
As Isaac showed, implements are doubtfully present at Hadar but definitely appear at Omo,
Olduvai and Koobi Fora from *ca.* 2 Ma ago. Reduction in the sizes of jaws and teeth also seems
to have proceeded rapidly from about 1.6–1 Ma ago. However, there is no evidence that there
were any hominids before 1.6 Ma ago with brain size more than half that of modern man. Of
course larger skulls may yet be found, but it seems that the freeing of the hands by bipedalism
was neither concomitantly nor even shortly followed by increase in brain size and use of
implements.

This further evidence of the mosaic character of human evolution makes it more than ever
difficult to give a clear answer to the question 'What is man?' The question is as hard to
answer professionally as it is colloquially and is the nightmare of systematists who describe new
material. Further, as Tobias emphasized, it is most important to consider variation in space as
well as in time. For this and other reasons the use of subspecific groupings and names seems to
have many advantages. They may be clumsy and unglamorous, but the possibility of their
impermanence is an asset, and they should bring more honour to their creators than the
founding of an unsatisfactory species or genus.

Of course any attempt to follow the emergence of man demands that we face the question
of whether evolution has been continuous, or interrupted by quantal jumps of appreciable
size (Gould & Eldredge 1977). This problem was raised occasionally in the symposium but not
decisively answered. Tobias suggested four stages of evolution of brain size, micr-, meso-,
macr- and gigant-encephalic. But have we enough skulls to be sure that the gaps are anything
except accidents of discovery? Anyhow, size is not everything, and Holloway has provided an
attempt to show when various *parts* of the brain developed. Surely such changes as may have
occurred in the proportions of the visual or prefrontal areas must have proceeded gradually or

by small steps, and probably on several lines. Similarly, development of the capacity for sequencing movements by the premotor area, which as Passingham showed is necessary for speech, could well have been gradual.

Probably most biologists believe that evolutionary change occurs in small steps, even if these steps are sometimes discontinuous because they result from foundations by small colonies and geographical isolation. But ice-core evidence shows that large climatic changes have often occurred over quite short periods (Dansgaard *et al.* 1971). Moreover, the palaeontological record shows repeated extinctions of whole groups of animals and plants, often sufficiently rapid to be called catastrophic (Hallam 1977). Some molecular biologists are inclined to believe in evolution by small steps. Indeed, as Bodmer showed, the discovery of the close similarity of many molecules in creatures as different as man and chimpanzee makes the problem of defining differences between closely related groups very difficult. The extensive polymorphism indicated by Balner certainly provides the basis for gradual change. Further, as Jope and others speaking in this symposium explained, the complexity of the process of change of even one amino acid in a protein chain makes it unlikely that abrupt changes could be successful.

Questions about continuity lead to the problem of whether we should use concepts of genus and species to define horizontal or vertical groupings. This was also raised implicitly, but is not often faced by anthropologists any more than by other biologists, which is not surprising since in principle there can be no clear answer to it. The extension of *Homo* to include the specimens known as *H. habilis* may appear as a concession to cladistic concepts of linear classification (always assuming that the phylogeny is correct). But for fruitful discussion we often need to refer to *stages* of evolution, and for this horizontal definitions are better, with the assumption again that we must have names. Cladistically speaking, *Ramapithecus* might be made part of *Homo* (or vice versa). Such excesses lead to the situation that the word 'man' becomes more precise than *Homo*. I suggest that we should be very cautious about including small-brained creatures in the genus *Homo*, however we (re)define it. Whatever features we decide are characteristic of 'man' should surely be incorporated in the definition of the genus *Homo*.

The question of continuity is particularly important for evolution of the brain since study of fossil brains is one of the few ways of approaching the key problem of the origins of 'mental' characteristics. I was particularly sorry that in a joint meeting of the British Academy and the Royal Society there was little reference to the first appearance of these mental qualities that many philosophers and theologians regard as unique characteristics of man. Of course this was largely our own fault for not allocating time for appropriate speakers. But there is scope for another full meeting here, and indeed one is planned. It is important that we should not allow our Discussion to seem to ignore such questions, and indeed some were treated implicitly. So far as language is concerned, Brown's analysis suggested that there is no evidence that apes have the power to use symbols in syntactic combinations. If this power is unique to man could it have appeared gradually, and if so when? The assemblages of instruments in Olduvai bed 1 suggest that even around 2 Ma ago there was the ability to create distinct *classes* of instruments. This indicates the presence of a kind of segmented and symbolic conceptual ability. As Isaac showed, the development of such capacities was correlated with increase in brain size that seems to have occurred most rapidly from about 1 Ma ago. This might therefore be suggested, very tentatively, as the time for the appearance of rudimentary capacities for grammar and logic. The great selective advantages of these for social life may then have quickly produced still further enlargement of the brain. An inherited character such as an effective brain that leads to social competition is likely to proceed to a 'runaway evolution' (West-Eberhard 1979). Conspecific rivals then constitute an environmental contingency that itself evolves, increasing the stakes for access to scarce commodities. The advantages conferred upon groups by more intelligent and plastic behaviour could only be met by still further increases. If this analysis is correct it further emphasizes the interdependence of genetic and extrasomatic inheritance.

The evidence that instruments were used mainly for butchery also allowed Isaac to make one of the few suggestions as to 'why' human characteristics have appeared. Accepting the function of butchery, he suggested that the diet of big game necessitated specialization and social organization for food-sharing throughout kin groups. Jones showed the influence of material on the kind of implements that were made. He followed the ideas of the late C. B. M. McBurney as to the possibility of learning from the wear on the edges how implements were used and for what purposes.

Much of the evidence thus seems to suggest that about 1 Ma ago there were creatures with physical and cultural characteristics at least somewhat like those of modern man. This is such a long time ago that we have to look hard to find evidence of the culture and of the extent to which the proto-humans at that time were really like ourselves. Had they the elements of intentionality, of logical and syntactic powers, of aesthetics and religion? Did they believe in spirits? Oakley showed us that features of manuports, implements and pigments from more than 1 Ma ago already suggest considerable interest in symbols, aesthetic feeling and, from 0.2 Ma B.P., possibly even thoughts about the stars.

So the evidence, fragmentary though it still is, indicates that the bipedal hominids underwent great changes between 1.5 and 1 Ma ago. It may be significant that the particularly severe cold, with formation of Arctic as well as Antarctic ice caps, began about 2–3 Ma ago (Kennet 1977). The subsequent oscillations of climate of the Quaternary ice ages were often rapid and accompanied by a series of extinctions of plants and animals as great or greater than at any other time in geological history. The hominids proved able to survive these great changes, which occurred all over the world. Such conditions may have placed a special premium on the capacities conferred by social life and large brain. The later stages of the Pleistocene included some periods of extremely rapid change. The Greenland ice sheet record shows a variation at about 90 ka ago from warmer than today to fully glacial *in less than 100 years* (Dansgaard *et al.* 1972). There is evidence of this event also from stalagmites in France and foraminifera in cores from the Gulf of Mexico (Kennet & Huddlestun 1972). Such changes, however they were caused, may have provided the strongly selective conditions that encouraged the final development of the adaptive powers of *Homo sapiens sapiens*.

More precise dating thus allows us to see the outlines of human history, but the details still remain tantalizingly uncertain. The evidence of 'catastrophic' climatic changes perhaps increases the possibility that human characteristics appeared suddenly. The long survival of early hominid types is also used as negative evidence for rapid change by those who believe in punctuated equilibria (Gould & Eldredge 1977). A sudden emergence of man is certainly an attractive proposition for those who believe that his features are in some way 'unique'.

So we may suggest the hypothesis that the emergence of man has been the consequence of a series of climatic changes spread over some 14 Ma from a *Ramapithecus* stage. The dry conditions determined the adoption of a partially terrestrial life and the eating of meat, first as part of a mixed diet. The Australopithecines and such types as KNM-ER 1470 represent this stage, whether or not they are on the direct line of human ancestry. Then from about 2 Ma ago, with rapidly varying and often severe conditions came the changes in the brain and endocrines by which the hominids became social hunters, such as *H. erectus*, using implements, sharing the products of the quest for food and developing a simple culture. The advantages so conferred led to still more rapid increase of brain power, which allowed for survival through the often harsh conditions of the later Pleistocene. Finally further developments in the same directions made possible the logic, language and culture that marked the emergence of man as we know him when conditions became milder in the Neothermal period.

REFERENCES (Young)

Dansgaard, W., Johnson, S. J., Clausen, H. B. & Langway, C. C. 1971 Climatic record revealed by the Camps Century Ice Core. In *The late Cenozoic glacial ice ages* (ed. K. K. Turekian), pp. 37–56. Yale University Press.

Dansgaard, W., Johnson, S. J., Clausen, H. B. & Langway, C. C. 1972 Speculations about the next glaciation. *Quat. Res.* **2**, 396–398.

Gould, S. J. & Eldredge, N. 1977 Punctuated equilibria: the tempo and mode of evolution reconsidered. *Paleobiology* **3**, 115–151.

Hallam, A. 1977 Patterns of evolution, as illustrated by the fossil record. *Developments in palaeontology and stratigraphy*, vol. 5. Amsterdam: Elsevier.

Kennet, J. P. & Huddlestun, P. 1972 Abrupt climatic change at 90,000 yrs. B.P.: faunal evidence from Gulf of Mexico cores. *Quat. Res.* **2**, 384–395.

Kennet, J. P. 1977 Cenozoic evolution of Antarctic glaciation, the circum-Antarctic ocean and their impact on global paleoceanography. *J. geophys. Res.* **82**, 3843–3860.

West-Eberhard, M. J. 1979 Sexual selection, social competition and evolution. *Proc. Am. phil. Soc.* **123**, (4) 222–234.